Lost Teams of the Midlands

Lost Teams of the Midlands

MIKE BRADBURY

Copyright © 2013 by Mike Bradbury.

Library of Congress Control Number:		2013916142
ISBN:	Hardcover	978-1-4836-9530-3
	Softcover	978-1-4836-9529-7
	Ebook	978-1-4836-9531-0

All rights reserved. No part of this book may be reproduced or transmitted in any form or by any means, electronic or mechanical, including photocopying, recording, or by any information storage and retrieval system, without permission in writing from the copyright owner.

This book was printed in the United States of America.

Rev. date: 10/18/2013

To order additional copies of this book, contact:
Xlibris LLC
0-800-056-3182
www.xlibrispublishing.co.uk
Orders@xlibrispublishing.co.uk
306277

Contents

Dedication

This book is dedicated to my daughter Kimberley.
I would like to thank the following people for their encouragement, guidance, faith, and, above all, for putting up with me when my only conversation was about this book and the knowledge and discoveries that lay inside:

Mrs Diane Bradbury
John Green
Steve Carr
Terrance Fletcher
Lee Gauntlett
Geoff Fletcher
David Shaw

Timeline of Events in Midlands Football Up to 1901

1860 Oswestry Football Club founded

1862 Notts County FC founded

1863 The formation of the Football Association in London/Stoke FC founded

1865 Nottingham Forest club founded from a shinty club

1867 Stafford Road Football Club founded in Wolverhampton/offside law required three defenders between the forward and the goal

1868 Notts Rangers Football Club founded/Rushall Rovers founded near Walsall/Aston Unity football club founded

1869 Excelsior, and Victoria Football Clubs founded in Aston/Birmingham Cricket and Football Club founded

1870 Elwells Football Club founded in Wednesbury/Saltley College FC founded in east Birmingham

1871 English FA Cup begins/Burton Swifts club founded

1872 The first International games: Scotland v England/Shropshire Wanderers and Tipton FC founded/free kicks given for handball

1873 Calthorpe FC founded in Birmingham/Wednesbury Strollers founded

1874 Shin guards introduced and the crossbar replaces the tape/Aston Villa, Walsall FC and Wednesbury Old Athletic founded

1875 The formation of the Birmingham Football Association/Victoria Swifts FC founded

1876 Welsh FA founded/Shropshire Cup started/Aston Shakespeare, Derby Town, and Aston Victoria clubs founded

1877 The first Birmingham and District Cup Final/Wolverhampton Wanderers formed

1878 First use of a referee's whistle in an official game at Nottingham F v Sheffield Norfolk/Stoke FC wins first Staffordshire Cup final

1879 Walsall Swifts v Stafford Road cup tie draws the country's first ever 10,000 crowd in Wednesbury, Staffs.

1880 Wednesbury Football Association Cup started/West Bromwich Strollers change their name to Albion

1881 Derby Midland Football Club founded

1882 Two-handed throw-in introduced/Long Eaton Rangers FC founded

1883 Singers FC founded in Coventry/Nottinghamshire county cup started/5-3-2 formation commonplace

1884 Notts Olympic, Leicester Fosse, and Derby County founded

1885	Legalisation of Professionalism
1886	The first of three consecutive Cup Finals for West Bromwich Albion
1887	Aston Villa win the FA Cup for the first time
1888	The founding of the Football League/West Bromwich Albion wins FA Cup/demolition of the Aston Lower Grounds/Walsall FC founded
1889	Aston Victoria wins the first Birmingham Junior Cup/The Football Alliance formed
1890	Kidderminster Olympic are unbeaten champions of the first Birmingham & District League
1891	Introduction of goal nets and penalty kicks
1892	Inter-League matches introduced by the FA/Football League embraces Football Alliance as its Second Division/West Bromwich Albion win FA Cup
1893	FA Amateur Cup started/Small Heath are first ever Division Two champions/Wolverhampton Wanderers win the FA Cup
1894	Aston Villa win Football League for the first time/Notts County win the FA Cup
1895	Aston Villa win FA Cup/FA Cup stolen from Birmingham whilst in possession of Aston Villa club
1896	Extra-time made compulsory in cup-tie replays/Aston Villa win Football League
1897	Aston Villa win Football League and FA Cup double/Notts County win Division Two title
1898	Football League introduces promotion and relegation concept/ Nottingham Forest win the FA Cup beating Derby County
1899	Aston Villa win Football League/Derby County lose Cup Final
1900	Aston Villa win Football League again
1901	First footballer's maximum wage rule introduced by the Football League/ Burton's two clubs amalgamate

Introduction

Foreword

Like most lads of my age (I was born in the early fifties), I wouldn't just play football after school, rather, we would take a ball with us, pass it to each other all the way to school, then again all the way home. Sometimes, we might come across some lads playing '3-and-in' on some waste ground (one goes in goal, the others – usually just two or three – take his place when they've scored their third goal) and challenge them to a game which might last till it was too dark to see, and boy, did we hear about it from our mums when we eventually got home, our teas long gone cold on the table.

Let me say from the outset that this is not one of those scientific books just crammed with facts, figures, and minutes. Rather it is a layman's attempt to provide a picture of what thing must have been like in the early days (1870s-90s) of Victorian football in the Midlands and to give an insight into over fifty teams whose names were featured in the football reports in the last three decades of the nineteenth century. However, there will be found some new snippets of information within the book that have either not previously been published, or shed new light on accepted facts. In reading through several hundred match reports from the Victorian newspapers in a dozen libraries around the Midlands, I frequently discovered a new truth against certain so-called facts reported on the Internet. May I take this opportunity to thank the publications of Steve Carr, whose definitive works on the Birmingham Cup, West Midlands League, and some of the Black Country teams has been invaluable, so too the help of staff at Walsall and Sandwell Local History Centres? Special thanks, too, to David Shaw the Hednesford Town FC historian, who offered all his research web site to me, and to Geoff Fletcher at St. George's Club (Wellington), who spent a whole day turning out the club's entire history records and photographs and filling the boardroom table with unseen delights for me in the autumn of 2012. A debt of thanks are also due to Terrance Fletcher of Belper, who helped me for most of a week by taking me to find the various Derby grounds and following up leads using his years of experience as both a player and referee and his immense collection of football photographs from Derbyshire.

Some of the teams in this book came and went like moths into a candle; some lasted a decade or two, whilst some of the more enduring names made it into the twentieth century. The teams I've chosen had either featured prominently in the Birmingham Cups (senior and junior), their respective county cups, or leading leagues of the day, or the team had been pioneering or instrumental in the development of football in the region. The apparent imbalance of teams from the West Midlands, as compared to the East, was a reflection of the natural order of the day; the Industrial Revolution had made great social impact in the Birmingham and Black Country districts, with the commensurate high employment and high density of population in these areas which provided the social raw material for the nurturing of the game. The East Midlands, albeit with thriving towns such as Derby, Nottingham, Leicester, tended to have one principal city or town for that county, and there was much farmland and agricultural employment which did not lend itself to creation of anything other than small village sides. The principal teams from the major East Midland counties became professional and of course survive to today and are well-known names, outside the scope and focus of this book. The Birmingham Cup assumes importance, because, quite quickly, it became, in effect, the unofficial 'Midlands' Cup. Only the English FA Cup was of more importance and only challenged for its desire by perhaps the county cups. The Football League, and then the Football Alliance, were of course the preserve of the professional teams, who couldn't wait to trample these little amateur teams underfoot. Let us see.

Social Advances

In and around Birmingham by 1860, something of social importance occurred; the working half day Saturday was introduced. The 1850 Factory Act, limiting the working week to sixty hours, released hard-working men from their grimy drudgery for a Saturday afternoon all to themselves. Primarily intended to limit the maximum number of hours worked in the northern textile industry, where twelve to fourteen hours a day was commonplace, hours were brought down to around a fifty-four-hour week by the 1870s. The thought of any activity on a Sunday was of course out of the question; Sunday meant church or chapel in the morning, and perhaps again at teatime, and maybe spending a few hours with family members until the week started all over again. In any case, there was strong moral and religious opposition to the idea of manual effort on the Lord's Day. Wages had slowly risen in real terms during the 1860s and 1870s, and hours had been gradually reduced with it; in many aspects of life, there had been economic and social advances throughout the last quarter of the nineteenth century. A semi-skilled worker might expect to earn up to twenty shillings (£1.00) a week by 1895, but of course, boys and women more like eight to ten shillings. Men (and women and boys) could now find escapism from their turgid lives, and football was the sport which drew the common man to follow his chosen team in ever-increasing numbers. During 1870-90, with the advent of mechanisation in the textile and food industries, plus new higher paid jobs created by social and economic progress, basic living costs actually went down on food and clothing, which gave rise to a general feeling of increased security of life. A second major factor came along in 1871 with the proclamation from Parliament of the country's first National Bank Holiday, which was to be known as St. Lubbock's Day for the rest of the century. Other bank holidays were to follow, giving the nation's workforce ever more freedom and leisure time, and most of it was spent at football matches. A third moving force which helped football become established as the game of the school playground was the 1870 Education Act which increased school-leaving age to fourteen and also made schooling provision compulsory and under the control of the local education authority. By 1880, schooling was compulsory, but a decade later, it was free. During 1870-90, this increased the general level of education for children and youths, enabling new readers and writers to take up the new employment opportunities arising in the new service industries, the railways and the police for example. This also now meant that pro-physical education headmasters and teachers were provided with a continuous stream of a captive raw material of youths into which they could pour their wholesome Christian exercise beliefs. In short, it had created an assembly line of future footballers. These young men and boys would later emulate their football heroes in the playground and develop their skills and strength for later life.

Jack Allen, in his dissertation on the growth of football as a spectator sport in the last quarter of the nineteenth century, writes that 'working class men experienced victory in a world in which they otherwise felt defeated.' This is in reference to attempting to understand how it came about that workmen, newly released for Saturday afternoons, found a vehicle to release their daily frustrations. Men began the process subconsciously as a local body, of forming an allegiance to one football club over another, even within the same town of upwards of four sides to chose from. Football became a way of establishing social links with one's town or community, and individuals and groups of people could share in the successes of their chosen team. Rivalries began to form – sometimes within the same town – and the bonding structure grew stronger with the passing generations. Fathers began to pass on their team loyalty to sons whom they'd taken to watch their team play. Businessmen were quick to see the potential for profit in football clubs and began to invest in the clubs' infrastructure. Grandstands would be built, which of course meant charging double for the pleasure of sitting on wooden seats, yet still receiving the rain in one's face! Club directors knew that a football club was yet another business; more success on the football field meant more spectators, which yielded more income and profit for them. More income meant your club could afford to pay for better players, coaxed from rival clubs, thus improving your team whilst reducing their team all in one move. This cycle would continue, and with the advent of legalised professionalism after 1885, began the gap between the top professional teams clammering to join the best leagues and those who were left behind as amateurs. Many of the small amateur clubs, unless from a parent company such as a large factory employer, or a general sports club with other interests (i.e. cricket or athletics), would disappear by the end of the century. The collapse of a football team in its second decade was not exclusive to the struggling amateur; many teams tried to make the transition into professionalism too quickly. If the town was not large enough, maximum possible attendances would be below survival levels, exacerbated if a small town was trying to support more than one team, such as in Wednesbury, Wellington, Derby, and Walsall. Expansion was a two-edged sword; bigger crowds meant more money for better players, but in a town like Wednesbury with only 24,000 people, no club was likely to get more than the minimum 3,000 gate every week to sustain the club's outgoings.

Strangely, by the mid-1890s, social commentators might have observed that hard-working men who were seen to be oppressed and over-worked with poor pay and conditions in factories, mills, and foundries who had turned their lot into becoming a professional footballer might have seen the irony of the deja vu. Ten years into professionalism, huge crowds had swelled the coffers of clubs, directors, investors, and backers, and most of these people were those who were already wealthy. Businessmen, industrialists, factory owners, and politicians alike were the ones who were reaping large rewards. The man who was missing out, with his paltry fifteen shillings a week (for the top teams), who gave his all to the loyalty of one employer was the footballer himself. With a crowded week of league matches and various cup ties and replays, he was being overworked and underpaid all over again. It would remain this way until the 1930s when footballers' pay went up a little; however, in real terms, by the time the 1960s came along, footballers were on poor money again.

There are over sixty teams who receive a spotlight before the end of this book is reached, and they are from the counties of Staffordshire, Warwickshire,

Worcestershire, Derbyshire, Nottinghamshire, and Shropshire. I thought long and hard about including the Sheffield Association clubs, but I decided that they weren't in the 'Midlands' as a Midlander might acknowledge it, as they were indeed from south Yorkshire. Their contribution to the birth of organised Association football is clearly acknowledged as being significant, to say the least, but a club like Sheffield FC would and does need a whole book just to itself! Clearly, the Derbyshire teams had a lot of exposure to Sheffield clubs and the rather excellent Sheffield Rules between the mid-1860s and the mid-1880s, and I have tried to give a mention to Sheffield teams when it arose. They were years ahead of London thinking and were pioneers in terms of crossbars instead of tape, free kicks from the spot for handball offences, corner kicks, and corner flags too. As early as 1877, there were no less than twenty-six registered teams belonging to the Sheffield FA. Eleven of those teams alone were formed before 1870 and include the well-known sides Sheffield *(1855), Hallam (1857), Norfolk (1861), and Heeley (1862), as well as the unlikely but true Sheffield Thursday (Wanderers). Owlerton, for example, were formed in 1873 and played in scarlet and black hoops at their Rawson's Meadows Ground. They used the Victoria Hotel for their headquarters. There were also the misleadingly named Oxford FC (1869) club, who played in blue and yellow, Surrey FC (1870), who played in scarlet and white, and Philadelphia FC (1873), who turned out in only blue caps to identify themselves.

* some give 1857

Professionals Win Out

Nearly all the teams I've chosen ultimately folded, because, despite the rapid rise in football as a spectator sport from say, 1874-88, when the Football League was started, these local teams, however successful had been on the minor circuit and couldn't compete in what they had to offer to a footballing public. Imagine you lived in Aston near the town of Birmingham (for, in those days, Aston was the parish town and Birmingham no more important), who would you rather see at the Aston Lower Grounds: Aston Unity, Aston Excelsior, Aston Shakespeare, or the Aston Villa?

It was the same story if you lived in Smethwick (a town between West Bromwich and Birmingham); there was the quite successful Birmingham St. George's FC at Cape Hill, Smethwick Centaur, Smethwick Carriage Works, or you could just go and see the West Bromwich Albion instead. And so, most people did. There was nothing to prevent a good player from turning out for two, three, or even four teams in his area; equally, there seemed to be little club loyalty since most clubs lost their best men to the faster-rising clubs, especially to Aston Villa, West Bromwich Albion, Wolves, and Derby County. Those four clubs alone contributed directly to the downfall and closure of perhaps a dozen smaller clubs, since it was only natural that a top player would want to join a top club; it was a pity that the men who did, didn't look back over their shoulders and see the damage it had done to their founding team – in true Darwinian fashion, the weakest fall to the wayside, and the strongest take the spoils. The spoils being, for the Albion, Villa, Derby, and later the Wolves, the English (FA) cup and entry into the new Football League of which Villa's celebrated William McGreggor was the founding figure.

The big clubs, by this stage (mid-1880s), were heartily fed up with: (a) easy double-figure wins in friendly and local cup competitions and (b) teams simply failing to turn up after the home club had spent a lot of time and trouble putting up adverts, posters, etc., and selling tickets. Some games started so late due to errors in their travel plans by visiting teams, such as missing the train from Derby to Wolverhampton, getting off the wrong station and having to walk five miles to the ground so that you're too tired to play a decent game when you get there! All these things have happened, even into the 1890s. Remember, too, that men still had to work until 1 p.m. on a Saturday, so even travelling to and getting ready to play a home game was a rush for the amateur footballer.

What teams and their financial backroom committee men needed was a guaranteed weekly income from a good quality fixture against teams that were assured to turn up (and on time), thus providing the best clubs with regular top-class football to keep the crowds pouring into the grounds. Most definitely, the legalisation of professionalism in 1885 was a leading factor of making the big split between the haves and the have-nots in the years to come, but the formation of the Football League in 1888 created an elitism that only served to alienate small amateur local clubs from their thriving professional neighbours.

Wednesbury Old Athletic, for instance, drew 5,500 for their local derby with the Wednesbury Strollers in 1880, and the largest crowd ever yet assembled for a football match in England in April 1883 when 10,000 turned up to see them play the Aston Villa in the final of the Birmingham FA cup at the Aston Lower Grounds. This was a bigger crowd than ever assembled at the London Oval for the final of the English Cup that year (8,000), yet a decade later, Wednesbury crowds were down to 500 or 1500 for the most attractive visitors.

One common denominator in all the original twelve professional League teams was that they all possessed their own ground. Walled or fenced in, not always owned by them, otherwise on long-lease rents, they had one huge advantage. They could charge a gate (entrance) fee. Usually 3d (1.5p) would get you in, or 6d (2.5p) to a shilling for a seat in the wooden primitive stand that at least afforded you some protection of the worst of the weather elements. In the early years at Aston Villa's first Wellington Road ground in Perry Barr, you could literally drive your horse and wagon-cart into the ground and get a position at the edge of the pitch for 5d (2p) and then sub-let a bit of your vantage point to one or two others for a penny and get most of your money back!

Crowd control before the Football League scarcely existed if at all. Clubs didn't see it as their responsibility to look after, and provide anything other than, the most basic facilities for spectators. Indeed, in the late 1860s, spectators were positively discouraged until clubs realised that they could charge people a small fee to let them watch the games. At Wellington Road, there were no perimeter walls, no terraced banking, no ropes to define the pitch extent and thus hold the crowd back; indeed at one end the locals were known for encroaching so close under the goalposts that on more than one occasion, a goal was prevented from being scored by the visiting team because they were standing on the line with the goalkeeper! Two grandstands were added in the 1880s, though, along with perimeter ropes.

Stands

Sometimes, but not everywhere, a club might erect a grandstand, although the word *grand* was hardly a fair description.

A wooden structure, nothing more than a glorified large shed with tiered planking, might give cover at extra cost to between 50 and 300 people. By the 1890s, some grounds would have just one central grandstand, but it would often be very ornately decorated with cast-iron embellishments and might have two or even three tiers, the old stands at the Small Heath Muntz Street ground and at Long Eaton Recreation ground being two prime examples. Changing rooms, purpose-built, did not exist. Instead, any nearby structure, however small, inappropriate, or inconveniently situated would be pressed into service. Since players would likely need a wash afterwards, all the better if you could use a building near a water pump. Even when Aston Villa were drawing five-figure crowds at the end of their twenty-year tenure of Wellington Road ground, players changed in the blacksmiths forge across the road! That forge, by the way, is still there today, used now as a carpet shop, adjacent to the Crown & Cushion pub which was the club's HQ at that time.

Fixtures we take for granted at a modern football ground, such as the goalposts themselves, were kept by the football club and carried to the field they intended to play on, erected on site just before the match. Don't try to imagine half the team struggling to carry a heavy metal twenty-four-foot goal frame like we have today. Instead, there would have been two pairs of wooden upright posts, often square as opposed to round, and a crossbar made of rope or tape would be nailed or tied to them at the appropriate height (eight feet). How they measured eight feet would have been in a variety of ways. If you had someone in the drapery or tailoring business in your team, you may have used a cloth tape or carried a folding wooden rule. At its most basic, however, was the idea that a tall man (about six feet) would raise his arm aloft, and that would be your crossbar height. In early matches in the 1870s, teams just got on with it if the crossbar tape seemed about the right height, but as the fierce competitiveness of the English Cup took a grip with the nations' young teams, it was not uncommon for a losing team to find any excuse after the game to lodge a protest about the height of the goal, the ineligibility of a member of the opposing team, or the excessive slope of the ground! Interestingly, these 'protests' didn't seem to be made before the game commenced! Or by the winning team! A common tool in Victorian use was the hinged wooden rule. A brass centre hinge allowed it to open out to exactly two feet, and this would have commonly been used to set the height of the cross tape or bar. Unfortunately, a common mistake was to measure to the top of the crossbar, and not the underside, as that was the true measurement, and this was the case in the infamous Crewe Alexandra v the Swifts tie which became embroiled in the amateurs v professionals wrangles of the mid-1880s. Until the advent of the FA Cup in 1871, there was no maximum height restriction of a goal frame, and it was difficult for the umpires to judge whether a high punted ball was going to count as a score at all.

Grounds

In the 1870s, what we talk about as a teams' home ground today was, in reality, often nothing more than a nearby available field of grass which was owned by a local farmer, or pub, or a family that had lived in the town for generations. Some teams used common land or parks, which meant that they didn't have to pay any rent. However, the big downside was that neither could you level it off, enclose it with a boundary fence, or even make the presumption that yours was the only team hoping to play on it! More than once, Wednesbury Old Athletic men walked to the Elwell's ground to find the Strollers already playing on it and had to make do with playing their game on the adjacent side of the Oval which hadn't had its long grass cut. Many of these fields were rough, lumpy, uneven, and had slopes from top to bottom, side to side, or even both! Many teams, once they had secured the rental or free use of a field for a few years, might make a good attempt at levelling it out and making it into a reasonable playing surface, although by today's standards, they would still be pretty rough. I visited the site of the first ever pitch used by Wednesbury Strollers on the highest part of the town by the two churches. Long since built over, it is still clear that the ground must have been like the grazing ground of an Alpine mountain goat, as the houses in both directions are all on a considerable slope! The best football was played on long-established cricket grounds, such as at Kidderminster Olympic, Aston Unity, Wellington St. George's, the Gregory Ground, Nottingham, and the Derby Racecourse.

The biggest downfall of not having exclusive use of your pitch was that you weren't able to develop it and charge the spectators an admission fee. Now whether you develop into a professional club or not, money would still be very useful to your team so that you could, for example, pay someone to look after the playing area and mow the grass, prevent gypsies making camp on it, stop people from grazing their animals on it (although grazing would keep the grass short, you might still have the problem of making sure the cattle or sheep weren't there on match day). Balls weren't exactly cheap in those days either, if you could get one. In 1877, a Walsall leather shop was advertising footballs for 8/6p (42.5p). To put it in perspective, that was almost a week's wages for a non-skilled man or servant. Clearly, it needed seventeen men to each give a sixpence to obtain the golden globe. You could rent a ball too, but that was about a shilling (5p) a game, which worked out even more expensive. You could buy 2 lbs of tea for the price of a football in 1880, and tea was a valued commodity. West Bromwich players had to walk to Wednesbury in 1878 to buy one. And one is all you would have possessed as a club, and you would look after it properly with leather dubbing and new laces, etc., and woe betide if the worst were to happen – a burst ball – for unlike in later years, there would be no spare ball to carry on with the match. A football shirt circa 1880 would set you back six shillings (30p); cheaper by the dozen – as the saying goes – but still three days' wages for a labourer. One can now begin to see the advantage of an amateur village side sticking to a plain white, red, or blue shirt – they probably already possessed one, and thus money was saved. One example of this was the Small Heath Alliance club, who all simply agreed to wear any blue shirt which they already owned.

Colours

As we research today for the early team colours, it must be understood that at first (1860-70), it was not recognised that a team needed to identify itself by all wearing the same colour jersey, just as, in the school playground, two teams of schoolboys, picked alternately by the two captains, would instinctively know who their fellow teammates were, even though they were in everyday school clothes. However, any teacher or parent trying to watch the proceedings would have no idea who was in which team. So the reason for all players of a team to wear the same colours is as much to do with making it easier for spectators to readily recognise the two sets of players as much as for instant identification of who is near you on the pitch itself. Who has not, in the school playground, wrestled the ball of some chap, only to find he was on your team, and in retribution, find that no one gives you the ball again for the rest of the game?

Oxford University Football Club were one of the first teams to become identified by their club colours. There exists a picture of their eleven men in dark blue and white halves with black knickerbockers in 1871, and you can sense from the photo as they pose outside the college walls that here is a team with a true identity as a body of men, and proud of it too. Creating an identity like this helps turn a team into a football club. Of course, many football team wore colours before 1871, but it doesn't help in creating your identity if you keep changing those colours. Some sides, like the Wednesbury and Burton teams, seemed to have a different shirt almost every year. Nottm Forest, on the other hand, have never moved away from red, and they are associated with that colour. True, having your own ground is a big part of it, but having your colours known across the land helps forge an identity for your club wherever you play. As Oxford University travelled the country, local teams would copy their idea of 'team colours equals an identity'. The same thing happened when Queens Park and Royal Engineers went on tour. The local teams would be very impressed by the combination play of those two teams and often switched to the black and white hoops of Queens Park or the red and blue hoops of the Engineers. Additionally, if your team plays in red and white hoops, it would be very helpful to know that your visiting opponents didn't play in the same colours! Or, if they did, to have a change of jersey available to avoid the colour clash. There is good evidence that Notts County were wearing orange and black hoops as early as 1864.*

They must have resembled a swarm of wasps as their forwards chased around the ball!

In the embryonic days of football teams (1860-70), players identified themselves by wearing caps with coloured hoops or quarters and socks to match. Unfortunately, these tended to be from their former school, college, or university for whom they intended to demonstrate their continued affinity, and these caps would all be different amongst players of the same team! Players in those days, particularly university old boys' teams, were more interested in being admired for their individual plucky and robust play, and gaining a mention for it, rather than simply being just another member of the team. Velvet caps were awarded to men selected to play for the country or county representative side. This is the origin of the phrase 'being capped for England/Wales'. Many Southern and old boys' sides wore fanciful caps, peaked or pill-box style (all the fashion circa 1865-80), in velvet, complete with tassels and embroidery.

The earliest known photo of the Forest club – later to evolve into the celebrated Wanderers – shows the men standing in various 'poses', as was the Victorian custom, all wearing white, including long trousers, but with coloured caps, only to distinguish themselves from the opposition. However, that was 1860, but as the 1870s approached, teams began to wear colours and, of course, caps in various styles, such as pill-box, with or without tassels, peaked and no-peaked, or caps with a peak both front and back (Sherlock Holmes-style), and in the 1860s, they wore cowls, knitted woollen hats, which looked like you might go to bed in it. Individuals would also pay homage to their school, college, or university by wearing socks representing the colours of that institution.

Team colours, as the 1870s developed, got ever more bizarre. Whether a team thought that a simple red or blue shirt would cause frequent colour clashes, I don't know, but hoops and quarters and halves were the order of the day, with gay colours such as pink (thought of as representing health and vitality then, hence the phrase 'I'm in the pink') and various shades of purple (a newly created dye colour), and chocolate or amber! It wasn't until the end of the century that colours settled down into plainer colours, mainly led from the Football League sides. The two most common outfits were still either a white or a red shirt, however, even by 1900. It is thought that the manufacture of striped shirts was not possible until around 1884, and so a club whose colours are said to be red and black, for example, would probably be either halves or hoops. Only the shirt colours counted in team colours as registered with the F. A; trousers, knickerbockers, or shorts were worn randomly. In this way, we often see pictures of teams all wearing different coloured legwear. There are two words to be wary of when trying to interpret Victorian football kit information: *stripes* and *red*. 'Stripes', up until the early 1880s, usually meant 'hoops', as the Victorians used that word to describe horizontal stripes. The colour *red* as a word was not in popular use until circa 1900, with scarlet usually used in its place. Other shades of red, such as vermilion, wine, maroon, magenta, and claret were frequently in use.

* This was virtually confirmed when Notts County played away games in the Football League wearing thin amber and black hoops in season 2011/12 for their 150th anniversary.

Formation

Generally speaking, teams were formed in one of the four ways: a cricket club wanting a winter activity; a church group of fellows wanting to express their muscular Christianity in a wholesome, manly way; a factory entrepreneur or businessman wanting to make his name in the town as a philanthropist, so becoming a benefactor to a football team drawn from his workers. By 1885, a quarter of the Birmingham FA's 350 registered teams were church-based organisations. The fourth method was the least popular, being a group of men or youths who simply met up in the same pub but who were employed in a similar trade, as in the case of Walsall Victoria Swifts and Birmingham Excelsior.

Away from the Midlands, that black, sooty, grimy, dreary region, its sky, choked with hundreds of smoke-belching chimneys from forges, foundries, factories and mills, your team might be an old boys' team where you could stay in touch with your old chums from the public school and university that your privileged background enabled you to go to. And 'go to' would be what half these chaps did, often doing very little work, yet still being placed by their influential, yet still disappointed fathers, into a good post in the city, or in the Forces at home or in India. However, back in the real world of the noisy, blackened, chimney-filled skyline of the Black Country, I never cease to be amazed at how a group of a dozen men, after six and a half days' hard manual labour, had the strength or desire to go out on a muddy or frozen football field and endure up to two hours of muscular effort in order to force a heavy leather ball between two wooden poles 8 yards apart.

By 1875, both the Sheffield F.A and the Birmingham F.A had been formed, with its officers and committees established. Importantly, in 1877, the

Sheffield Association fell in line with the London FA and conceded the last few sticking points on the rules of play which had hitherto prevented national unity. This helped further in the standardisation of the game, by compelling all aspirant clubs to register their colours, ground, and secretary contact details. The club secretary was often a player or an old player who wanted to stay on and help the club, not usually a schooled cleric, but nonetheless, he played an important role. He would try to attract opposition to his team's ground that, hopefully, would bring in a larger crowd than usual, although if the new visitors proved too strong, the embarrassment of a humiliating big home defeat wouldn't exactly help to keep the crowds coming in the following week. In the 1870s, there was frequent mismatching of teams' abilities with scores of more than 10-0 not uncommon. Now you might think that, if you were running a football club, this was a good idea. After all, who doesn't want to see loads of goals, especially if it's your side that's putting them in the net? Well, actually, many a football crowd got bored with seeing their team thrash hopelessly outclassed opposition, and they would drift away long before the end of the ninety minutes, much as if their team was losing, say 0-4, with ten minutes to go. Whether they turned out in numbers depended very much on who the visiting team was and its reputation. Teams published probable team line-ups on posters near the ground and promised that the visitors would be bringing their 'star' players. If word got out that these star players were not coming down with the team, then the turnout would be decimated and a profit turned into a loss. Such is the fickle public.

The club secretary of the Birmingham St. George's FC, for example, Mr William Stansbie, would write letters to his counterpart at distant clubs such as Sunderland Albion, Druids (Ruabon), and Darwen, promising them a percentage of the gate money (sometimes more than 50 per cent), hoping to secure a large crowd at their Cape Hill ground, in an attempt to strengthen the clubs' intention to turn professional in the years to come. This continued into the 1890s, even after the Football League had created the new elite gulf between the top professional sides and the amateurs of the Midlands and the South, and clubs with just one or two paid players on their books, like Willenhall Swifts, Wednesbury OA, or Aston Unity struggled on trying to keep their heads above water. Alas, all too often without success.

There is an accepted culture in this country which follows the oft-cited theme that rough-house street and field football was formulated and fine-tuned by the universities and public school boys' teams into the modern game of today, and without those clever souls, we might not have the version of football which the world plays today. I don't deny that astute men of passion sat around tables long into the night at Cambridge University and Harrow and Charterhouse, with candle wax dripping on to their quill-penned manuscripts and notepads, but it is plainly clear that football was beginning to organise itself to a degree all across the land throughout the 1860s. Shrewsbury School were playing around ten matches a year in the 1860s, against other public school and colleges such as Malvern and Reigate, and indeed, many Midlands grammar schools and colleges were doing the same in that decade. Some parts of the country were even in front of Alcock's Football Association itself. The Sheffield FA were in many ways decades ahead of London thinking at the time. Their version of offside was to have three defenders within 15 yards of goal in front of the attacker before he was given offside, when everywhere else forbade the forward pass altogether, and later, when the forward pass was allowed – which revolutionised the game – Sheffield were using modified rules that now said that only one defender was needed for the offside law, which of course was the basis of the World game throughout the twentieth century. Goal nets, crossbars, shin pads, corner kicks and corner flags, referees, whistles, floodlit matches, professionalism were all concepts invented or first used in the Midlands and the North of England quite outside London's FA rulemakers. The Midlands and the North, and obviously pioneering teams like Queen's Park, Sheffield FC, Nottingham Forest, Shropshire Wanderers, all gave as much to the development of modern football as did Royal Engineers, Corinthians, and the Wanderers, who seem to get all the popular credit.

Without being aware of it, I was surrounded by local football history as a boy. I can remember the coal man bringing his coal sacks to my grandmother's house in Walsall, and in the 1960s, the local mobile grocery van on Sunday mornings, so useful if you had run out of Oxo cubes for the Sunday dinner gravy. I later found out that the coal man was called Bassett and he was a relative of the famous William Isiah Bassett of Albion and England fame; the mobile van belonged to a Mr Devey of Bloxwich.

He was a relative of the famous John Devey from the 1897 Aston Villa double winning team. My father's business partner turned out to be Laurie Percival, Hednesford town's centre forward, and when the Sunday team I played for ended up being absorbed into Hednesford's reserve team, I discovered that my girlfriend's uncle was the team chairman, and the brilliant midfielder I admired on the pitch for the 1st team turned out to be Brian Horton, later First Division player and manager of Brighton & Hove Albion at the FA Cup final.

So where did my interest in early football teams originate from, and why do I have a fascination (obsession!) in finding out the team colours of long-gone teams?

Well, for over twenty years, through the 1970s and 1980s, I was associated with Waddington Games who had purchased Subbuteo Games Limited in the mid-1960s. Subbuteo was probably played by most young lads up until the advent of computer games in the 1990s, and at its peak of popularity, there was a league in most towns of the UK, and there were numerous local, regional, and national championships. Indeed, after 1974, there was a real World Cup held every four years, with the national champions of different countries playing for the world champion title, all backed up by the wallet of the sales and marketing side of Waddington Games. The top players were very serious about it indeed, obsessional in fact.

It was here that I became involved; already the county champion, and later having played at national and international level, I had a great knowledge of how the game was played at the very top level, what players and leagues needed and wanted, and I happened to be a very good organiser. In fact, after creating the largest and strongest club in the country based in south Staffordshire, I travelled the greater Midlands, setting up new clubs in schools, youth clubs, or church halls. By 1980, I had an organisation of over fifty such leagues; I later went on to organise the National Club Championships, where I hired Walsall's Bescot stadium where 300 players took part and did TV interviews for BBC Midlands and Central TV. I raised the standards to a high level in an effort to have the game recognised nationally as a sport (at its top level) and to get the newspapers to give important events some press coverage. This worked to a degree, for, as I was returning back to the Black Country on the train, having reached the semi-finals of the British championships at the 1974 World Cup in London, I read about myself in the *Evening Telegraph*. I was lucky – and privileged – enough through organising and playing Subbuteo at national level, that I was able to meet quite a few top footballers of the age.

I've played table soccer with Bobby Moore, Gordon Banks, Pat Jennings, Bob Wilson, Bill Shankley, Gary Shaw, John Wark, and Allan Clarke.

It was with this background that Subbuteo Games would contact me for advice and opinion with regard to important future competitions and playing rule alterations. I would organise the Midland championships on their behalf and be lucky enough to get to keep all the teams, pitches, and goals, etc., that the sales rep would fill his boot with as a thank-you.

One day, George Underwood, a director and friend of the now deceased inventor, Peter Adolph, said to me, "Mike, what do you think of the new Wimbledon FC Subbuteo team (they had just won the FA cup)? We now have produced the teams for every side that's ever won the FA cup."

"No, you haven't," I replied.

"What do you mean?" said Mr Underwood. (I would never have dreamt of calling him by his first name.)

"Well, there's the Wanderers for a start, then there's Royal Engineers and Old Etonians . . ."

"Who are they?" he asked.

"The first early winners," I replied.

"Mmm", he said, "no one's going to buy those. We need to make at least 10,000 of each team (box)."

So that's why Subbuteo never made teams of Wanderers, Old Boys' Clubs, and the Corinthians.

And that's why I was determined to find out what all the colours were of the teams with strange names.

Team Colours

It took me over twenty years to discover the colours of the famous Wanderers from London, who played variously in Battersea Park, the Oval Cricket Ground or Crystal Palace Park. Dazzling hoops of black/orange/mauve with white flannels were tucked into black stockings, and the only flesh on show was that of their hands and faces! Most bizarre was probably the Forest (Epping) team.

They were all red at the front and all black from the back! Others quickly followed: the red and navy hoops of the Royal Engineers FC, the orange and blue hoops of the Civil Service club, the light blue-green and white halves of the Old Etonians . . . after a few years, I had amassed the colours of over

100 early teams. Needless to say, I would paint up my Subbuteo teams in those colours, but eventually I thought it would be better to make up a large display case, with each team being represented by one subbuteo figure in those colours with the date of that club's formation printed underneath.

It wasn't long before I ran out of purple, orange, green, gold, and chocolate colour paints, as I made up the garish colours of the Southern Old Boys' teams. One of my favourites was the chocolate and pink halves of the Casuals FC, from the racing silks of the horses owned by their patron, the (Winston) Churchill family, although they were a much later team from the 1930s.

Midlands and Northern sides seemed to show greater restraint with their palette. Sheffield Heeley wore plain green shirts after starting out in grey and white stripes, with rivals Hallam in plain blue; old Sheffield club wore scarlet shirts, but later changed to red and black halves. I am, by the way, a member of that club, and last year, I saw them play twice in my area, against Rushall Olympic and Willenhall Town. There's a picture of Olympic's predecessor, Rovers, on a Rushall pub wall showing them in 1876, wearing all-white with a large black Staffordshire knot across the chest.

Birmingham St. George's played in white shirts and black shorts during the 1880s, and Aston Unity, the winter arm of the well-known cricket club, played in claret and light blue long before Aston Villa adopted those colours. Plain or halved shirts, sometimes hoops, seemed favourite outside of London, whereas rugby-style hoops were favoured in the capital.

You might think that, after setting up a club identity with a ground, maybe a nickname yelled from the terraces, a team would stick to the same colour scheme from year to year. Far from it, in places like West Bromwich or Wednesbury, the Albion and Old Athletic changed their colours almost every season during the 1880s. Albion went through every colour combination you could think of: yellow and white quarters, chocolate and blue halves, red hoops, red and blue hoops, scarlet and blue stripes . . . W.O.A weren't any better: maroon and white, scarlet and blue hoops, amber and black with navy shorts, scarlet and black hoops . . . make the present-day Manchester United and England kit changes look infrequent by comparison! How on earth did they expect any supporters to display their allegiance in terms of rattles or banners, etc.?

A game between Wednesbury Old Athletics and WBA in 1884 would have seen the home team in scarlet and blue hoops, with the visitors in chocolate and white halves; the same fixture in 1890 would have seen amber and black stripes versus scarlet and blue stripes, black shorts!

In terms of doing research for this book, I have made a combination of my memory from the forty or so old football books which I possess, some details being oft repeated so that no one book or author could be given the acknowledgement; some Internet searching has gone into it as well, although there is very little new stuff to be found there. Mostly though, I've travelled to these places and spent the day in each town, at the local history dept. of that library, waded all through the local papers of the 1870s and 1880s and been and found out the exact location of the extinct football grounds or areas of land used, and stood on the very spot where, almost one and a half centuries before, the very beginnings of football as we know it today were put in motion by enthusiastic men and boys, scrambling to kick a heavy wet leather football under the tapes of a primitive wooden goalpost, devoid of any pitch markings or officials.

Umpires and Referees

At the beginning, each team would put forward one man to act as umpire in each half of the pitch. Naturally, there were many times the two umpires couldn't agree, as each goal scored had to be claimed by the player raising an arm, hopefully being returned with a nod from the umpire. Offside claims, too, were numerous and hard to discriminate. These too had to be appealed to with the umpire, there being no linesman (yet) to run the line and keep up with play. Eventually, a third, independent person, who stood off the pitch, would give judgement on disputes which the umpires 'referred' to him.

He of course became the referee, and later development saw him alone remain on the field of play. The umpires returned, each running along the touchline, and now are known as linesmen (assistant referees, after 2009). Some referees were themselves famous players, such as Major Marindin of the Royal Engineers and FA committee fame. Charles Crump, the well-known Wolverhampton dignitary, being president of the Birmingham FA, FA committee, and Mayor of Wolverhampton as well as being Chief Clerk at the G.W.R loco repair depot in Bushbury, was not unknown to referee the Birmingham Senior Cup final or the final of the Staffordshire cup. Throughout this early period, umpires or referees did not have the whistle, despite that sound being a constant familiar noise to the men who worked at Crump's railway depot being the players of the Stafford Road FC. Rather, a white or red handkerchief was raised or waved to indicate a goal given. The referee's whistle is claimed to first have been heard at a match in Nottingham in 1878. This could have been at a game where the official had links to the Midland Railway. Is there any truth in the idea that the umpire or referee couldn't make himself noticed with just a red handkerchief or small flag and in an impromptu moment of inspiration took out his railwayman's whistle from his waistcoat pocket and startled everyone with the first ever shrill single-whistle blow?

Joseph Hudson, a Derbyshire farm worker, moved to Birmingham in 1860 and set up a small workshop at the back of his house in St. Mark's Street, in the Jewellery Quarter, making anything that he could to provide his family with an income. Alongside snuff boxes and boot repairs, he began making whistles after the Metropolitan Police were looking for something to supersede the old rattle which up to then had been the policeman's only communication device. After 1883, his ACME Whistle company greatly expanded its output as his range of whistles diversified for different types of occupation, and ACME is now recognised as the world's oldest and best maker of cup final whistles.

Referees had a hard time of it too, especially in the pre-Football League days. Forced to get changed in the most primitive of conditions, such as a shed or a pub involving a long walk to the ground, with no security for his belongings or workday clothes, he came in; he was an overlooked and maligned character. Even when the Football League started, and referees were awarded a Guinea (£1/1/0) = £1.05p) to cover all travel, refreshment and lodging expenses, he was lucky to get it. He was required, after the match, when everyone had gone home, to seek out the home club's financial secretary and ask for his money. If our poor referee was pressed for time to catch a train home, or couldn't find the secretary, he would have to apply in retro by letter a few days later for a cheque to be forwarded to his address. Often, if he should think himself lucky to be offered changing facilities with one of the teams, he would regret it after the match, should that be the losing team, especially if they felt aggrieved at some of his decisions!

According to 'Association Football' Charles Alcock's 1905s handbook on the potted history of the Football Association to date, and how to play the game according to the current rules, the standard pay to a referee for ordinary cup ties was 10/6 (ten shillings and sixpence=53p), with any overnight stay expenses being met by the home club. The referee would, even in the last two decades of the nineteenth century, do a pitch inspection two hours prior to the advertised kick-off time, and his decision was final. If a cup-tie was called off due to the state of the pitch, clubs were not allowed to play a friendly or league match instead, although I have read several newspaper reports where this did indeed happen.

Equipment

The great joy about football, like cricket, is that all you need is a ball and four sticks of wood. But even cricket needs a bat of course, as well. So 'footer' was a street game that could now relatively safely be played by children, youths, and men of all abilities on almost any surface, be it grass, concrete, cobbles, or courtyard, and in any type of weather, and thus took hold of the masses. Cricket lost out on the last point, working best on a dry spring or summer's day, and thus by 1895, this country's greatest ever all-round sportsman, Charles Burgess Fry, proclaimed that football, not cricket, was now the national game. Up until say 1950, no one would need to be reminded of Fry's fantastic abilities; he played both cricket and football at England level, one of cricket's all-time batsmen, world long-jump record holder, a supreme athlete the like of which modern sport has seen no equal. It would be like combining Daley Thopson with Alan Shearer and Ian Botham. Modern-day readers would do well to read one of his biographies and be startled at his achievements compared to today's so-called football superstars.

And thus, with such rudimentary equipment, football took root in England's schools, factories, and Universities. During the embryonic 1850-60 period, when the basic elements of the modern game were being fashioned into shape in the public schools and the universities, each establishment designed its own version of the basic premise of getting the ball in between the sticks at the other end of the playing area. Some colleges were limited to cloisters and narrow passageways within their ancient buildings, and thus a dribbling game backed up with pack-like rushes developed in those places. Others had more room on their playing fields (Eton), and goals were placed wider apart (up to 20 yards apart at Uppingham, Rutland).

But of course in terms of this book, concerned as it is solely with Midlands' teams, much of this is academic, with most Staffordshire and Warwickshire teams adopting a goal of 8 yards x 8 feet. The Hallam & Sheffield brigade, certain that their rules should be followed even by the London FA, persisted for some time with nine-foot high goal tapes and with rouges. In the rouge scoring system, four poles are driven into the ground, each one four feet apart from the next. The centre two poles count as a goal, whilst the outside poles count as rouges. It was an attempt to give recognition to a near miss, although today of course, we just award a goal kick.

It was really the installation of the FA Cup in 1871 which provided the benchmark on the national scene, because all entrants had to follow the London FA rules and regulations. It was the Sheffield club which introduced goal nets, crossbars, and floodlights to the game, however, so we must thank them for that, and Nottingham gave the game ref's whistles and shin pads.

By the mid-1880s, most of England was singing from the same hymn-sheet, as we say today, and a match in Derbyshire was no different to the one in Worcestershire. Major Marindin of the FA had brought the four home countries together in 1882 to agree on a unified set of rules and regulations.

Samuel Widdowson came up with one of the most useful inventions in 1874. He was a keen player who played for several of the Nottingham sides, but principally the Forest side. He was also a first-class cricketer and came up with the idea of wearing modified cricket pads on the outside of football stockings to protect the lower leg from the hacking and heavy tackling which was still permitted then. Very quickly, this idea was taken up throughout the Midlands, and eventually, these 'shin guards' came to be worn inside the stockings instead. Forest were a pioneering team in many ways; their men were the first to use goal nets attached to the goals (Old Etonians had used a catch-net behind the goals earlier, but not attached), and the referees' whistle in a game against Sheffield Norfolk, who, incidentally played in mauve and black hoops.

As transport facilities progressed, with the coming of steam and electric trams (steam train travel was beyond the purse of most working-class folk), a whole industry sprang up to furnish and support the players and fans of organised football. Wool-mills and drapery shops would be making, advertising, and selling all types of football shirts, hose, and boots, and rosettes, rattles, and scarves for the fans. The printing industry found a new friend in the demand for posters and leaflets advertising not just football matches, but all the ointments, lotions, and remedies which sprang up with eye-raising claims as cure-alls for sprains, lesions, and aching muscles. Long gone now, the wooden simple goalposts, there were companies making fold-down or easy dismantle goal frames, corner flags, and even small grandstands. By the end of the 1890s, outfitters and manufacturers were selling shirts, knicks, and stockings in every available colour and size, offering up to three standards of quality too. Gammages of Holborn, London, were advertising standard shirts at 2/8d (13p), knickers at 1/10d (9p), and shin guards at a shilling (5p). The Universal football boot was 5/11d (30p) and a match ball cost 10/6d (52.5p). Even goal nets were in their catalogue, although at over 30/-(thirty shillings = £1.50), this represented about a week's wages for most folk.

Popular in the day were the cards printed with such phrases as 'Play up, Swifts!', or some were called cemetery cards, which took the mickey out of the demise of the vanquished club, especially where a local derby was concerned, with that team's name printed in black inside a coffin or suchlike. Football clubs began to print match cards, listing the anticipated line-up of both teams, hoping that the curious public would turn out in numbers should the visiting team promise to bring their 'star' players, or 'cup team' as they were known then. The iron and steel industry too, centred in the Black Country, but also in Manchester and Sheffield, found a new product in cast-iron turnstiles and ornate railings and gates at football grounds; Wednesbury tube would make steel crush barriers and goals, and well-to-do teams might have a dressing room containing several cast-iron baths. The country's leading leather town of Walsall would also discover a national demand for laced leather footballs, or supply the leather almond cut shapes and send them to manufacturers around the country, who stitched them together. An India-rubber bladder football would cost you around 7 or 8 shillings in 1878, depending on quality. Prices rose slowly in the last quarter of the nineteenth century, but as wages crept up above the level of inflation, it was getting less expensive to kit out a football team.

Research

In reality, I had been collecting historical football information for over thirty years, ever since I discovered the nostalgia of the Wanderers FC (London), the five-times FA cup winners in their short history. I had a wealth of information about the Old Boys' teams, some of which still play today because the institution from which they sprang is still there, be it a university, public school, or the Forces.

For the purposes of this book, however, I kept myself to Midlands teams, who, unless they developed into a current team, such as Small Heath, Fosse, and Singers did, are all dead and buried in an age when football was of little interest to the press, and consequently, as all football historians know, makes it very difficult to find any new material. What I have done, however, is many miles of legwork added to Internet research. I have stood on the spot of most of the defunct teams' grounds in this book, and I do believe that I have photographed the actual sites of where they played. Many have been built over, and what was built has been knocked down again and rebuilt in modern times. During the 1890s, much land was given over to the very lucrative concept of house-building on a wholesale scale. The old Bournbrook Grounds on the Bristol Road at Selly Oak near Birmingham University and the nearby tram depot were built over in 1900 and built over again for student accommodation flats exactly a century later. However, some of the places are still to be found, once you have worked out where they were. Often, disappointment was the host to my travels, but sometimes a quiet inner joy when I would stand on a grassy forgotten field, to be stared at by a passing dog-walker, who would not know my entirely different reason for being there. More than once, it has to be admitted that I went to the wrong place, sometimes only by a few hundred yards, then later to return to the true location once I had realised my error. More than once I discovered that an old public house, which had been quoted as a reference point to a ground, used to be on the other side of the road in the 1870s but was knocked down and rebuilt in its present location! I have surprised more than one householder when informing them that what is now their back gardens used to be an old football ground where perhaps 2,000 or 3,000 people would gather to watch a team that they (today) had never heard of. That was the case for Wednesbury's Trapezium ground.

I have also tried through many hours of searching in each town's local history section, to discover the colours of the team I was researching on that day, only to be foiled at every turn, as in the case of the Wednesbury Strollers.* There was no shortage of column inches in the Wednesbury press, with match details and annual presentation evenings, but nowhere could any reference to shirt colours be obtained. This was particularly frustrating, as I live only a few miles from that town. It was only a few months before going to the publisher that I discovered the Stroller's colours.

Indeed, all the Aston, Birmingham, Walsall, and Smethwick teams were on my doorstep; also as I worked as a manager for the Birmingham City Council, I had access to places with council links such as Saltley College, Calthorpe, and Warwick County. I also had the good fortune to go and visit Mr Roy Burford at his home at Cape Hill many years ago, and we went through his amazing collection of Mitchell St. George's memorabilia, including Victorian postcards for the team, the players, and the ground. A few days doing site visits to the East Midlands was greatly enhanced by the help of Buxton football historian Terrance Fletcher. He came out and helped me discover seven grounds in Derby, including the lost grounds of Derby Midland, Derby Junction, and Derby Town, and he continued to keep in touch whenever new information came to light regarding my theories. One discovery was the Vulcan ground, and another being the realisation that Derby Junction Street School FC didn't come from a proper school! The Derby Junction photograph came from his vast football photo collection too.

There must be many households in towns around the Midlands, where their great-grandparents played for these long-forgotten teams, and people like Roy are in possession of boxes of old photographs to which they attach little importance to the funny old sepia-tinted photographs of great uncle Ezra in his hooped top and trousers cut off below the knee!

The Press

Newspapers of course played an important part in popularising the game of football. The nationals were only really interested in the most important matches – the Cup Final of course – and the representative games, which were popular in the 1870s and 80s, and the annual international matches, limited in the nineteenth century to games between the home nations. Regional games were reported in the local newspapers of each town to a varying degree: many games were simply nothing more than a statement of the score itself, other town papers quickly got behind the town's leading team and gave fuller accounts.

Having now read hundreds of local papers of the period from all over the Midlands, I soon realised that they were not 'local news' papers at all. There was news from all around the world, with all manner of political, agricultural, industrial, and social reports and comments throughout. They were in effect a locally printed version of the BBC World News. When you think about it, we are so used to finding about what's going on in the world all around us today from the radio, television, Internet, and all the other new technology devices which continue to be created, we forget that a one-penny newspaper, purchased and printed locally, was the only way that most of the populous got to hear about what was happening outside of their own town. The front page of the *Walsall Observer* in the 1880s for example would carry leading articles on the war in the Pacific in South America, letters from Florence Nightingale, an explosion in an African gold mine, the death of a leading member of the government, and ships sinking in Argentina! The inside pages would be full of helpful hints for the housewife, the latest washing machine (a new invention), the tonnage output figure for the iron and steel industries, and the reports of various committees representing all the trades prevalent in the town. Buried amongst advertisements for pills and cures for everything from colds and flu to artificial legs and corsets, one might be lucky to read about the sports events of the day.

Cricket, of course, being an older sport by almost a century, was well reported, with a resume of the match, a list of all the batting and bowling details, and a few players picked out for merit. Quoits, archery, and rifle-shooting were popularly reported in the Staffordshire and Warwickshire papers too. When football first began to be reported, in the mid-1870s, reports were both brief and often inaccurate. Names would be spelt incorrectly: written more often, as they were spoken. Dyass would be Dyoss the following week, Davis would become Davies, and so on.

The newspapers, of course, did not despatch junior reporters to all corners of the district to watch and report on any of these games; rather, it was up to the home team secretary to send in a report to the papers, and in order to secure publication, he would have to be there in time to meet the printing deadline as advertised. Naturally, with the report coming from the home team – often the victors – the account would hardly be expected to be a neutral or objective one. A big win for the home team would illuminate certain star players from the match; goals scored by the visiting side would not even include the goalscorer's name, and quite frequently, at the end of the report, only the names of the home team players would be given. Reading these match reports was also somewhat infuriating. There might be a proper description of how the home team went 3-0 up, with goalscorers' names and how those goals were obtained, etc., but if the away side scored 3 to draw the game, you would be lucky to read their names or even have the goals mentioned at all! I have read several so-called match reports where you read the sequence of events, of the description of how and when the goals were scored, only to find that that match ended 7-2, but you only read a description of five of the goals. You would also read about things which don't seem to matter to us today-'a light westerly breeze prevailed' at the kick-off; the home side 'kicked-off towards the church'; the visiting team 'were comprised of heavy-looking men', and so on. Unfortunately, it was what one didn't read which, frustratingly, was more important.

What colour shirts did both teams play in? What was the name of the ground, and where was it? Did the referees blow whistles or wave flags, etc.? Almost never in nearly 300 match reports did I read what colour shirts the teams played in. The venue was always simply described as 'the ground of the former/latter', with no location given or alluded to. The crowd, of course, was only estimated before the advent of turnstiles and was generally reckoned thus: each single layer of spectators around the pitch would count as half a thousand spectators. This is devolved from the idea that a pitch 120 × 80 yards would have a perimeter of 400 yards, and that each person would need about a yard of space to himself, thus say 400 persons per 400 yards. Therefore, a crowd of five persons' deep all around the ground would be estimated as being 2,000. The home club secretary could of course submit the paying attendance to the press, but to reveal publicly what the gate receipts are each week would put the football club open to the suspicions of prying eyes and ears of those members of the community who viewed the trend towards a professional football system with disapproval, to say nothing of the local tax inspector!

Many clubs of course gave a goodly portion of their income to local charities, but this was a double-edged sword, as it was also the downfall of many a local team with Christian or charitable beliefs, who found themselves short on funds when ground improvements or new kit were called for. The whole reason d'etre of the Wednesbury Football Association was to use the popularisation of football to furnish funds for the town's charitable causes. In this regard, they were entirely open and above board, and published full accounts and balance sheets annually in the newspapers, demonstrating how they had distributed the monies set aside. Most went to up to thirty small charities, such as hospitals, almshouses, widows, and orphanages, and small amounts as pensions to footballers whose career had ended due to broken limbs.

Returning to actual newspaper match reports, it is here where the sleuth would detect an element of repetition and be able to join up the dots to discover a bit more about the lives of the leading players themselves. Many footballers had unusual surnames: Greatorex, Dyoss, Kilpin, Danks, Addenbrooke, Amphlett, and so on. One then begins to see these surnames appearing for different teams, perhaps up to ten miles apart, and one can begin to see that those very keen men who helped to start a football club in one town or village would go on and do it again in their workplace town, or if they moved to another location. Sometimes, a player could be spotted playing for up to four different sides, all at the same time, since players were free to do as they wished in the amateur days, and even to a degree, if they were paid as a 'professor' or professional by one club, they might still turn out for another. However, this is the root of many of the claims read about in the newspapers, where a losing team (usually) lodges a protest against the winning team on the basis that so-and-so who happened to have scored the winning goal also turned out for another team either concurrently or earlier in the season.

For myself, in researching this book, where I have discovered the colours of a team which were hitherto unknown, I have sometimes had to piece together snippets of information which I have gathered over many years. A black-and-white photograph seen in 1985 might have to wait twenty years before I read that 'the sky blues' played 'a plucky game', and that the 'ground of the former' was the Derby Turn, for example. I have also learnt to take the ground location with a wide brush, as the actual pitch has often turned out to be several hundred yards from that as given. In the 1880s, clearly the road infrastructure was primitive compared with today's network.

In that time, there would only be perhaps two or three lanes which ran out of a town or village to its neighbours. Thus, a team renting a field from a farmer or landowner, which might be a five-minute walk off the beaten track, would give the ground location as being the nearest well-known road.

Within ten years of the game being played formally, the newspapers soon carried advertisements of outfitters selling shirts, caps, and 'hose' of the local football team. In those days, if you agreed to join a club, it was down to yourself to go out and buy your own team shirt. This explains why you see a team photo where there are seven men in identical thin hooped shirts and the other four are in wide hoops. It's because they purchased them from different shops. Adverts also appeared for every type of treatment and relief from cuts, sprains, bruises, and for all sorts of elixirs which would give you more strength and vigour.

As time went on, I detected a shift in the attitude of the newspapers to football. In the 1870s, the novelty factor was high, and even though a club might only play five or six games a season, they would generally get mentioned. By the 1880s, there were so many teams turning out every Saturday in each town that up to half a page would have to be given over to football reports, whereas in the summer, cricket games only took up a quarter column. As a consequence, papers had to limit the size of match reports according to the importance of the teams in question. The Walsall press, for example, gave about 25 per cent of their half page to the Town side, slightly less to the Swifts, and up to thirty lesser sides would share out the rest of the column inches. Minor teams would be relegated to simply having their scores listed. Unfortunately, many of the teams in this book are in the category of a 'brief report'. It would need many reports from different newspapers before

I could piece together enough detail to bring together the story of even the more well-known teams.

At first, and because it was a new sport, newspapers did not have the terminology at their disposal to describe a football match in a way which modern readers would obtain a clear understanding. Modern-day phrases such as 'he sent over good cross', 'a diving header', 'a bending shot', 'the goalie dived to save', 'a dummy or nutmeg' had not been created then, and so the match reports are full of alien phrases and clumsy descriptions. Centring the ball was called 'middling'. A swerve or bending shot was called a 'screw shot', and phrases such as 'a goal was obtained by judicious work' and the goalkeeper was 'forced to exert himself to the fullest' were the order of the day. Even a goal was often called a point. 'The Swifts added another two points to their tally' or 'the goalkeeper prevented the point by use of his hands' being the Victorian descriptions of events. In the early 1870s, goals were augmented by rouges, especially if the teams were playing to Sheffield rules. Rouges were either the ball being propelled between outer sticks either side of the goalposts, or rugby-style, the ball being carried past the defence to the goal line. Today, this would simply be a goal kick unless the ball comes off a defender, in which case it's a corner kick. The papers thought they needed to mention that the ball had been carried to the opposing goal line, but didn't seem to know what to do with this detail. In the late 1860s, rouges would be used to decide the winner of a match if the scores were level at ninety minutes. The opposing goal was described in the papers as the 'citadel'.

It was as if the newspapermen were trying to compare the game of football with a battle, where the object is to assail the castle, storm the citadel, and lower their flag. Such phrases were also used in match reports too; the 'visitors flag was lowered'; the 'away team's fortress was subjected to constant attacks', and so on. Despite their stilted and outdated phraseology, those Victorian match reports make for enjoyable reading and actually tell the reader much more of what went on in the game than today's so-called match reports, where tabloid scandal, sensation, and speculation are placed before a description and assessment of what has actually taken place over those ninety minutes.

As more time went on, into the 1890s, football had become a big business, with hundreds of teams either entirely professional or had one or two star attackers paid by the game. Many local newspapers were beginning to lose interest in the direction that things were going. Articles began to appear, complaining that the wholesome and original idea of mainly amateur sportsmanship was being lost to the game and that money was the new prize and not success in itself. The top teams employed players, who sometimes would deliberately set out to injure opponents because they had to have success at all costs. Even after professionalism was legalised in 1885, many so-called 'amateur' teams were paying their men under-counter money above and beyond out of pocket expenses for turning out. Even the Corinthians were not beyond criticism in this regard.

By the late 1890s, many of the early pioneering sides had fallen by the wayside, and thus local papers could focus their attentions on the principal one or two teams in their town, although Derby still had most of theirs, and Burton still had more than it needed. In the Birmingham area, Aston Villa were so huge nationally that even Small Heath struggled for column inches. After the 1910s, the papers had something much more important than even football to report on. The Great War was around the corner, and much of football was suspended for the duration. It was whilst searching through newspapers of 1916 for football that I became aware of a feeling of guilt which had come over me. I was ignoring the whole newspaper which was full of epitaphs of soldiers and sailors, mostly under the age of 25, whose lives had ended on that day, to look for the results of a football match! As I stood back to realise what it all meant, and read about young men killed in action in horrendous conditions, I had a cold sharp reality check on the comparative non-importance of the research that I was doing. Whilst Bill Shankley may have famously said that "football isn't like life and death – it's more important than that", those 1916 newspapers taught me that nothing is more important than life itself.

Football was expected to lead the way in terms of volunteering its men for conscription, and it did. Many teams had their entire playing staff sent off the war; many teams never got them back, and 1915 drew a line under football. Things would never be the same again.

An early attempt by the newspapers to provide a comparison table of Midland teams was based purely on the number of games won during the 1884/5 season, having no regard to the varying quality of the opposition! Note the wording of goals obtained/lost as opposed to For/Against as used today, and the fact that the team with the most wins (nineteen) are below halfway –

Presumably the goals record for Birmingham St. George's had not been recorded.

Club	PL	W	L	D	Goals obtained	Goals lost
Wolverhampton Wanderers	22	15	2	5	95	19
Birmingham St. George's	22	15	4	3		
Leek Town	20	14	4	2	80	39
West Bromwich Albion	21	14	4	3	88	22
Walsall Swifts	25	14	6	5	63	33
Walsall Town	22	13	7	2	103	24
Aston Excelsior	13	10	2	1	49	18
Aston Villa	18	10	6	2	53	37
Small Heath Alliance	27	19	6	2	38	31
Stoke	19	9	9	1	50	41
Wednesbury Town	13	6	6	1	29	35
Stafford Rangers	18	5	5	8	32	25

* Finally discovered thanks to Steve Carr on the eve of publication.

The Administrators

1. The Wednesbury AFA

The Wednesbury & District Charity Football Association. Doesn't sound much, does it? But this little town just three miles from both Walsall and West Bromwich was instrumental and progressive in promoting the ordered growth of football and football clubs in the West Midlands region throughout the 1870s and 1880s.

Frederick Hackwood (1851-1926) was Wednesbury's most illustrious citizen. He was a leading light in bringing about the general improvement of every social and economic aspect of the town throughout his life. He was a Justice of the Peace, deputy to the town's Member of Parliament, secretary of the Freemasons Lodge; he set up the Wednesbury Institute, its Horticultural Society, and was a prolific local history bookwriter, with over forty published books on every aspect of Wednesbury life. He went through that breeding ground of so many others who went far and wide and promoted healthy sport, especially football, wherever their teachings took them, Saltley College in east Birmingham, from 1870 to 1871.

Hackwood set up Wednesbury's first football club, at first simply called Wednesbury FC, but later adding the suffix of Strollers to their name as other teams started up in the town. This was in 1873, and soon, rivals Wednesbury Old Athletics and Elwells started up too; by 1881 the Wednesbury Association had no less than 45 teams within its wings. This bringing together of what must have felt like a family of Staffordshire clubs was the vital factor that in order to compete for the Wednesbury Cup, a club had to become a member of that Association. Without realising it, Wednesbury, Birmingham and then the Walsall Associations, through this membership – to – compete rule, drew together clubs from the region into a family body, and much rivalry and friendships became of it, cemented by the association's annual presentation of awards ceremony, in Wednesbury's case, at the Anchor Hotel on Hollyhead Road.

The Wednesbury Charity Cup doesn't sound worth playing for either, by today's standards, but the committee of prominent businessmen and civic dignitaries who commissioned it from the finest silversmiths (White &

Hawkins Co.) in Birmingham's Jewellery Quarter at a cost of 60 guineas intended it to be the finest football trophy in England. And it was. The 30" high solid silver cup was about five year's wages for a skilled labourer at the time. It was a knockout competition limited to just eight selected teams for the first decade, and to be selected to take part meant your team was one of the best in the Midlands. Of course, the Wednesbury sides usually took part, but teams as far as Nottm Forest, Oswestry, Stoke (a minor team at the time), Chesterfield Spital, Aston Unity and Calthorpe were all eager participants.

The first cup draw didn't take place until the Association had been going for a couple of years. On 13 February 1880, President Isaac Griffiths, the Associations' co-founder, drew the following names out of the hat:

Derby Town v Stafford Road (W'ton)
Wednesbury Old Athletic v Aston Unity
Wednesbury Strollers v Elwells FC
Stoke v West Bromwich (Dartmouth)

Twelve teams entered in the second year, including Nottm Forest and Oswestry.

The committee controlled every aspect of the competition; they named the dates of the fixtures and appointed the referees for each game. Courtesy of a Mr Watson, the proprietor, they met once a month at the Anchor Hotel in committee, with Hackwood, Tranter, W. H. Jope, and J. Arnall in the senior positions, and each club sent along its representative. Crump for Stafford Road, of course, for he was to become president of the Birmingham FA, George Salter for the West Brom Dartmouth, E. M. Scott for the Strollers, Allden for the Elwells, and S. Durban or such for the Aston Unity. They would witness and report back on the cup draws and hear the committee announce their decisions on the many and various appeals from the previous month's games. It was still all too common for teams to turn up late (sometimes so late, it caused the last half hour to be played in darkness), or worse still to not turn up at all; public transport was still in its infancy too. Many a team, some never having left the town they were born in, and some travelling by train for the first time, alighted at the wrong station and had to endure a couple of miles' walk to their opponent's ground. Arriving weary, they would be in no state to give a fair performance with the inevitable easy home victory to cap a sorry day all round. The Old Athletic team, who travelled to Derbyshire to play the Spital team, set out at breakfast, caught every connection without delay, and still didn't get back to Wednesbury until almost 1 a.m. the next morning! Good job, but it was only church the next morning.

In the above 1st round draw, you may like to know that Stafford Road had an easy 6-2 win at Derby, Elwells had a thrilling 3-2 win at the Oval, and unknown Stoke surprisingly beat the Dartmouth team by 3-1. Aston Unity scratched to the Old Athletic; the reason? They had a much more important cricket match that day, and their best four players were key to the cricket team! Those two teams did meet, in the final the following year, when after a 2-2 draw, Old Athletic edged home 3-2 over the cricketers from Aston.

The Wednesbury committee were also looking after the social well-being of its townsfolk; Hackwood, Scott, and Griffiths were all staunch Christians and held office at the Wednesbury parish church; indeed several of the Strollers' leading men all lived within a few hundred yards of the parish church on the hill. The committee would award small monetary sums to local footballers who were sufficiently injured to prevent them from going to work for the next week. A few shillings here and there all helped, and a broken leg which ended your footballing days might get you a few pounds. Most of the Wednesbury committee were wealthy men: Isaac Griffiths, Elwell, and Knowles had their own steel tube mills or foundries. The new middle-class men were facilitating the working-class men of Wednesbury to compete in a way which was both healthy to their minds and bodies.

The competition grew and grew year on year, and by 1896, the entrants numbered over forty, drawn from five counties. Accordingly, the early rounds were regionalised to limit travelling expenditure, but this had its downfalls; teams would find, as in the English Cup after it was regionalised in 1888/9, that you were drawn against the same one or two sides every year, and the public – if not the teams and their officials – got rapidly fed up with this.

Nonetheless, by 1890, Wednesbury Association were running both a Junior Cup, and a minor cup for school teams, to promote the introduction of athletic sports into school curricula. Teams which had earlier made their name in the senior event were now to be found in the junior ranks; this was the same story across in the Birmingham Association, and in Derbyshire and Nottinghamshire too, as the early pioneering teams gave way to the professional teams we know today.

When Frederick Hackwood died in 1926, he was given a civic funeral of honour by the people of Wednesbury whom he had served so well. His legacy to football still continues today, as the Wednesbury Charity Cup, which since its inception gave all the cleared funds to local hospitals and charities, is still played for over 130 years later.

Wednesbury Charity Cup-the early winners were:-

1880	Stafford Road
1881	Wednesbury Old Athletic
1882	Wednesbury Old Athletic
1883	Nottm Forest
1884	Wednesbury Town (Strollers)
1885	Birmingham Excelsior
1886	Walsall Town
1887	Wednesbury Old Ath
1888	Wolverhampton Wanderers
1889	Wednesbury Old Ath
1890	Wednesbury Old Ath
1891	Wednesbury Old Ath

References

F. W. Hackwood: *The History of Wednesbury*

The Wednesbury Football Association's committee books 1879-1900, volumes 1-5

Sandwell Archives Library, Smethwick

The Wednesbury Herald 1879-1885

2. The Birmingham FA

The Birmingham Football Association started life in 1875 when the Aston Unity and Calthorpe clubs were weary of friendlies, cancelled games, a lack of unity of rules, and the general lack of organisation amongst the football team of the Birmingham and Aston districts.

"We felt severely the want of a Union and the inconvenience of playing different association rules." These were the words that caused the men from Aston Park Unity and the Birmingham Clerks Association (Calthorpe FC) to form the Birmingham Football Association, twelve years after the Football Association itself had, after a lengthy and protracted wrangling, set down a universally accepted set of playing rules for affiliated clubs throughout the land. At first (1875/6/7), the Birmingham FA adopted the Sheffield Rules, but switched to the London (FA) Rules in 1877, presumably because Birmingham area teams wanted to compete in the English Cup.

Cricket, of course, had a long start on football, and although the world's first ever competitive cricket league didn't start until 1889, the Birmingham & District League, the leading players of the famous cricketing Aston Unity and the middle-class well-educated men of the Calthorpe team (they were comprised of articled clerks in the town centre) knew that somebody had to take control and set up an organising body to bring together the Birmingham clubs. The London FA was thought of as just that: controlling the capitals' footballing affairs but not suited to Midland matters as it was too remote. Yes, Major Marindin of the Royal Engineers FC and Football Association committee would come up to Birmingham to be the final arbitrator on disciplinary matters in later years, but just as some people in Scotland and Wales today judge Parliament to be too remote from local matters, so it was in the 1870s Midlands' football.

A primary aim of the new Birmingham FA was to set up a Cup competition, and this they did in December 1875. However, it was too late in the footballing year, and so they launched it in the following Autumn. The following clubs attended the launch meeting at Mason's Hotel, Birmingham.

Calthorpe, Aston Unity, Wednesbury Town, Wednesbury Old Athletic, Stafford Road, Birmingham FC, (not Small Heath), Saltley College, Aston Villa, Tipton, St. George's FC, and West Bromwich (Dartmouth). Charles Crump of Stafford Road FC was elected president, and J. Campbell Orr (Calthorpe) was elected secretary, with Swallow of Saltley College as treasurer.

Each club was asked to donate towards the purchase of a silver cup. Calthorpe gave seven guineas (a guinea was one pound one shilling); whilst Wednesbury Old Park gave just ten shillings. Apparently, three teams gave nothing at all! Seven guineas from Calthorpe was a considerable sum in 1875; a domestic servant might only be paid around £10 per annum in those days.

Many publications give the 1875 match between Tipton and Aston Villa as the first Birmingham Cup final; but it was not so. What happened was that the Birmingham FA selected a venue, Wednesbury Strollers' Crankhall Farm Lane ground, and selected Tipton and Villa to play an exhibition game to see what the public response was. The response was very promising, since Wednesbury was football – mad. Tipton won 1-0, but there were no other teams involved in 1875: no knockout rounds, just that exhibition final. The Birmingham FA centenary yearbook of 1975 lists it as their first final, but reading the book, it is littered with errors, odd dates, and wrong team names. I have read the exhibition final story in the Wednesbury newspapers of 1880 for confirmation.

By 1885, many towns and cities had their own Challenge Cups; most county associations did too. But in terms of importance, it was fair to say that after the English FA Cup, the Birmingham Cup was next in succession of desirability and importance, even over say, the Staffordshire Cup. It is for this reason that one of the selection factors in writing this book was to choose teams that had enjoyed success or contributed to that competition's success, both at senior and junior level. Apart from Stoke in 1877-78-79, Birmingham area teams had won the Staffordshire Cup anyway until the advent of the Football League, and so for the purposes of this book, I rank the achievements of clubs in the Birmingham Cup higher than for example, the Nottm, Derbyshire, or Shropshire county cups.

In their centenary publication of 1975, the Birmingham Football Association reflected on their founding fathers and singled out the immense achievements of Charles Crump and James Campbell Orr, who both gave a lifetime of dedication to the association and the promoting of football in general throughout the West Midlands region. Orr was either the Association's secretary or the treasurer from 1875 until his death in office in 1921. The hard-working Crump was also on the board of directors at Wolverhampton Wanderers. These two men were the giants of Midlands football, along with William McGreggor.

The B.F.A. committee and sub-committees were concerned about every aspect of the game at both amateur and professional levels, and schoolboy level too; by 1900, there was a thriving B'ham schools organisation. They had little or no precedent; yes, the London FA since 1863 had formulated the game and attended to disciplinary matters, but 1870s London was very remote from the centre of the country. The Birmingham FA had had to set the benchmark for truth, accuracy, and fairness and what a success they made of it! Their empire flourished and expanded at an alarming rate, with dozens of affiliated teams turning into the hundreds by 1883, and then into about 3,000 by the First World War. They also administered the ever-growing number of leagues, cups, and inter-league competitions which went past the 300 mark by 1920. Today, Campbell Orr is remembered in the competition which bears his name, played for by inter-league representative sides. Even Premiership clubs like Aston Villa, Birmingham, Coventry City, and Wolves are all still affiliated to the Birmingham FA.

The first ever Birmingham Cup final was played between Wednesbury Old Athletic and Stafford Road, a work's team from the large GWR locomotive repair depot in Wolverhampton. Over 2,000 spectators paying 3d, each gathered behind the Bournbrook Hotel on Bristol Road Selly Oak at Calthorpe's ground to see a five-goal thriller, with the Wednesbury men taking the cup home in a 3-2 win. Amazingly, after paying the expenses of the two clubs involved, the bulk of the gate money was given to various local charities! A surplus of money was actually an embarrassment in the early years, and the various associations did not want it on their hands.

It was this cup final, claimed the *Birmingham Daily Post* on 15 October 1886, that really sparked the flame for football in the region; it was the catalyst for the explosion of the game, both for spectators, who could now start to show their allegiance to the team of their choice, and for new teams to flourish in the area.

As the years went by, the entries to the Birmingham Cup of course, grew and grew, until by 1880, almost every club with aspiration, was entering. Some clubs would rely on a fixture card of cup ties assembled by entering the Birmingham, Wednesbury, Walsall, and Staffordshire cups. As the 1880s went on, other town cups sprang up all over the place, each one catering for the different levels of senior and junior and schoolboy football.

The concept of arranging your cup competition to have multiples of four in order to eliminate down to a four-team semi-final had not been thought of in the early years, and quite often there would be five teams left in the cup after four rounds, or a three-team semi-final, leading to one lucky side getting a bye into the final; how aggrieved one wonders were the teams who lost the one semi-final game which was played, especially if they had a better chance of being the 'bye' team in the final, had they got there.

Early years' results (1870s) saw some which might raise an eyebrow today; Aston Unity beating the Villa 5-0; unknown St. George's from Aston beating the Wolves; Stafford Road putting seven past Walsall (Swifts); and Wednesbury Old Athletic beating West Bromwich Albion. These were in the days when the roles were reversed to today; most of today's football league or premiership teams weren't formed until these early amateur sides had had their day, their brief decade of glory in the sunshine of association football hall of fame.

Of course, as the decades moved on, by 1890, the semi-finalists each year were familiar names from today's football: Aston Villa, Albion, Wolves, and Walsall or Stoke. The Birmingham Cup, by then, had swollen to an unmanageable near fifty teams; regionalisation and then, the same year as the Football League started, a separate qualifying competition.

However, once the Football League had taken the public's heart, with regular guaranteed top-draw opposition from all over the country, the Birmingham Cup began to lose its appeal, as one by one, the league sides just entered their reserve sides. Crowds dwindled, entries got fewer, until it was back to eight, and small-fry thanked the Lord for the Birmingham Junior Cup, first won by Aston Victoria in 1888/9. The *Birmingham Daily Post* in 1886, however, ran an article on the state of football nationally; a resume of its first twenty years. It seems that all was not well and that the newspaper editor had some scathing things to say about the way the game was changing. The game was past its zenith, it said; amateur spirit and good sportsmanship had gone forever; and that 'men no longer play for true honour but to the highest bidder for their services'. Hard words, almost alarmist, but we, for whom true amateurism is a bygone concept, can only imagine their angst.

Weeks of searching through newspaper reports from 1873 to 1900, however, left me with one impression, that at first, when football was a novelty, a paper would print match reports from perhaps twenty local games, even though it was the responsibility of team secretaries to send them to the press. By 1895, the *Walsall Observer and South Staffordshire Chronicle*, for example, would only run match reports from Walsall Town-Swifts and Bloxwich Strollers. The papers had become bored with football.

Birmingham Football Association Cup Finals (up to 1900)

	Senior	Senior venue	Junior (begun 1887/8)
1876/7	Wednesbury Old A. 3 Stafford Road 2	Bournbrook Ground	
1877/8	Shrewsbury FC 2 Wednesbury Stroll. 1	Wellington Road	
1878/9	Wednesbury Old A. 3 Stafford Road 2	Wellington Road	
1879/80	Aston Villa 3 Saltley College 1	Aston Lower Grounds	
1880/1	Walsall Swifts 1 Aston Villa 0	Aston Lower Grounds	
1881/2	Aston Villa 2 Wednesbury Old A. 1	Aston Lower Grounds	
1882/3	Aston Villa 3 Wednesbury Old A. 2	Aston Lower Grounds	
1883/4	Aston Villa 4 Walsall Swifts 0	Aston Lower Grounds	
1884/5	Aston Villa 2 Walsall Swifts 0	Aston Lower Grounds	
1885/6	Walsall Swifts 1 West Brom Albion 0	Aston Lower Grounds	
1886/7	Long Eaton Rangers 1 West Brom Albion 0	Wellington Road	
1887/8	Aston Villa 3 West Brom Albion 2	Aston Lower Ground	Aston Victoria 2 Unity Gas Saltley 0
1888/9	Aston Villa 2 Wolverhampton W. 0	Edgbaston County Ground	Aston Victoria 2 Wolverhampton Druids 0
1889/90	Aston Villa 2 West Brom Albion 0	Wellington Road	Smethwick Carriage Works 2 Packington 0
1890/1	Aston Villa 3 Wednesbury Old A. 0	Wellington Road	Singers Coventry 1 Willenhall Pickwick 0
1891/2	Wolverhampton W. 3 West Brom Albion 2	Wellington Road	Singers Coventry 2 Willenhall Pickwick 1
1892/3	Wolverhampton W. 3 Aston Villa 1	Wellington Road	Lozells FC 2 Park Mills 1

1893/4	Wolverhampton W. 3 West Bromwich A. 3	Wellington Road	Willenhall Pickwick 4 Lozells FC 1
1894/5	West Brom Albion 1 Aston Villa 0	Muntz Street after 0-0 at A.L.G.	Walsall Unity 1 Windsor St. Gas 0
1895/6	Aston Villa 3 Sheffield Utd 0	Wellington Road	Bilston United 2 Lozells FC 1
1896/7	Walsall FC 2 Wolverhampton W. 0	Wellington Road	Rudge Coventry 3 Warwick United 0
1897/8	Walsall FC 3 Wolverhampton W. 0	Aston Lower Grounds	Darlaston Town 4 Hoobrook Olympic 2
1898/9	Aston Villa 4 Burslem Port Vale 0	Aston Lower Grounds	Coombs Wood 3 Bournbrook 2
1899/00	Stoke FC 4 Aston Villa 3	Aston Lower Grounds after 1-1 at Hawthorns	Bloxwich Strollers 2 Bournville 1
1900/01	Wolverhampton W. 1 Aston Villa 0	The Hawthorns (WBA)	Bournville 2 Bloxwich Strollers 1

Birmingham Senior Cup

The Grounds

THE WEDNESBURY OVAL

ONE OF THE TWO PRINCIPAL venues for important football matches in the Midlands during the 1870s and 1880s were the Aston Lower Grounds opposite the seventeenth-century Aston Hall, in Birmingham, the other being the Wednesbury Oval. Nottingham, with its large Recreation Ground, Gregory Ground, Derby Racecourse, and County grounds, were equally as large, but naturally, the Birmingham FA favoured venues of which they were more familiar.

Wednesbury is a small market town about four miles from Walsall, then both in Staffordshire. The population of Wednesbury around this time (1880) was 20,000. Nonetheless, it seemed to be football mad, with three principal teams in the 1870s: the Old Athletic, Elwells FC, and the Strollers (later Town). Later on, this number swelled to twenty-two clubs in Wednesbury alone, with the next best side being the Wednesbury Old Park.

In modern times, venues for important cup ties, etc., would be chosen for a variety of reasons: ease of accessibility and public transport, covered seating capacity, spectator toilet and refreshment facilities, and quality of playing surface.

The Wednesbury Oval had none of these: It was chosen instead by the Birmingham and Staffordshire Football Association committees simply because of its vast acreage and an ability to hold a crowd in excess of 10,000.

There was nothing but a dirt-track lane – St Paul's Road at the rear of Brunswick Park – which led to Elwell's forge mill and to the ground; there was no banking or terracing of any kind, which meant that only the first few rows deep could actually get a continuous view of what was going on. I can find one record of there being a temporary wooden stand, probably on wheels, moved into position depending on which pitch the match was on, whether football or cricket. The only method to contain the crowd was a perimeter line of strong rope, which of course the crowd – especially behind the goal – had a local habit of pushing forwards as a body and, on more than one occasion, preventing the ball from crossing the line. The Elwells

FC supporters were the usual culprits for this. The Walsall Swifts v Stafford Road tie for the Wednesbury Cup on 15th March 1879 had to be abandoned before the end because the huge 10,000 crowd kept on spilling on to the pitch and coming right up to the goal line, thus preventing Stafford Road from scoring. It was said that the crowd formed into an oval, thus cutting off all four corners of the pitch. The road leading to the ground was known as Forge Lane in those days, but it is called St Paul's Road today.

The Oval's correct name is Elwell's Field, owing to a well-known local man having a forge on the far side, next to the river Tame. He later relocated into Wednesbury town centre, but the name remained, so when a group of men from the Elwell's forge section of the Patent Shaft Steel Works at Old Park started a football team, they called themselves after the name of owner of the ground they played on. Elwell's name is now better known as Spear & Jackson, maker of shears, knives, and gardening tools.

For several decades, the semi-finals of the Birmingham, Staffordshire, and Walsall Cup ties were played there, attracting large crowds. Once or twice, a crowd bigger than even the FA Cup Final at the London Oval saw matches there between Walsall Swifts, Aston Villa, Wednesbury Old Athletic, or the Albion.

The ground was heavily used too by all the Wednesbury teams, and with a river nearby and it being a low-lying flat land which had previously been the site of Elwell's two artificial lakes, it often became very muddy and heavy going. Such conditions did not suit teams like Aston Villa, whose passing game needed better conditions, and they never did as well at the Oval as might be expected. Kick-and-rush sides like Wednesbury Old Athletic and Strollers fared better.

Even in the mid-1890s, Walsall Town-Swifts played here for the odd Football League Division 2 match, when their short-lived Fullbrook Ground on the West Bromwich Road used to get flooded. The Walsall TS v Small Heath Alliance match on 2nd September 1893 drew 5,100, for example. The ground record is believed to be 12,000 who assembled to see whether the Albion or Aston Villa would win the 1884 final of the Staffordshire Senior Cup.

The Wednesbury Oval is still there (largely) today (2012). Teams still play there, not just for football, but rugby and hockey too. There remains three or four marked-out football pitches with goalposts, a rugby pitch, and the remains of some tennis courts. More and more each year though, the Wood

Green High School acquires a bit more of it, and they've put some school extension buildings up on one side. The 'Oval' is in fact a squared-off triangle, with the original three boundaries still in place – the railway line embankment, the little river Rea, and what's left of St Paul's Road, which is now derelict beyond the building which was the original St John's Night School. It was scholars from here who founded Wednesbury Old Athletic club in the winter of 1874. When I went to the Oval a decade ago, all the original high brick wall running down St Paul's Road was still there, complete with one or two green doors from which the public would pass through and pay their 4d (2p). The pitch itself had the one goal end running parallel to the wall on the road to Elwell's, and the touchline ran not quite parallel to the railway embankment, which would loom over the pitch by over twenty feet. There was a row of trees at the base of the railway embankment. The goal at the other end was somewhere near the middle of the large field, and school pitches which are on it today run at right angles to the old pitch. There were no embankments or shelter, save the small pavilion at the foot of the embankment. Once the site of Elwell's lake, the ground soon became boggy, and spectators who knew what to expect took boards or planks with them upon which to stand and keep their boots out of the mud.

Sadly, only a short section remains today, and gone are all the memories of the glorious important cup ties which drew thousands there to see all the top local teams battle it out for Midlands supremacy in the Victorian days. It won't be long before nothing at all remains. Today, the dog walkers and joggers are completely oblivious to its former glory days and the important position it held for Staffordshire and Warwickshire football.

To visit the Wednesbury Oval today, come off the M6 at Wednesbury (J9) and follow Wednesbury signs, but only 500 yards to the traffic lights by St Paul's Church. Turn left into Wood Green Road, then first left into St Paul's Road. The road is impassable after the railway bridge, so go on foot for the last 100 yards. All the area to your right once under the bridge is and was the Oval, the scene of so many important football games 140 years ago.

The Aston Lower Grounds

As football teams began to look for meadows, waste ground, farmers' fields, etc., there were already some ready-made areas in use. Cricket clubs had already been formed some decades before, and there were cricket and sports clubs already in existence. Some cricket clubs had turned their hand at football anyway in the winter months, both to stay fit, but also for its members to stay in touch and keep the unit together, as many players had work or business interests which of course took priority. Employment was, of course, the principle provider for all things. Aston was then a separate town to Birmingham until the late 1890s when the city council was created and a rapid development took place with grand public buildings and improved public transport infrastructure as a result of the metal and manufacturing industry expanding at a pace.

Both Aston Villa and Aston Unity had their origins from cricket clubs. At first, Villa were using the grounds of Aston Hall, although from my visits there, it seems to me that as the Hall is some fifty feet higher than the road, most of the park is on quite a slope, so finding an area anywhere near flat must have meant the grass they used would have been either at the bottom of Trinity Road down by the old bowling green, opposite the 'magnificent meadow' where the Birmingham football and cricket club played, or at the back of Aston Hall underneath where the ghastly Aston Expressway now looms overhead.

Many other Aston teams, like Trinity, Excelsior, Florence, St. Mary's, and Victoria, also used the park and the Aston Lower Grounds, much like today where many teams play on the same park pitches without having any ownership of them.

Occupying some 50,000 sq yards, the Aston Lower Grounds was, at its height, the largest, most grand complete amusement and sporting arena in the Midlands bar none. It had originally been part of the Aston Hall estate, but this portion of land had been given to the people of Aston to use for their recreation and amusement. Broadly triangular in shape, it was defined on three sides by Trinity Road, Witton Road, and Witton Lane. Trinity Road cut across the land, defining the boundary of Aston Hall park with the Lower Grounds. Witton railway station was only a few hundred yards away on the Grand Junction line of the London and North Western (L&NW) Railway. The railway tracks ran roughly parallel to Witton Lane, and between the two was a very useful piece of land of some 16 acres. The sports field playing surface of the A.L.G. was highly regarded as the best around at the time and was known locally as the 'magnificent meadow'. As early as the 1860s and 1870s, crowds of up to 5,000 would assemble to watch (and bet on) the outcome of pedestrian and bicycle challenges. Some pedestrian events would last for several days! During the 1870s and 1880s, it was used for all manner of top-flight events, including a W.G. Grace-led international cricket match, England v Australia, many Birmingham Cup finals and semi-finals, and even the semi-final of the English FA Cup in 1886, which saw Blackburn Rovers victorious. Until the County Ground was built at Edgbaston, it was the home of first-class cricket in the region.

It was the first choice of thought for the committee of the Birmingham Cup, who made a ruling that all ties from the quarter-final onwards were to be played there. It was not until Villa began to develop their Wellington Road ground capable of holding nearly 20,000 that the ALG was challenged as a cup-final venue.

Famously, Buffalo Bill's Wild West show even came here, in 1885, being the catalyst for the long grandstand to be built along the Trinity Road side and a banked cinder bicycle and running track around the pitch. The outer buildings which housed the various amusements had a wonderful glass conservatory which faced on to the cricket ground. It also became the principal venue for important bicycle championships and challenges, with prize money at stake and betting done openly around the ground, and, of course, fairs and circuses would come here too.

Villa would later give some consideration to setting up home near here, right opposite to where Villa Park is now, but the land was too marshy due to a nearby river and a brook. There were plenty of ways to get to the Aston Lower Grounds. Well-made roads with pavements, the railway station close by, plus the fact that the area was well served with tramlines. Indeed, the Aston tram depot was right opposite the refreshment rooms and the bandstand pavilion. People flocked there in their thousands for every kind of amusement and to spectate or participate in all kinds of sporting activities. At the top end, towards the Hall, there was a large lake with pleasure grounds, some 1.35 acres, allowing that favourite Victorian pastime to take place – promenading. Here too, was a polar bear house, a wooded area, and the Holte Hotel. There was a small grandstand on to which was depicted a simulation of the eruption of Vesuvius at a charge of sixpence (2.5p)!

Here, you could watch fireworks displays, hot air ballooning with parachute jumping displays and other Victorian oddities. At the bottom end of the venue, at the junctions of Witton Lane and Road, there was a toboggan slide, ice skating rink (the first in the country), a huge aquarium building, and the Great Hall (built in 1879). The L-shaped group of buildings were impressive in the high gothic Victorian style, and only the newly refurbished Holte

Hotel today can give an impression of what they were like. The whole site and all its activities came under the management of one man: George Henry Quilter (see Birmingham C & FC).

Owners of all this splendour were George Reeves and his father, who went on to use the profits from the venture to build the Central Restaurant in Corporation Street in Birmingham city centre, at a cost of almost £20,000. However, the man who spent half his life promoting, managing, and was otherwise responsible for the success of the Lower Grounds as the region's premier entertainment and sporting venue was showman extraordinaire Charles Henry Quilter. Quilter and his family put all their time, effort, and money into the place, only to eventually see it go broke, and he retired to the Bath Hotel, Felixstowe. He read in the papers about it being demolished in 1888, and he was embittered when he nowhere read his family name in the tribute to the passing of the grand old venue. In the November of 1888, he wrote a vitriolic letter to the Birmingham Mail, reminding the people of Birmingham that it was he who gave half his life to making it a success. He managed a sizeable staff, including the husband-and-wife team of Martin and Emily Fox as lodge-keepers. There was never a week that went by when Quilter hadn't got an advertisement in the Birmingham papers, announcing to the citizens all about the forthcoming attractions. Quilter was a keen cricketer as well as footballer. He played for Birmingham as a youth, and I found his name listed in the Birmingham cricket team which played Walsall at the Chuckery ground in 1873. He was never given the credit he deserved after twenty-four years of hard work, and here I hope to put the record straight, albeit over a century too late.

So everything came to an end, one sad day, the 29th September 1888, when the demolition team moved in. The track was dug up, the 'magnificent meadow' was ploughed up, and a quarter of a century of the happiest memories of the people of Birmingham, Aston, and Walsall all went with it. Three long parallel streets of terraced and villa-style houses were built in its place, and they remain today as in 1888: Jardine, Nelson, and Endicott Roads. Birmingham had been left without a major sporting venue for the first time since organised sports had begun.

Across the Witton Road, there was another large lake, called the Staffordshire Pool, some 5 acres with a wooded island, facing the toboggan slide. This was used for pleasure boating and fishing. The pool was later drained and filled in to make way for rows of houses in the late 1880s, and no sign of it exists today.

Some years later, the Aston Lower Grounds were sparked back into life, when Aston Villa were looking for a new home because their great successes had meant that their old Wellington Road ground at Perry Barr (capacity 22,000) could no longer hold the increasing masses who were coming to see them play. Wellington Road, incidentally, became the main home for the Birmingham Cup finals, as it was easier to control the crowd, and much less easier to get in without paying!

The Villa directors purchased the section which remained from the demise of the sports ground, filled in the large lake to make room for the new pitch, and moved into their new home in time for the 1897 season. Villa at this time were at their historical peak, and although the opening crowd was only around that of a full house at Wellington Road, ground expansions soon got the capacity up to over 70,000. Several of the old Victorian buildings from the glory days still remained in situ for half a century or more. The Aquarium became Villa's administrative offices, the bowling club remained in use until the 1970s, and the ornate gothic-style Aston and Holte hotel/pubs at each end of Villa Park, are of course still here today, having recently been brought back to splendour by Aston Villa themselves. The old tram depot which brought thousands to the ground a hundred years ago became the Aston Transport Museum.

If you want to get a good perspective of the area, and try to imagine what size the Aston Lower Ground used to be, then walk through the main gate of Aston Hall, to the top of the hill. Go round the side of Aston Hall, and you will be able to see the roof of the stands of Villa Park. Look over to your left, past the car parks and Villa village, and you will see those three streets which used to be the cricket and football ground where, 140 years ago, all of Birmingham's top sporting events took place.

The Chuckery Ground Walsall

This large sports ground was created in 1833 when land owned by Lord Bradford was set aside for public use as a cricket and recreational ground. Previously used for grazing, the land was on the high hill on the south side of the town on the way to Great Barr, which is now a district of the city of Birmingham. Considerable in size, the Chuckery had room for no less than fourteen football pitches and four cricket pitches, despite there being a steep slope back towards the town centre.

Walsall cricket club (now at Gorway grounds since 1908) were based there for many years. Both the town's top two football teams, the Swifts and the

Town, played on adjacent pitches. One remarkable day saw the Swifts hit 19 goals against hapless Nettlefolds, whilst the Town put 17 past Willenhall. There must have been almost non-stop cheering for ninety minutes! No wonder the residents of Sutton Road (a premier residential district) complained to the authorities long enough for the later Walsall Town-Swifts to be issued with an eviction notice in 1893!

The site was, like many other edge-of-town sites, sold at a large profit to be built over with streets of cheap Victorian terraced or villa houses.

Today, Crabtree Electrical works occupy some of the land, and streets such as Lincoln Road and Chuckery Road now occupy the land where once crowds cheered willow on leather and 36 goals in an afternoon. Walsall Arboretum, bequeathed to the townsfolk of Walsall by the Earl of Dudley, spans from the Queen Mary's grammar school on Lichfield Road in the town centre, up the famous Arboretum hill, and up to the Sutton Road some one kilometre away; this pleasure ground today would give a good idea of what the Chuckery sports ground looked like. The grammar school themselves had a football team from the early 1880s and often played on the Chuckery ground, as did other minor teams. I was delighted to read about Queen Mary's school football team as far back as the 1880s, in the Walsall press. When, as a third-year boy there in 1967, I tried to start up a school team (the school was rugby and cricket dominated and had produced several international players and athletes), I was told in no uncertain terms by the gown-and-mortarboard-wearing headmaster that 'this school has never played football, and never will!' It now seems that there was some connection with Queen Mary's Grammar School (founded in the sixteenth century) and the start of the Walsall Football Club at Chuckery, as the then headmaster played for both Walsall cricket and football teams at the Chuckery, and the school did too.

The land had been bequeathed to the townsfolk of Walsall in 1832, to be developed from rough fields into providing sporting and recreational facilities for Walsall people at no cost. Walsall Arboretum, opened in 1877 by Lady Hatherton, had an entrance fee depending on your status; a penny for a child, 2d for an adult, and so on, according to whether you took your carriage or bicycle in with you; you could also subscribe to an annual pass. Within months, the rough fields had been cleared, mown, and fenced. Walsall Cricket Club set up permanently there in 1832 and stayed until 1908 when they moved to Gorway Ground which they still occupy. Fortunately, for the two leading Walsall football clubs, Town and Swifts, by the time they moved in, the cricketers had already built two pavilions, one wooden, the other of brick, and had made a perimeter fence around the cricket area. The Swifts and Town played adjacent to the cricket pitch and on side-by-side pitches. I say pitches rather than grounds, for, apart from sharing the pavilions with the cricket team, they didn't seem to make much of an effort to turn their two pitches into separate grounds, with a grandstand for example not being built for some time, and the high aspect of the land put them at the mercy of high winds. This inability to develop the grounds with stands and facilities was probably down to the cricket club, who would have vetoed any such proposals. After all, they saw themselves as the town's oldest sporting club and didn't wish to see their peaceful arena taken over by noisy hordes of football fans. They would not have wished to look up from the crease to see the skyline blotted out by several high stands. They could not have objected to any professionalism on the part of the footballers, for they had at least one paid professional themselves in the 1880s.

Despite its large acreage, the Chuckery ground was only suitable for cricket and football at the top end, where the Shrubbery House was situated. The topography was hilly in all directions, not so much of a problem to the cricketers, but the two football pitches occupied the only area that was anything like level.

By the 1890s, as elsewhere, much land was given over to the very profitable business of house-building, and so it was that piece by piece, the Chuckery became built over with four or five parallel streets of cheap terraced houses. By the end of the 1890s, the Chuckery was the playground of Walsall's high society, with galas and events taking place featuring top-hatted dignitaries and champagne parties. Lumley and Florence Streets now occupy those two football pitches. Houses still there today in Walsingham Street would have had their back gardens looking on to the Town pitch. The Shrubbery is still there, no longer the residence of the town's Justice of the Peace or mayor, but a private nursing home, and this still has its old original boundary wall. Cricket Close now stands on the spot where once stood the two old pavilions.

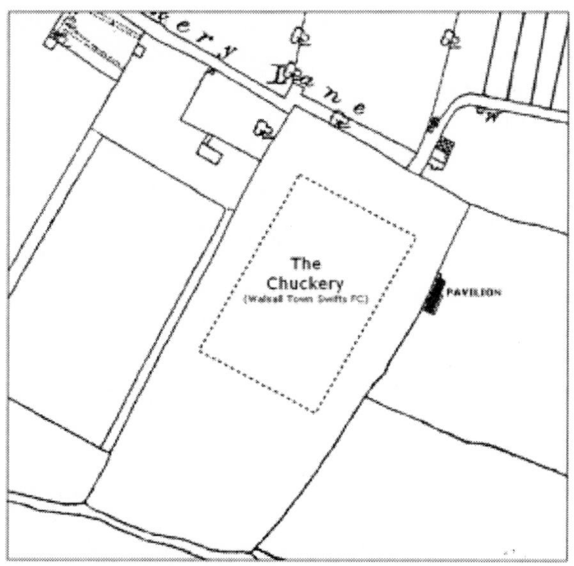

Walsall's Chuckery Ground 1885

Wednesbury Oval Today

Aston Hall

Aston Lower grounds

Imaginary Games

Imaginary Game #1

The year is 1863 and none of the true football teams in the Midlands have been formed yet; games would have been impromptu between local youths on village greens, fields, or meadows at the edge of town or village. Far away, in London, the Football Association is being formed by leading and influential men from the leading public schools and the Universities. They are busy experimenting, debating, and fine-tuning a set of laid-down laws of the game that, whilst no two clubs can totally agree upon, nevertheless permits clubs in the association a common ground for matches between clubs from different towns and cities. Sheffield and Nottingham, even before that, have their own ideas, and it will be some time before the whole country can be unified under one banner, and the vehicle which drew the whole country together was Alcock's brainchild, the FA Cup. It was fiendishly clever; all top clubs wanted to show who was top dog – or cock-house kings, as the Old Harrovian element remembered it from their school days. In order to achieve this, the FA cup provided the vehicle on which to decide – albeit only on the day of the cup final itself, as the later Football league would demonstrate – who was top team in England.

And in order to take part, you had to sign up to agree to play the one and only set of rules that had been bashed around from pillar to post by Cambridge University in the 1850s, schoolmaster of Uppingham school J. C. Thring in 1861, and the Forest, Sheffield, and Harrovians teams of the 1860s.

However, none of this pretty arrangement has reached our imaginary game somewhere in Staffordshire in 1863; it would take another ten years at least before a game we might recognise today as association football between two teams who could agree on the same set of rules without fighting over it or protesting loudly afterwards. No, what we see are two teams made up from the ranks of the same club, whose numbers vary from 11-a-side to 22-a-side, often 15. The pitch is a plain meadow or suchlike, with no markings whatsoever, perhaps sticks or flags around the perimeter. Although finding a level field is obviously better, even football grounds throughout the Victorian era had considerable slopes or bumpy ground. Goals would be two sticks at either end of a pitch roughly 100-200 yards long and half as wide (although some public schools playing areas were much narrower). Maybe not even a tape or rope to determine the height of the goalposts, so that a kick between the sticks at any height would count as a goal. Rouges, too, were a part of the very early game.* They recognised that propelling (or carrying) the ball to the opponents' goal line was an achievement second-best to a goal, and thus deserved some mention. Much later, we would call it either a goal kick or a corner kick. A ball in the air could be caught and brought down to the foot, and the player would make a 'mark' on the ground, and from this he could make a 'free' kick goal-bound. Catching and moving forward with the ball, or knocking it on with your hand was quickly eliminated in the London rules. The game we saw would owe much to elements of the rugby game too, with much mauling or scrimmaging for the ball, with a ruck of men attempting to carry the ball through the posts. The spectator would have great difficulty in telling the two teams apart. Both sets of men come on to the field in white shirts. The two teams are only identifiable by one side wearing blue caps, the other, red. Some men are in everyday black work trousers, some in cricket flannels. They wear the boots they went to work in. There would be no offsides; as in school playground football, it was common for one forward to stand right by the opposing goalkeeper and shoulder charge him out of the way of a shot, or try to knock him and the ball into the goal. The duration of the game would have been pre-agreed, at an hour or ninety minutes or perhaps two or even three 'halves' of thirty minutes each. Remember though, that finding someone who owned a watch might be difficult! The game would be a rough maul, with most players sustaining bruises or sprains. A modern-day spectator would think he was at a rugby match!

No doubt the town or village clock, chiming the hour, would be useful for deciding the end of the game. The final result is likely to have been either no score, or the score not being agreed upon by both sides afterwards, or the ball burst or lost in a stream or suchlike. Crowds of locals might gather to watch for their own amusement, perhaps with a half pint mug in their hand and a chance to call out names and abuse to the rough-house participants, no doubt with much cheering and booing! Even up to twenty years later, it was not unknown for spectators to encroach the field of play, or interfere or worse, with the actual players. If a visiting player hacked a home player too roughly, it was likely to trigger a mini-pitch invasion of the player's relatives to run on the pitch and assault the perpetrator! Matches in the Black Country were particularly known for this violence.

*Sheffield Rules, during the 1860s, had four poles, each one four feet from the next; the centre two were the goal, and the ball between the posts either side was called a rouge. For a while, until about midway through the 1870s, a game might be described as 'two goals and two rouges to nil'. If teams were level at the end of the game, rouges would be used as the winning factor. A rouge was counted regardless of which side propelled or forced the ball through the outer sticks. It was 1876 before Sheffield and London agreed to the same set of laws.

Imaginary Game #2

A few years have passed, and it is now 1876: perhaps we are at the Aston Lower Grounds watching Birmingham Excelsior play Calthorpe from Edgbaston. The Excelsior team are out first, led by Captain Thomas Spriggs, resplendent in maroon and yellow. Calthorpe, being formed three years before Excelsior, have older men in their side who enter the field in red and blue hoops. There are now some markings on the pitch, albeit only to define the touch and goal lines, but goals have come on a bit. We now have sturdy and straight wooden posts, and a new idea has come in this year: replacing the rope marking the height of our goal is a wooden crossbar at eight feet. Rouges have now developed into the corner kick, or a goal kick, depending on who put the ball beyond the goal line; teams would only change ends now at half-time, not every time they scored a goal as before. In the early version of a corner kick, the ball was brought back on to the pitch to a point 15 yards from where it went out of play beyond the goal line, and the attacking side had a free kick at goal, thus a near-miss shot would have brought the ball back almost to a modern-day penalty spot. High-scoring matches must have felt like a merry-go-round in years gone by, with ends being changed at every goal. The referee (umpire) was now on the pitch in authority over the two umpires running the line with their flags.

Team formations have slowly got more defence-based. Almost every man was a forward in the 1860s, with only one 'back' and a man defending the goal. The sole purpose of the back was to boot the ball upfield so that the forwards could chase after it. Slowly, for the next few years, the formation will go from 8-1-1, to 7-2-1 and 6-2-2, with the goalkeeper being given his own responsibilities. At first, anyone could be a goalie, not just the nearest man to the goal line; then you would choose some big hefty fellow who could not easily be shoulder-charged into the goal. At this time, however, he was permitted to handle and carry the ball anywhere in his own half, and some men made all the difference by this tactic. They would carry or bounce the ball, basketball style-up to the halfway line, before throwing the ball to a winger. As time went on, the handling goalkeeper would be restricted to his own small area.

Suddenly, there's a tackle and the ball goes over the touchline for a throw-in; today, in 1876, the team opposite to the one who put it out takes the throw, just like in modern times. A decade before, it was the first man to get to the ball which went out, who threw it back, and one-handed too, like a hurled missile. There were headers and tackles, and maybe a lot of heads-down dribbling, just like the old days in the 1860s, but crowds were beginning to boo the selfish player who held on too long and see it come to nothing. After a hard and fair tussle, the game ends without a winner, as neither side has been able to score a point, and the two sides retire for an evening supper at the Aston Hotel.

One key element of our 1876 match is the new offside rule. At first, everyone in front of the ball was offside: just as in rugby football today. This meant that you could never make a forward pass. Any player in front of the ball had to quickly run back to get behind it, just like Rugby today. Imagine that in a game today! In the revised set of FA rules of 1867, there needed to be three men between you and the goal line in order for you to be onside.* This took a lot of getting used to. It would have been difficult for the umpires to make the right decision, and no doubt many an offside goal was given and vice-versa, and often was the time that a team left the field en masse to protest about a fair goal unjustly disallowed. This probably made life very difficult for the linesmen or umpires to adjudicate. Nonetheless, as the 1860s and 1870s progressed on, teams got used to it and tactics changed to make the best of it.

The forward pass made all the difference in the world to the development of association game, and with hacking and handling, it became the major reason behind the rugby and association forms moving apart in different directions. Remember that the Football Association had, in creating the FA Cup, forced teams from all over the country to play to the same set of rules, for the first time; this was a very important factor in the growth and progress of association football towards the modern game we see today. There is a school of thought that believes that team shirt colours came about partly because a team needed to create an identity so that the spectators could identify who belonged to which team, but also it became necessary of the field of play. In the earliest days of no forward passes, a man would not have anyone in front of him if he was running with the ball at the defence. Therefore, he never saw, or needed to look out for, any team members. When the forward pass was allowed, and the various levels of offside introduced, it became necessary for forwards running to attack with the ball to be able to identify their colleagues. It therefore became a need to have everyone on the same side wearing the same shirts. Our game of 1875 would see the disappearance of handling, although the game was still rough and robust. Goalkeepers were still being bundled into the goal, whether holding the ball or not, and there was a lot of shoulder-charging, not just on the man with the ball, but to block people out of the way too. But the game was quickly evolving into the modern version.

Even so, at a local level, some teams were reluctant to let go of their own versions of offsides, tripping and so on, and it wasn't until the end of the 1880s that the old ways died out. Wednesbury football kept hold of its rougher side later than other towns, with rouges or touchdowns and scrimmages in front of goal common. Sheffield, with their determination that their version of the rules would win out over the London FA, kept a nine-foot crossbar when most others had the usual eight-foot version, but also led the way with developments such as corner kicks, crossbars, etc.

* Sheffield FA wanted it to be just one defender, just as it was a hundred years later. In this and many other respects, Sheffield were years ahead of London thinking.

Imaginary Game #3

We are now at the final of the 1883 Staffordshire cup final at the Stoke ground. The first thing you notice is a jolly good crowd of some 5,500 people; some lucky ones are in the stands, paying an extra threepenny bit (1.5p) to stay dry. The St. George's team are first out, in their colours of white shirts and black shorts, although they mostly look like trousers cut off at the shin. They've all got heavy leather boots on, and there's a rumour that at least one of their team is a professional. You notice the black badge of a cross on the shirt of a St. George player as he stands near you to take a throw-in; these days it must be with both hands on the ball since they changed the rules in 1882. The game is both muscular and fast, and when the ball is in the air, some players attempt to head it rather than jump up and try a fancy kick. Most of the twenty-two players wear long moustaches, to which they attach great importance, and frequently try to gain the eye with fancy kicks, screw-shots, and long dribbles with the ball, sometimes over-selfishly. Teams are beginning to copy the new 2-3-5 formation displayed by Nottingham Forest and Cambridge University, where one of the three centre forwards has been pulled back into the new centre-half position. It is his job to be the linkman between defence and attacking play. Previously the ball was just booted unceremoniously upfield and chased after. Now, with the passing game becoming the norm, the play is beginning to get a bit more scientific, with defenders working the ball upfield to the wingers. The defence are now also starting to make short passes between themselves to evade the threat of the forwards, and our team of 1883 is more balanced now between attack and defence. W. N. Cobbold, the great Old Carthusian and Cambridge University centre forward, spoke in 1885 of not waiting until the wing-man had reached the corner flag before 'middling' the ball, but to send it hard and low into the centre before you reach the last back. Of the five forwards, there is a pair of wing-men on each side of the field who work together to centre the ball, or middle it, as it was called in the day. The single centre forward – there used to be three centres a decade before – needed to be a big, strong, preferably tall specimen of a man who could throw all his body weight into connecting with the cross. Goalkeepers frequently ended up in the net still clutching the ball. Despite teams employing a more thoughtful approach to playing the game, there are still half a dozen men chasing the ball all over the pitch, like a kaleidoscope of ever-changing patterns.

The Albion team from West Bromwich are resplendent in their red and white hoops, instead of the chocolate and white halves of at the start of the season. Maybe they will stick with these colours and not change them every year, as before. It's said that not only are all the Albion team from their own town, but nearly all of them work together at the same Salter Springs factory. The St. George's team are said to include men they've paid to join them from teams all over Birmingham. It's a close game, but the St. George's have a narrow 2-1 win and thus are presented with the cup.

On the way home, as you read again the printed match-card showing all the players in their positions, you reminisce of how the game has changed quickly over the past ten or so years – the funny old days when some teams didn't even have their own colour shirt had to carry their own goals around till they found an empty pitch, and some games were played one half rugby and one half association rules! On this occasion, you had travelled to Stoke by steam train from Birmingham to follow your team, something not easily possible fifteen years previously, which limited not only football teams' mobility and range, but their fans too.

The railways had been a significant factor in making football into a national game; by the 1880s, almost every town could be reached from anywhere in the country, and many villages had their own railway station or halt. As time went on, journey times were dramatically reduced, and an unthinkable journey from say Shrewsbury to Sheffield was now possible all in the same day, with a change at Birmingham. Railway companies, like shops and manufacturers, were quick to see the huge potential of football trade, and cheap day excursions were soon laid on to attract the masses. As the decades wore on, whole trains were set aside for important cup ties. The social impact for many people, hitherto never having left their town of birth, to travel at unimaginable speeds of over 40 mph and take in the splendour of the capital city or seaside resorts would have been indelible from their parochial minds. Hordes of men from Derby or Sheffield would mix with their counterparts from say Worcester or Stoke-on-Trent and experience each other's dialects, fashions, and habits. Men from different cultures would remark on their regional differences yet find a common ground in the game they adored and, of course, in drinking and gambling, those time-old pursuits of the reckless.

The London & Birmingham Railway, formed in 1837, quickly became the most important in the UK, and was the forerunner to the Midland, then LMS (London, Midland & Scottish) Railway Company founded in 1922. Rapid design improvements throughout the 1860, 1870, and 1880s saw locomotives increased in size and tractive effort (pulling power), as more efficient wheel arrangements and steam compounding techniques were created by men such as Robert Stephenson, Brunel (GWR), Edward Bury, Francis Webb (LNWR), and Samuel Johnson (MR). These legendary railwaymen were not as you might imagine, railway engine builders at those great loco works at Derby, Crewe, or Swindon, rather they were designers and experimenters, often holding the rank of Superintendant of Works at one of the big railway companies, who commissioned their designs to be built, often in large numbers. Broadly speaking, train speeds increased by 20 mph for every decade in the second half of the nineteenth century. The Midland Johnson Single 4-2-2 locomotives, first built in 1887, were reaching speeds of up to 90 mph in the 1890s, halving long-distance journey times across the Midlands.

Things were not without their problems however, since for most teams travelling by steam train, it would be the only time they had made that journey, and the perils of changing trains at Birmingham, Derby, or Shrewsbury, for example, would and did lead to many teams taking the wrong train, or getting off too soon or too late. This was frequently reported in the papers as being the reason why a game, scheduled to commence at 3.30 p.m., would kick off so late that it went dark well before the ninety minutes were up, and usually why a visiting team would refuse to play extra-time if the cup tie was drawn. Horse-drawn and steam-propelled vehicles and carriages were still the main method of travelling locally. It was not unusual for a team to walk up to five or six miles in order to save what little money they had.

Imaginary Game #4

This time it's 1889. We are in Shropshire at the Birmingham cup-tie between Wellington St. George's and Warwick County, the Birmingham footballing side from the Edgbaston county cricket ground. The visitors are all professionals, and it's all above board, since, after a few years of protracted wrangling in the early 1880s, the FA has finally allowed professionalism.

It had been a long and vociferous battle to reach this state of play. Leading officials of the Sheffield and Birmingham associations were, and remained, against it, and all of London was full of well-known amateur clubs, still going strong, such as the Old Carthusians and the Casuals.

The home side, all amateurs from the village, walk on to the field from the pavilion in their claret shirts and white trousers. Warwick are in royal blue. Vicarage Field looks picturesque in the November sunshine; the trees surrounding the field are half-empty of their golden leaves. The church overlooks the proceedings, and as the bells chime 3 o'clock, the game gets under way. The usually manicured grass of the cricket pitch has been left to grow long in the winter months, and the heavy pitch begins to contribute to defensive errors on both sides as the goals flow. Rose has been kept busy in charge of the Warwick citadel, but Ollis and new man Pangbourne shine in the visitor's attack. The Jones brothers form the home side's spearhead. At the call of time, the scores are level at 3-3, but the match can't be decided, because, even at 4.45 p.m., it's getting too dark to see properly, and so extra time is not possible. The light from the gas lamps on the main road are no use to the players. The cup tie will have to be decided after a replay, probably in the new year. After a supper at the Bail and Balls public house across the road, the Warwick team sets off for home, some forty miles away. The steam train from Oakengates station will take them to Snow Hill station in Birmingham, where they will disperse by hansom cab to their homes.

The ground had looked just like a football ground that modern folk would recognise, a properly defined, fenced-off and well-marked out playing field, with halfway line and a centre circle. The goal area though has yet to be changed to the twentieth century shape of a small rectangle within a large rectangle, and instead we see two half-moon shapes in front of each goal area, defining the area that the goalkeeper could handle the ball. In a couple of years (1891), there were two lines added to the pitch, which may seem strange to the modern eye. The ground has grandstands down each side, and the crowd benefits from earthen banking behind the goals.

A continuous line painted across the pitch 12 yards out described a point at which penalty kicks could be taken in an attempt to score. It was a one-on-one situation where the man with the ball had a chance to either shoot from where he was, or dribble around the goalkeeper and score. This, of course, was an early attempt to punish a foul or handball misdemeanour and provide the attacking team with a strong chance of scoring from the opportunity, the penalty spot itself finally appearing on the pitch in 1891. Also, a dotted line, painted 18 yards out described the restriction of the defensive zone in which a forward had to be in before being called offside. There are now long grandstands some dozen rows deep, seating made of wooden planking for a charge of double the standing admission fee. Most of the village has turned out to see this exciting match, and the 600 who each paid 4d (1.5p) will have helped the team to keep the club going for a while yet and give the visiting team a contribution towards their travelling costs.

Imaginary Game #5

For our last visit into the past, we now take a tram to the new Villa Park, get off at the terminus in Witton Lane, and walk the last few yards to where only a few years before once stood the magnificent Aston Lower Grounds.

The year is 1897 and Villa are now the top team in England, which means the world. They had risen from humble beginnings twenty-three years before and had returned to the scene of their earliest friendly games in Aston Park, having left the old and outgrown Wellington Road ground behind them. At their old ground, they had become known as the 'Perry Barr pets', but here, they had a new nickname of the Villans. All the players were professional and earning up to £6 a week (Devey and Cowan). Most people arrive on foot or the very popular bicycle, although horse – and steam-driven trams bring thousands right outside the ground from Aston, Walsall, and Birmingham. Curious folk look in amazement at the new fangled motorised carriages.

Their colours having ranged through red and blue stripes and chocolate and pale blue halves (I still wish they were-Ed.), Villa come on the field in their famous claret and blue strip. Legend has it that a printer's mistake caused the chocolate to become claret when the team kit secretary posted a picture of the team to a new football outfitters which had been recommended to them, and when the Villa men saw the claret and blue, they decided to stick with it.* The purpose-built magnificent stadium is complete with concrete bicycle track (still a very popular sport, eminently suitable for betting and gambling!), gymnasium, dressing and treatment rooms, and dozens of turnstiles all the way along the Witton Lane, collecting tens of thousands of sixpences, pennies, and threepenny bits at every home game.

The limit at Wellington Road had been 20,000. The final match at Aston Lower grounds drew 13,500. Villa Park was built for over 75,000, and indeed, 35,000 poured in for its second ever game, a league match against local rivals, the Wolves.

Everything would now appear relatively modern to today's spectator, after his 'travels through the ages'. There were large grandstands, built along both long sides, and an open high-banked terrace, or 'kop' behind each goal. The word *kop* was a recent nickname drawn from the Boer War, it being Africaans for hillock. There were bold advertisements everywhere; even the roof of the long stand bore the words 'Ride Palmer Tyres' – an advert for bicycle not motorcar tyres! Other prominent adverts proclaimed the virtues of 'Oxo', 'Gaiety Theatre', and 'the Hippodrome'. A flagpole adorned the stand by the halfway line, and the crowd were allowed to stand on the concrete cycling track when the stand terraces got full. The outside of the ground was a riot of advertisement posters and boards, and there were street sellers and hawkers, and spectators could buy rosettes, hats, and rattles in their team's colours. The wooden rattles became an essential part of going to the match right up until the end of the 1960s, when, for some reason, they just gradually died out of use. Inside the ground, there were refreshment stalls and kiosks, selling hot beverages and beer and pies, and there would be gambling and betting.

The Villa men, seven of them sporting well-kept moustaches, laid waste the lowly visitors, Wednesbury Old Athletics, scoring double figures without reply in this local cup tie. The new Villa, a team at first assembled from the best players in the area, was now comprised of the best men in the country, funded by ever-increasing attendances and a very committed management team of Rinder, McGreggor, and Ramsay.

Once, twenty-five years before, these two teams were equals without peer in the whole of the Midlands; now, the tragedy of the demise of the 'Old Uns' compared with the meteoric rise of the powerfull Villa rawly illustrated the vast chasm in all aspects of the footballing world between these two famous old teams. The glory days of the Old Athletics had long since been over, and their best players were long gone, being too old or crocked. Not enough good quality players have been introduced into the side to replace legends like George Holden and JEM Bayliss. Failing to turn professional when they were at their peak, instead of waiting until the side had grown old together was to be their downfall. Villa, on the other hand, had turned professional relatively quickly, and success had attracted better players, which in turn led to more success, and more income from bigger crowds. The Old Athletics, the Midland's first footballing giants, had lasted barely two decades at the top. The club would linger on for just a few more seasons as a junior club, their black and amber colours lying in the dust. For teams who made the right choices, at the right times, and added a bit of good fortune to their solid management team, like Villa, Albion, and Wolves, their future would be a bright one.

The twentieth century was about to begin.

* See Aston Unity.

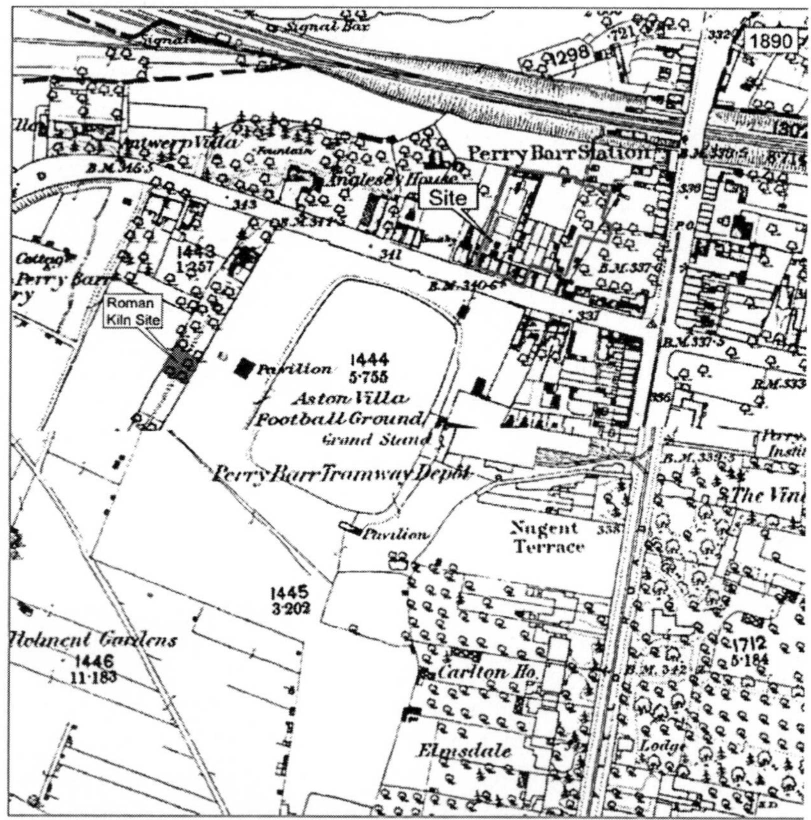

Wellington Road AVFC

The Teams

Aston Shakespeare FC

(1876-1889)

Origin of team – possibly the Midland Vinegar Company of Tower Road, Aston Cross, as the football ground was owned by Edwin Samson, who owned the vinegar factory, and both the teams and the factory are from the same year. Samson had the sports ground 'built for his employees'. A stronger candidate is that the teams were formed by men from the Shakespeare Inn on Park Lane (B4144), which was a street away.

Ground

1. Aston Cross:
   There was a large football ground behind the Aston Tavern on the corner of Rocky Lane and Aston Road North (A5127). A site visit during autumn of 2012 with my Aston guide, John Green, who used to work at the HP Sauce factory, revealed that the Aston Cross Business Centre occupies the old ground today (see photo). The Vinegar factory was across the road in Tower Road. Another leading Aston team, the Victoria also shared the ground, which was used extensively for athletics and bicycle races, and the Aston Tavern would have received a huge revenue from these crowds. The Aston Tavern, dating from 1776, despite several renamings in the twentieth century, is still there on the corner, as a group of gothic Victorian buildings along with the library building, which is now rented accommodation.

2. Thimble Mill Lane, Nechells:
   This was known as John Wright's playing field – access was through the rear of the churchyard! Aston Shakespeare were using this ground in the mid-1880s. This football ground was one mile from the Shakespeare Inn, reached by walking to the end of Park Lane to the Aston Cross, continuing down to the bottom of Rocky Lane, turning left into Walter lane, thus bringing you to Long Acre.
   The ground was in use into modern times (1980s) when the Long Acre Industrial estate was built over the site of the pitch.

There was also a bowling green by the pitch which was hemmed in a triangle by Long Acre, Thimblemill Lane, and the railway line.

3. 'Showell Green Lane':
   After on-site investigation, this turns out to be the back end of what is now Sparkhill Park (photo). They played here from 1887/8 onwards.

Representative on the Birmingham FA committee – C. Easthope

Edwin Samson had set up his Midland Vinegar Company on Tower Road off Lichfield Road Aston Cross by 1877. In Victorian times, Aston Cross was a busy and thriving centre with a high-density but cheaply housed population, and four of Birmingham's largest and most well-known factories: Midland Vinegar, HP Sauce Co., and Hercules Cycles (later Dunlop), plus Ansells brewery, were all virtually next door to each other. So there were plenty of employment possibilities; there were several theatres and halls, and grand shops, right up until a generation ago. Then, one by one, these famous names started to disappear, in an act of gross social vandalism. Hercules was the largest bicycle manufacturers in the country once; that was the first to be demolished. Ansells brewery went in the 1980s, and despite making million-pound profits and employing a long-serving workforce, the world-famous HP Sauce Co. was demolished early in the twenty-first century after the parent company Kraft moved production to Holland amid public outrage. Anyone looking at pictures of Aston Cross in the 1890s would think it was the city centre, with its Carnegie-funded high gothic library and public houses and theatres. And what is there today? Unless you value the architectural gems of Staples office equipment and the new business centre, and an immense and anonymous shed of a building where once stood the mighty HP factory, now a warehouse for a Chinese food empire, and the Volvo car showroom where once stood the Aston Football Ground.

The employees of the Hercules Cycle Co. too had their own sports ground. Curiously, this was next door to Aston Unity's ground on Trinity Road and was only built over in the 1980s. Towneley Gardens now occupies the sports ground location.

It was on land belonging to the aforementioned Edwin Samson that the Aston football ground was created. It had a running and bicycle track around the pitch and a small grandstand down one side. It seems to have been used for anything that the Victorians were crazy about, including running, racing, archery, etc. The ground was already established by 1850, as an athletics and pedestrian ground. The *Birmingham Post* mentions a race meeting there on 7th June 1870 which attracted 600 spectators.

I can see now, how letters in an 1888/9 red leather book owned by Mr Roy Burford, connected with the M&B FC (formerly Mitchell St. George's), simply addressed to 'Aston Shakespeare FC, Aston Cross' would have found their delivery mark, as the ground was right by the famous Aston Cross clock tower, behind Aston Cross post office itself. It seems that this old athletic ground was set up as a sporting ground for the Midland Vinegar Co. employees, but later became used (or rented) by Aston Shakespeare (no doubt among others). Charging 2d (1p) for regular games and 3d for cup ties, Shakespeare FC were drawing crowds of around 1,000 by 1891. I could not find any factories or businesses in Aston or Birmingham called the Shakespeare works.

Maps for both 1878 and 1902 show the football ground as being directly behind the Aston Cross Tavern on the corner of Rocky Lane with entrances from both an alley by the munitions factory next to the site of the library and also from an alley at the side of the P.H. between the pub and the site of Aston Cross tram depot. Both the Tavern and the tram depot are still there today, the Aston Cross business centre occupying exactly where the pitch was. Early into the twentieth century, the huge Hercules bicycle factory was built down one side of the ground and occupied a large part of Rocky Lane, providing employment for hundreds of Astonians. Part of the original wall down the alley between the Aston Tavern and the tram depot is still there, also part of a wall containing two doorway entrances into the ground, now occupied by a large Volvo car dealership showroom.

As to the origin of the team, speculation is regretfully called for. A simple explanation comes from Birmingham football historian Lee Gauntlett, who suggests they were simply a pub team from the Shakespeare Inn, which was on the corner of Park Lane and Parliament Street at Aston Cross. This would have been very close to the Vinegar factory, only 500 yards up Park Lane from the Aston Cross ground, halfway between the Barton Arms and the Aston Cross. By 1901, the Shakespeare pub had fallen into disrepair as well as disrepute, and the owners were losing money and closed the pub. This may have led to the demise of the football club. From 1901 to 1915, the Dunn family took part of the building over and ran it as a fruit and vegetable shop, and the Shear family then took over from 1915 to 1930, after which time it became, of all things, a pet shop. The Dunn's recalled a pair of large busts of William Shakespeare and Anne Hathaway prominently holding up the main fireplace. The pub had its own brewery in the backyard, and the original copper vat, stables, and yard gates were still there in the 1950s. I would choose this as the most likely origin for the team. Today, 115 Park Lane occupies the location of the old Shakespeare Inn, and Parliament Street no longer adjoins Park Lane for vehicles.

Another avenue of research points to a connection with Aston Hall. As is well known, William Shakespeare married into the Aston family, but this leads us nowhere. However, in 1864, a Shakespeare Library and exhibition was set up at the original Birmingham central library, by the combined efforts of George Dawson, Samuel Timmins, and the Rev. C. Evans, who was headmaster at King Edwards School. It became the world's largest library dedicated to the Bard, with over 8,000 books, manuscripts, and paintings, but sadly, much of it was destroyed in the fire of 1879, and only 500 books were saved. When it outgrew its allocated room, the exhibition was moved to Aston Hall whilst the new town library was being built.

Now Aston Shakespeare's most famous player, Billy Garraty, who made his name at Aston Villa and was capped once in 1903, had started out as a fourteen-year-old with a little known team called Aston Hall Park FC; this suggests a good link between employees at Aston Hall with its square kilometre of parklands used by most of Aston's fledgling sides and a team using the suffix of Shakespeare.

Aston Hall park was so heavily used by all and sundry that, in 1885, the council parks department had suspended the use of the grounds by football and cricket teams, banning these sports altogether in 1887 when the football pitches had been churned into 'a sea of black mud'. For the next few years at least, local teams would have to find an alternative pitch to rent with their shilling. Some teams in the early 1890s moved so far away from their area roots that they ended up changing their name to suit their new district location. In 1887, Aston Shakespeare FC entered the inaugural Birmingham Junior Cup, and their first opponents were a small local side, the Witton Wanderers, who may have had connections with Kynock's munitions works, as it was virtually the only factory there at that time.

On Saturday 27 April 1889, Aston Shakespeare reached the semi-finals of the Warwickshire Cup but were easily beaten 6-0 by Small Heath, the tie being played at their Coventry Road ground. The Shakespeare side that day was:

Dunnall (goal); Roberts, Ravenhill (backs); Solloway, Hunter, W. Roberts (halfbacks); Stanley, Walker, Turner, Taylor, E. Roberts (forwards).

As to what happened to them: Since Shakespeare stopped entering the B'ham Senior Cup in 1889 coinciding with when the Aston Victoria name began to enter it, I think the Shakespeare were absorbed by Aston Victoria, or amalgamated with them. At one stage, both clubs used the same Aston Cross ground, and if indeed the two clubs were pub-based, they would have only been 800 yards apart. Aston Victoria had met Aston Shakespeare way back in 1877, and so the two clubs may have shared players. The Aston Cross Tavern, with the football ground immediately behind it, may have been unhappy about a team from a rival pub using their facilities on match days, and then this is likely to have led to commercial friction, especially after 1901, when the Shakespeare pub had shut down.

After the mid-1890s, we hear no more of Aston Shakespeare, whilst near rivals, the Victoria, won the 1888/9 B'ham Junior Cup 2-0 over Unity Gas Works FC and joined the Birmingham and District League from 1889.

No FA Cup History

Aston Shakespeare never made it to the 1st round proper of the FA cup. They were beaten 2-4 by Warwick County in the Second Qualifying Round in October 1888.

Birmingham Cup History

1884/5	1st round: 7-1 v Asbury	2nd round: 1-9 v Walsall Town	
1885/6	1st round: 2-6 v Mitchell St. George's		
1886/7	1st round: 1-4 v Darlaston		
1887/8	1st round: 3-2 v Stafford Road	2nd round: 5-0 v Excelsior	3rd round: 0-3 v West Bromwich Albion
1888/9	1st round: Bye	2nd round: 2-2, 3-1 v Birchfield H.	3rd round: 2-2, 1-4 v Shrewsbury

Their 1887/8 results against some decent teams suggests that this was their peak season, although this looks like the year they moved out to Showell Green Lane. This is in Sparkhill, some four miles away from their Aston roots, and a team which is forced further out from its home base to play home games on a strange pitch; and presumably losing its entire support base, it is a team that is on the way out. Perhaps an amalgamation with Aston (County) Victoria was their only survival choice.

Severe fortunes were with the club in their 1884 Birmingham Cup run. They thrashed Asbury FC 7-1 at home but were themselves thrashed by 1-9 in round 2 when an on-form Walsall Town side came to the Thimblemill Lane ground on Saturday 15th November. Despite the Walsall team complaining about the narrowness of the pitch, they soon settled and opened the scoring after just two minutes. Later checked, the pitch came out at 2 yards above the minimum FA requirement of 75 yards. If you want to see where that game took place, drive to the corner of Thimblemill Lane (B4132) and Long Acre, and you will see the St. Joseph's R.C. church. The football ground is at the back of the old churchyard, high up behind an old wall, and is now the Long Acre Industrial Estate.

Their 1887 Birmingham cup tie against the Albion at Stoney Lane on 21st November saw the Shakes give a good account of themselves, despite the 0-3 scoreline. A goal down at halftime, they had the better of the second half and were unlucky when the Albion scored twice on the break. In the November of 1886, Shakespeare held Wolverhampton Wanderers to a 1-1 draw in a Walsall cup tie at Aston, before going out in the replay, although it must be admitted that Wolves also sent a mixed team of 1st and 2nd team players to beat Leek away on the same day.

The team which defeated Walsall Town by 4-1 at Aston Cross in 1888 was:

T. Garvey (goal); Yates and Ravenhill (backs); Solloway, Roberts, Ludford (halfbacks); W. Garvey, Wilcox, B. Garvey, J. Turner, Clive (forwards).

Shakespeare's star players were: Billy Garraty (b. 1878-1931), also 'Bat' (Bartholmew) Garvey. Billy Garraty, born on Rocky Lane near the Aston Cross ground, but mostly lived in Saltley, went on to have a famous career with Aston Villa and later Leicester Fosse. He was their star player from 1895 to 1897. Despite not being played up front as an out and out striker, he scored 96 goals from midfield. He kept his trademark handlebar moustache throughout his football career. After a spell at West Bromwich Albion and Lincoln City, he returned to the Villa as a trainer. After leaving Lincoln and retiring from football, he became landlord of the Old Green Man pub in 1912, Birmingham's oldest pub after the famous Old Crown (1368) at

Digbeth. In 1915, he fell ill with respiratory problems and became a beer delivery driver with Ansells brewery at Aston Cross.

His early schoolboy/youth teams included:

Ashtead Swifts–St. Saviour's (a Perry Barr church team from Wellington Rd); Highfield Villa–Lozells FC; Aston Shakespeare–Villa. He went to the Villa in 1897/8. He became top scorer at Villa in 1899/00, with 31 goals in 40 games, and altogether 96 goals in 224 appearances.* He was a fit 5 9 and 12 stone. Honours: Capped once for England. He is buried in St. Saviour's Churchyard at Saltley.

It was said that once Garraty, their star player had gone, Shakespeare were never the same team again. If they were a pub team, then they would have found it difficult to keep the standard of the team up as the years went by, and it's quite possible that the team grew old together, and they decided they were too old to carry on.

Their early team of 1877 against Victoria Swifts of Walsall was:

H. Dyass, Mason, Thornton, Hill, Wootton, C. Dyass, Lawton, Spriggs, Wilcox, Chambers, Longstaff.

The team of 1879, including the three Garvey brothers, was:

T. Garvey, Merritt, Lawley, Cox, Foster, Morris, Hurley, W. Garvey, Fox, B. Garvey, Walters.

Note that the two team sheets are completely different from one another, yet only two years apart. Such fluidity of player movement is a recipe for ultimate demise.

Captain Henry Dyoss moved to Walsall Swifts in 1885 along with his brother Charles. Their names are often misspelt in the press, frequently given as Dyass, but no such surname was registered in either the 1871, 1881, or 1891 Censii of Birmingham or Walsall inhabitants. There was also a third brother, Edward, who played for Walsall Swifts during the late 1880s. The Dyoss family seem to have been employed in the horse industry in Walsall; Edward was a bridle-stitcher, and Henry was a silver-plater.

The Spriggs brothers also played for Walsall Swifts, and Walsall Robin Hood circa 1877/8. So either the Dyass and Spriggs brothers all lived in Aston and worked in the Walsall leather trade, or lived in Walsall and were employed in the Jewellery Quarter, as their occupations involved the silver-plating trades. Walsall FC expert Kevin Powell thinks that the 'Shakespeare' team are not from Aston, but Walsall instead.

To find Shakespeare's grounds today, take the A41 Stratford Road from Birmingham to Sparkhill (three miles) until you see a tall clock tower by the police station and swimming baths. The Sparkhill Park is up a side street by the police station.

Aston Cross directions are given under Aston Victoria FC.

Directions to Thimblemill ground are given in the text above.

References

Birmingham Daily Post
1871 Census
1881 Census
Billy Garraty family history web site
The Aston Manor History Society
The works of Steve Carr

* Others give 112 goals in 300 appearances.

Bat Garvey of Aston Shakespeare

Billy Garraty of Aston Shakespeare in his Villa days

Home to Aston Victoria and Shakespeare-Aston Park meadow

Aston Unity

By the time Jack Hughes and his three cricket pals from the Lozells Wesleyan Chapel met under a gas lamp on the corner of Heathfield Road and decided to form a football team (Aston Villa), Aston Unity had already been playing football for a few years and cricket for decades before that.

Founded in the winter of 1868-1896 by members of Aston Unity cricket club (still playing, now at Sutton Coldfield)

This means they were probably Birmingham district's first football team, and one of the most important of the early Birmingham area teams.

They co-founded the Birmingham Football Association and were also founders of the world's first cricket league, and so in terms of establishing both cricket and football in Birmingham, Aston Unity are a very important club.

Grounds

1. Played in Aston Park until 1875
2. Aston Lane using the Witton Arms as HQ from 1876 to 1878†
3. itton Lane during 1879‡
4. Aston Lower Grounds (1880-1881)
5. The walled Unity cricket and football grounds on Trinity Rd from 1881 until 1908. The ground is now owned and used by King Edward VI School for rugby, cricket, and hockey.
6. Trinity Road cricket ground, now the site Towneley Gardens, later known as the Hercules Sports Ground

Colours

1. claret and pale blue until 1875*
2. royal blue and white hoops (1876)
3. blue and white (1877)
4. brown stockings added (1877)
5. blue and white stripes (1879)
6. red and black (1887)

*Colours: The first colours are believed to have been claret and pale blue. Unity's present-day club chairman, John Reeves, tells me that there has been a long-held belief that Unity's colours of claret and blue were taken up by

Aston Villa after their chocolate and blue years. However, a comparison of the two side's shirts throughout the 1870s and 1880s shows that Villa didn't start to wear claret and light blue until around 1888/9. At the end of the 1860s, Unity are likely to have been playing in hoops which were then in vogue. Aston Unity also has the lion rampant on their club crest, and Mr Reeves also believes that the two clubs had strong links in the 1870s and 1880s, sharing players as well as colours. There is a claim at the Unity club, now at Bassetts Pole in Sutton Coldfield, that prior to Villa's first ever recorded match against Aston Brook St. Mary's, a local rugby team, that it was in fact Aston Unity who were the Villa's first ever opponents, but the details were never recorded. Villa were playing in scarlet and blue hoops from 1874 to 1877. Villa then had two seasons in their (in) famous black shirt before switching to 'coral and maroon' (1885) and then their chocolate and blue halves by 1887 in their Wellington Road days.

An early honour came to Aston Unity when their ground was chosen to host the Birmingham v London representative match which had attained some importance just below an international game. The quickly improving Brummies trounced London 7-1 on 15th January at their Aston Lane ground to send a message of rapid growth in the association game back to the capital.

The Aston Unity continued to play Aston Villa at cricket until the 1960s.

Until they got their own Trinity Road walled and enclosed grounds, the team played variously in Aston Park, the Lower Grounds and Cannon Hill Park. They were known as Aston Park Unity until 1888, even though they'd left the park some years before. From 1876 to 1878, the club used the cricket ground on Aston Lane, later better known as the Aston Manor cricket ground, and still called Manor Close today, but this now leads into Broadway School. They played on 'Witton Lane' during 1879, but this is probably just another way of describing the cricket fields at the side of Aston Hall (now almost under Aston Expressway).

The Aston Unity Cricket and Football ground at the junction of Trinity Road and Witton Road is still there today (see photo). Their later ground, used after 1908, was there until the late 1960s, and was literally next door. It became better known locally as the sports ground for the employees of the Hercules Cycle Co., also used by Aston Villa in the 1940-50 period as a training ground. Houses were built on the land circa 1970, now called Towneley Gardens. The present-day resting place for the Aston Unity cricket club is at Bassetts Pole, on the outside edge of Sutton Coldfield on the way to Tamworth.

"Aston appears to be taking a very active part in football exercise. There are numerous clubs in the district and many of them figure in the various contests that are taking place every week, sometimes on the losing side, sometimes on the winning."

The above words were written in 1876, by a newspaper reporter in the *Birmingham Post*, and went on to list that week's local football results, in which Aston Park Unity and Wednesbury drew 1-1. It was reported that Aston Park Unity were affiliated to the London FA Rules, whilst the Wednesbury and Walsall teams favoured those of the Sheffield FA. This would lead to games being played under two halves of both sets of rules.

Aston Unity were, and still are, one of the country's leading cricket clubs and have a place in the cricket hall of fame; they were the first ever champions of the world's first cricket league – the Birmingham and District – and in 1889, played the world's first ever league cricket match against Handsworth Wood. The cricketers set up a football team in the winter of 1868, although at such an early date, it would have included much of what we see in the Rugby game today, mauls, hacking, charging and ball-handling. Earliest cricket and football matches were played in nearby Aston Park.

Aston Park was the large area of parkland around Aston Hall, which had been built by Sir Thomas Holte in 1635 (hence the Holte end at Villa Park today). In 1858 the grounds were made open for public use for strolls and pastimes after originally being a deer-hunt park. The Manor of Aston, by the way, wasn't part of Birmingham until 1911. It was in Warwickshire, and indeed, Aston was bigger than Birmingham in the mid-nineteenth century.

Unity's star players were some of the best in the county and included:

Thomas Green (b. 1863)

J. Mathews: went to West Bromwich Albion in 1883, then on to Cowells FC in 1885

*Charlie Athersmith: who joined the Villa, as did several Unity men S. Saunders-went to WBA in 1895, and then on to local junior side B'ham Centinel FC in 1896.

Joe Wilson: also joined WBA in 1887. He came from Hamstead Swifts in 1877.

Arthur Brown: top goal-scoring centre forward (1859-1909) went to Villa and then Mitchell St. George's. Won 3 England caps. Played for Unity in 1876/7 as an inside right.

John Burton (1863-1914): a fullback who went to the Villa in 1885.

Harry Pallet: He was also a Warwickshire and England cricketer who joined the Villa in 1881 – the team captain and a mainstay of the midfield for a decade.

In 1882, they, along with St. George's FC, Villa, Walsall, Stafford Road, and the Old Athletic, entered the English FA Cup. At this time, an ever-growing number of clubs from outside London and the home counties were entering year on year, and the FA had to regionalise. Unfortunately, this meant that the Staffordshire and Warwickshire teams were grouped against each other until one team survived through to the fourth round. This time it was the Villa, who met the North Midland section winners, Notts County in round 5.

Despite regular jousts with nearby Aston Villa and the other Aston sides, Unity never won any football competitions. They reached the final of the 1883 Wednesbury Charity Cup but were narrowly beaten by 1-0 to West Bromwich Albion before a 4,000 crowd at the Oval ground, Wednesbury. They also got to the final of a six-a-side event held at the Walsall Chuckery ground.

Entering the FA cup in 1882/3, they did very well in reaching the 3rd round, before Aston Villa put them out by 3-1. Villa then went on to play Walsall Town to see who would be representing the Birmingham and Staffordshire teams in the last eight.

By 1883, the football team was in rapid decline. Many of its best players had all gone to the now mighty Aston Villa at Wellington Road. Unity were humiliated 0-16 by the Villa that season, although that was a freak result, since only five weeks before, the Villa had only beaten Unity by 4-1, and there was an explanation for it.

FA Cup history	1st Round	2nd Round	3rd Round
1882/3	Bye	3-0 St George's (H)	1-3 (A) Aston Villa
1883/4	1-5 Stafford Road		
1884/5	0-5 B'ham St. George's		
1885/6	1-5 West Bromwich Albion		
1886/7	1-4 Derby County		
1887/8	1-6 Small Heath Alliance		

The team was a mainstay on the Birmingham football scene, during the 1870s and 1880s, and were Aston Villa's first proper local rivals, and local they certainly were, since they were only a mile from Villa's Wellington Road ground, and you could almost see the Aston Lower Grounds from the Unity ground on Trinity Road.

Unity, of course, were primarily a cricketing side, and a top one too, becoming known on the national scene, but many of their men were all-round athletes and made good footballers too. Having your own walled ground helps a lot too, since you can charge admission money and get used to your own playing surface, and your groundsman can keep the grass exactly to the height that suits your style of play. Unity's ground was large enough for a separate cricket and football pitch area. With the permission of the King Edward VI School sports coach, I walked around the playing area, and even in late autumn, the ground was firm, suggesting good drainage. This would have led to good football conditions, and the six-foot wall would have kept the wind down too. It was in fact well protected from the elements on all sides, as there was a row of Victorian town houses on the far side.

Unity entered the Birmingham Cup right from the beginning and generally got to the 3rd or 4th rounds.

Their first meeting with the Villa makes good reading; they beat them 2-1 in 1878, before three thrilling games against St. George's from nearby Fentham Road saw them exit in round 2. Curiously, the next year (1879), they thrashed St. George's 9-1 on their own ground! They did not have to travel far for this away game as the 'Dragons' ground was in the next street!

The year 1881 saw a high-scoring tussle with the embryonic Small Heath Alliance in round 3, the Coventry Road team coming out 6-4 winners.

The Unity had had some good players through the ranks, such as Harry Pallett, Charlie Athersmith, and Arthur Brown, but as is usual with local amateur teams, the most promising players get snapped up by the local teams who have big ambitions to turn professional, and in Unity's case, they had too many other local teams within earshot, many who only had football as their interest. Crucially, they had mighty Aston Villa on the doorstep, with West Bromwich Albion and B'ham St. George's only five miles away. Football was not their main game; the cricket team held priority, and, in any case, a man like Harry Pallett could move to the Villa for football and still play for the Unity at cricket. How popular this would have made him remains unclear.

The infamous 16-0 humiliation by the Villa in 1883 requires some investigation, especially as the two teams had met only two months before, with a modest 4-1 Villa win suggesting the Unity were still a decent side. Indeed, Unity had been good enough to beat West Brom Albion 3-2 the previous season. It transpires that virtually the week before, Unity's best player, Arthur Brown, had 'defected' to the Villains and persuaded two others to go with him. Brown then had the temerity to score 10 of the 16 goals himself, playing at centre forward with the great Archie Hunter. I expect that the heart was torn out of the Unity, and they simply couldn't be bothered to play up. Another suggestion is that it was in fact the cricket XI who played the match, not the footballers! It had become commonplace when cup ties from different competitions clashed on the same date that a club would field its first XI for the most important game, its second XI for the other, or a mix of first and second teams. Wednesbury Old Athletic were known for this practice. The year 1883 also saw another couple of heavy defeats, when they were invited north to play at Preston and Halliwell. The Deepdale side thrashed them by 9-1 on 22nd October, and the home crowd were reported to have been surprised at the ease of the Preston victory, having heard that Unity were able to give Villa a game.

In a Birmingham cup tie in October 1887, Unity recorded their biggest competitive win when they thrashed Kidderminster Harriers by 14-0. The previous year, they had beaten Bournville by 8-0 away. At their best and with a full strength side, Unity were a match for anyone locally, but being able to consistently field their best eleven was something which they were rarely able to do.

For a short period in 1886/7 season, both Jack and Will Devey turned out for Unity. They were football mad and had played for several of the Aston sides, including, later, Small Heath.

Unity were still good enough to give the Walsall Swifts a fright in 1886, when their Birmingham cup 2nd round tie at the Chuckery ground went 5-4 to the Swifts. As was frequently the case in those days before player contracts, Unity claimed the Swifts had fielded an ineligible man, and the B'ham AFA ordered a replay, which Unity won 1-0. East Midland rising stars Long Eaton Rangers put the Unity out of this cup competition in the next two years, and after 1889, Unity fell back into the junior football scene. They decided to drop down to junior status, with the advent of Aston Villa going into the newly formed (1888) Football League, and Unity began to enter the Birmingham Junior Cup from the start in 1888. Their first ever game in that competition was a home tie with neighbours Aston Clifton. Unity were still putting in creditable performances and were only just beaten 4-3 when they travelled to play Nottingham Forest on Saturday 9th March 1888.

The cricket club had to move out of their Trinity Road walled ground in 1908, and the football team was sadly disbanded. A new ground, just a few yards along the Trinity Road towards the Walsall Road, became the new home for the cricket club. This large ground, literally next door, was almost exactly the same size as the old ground, but, of course, all the memories had been left behind.

Aston Unity team of 1885 was: Mathews (goal); Benson (back); Lloyd, Upton, Pallet (halfbacks); Coley, Rodgers, Heilborn, Ashford, Wilson, Fisher (forwards). Formation was 2-2-6, when many teams had moved on to the classic 2-3-5 one.

Compared to the Unity side of two years before, only the two fullbacks and two forwards had changed; Evans and Rodgers were the fullbacks in 1883, and Green and Dyer were 1883 forwards, suggesting a settled side based around the cricket squad. The midfield trio of Lloyd, Upton, and Pallet stayed together for some years.

ACKNOWLEDGEMENTS

Aston Unity Cricket Club, Sutton Coldfield
Birmingham Daily Post
Aston Local History Library, Perry Barr
Archie Hunters memoirs of Aston Villa
Aston Villa Football Club
Walsall Observer and *South Staffordshire Chronicle* 1880-1890

† This is now the site of the Broadway Community School. Aston Lane had a cricket and football ground on this site from about 1901. Prior to that, on the opposite site of the road, and laid well back in the fields, was the Broomfield cricket ground, which was probably the original ground refered to on Aston Lane, on the other side of the railway line. This very old (pre-1840) Broomfield ground is now waste land since the demolition of the large factory which was built on it in the 1910s.

‡ This may just be different parts of Aston Hall Park.

Aston Unity

Aston Unity's Joe Wilson

Tom Pank of Birchfield Harriers and Aston Unity

Victorian wall at Aston Unity ground

Aston Victoria FC

f. 1878*-1892

Grounds

1. Aston Park
2. Aston Lower Grounds (late 1870s)
3. Aston Cross Ground (1880s)
4. Fentham Road (1888-1890)
5. County Ground Edgbaston (1890-1891)

The roots of this team are unrecorded, although there are one or two small clues in Aston: by 1866 there was an Aston Victoria Bicycle Club, ** a horticultural club by the same name, and in Victoria Road there were several small factories and the town's swimming baths. Victoria Road was one of the new roads which led up to Aston Park, where several embryonic football teams were playing. As royalty-adoring folk, they may simply have added the Queen's name to their town. If the young men who founded the club worked together in the same factory, this could have been at Gillot's Victoria Penworks in the Jewellery Quarter, or perhaps at James Stevens & Co's Victoria Works in Dartmouth Street in the city centre. Another idea is that the team started over in Handsworth in Victoria Park, a mile from Aston, and when they started playing in Aston Park, they put the names of the two parks together. Unfortunately, this idea falls down when you discover that the park wasn't opened until 20 June 1888, a decade after Aston Vics had started. So one suggestion then is that they added the Queen's name to the Aston Park in which they played. It has to be remembered that Queen Victoria was immensely popular, as she ruled over the most successful era known in modern times, and everyone was jumping on the bandwagon by using her name to guild the new names of everything from parks and ships, to babies. Handsworth was a separate village in the 1880s with its own identity, but since 1911 was now a northern district of the sprawling city of Birmingham between Aston and Smethwick. Another nearby team, Lozells FC, also played in Handsworth and yet didn't use the word *Handsworth* in their title, and so one can see that a team born in one district but forced to play in another would keep its original district name. Victoria Park is now called Handsworth Park if you are trying to source it on a map. Following Queen Victoria's visit to Birmingham and Aston Hall in 1858, and Her Majesty granting city status to Birmingham in 1889, several new streets were named after members of the Royal family, including Albert Road and Victoria Road in Aston.

Birmingham football historian Lee Gauntlett prefers the idea that they were simply a pub-based team. If so, the best two candidates are the Victoria Inn at 319 Albert Road, and the Victoria Hotel at 88 Lichfield Road. Both of these are long gone, but they were only a few hundred yards from each other, both very close to the rear of Aston Hall Park. In 1880, one twenty-year-old Frederick Smith followed in his family tradition and opened the Victoria Brewery on Lichfield Road, Aston, presumably in the same building as the hotel/inn of the same name. However, this, too, is at least one year too late for our 'source' as there is a newspaper report of a Victoria v Shakespeare match in the winter of 1879.

The Aston Expressway, a monstrosity of the 1960s, has obliterated the way that Aston Cross used to look, chopping off several streets, cutting others in half, and causing others to disappear altogether. Google Earth 1945 gives a good aerial view of what the district used to be like, with many streets reaching over to the Lichfield Road from the Walsall Road. Both of those two pubs were within sight of Aston Cross itself and the Aston Cross football ground behind the Aston Cross Tavern (latterly called the Golden Cross) at the corner of Rocky Lane and Lichfield Road. Still standing (in 2013) is the Vine, halfway between Aston Cross and the Witton railway station, above the Lichfield Road, and this gives a good idea of what the pubs in the area looked like in the 1880s. There were many breweries and pubs in Aston Manor in the 1880s, and one, the Vulcan Brewery in Tower Road was sold to the HP Sauce Co. in 1899 after Mitchells & Butlers acquired the brewery.

The Aston Cross ground turned out to have a very long and ancient history. All through the 1850s, 1860s, and 1870s, it was used for running races, pedestrianism (walking races, often of hundreds of miles), pigeon shooting (not exactly p.c. in the twenty-first century!) and anything else which the Victorians could find to bet on. Challenge running races, often just between two 'champions', would attract up to 5,000 people there. The old boundary wall of the Aston Hall park grounds was said to have come right up to where the Aston Cross clock tower was, and, thus, the whole district would have exuded the air of almost being in the countryside, and it was popular as a gentleman's retreat in Georgian times.

Football took hold of the Manor of Aston, as it did in Wednesbury, and by 1890, it was said that every pub and church in the manor had its own football team, and some churches had three or four. One of the leading early church teams, Aston St. Mary's (famed as Aston Villa's first ever opponents) regularly played during 1876. One recorded match in the Aston News tells of their 2-0 win against the boys of Erdington Preparatory School after a two-hour game, played on Aston Park. By 1885, not just pubs and churches, but many schools were keen to promote football as a healthy exercise, and because a school had a continuous input of boys, they also had a continuous output of schoolboy teams, who went on to start their own teams when they started work (often aged 12-14). It was no surprise when in 1886, Mr Perry, Head of the Upper Thomas Street school (at Aston Cross, betwixt the Midland Vinegar Co. and Ansells brewery) introduced the Aston Manor Schools Cup, which from an initial entry of eight schools, grew year on year, and continued until the First World War.

The team was said to have comprised of 'youths aged between 12 and 18' in the local newspapers. Most of them grew into men together as the team matured.

In 1889, they were founder members of the Birmingham and District League; in fact, they were the originators of the idea. Mr A. W. Cooknell was their representative on the league management committee.

They only played in it for three seasons; 7 wins but 12 defeats saw them finish 8th of 12 teams in 1890.

The year 1891 was no better, with only 4 wins and 10 defeats, bringing them 9th place.

The year 1892 saw an improvement in form, and 9 wins, 3 draws, and just 4 defeats saw them finish in 3rd place. Even so, by playing in the Birmingham league suggested that, by around 1890, Aston Victoria were Birmingham's 3rd or 4th best side. In fact, the *Birmingham Daily Post* said on 19 September 1890 that the Victoria had been, for the past two seasons, Birmingham's best junior side by a margin.

In the 1st round of the Birmingham Cup, Victoria didn't have far to travel when drawn away to play Warwick County on the 12th October 1889. They both shared the same ground! However, on this occasion, Warwick won 3-1.

In 1890, they changed their name to County Victoria, because they had moved to the Warwick County cricket ground at Edgbaston but changed it back again in 1891!

In 1891/2, they were called B'ham Victoria.

In 1892/3, they were back to Aston Victoria again.

Two Victoria players were selected to play for the Birmingham representative side against Leicester in April 1890, and they were: E. James and A. Jenkins. Representative games were still popular right up to about 1910, even though they robbed leading clubs of key players when they most needed their services.

Early prominent players included Parker and Hatel. The team which travelled to play Bloxwich in 1883 was:

T. Dork (goal); Burton and Hunt (backs); Fisher, Cochrane, A. Dork (halfbacks); Rutter, Meadows, Poole, Randle, J. Dork (forwards).

Once again, we see three brothers forming the nucleus of a team, as with Excelsior and Walsall Town (the Keays). Incidentally, the 1881 Census shows no 'Dork' family living in Birmingham or Walsall, so that name could be spelt slightly differently.

The years 1887 to 1889 were the Vic's best years. They won the Birmingham Junior Cup two years running with the following team:

Withers (goal); A. Maynes, Price (backs); Corknell, J. Maynes, S. Vaughton (halfbacks); P. Vaughton, F. James, Marlow, Brookes, and E. James (forwards).

The Vaughtons were relatives of Villa's Oliver Howard Vaughton, and the James brothers, I believe to be the same two who founded Small Heath back in 1875. If so, they must have joined the Vics in 1886. The Vics defeated a good Unity Gas team 2-0 at Wellington Road to win the 1887/8 junior cup, and they retained their title the following season when they defeated the Wolverhampton Druids 2-0, after the first game had been drawn 1-1. They never again reached the final.

Starting off as a small junior team comprised 'of youth aged between 12 and 18', probably from Albert or Victoria Road in Aston, they slowly improved to one of the best four or five teams in the town by the late 1880s. They continued to play friendlies and local cup ties against nearby sides from Walsall, Aston, and Birmingham throughout the 1880s. However, in obtaining membership of the Birmingham League in 1889, they seem to have reached too far, and the reality of it was that they didn't have the foundations to compete at the higher level. They were an ambitious young team but without a ground or identity of their own. If they were indeed a pub-based team, then this fits the profile. They were soundly beaten when they travelled to Wednesbury on Saturday 11th October 1890, when the Old Un's beat them 8-1 in the Birmingham and District Association Challenge Cup. They fared no better when losing 0-9 to Brierley Hill the following season, and Wellington St. George's beat them 10-0 in the 1892/3 competition. Victoria were by now out of their depth and considered a junior team. Indeed, they elected to enter the Birmingham Junior Cup in 1888/89 season, which they went on to become that competition's first winners, having been drawn to play Saltley Gas FC in the 1st round. They had become the yo-yo team; neither good enough to win at the senior level, yet too strong on the junior circuit.

In January 1890, Victoria lost 1-5 away to Aston Villa reserves, with Shakespeare's former star player Bat Garvey netting a hat-trick against them. A decade before, they would have been able to give the Villa first team a game. Their best players circa 1890 were Clarke, the goalkeeper, Cook, E. James, and A. Jenkins.

From 1889, we no longer hear of their close neighbours, the Aston Shakespeare. This leads us to believe that Victoria amalgamated or absorbed Shakespeare. The fact that they both shared the Aston Cross ground also lends weight to the merger idea. Aston Victoria continued in the Birmingham and District League for four years: they reached their highest league position of 3rd in 1891/2, but, then to the surprise of all, they folded in the winter of 1892 and withdrew from the league.

The *Lichfield Mercury* of April 1900 gave a list of all the local matches played in the West Midlands, and I was pleased to still see such names as Aston Brook St. Mary's, Lozells, Birmingham St. George's, and Hanley Swifts. They were all playing reasonable opposition, but buried towards the bottom I saw the result: Smiths Arms 6-0 Aston Victoria. It seems that by 1900, the old club was a dim shadow of its former self, resorting to playing against pub teams in the park.

An entry in the 1929 Birmingham Football Association yearbook lists an Aston Victoria FC as an active junior club; there was no such entry in the 1930 yearbook. Their club secretary was listed as a Mr S. Brown of 82A Potters Hill, Aston.

To find the location of the Aston Cross ground today, take Park Lane (B4144) at the Barton Arms pub on the main Walsall to Birmingham road at Aston High Street. Drive to the end, which is the island at Aston Cross. The ground was directly behind the Aston Cross tavern which is facing you. The Volvo dealership occupies the site of the pitch.

I was quite surprised to receive an email back from the club historian at Aston Villa FC at Christmas 2012, stating that, sorry, they had no details of any matches or opponents that they had played before 1891! They said, 'Would a list of players from 1890 to 1900 from their old payroll records be of use?' I was quite staggered that a club as famous and rich in history as the Villa did not know about their own early history. I was sorely tempted to recommend several books on the subject to them.

REFERENCES

Midlands Advertiser
Birmingham Daily Post
Aston University Library
Edgbaston Cricket Ground
Aston Brook – through – Aston Manor web site

* possibly as much as eight years earlier
** based at the Aston Lower Grounds

Home to Aston Victoria and Shakespeare-Aston Park Meadow

Aston Cross Tavern

Berwick Rangers (Worcester)

f.1890-1902

Grounds

1. Barbourne Athletic ground early 1890s (now part of Worcester College sports academy)/also New Road ground (during 1894)
2. Severn Terrace, Worcester racecourse from 1897 to 1899
3. St. George's Lane ground (taken over by Worcester City)

Committee:
Joseph Cook (president); L. H. Burgess (hon. sec), A. Glover/T. Calder (treasurers); W. J. Digger (finance sec). Harry Smith was the club's representative on the council of the Worcestershire County FA.

Headquarters:
the Black Horse Inn, Lowesmoor. AGMs were held at the Bell Hotel.

Honours
Worcestershire Cup 1900/1, 1901/2

They were a mainstay of the Birmingham Combination during the 1890s until they folded in 1902 in financial trouble.

In their nine seasons in the Birmingham Combination, they mostly struggled near the bottom, except from 1894 to 1897, when they finished 5th, 6th, and 4th, but were bottom but one out of eighteen clubs two years later, with 20 defeats from 30 games. At this point, Berwick were playing adjacent to the New Road county cricket grounds (1894-97) for important cup ties where a large crowd was anticipated, such as the 4,000 who turned up on Saturday 8th December 1894 to see them beat Stourbridge 3-1 in the Third Qualifying Round of the Birmingham Cup.

Another 2,000 turned out for the next round (1st round proper) but Stoke crushed them 7-0 at home.

At their 1894 AGM at the Black Horse on 17th February, a large gathering of some forty of the club's players and officials heard a story of a struggling club, both in terms of finances and results. The club was poorly supported in the town, and because of the club policy of only using local players who lived in the town, results had suffered, but the committee were determined to see the policy through, even though there had already been suggestions that they should join forces with Worcester Rovers or another junior club.

They entered the Birmingham Senior Cup from the mid-1890s but rarely got past the qualifying rounds. Their 7-0 apparent victory over Kidderminster in the Second Qualifying Round was not what it seemed: the Harriers only fielded their reserves. Berwick didn't get through the qualifying rounds in 1895/6. A 3-2 win over Redditch was followed by a single-goal defeat to a fast-rising Singers FC. Singers had also eliminated Worcester Rovers in the First Qualifying Round, 2-1 after a 1-1 draw at Thornloe. 1896 saw the two Worcester clubs drawn against each other in the First Qualifying Round, and after two close tussles, Rangers got through 3-2 after a 2-2 draw. The 4,000 crowd drawn from the supporters of both clubs in the town suggests that this was the maximum number of spectators the town was likely to see turn out for a football match. In the next round, they got their revenge on Singers with a surprise 5-1 win, only to be drawn against mighty Aston Villa in the 1st round proper. No doubt the Villa sent a mixed team of 1st and reserve players to the Barbourne Athletic grounds on 14th December 1897, but only 2,000 turned out again to see Villa's class tell in a 5-1 win. The 1897/8 season was the last time the Rangers entered the Birmingham cup; they scratched when drawn away to Salop's Wrockwardine Wood village side on the same day that Worcester Rovers scratched to Salops' Newport.

Few, if any, Midland clubs bothered* with FA Amateur Cup when it was started in 1893 from the desire of the Southern amateur clubs to have a national cup for non-professional teams, which, by the 1890s, were monopolising national football events. Berwick Rangers were one of only a handful of Midland sides who took part, apart from Bournville Athletic, Shrewsbury Town, Leek, and Atherstone. They were drawn at home to Darlington from County Durham in the 1st round of the 1894/5 competition, and the northern side promptly withdrew on the grounds of distance. Round 2 saw Berwick play host to unknown Leadgate Exiles, who went away with the 2-1 victory to put an end to Berwick's attempt on the Amateur Cup.

At their AGM on 23 June 1894, held at the Bell Hotel, the secretary announced that the annual income of £336.9.11d left a shortfall of £52 on the season's expenses.

New players being pursued to strengthen the team included W. Jackson of Small Heath, and A. Edwards of the Lozells club. The kitty must have had a boost though when their home derby game with Rovers drew 6,000 to Thorneloe. This side won the 1895 game by 2-1 :

Potter (goal) Bevan, Reynolds (backs) Griffiths, Smith, Ruston (halfbacks); Jackson, A. Edwards, H. Smith, Roberts, Wigley (forwards).

Notable players were:

George Woodhall (1863-1924): joined the Wolves in 1892 (where he was twice chosen for England), and then in 1894, he joined Berwick from West Brom Albion. He played out the remainder of his career with Berwick, staying till he retired in 1898.

Fred Molyneux (b. 1873): came from Stoke during the 1900/01 season.

This team played the local derby against Worcester Rovers at Barbourne in front of 2,200 on Boxing Day 1893 :

W. Barnett (goal); H. Bevan and A. Clegg (backs); G. Griffiths, Bullock, H. Thomas (halfbacks); Feeney, J. Barre, H. Smith, A. Roberts, E. Smithers (forwards).

Smith and Roberts were said to be their best attackers.

During 1900 season, they ran up the club record score in an 11-2 win over the fledgling Singers FC (later Coventry FC).

They also won the Worcestershire Senior Cup two years in succession, 1900/01 and 1901/02, although, apart from the Kidderminster teams, the county suffered from a dearth of association clubs, rugby and cricket being more popular in the county of Worcestershire. Their local rivals Worcester Rovers were short-lived too. Berwick met the same fate as many other small clubs trying to offer professional football in a small town more interested in other sports (cricket and rugby here), and went bust and were wound up in 1902. At least this was two years more than rivals Worcester Rovers managed, and so the two clubs amalgamated in 1902 and became the present-day Worcester (City).

As all their grounds were next to the racecourse, which itself lies next to the river amidst meadows, any side from the industrial Midlands would have benefitted from the fresh countryside air when playing at either

Berwick Rangers or Worcester Rovers. In the 1880s, people did not move around freely as we do now; it was not uncommon for people from the Black Country and Birmingham to have never left the town in which they were born, and so visiting players from teams such as Great Bridge Unity, Wednesbury Town, or Old Hill Wanderers would have experienced the rural way of life, possibly for the first time. Football game aside, they would have returned to their dark and sooty industrial hometown with pleasant memories of a countryside venture.

Communications with Worcester City FC enquiring about the colours of their predecessors initially drew a blank. Eventually, club historian Julian Pugh unearthed an old Berwick Rangers photo from the late 1890s, with the stand in the background. Note the unusual shirts, a bit like Ajax Amsterdam with half sleeves too. If you intend to visit the St. George's Lane ground of Worcester City as it was at first the last home of Berwick Rangers, you will have to be quick, for there are plans to sell the ground for development in the summer of 2013. Severn Terrace is at the bottom end of the racecourse near the junction with the A449 Castle Street and Easy Row. Due to its close proximity to the river, Severn Terrace would have regularly flooded or been heavy underfoot.

* presumably due to the fulfilling popularity of the Birmingham Cup

References

Worcester Chronicle
Steve Carrs' *The History of the Birmingham Cup*
History of the Worcestershire Senior Cup
Julian Pugh, official historian at Worcester City FC (photo)

Berwick Rangers 1890 photo courtesy of Worcester City FC

Birchfield Harriers FC

(Athletic club f. 1877) motto: fleet and free.

Colours:
all black*

Nickname: The Stags
Football Club founded 1887

No, I haven't made a mistake and included this nationally famous athletics and running club in a book about Victorian football teams. They actually had a football team for about a decade from the mid-1870s to the late 1880s.

The Harriers were founded in the summer of 1877 as a result of an open athletics meeting at the Aston Lower Grounds in that year, put on by the Excelsior Club of Aston (see Aston Excelsior FC).

Apparently, the main event, a three-mile paperchase ended up a fiasco when the administration went awry, and there was much dispute as to who had won it (and the prize money), and in what order runners had finished. A group of disenchanted athletes met each other at the Lozells Sunday School in Wheeler Street and decided that they could do better, and so the Birchfield Harriers Athletic Club was born. Excelsior's Thomas Pank is believed to have been a founder member.

Their early headquarters were at Calthorpe Park in Edgbaston, some five miles away, a large area of fields belonging to the Gough family of Calthorpe estates. At that time (1870s), Calthorpe Fields consisted of just meadows for two or three miles from Birmingham town centre, all the way down to the Bournville estates down past Selly Oak. Today, of course, it has become the exclusive upper-class district of Edgbaston and is some of the most valuable land in the city. At this time (1877-81), they would have replaced the Calthorpe Club as main residents of Calthorpe Park, who left there in the autumn of 1876 when their lease prevented them from collecting a gate fee. In 1881, Harriers moved closer back home to their roots when they set up headquarters at the Aston Lower Grounds, which, by then, had been improved with extensive facilities by G. H. Quilter, who ran his own Birmingham Football Club team from his staff and groundsmen. No records of their football colours exist, but it's very likely that they played in their running vests which were black. Despite great success as a running and athletics club, by 1887, they had money worries; income did not meet expenditure, and so it was that Aston Villa and Stafford Road played a charity friendly which raised over £50, which cleared the Harriers' debts. There was a close relationship between the Villa and Harriers; four of the Villa team were actually Harriers' members, including Tom Pank and Oliver H. Vaughton. Also, leading industrialist George Kynock was Harriers' club president in addition to being a Villa director. He owned the large Kynock Works at Witton which was primarily a munitions factory. Being a staunch Scot, he had a larger-than-life-sized lion adorn the factory entrance gates, which curiously had under its paw – a football! This lion rampant found its way on to the Villa, Harriers, and Aston Unity shirts.

Admitted as a senior team, they became members of the Walsall & District Football Association on 10th October 1888 and proceeded to compete in the Walsall Senior Cup with the likes of Birmingham St. George's, Aston Shakespeare, Oldbury, Burton Wanderers, and the newly created Walsall Town-Swifts. They were drawn against Great Bridge Unity in round 1.

Playing mostly ad hoc friendlies, they did actually enter the Birmingham Cup in 1887/8 season, but were unlucky to lose by just 1-2 away to Oldbury Town on the 8th October. In the following year, they were drawn to play Aston Shakespeare, one of Birmingham's strongest sides. They surprised the home crowd at the Aston Cross ground on Rocky Lane on the 13th October, by coming away with a 2-2 draw. However, in the replay the following Saturday, they were beaten 3-1 at the Bournbrook Hotel ground (new home of the Calthorpe FC). In those days, replays were not held at the away team's ground as is today; rather, the Birmingham FA appointed a neutral venue, often resulting in a very poor turnout by the locals who saw little interest in going along to watch two unknown teams, sometimes from another town. After the 1888/9 season, the Birmingham FA introduced a Junior Cup, as there were so many new teams clammering for competition, and by then, the senior sides like Wolves, Aston Villa, St. George's, Walsall, and the Albion were on another level and needed the Senior Cup to be played without the lesser sides in the competition. Tragically, following a fire at the Birmingham FA's old headquarters on the Stratford Road, Hall Green, some thirty years ago, most of their historical records were lost in the fire, including early team records and the Junior Cup details. Harriers entered the first Birmingham Junior Cup in 1888 and were drawn to play the Unity Gas side.

It's possible that the Harriers continued to play in the Junior Cup after they moved to their well-known athletic stadium at the corner of the Walsall and Aldridge Roads in Perry Barr.

The only Harriers' match I could trace in the Birmingham press was their 4-1 defeat away to Small Heath on the 4th March 1889 in the 1st round of the Warwickshire Cup. The brief report describes the Harriers as having 'a powerful defence'. That probably meant physically athletic, as opposed to organised. Their goalscorer was named as Walters.

Harriers moved into their own athletics stadium in 1927, then moving almost next door in 1978 to the council-funded Alexander Stadium. The Alexander was used by Aston Villa for its 3rd team games in the mid-twentieth century. The Birmingham Brummies speedway team now uses the old Birchfield stadium, after a return to the sport after an absence of nearly thirty years, following the demolition of their own speedway stadium in the 1970s, now the One Stop Retail Park. Thus, for most of the twentieth century, Perry Barr had two 10,000 capacity stadiums, plus Villa Park less than a mile away.

References

Aston Library
Birmingham Daily Post
The History of Birchfield Harriers
Archie Hunters memoirs of the 1880s

Tom Pank of Birchfield Harriers and Aston Unity

Birmingham Cricket & Football Club

f. 1869-1884

Ground:
The Meadow, Aston Lower Grounds

Colours:
Scarlet and blue hoops*

Very little is known about this early team, based at the Aston Lower Grounds (next to Villa Park today). They must not be confused in any way with either Small Heath who became Birmingham FC or Birmingham City, as there was no connection whatsoever. This Birmingham FC was a team made up of the workers and groundsmen who were employed by C. H. Quilter to manage the Aston Lower Grounds' leisure complex, most of which is today's Villa Park. They were reported to have favoured the rules of the Sheffield FA, unlike their close neighbours Aston Park Unity, who were affiliated to the London FA. The Birmingham C&FC also used Aston Park in the 1870s, as did a plethora of other Aston-based teams. There was another short-lived team called Birmingham Heath Athletic, who were formed in 1877, and they played on Birmingham Heath (now the Winson Green district).

They were founded possibly as early as 1869, but certainly before 1873 by Henry Quilter, the proprietor of the famous Aston Lower Grounds, Witton Lane. They played regularly until the early 1880s, but between then and the demolition of the Meadow's cricket and football ground in 1888, they probably played only friendly and charity games, although they briefly entered the Birmingham Cup. Only Saltley College FC (1870) has a justified claim to be an earlier team in Birmingham. It is now believed that they started out as Grasshoppers FC.

The venue known to all Brummies as the Aston Lower Grounds was an extensive amusement park with facilities for cycling, cricket, football and athletics, as well as a fair, zoo, ice rink, roller skating, tea rooms, etc. This team had nothing to do with Birmingham City, Small Heath, and Villa, but comprised mainly the employees of the Aston Lower Grounds amusement venue. When this large site was sold off in sections in 1887/8, the southern end containing the large ornamental lake became the site for Villa Park. Anyone who has been to the Walsall Illuminations at that town's Arboretum would have experienced a small-scale idea of what the Aston pleasure grounds would have been like, if you add a skating rink, circus, bowling greens, and an international cricket ground, that is.

Charles H. Quilter was a great showman and entrepreneur manager; he worked tirelessly at promoting the multifarious attractions at his Lower Grounds amusement and sporting venue, the largest in the West Midlands. Barely a day went by when he wasn't running newspaper advertisements ranging from Wild West shows with 'real' Indians and cowboys to light shows, bicycle championships, and football and cricket. He also advertised that the grounds were for hire for every occasion. What a showman! No doubt he was the circus ringmaster too when the Buffalo Bill's Wild West Show came to Aston in 1885.

Notable players of this team included J. H. Cofield, a future leading member of the FA, George Tait, Charles Quilter – founder and captain.

Howard Vaughton (1861-1937) who came from local junior team, Waterloo FC; he later starred for Villa and England. He went to the Wednesbury Strollers prior to his legendary Villa years. Howard was also a noted cricketer in Warwickshire and played for the Mitchells & Butlers cricket team in the late 1870s alongside George Salter and Harry Mitchell.

This team received Derby Town at the Aston Lower Grounds on 6 February 1877: G. R. Quilter (goal); J. R. Riddell and H. Slack (backs); C. H. Quilter and captain Brindley (half-backs); H. Webster, E. Davis, J. Cartwright, G. Pears, F. Barnes, W. Nicholls C. H. Quilter, W. Evans (forwards). The team captain was H. H. Webster, and the E. Davis in attack was the Eli Davis who also starred for the Wednesbury Strollers and later joined the assembled forces of Aston Villa. The game lasted only one hour due to bad state of the pitch, and the Derby team were three men short of a team, and their 0-1 defeat wrapped up a wretched journey for them.

Not unduly concerned with becoming a force in football circles, Birmingham were almost a casual team, just playing friendlies against the other early sides. They would often be a new team's first opponents as they were one of the – if not the – earliest of the Birmingham sides, and of course, they had the famous Meadow football ground as their home, and who wouldn't want to play on that? They were the first opposition for West Bromwich (Dartmouth), for example, whom they met three times in the spring of 1874, winning the home games 2-1 and 3-0 and losing away 0-1. On 14th

December 1878, Birmingham FC travelled to Walsall to play the Town club at the Chuckery Ground. The Birmingham team were lauded for having 'survived encounters with the leading sides of the Midlands'. A 1,500 crowd saw Quilter's men come away with a 4-0 victory, with Howard Vaughton in notable form. The team for that game was H. H. Webster (goal); G. H. Quilter (captain), T. Butler, B. Stevens, R. Evans, C. Terry, J. H. Riddall, F. Bill, H. Vaughton, B. R. Quilter, A. Harvey, H. Cousins (forwards) – 12 men.

In 1879, they, with Villa and Stafford Road, entered the English FA Cup. Those two sides were drawn against each other due to an attempt by the FA at regionalisation to limit travelling expenses; the Birmingham club met the same fate as Wednesbury Strollers the year before and were thrashed 6-0 at Oxford University.

They also entered the Birmingham Cup that year, but were beaten 4-1 at home by Saltley College. For reasons unknown, they scratched in the following year (1880) when drawn away to Walsall White Star. The Star were an unknown new team without any pedigree, so perhaps it was just the idea of leaving town that the Birmingham team didn't fancy; perhaps it clashed with an important sporting event at the Lower Grounds, and they couldn't get the time off work. Whatever the reason, they never entered a major competition again.

The Birmingham club had an impressive fixture list, but their leading position could not be sustained beyond the end of 1880.

Their major legacy to Midlands football was the magnificent meadow otherwise known as the Aston Lower Grounds, where all the region's important cup finals would be played, an English FA Cup semi-final, and international cricket games. This, of course, led to the construction of Villa Park.

Their team of the mid-1870s included George Copley (goal), W. Burns (captain), Hubbard, Dutton, Dayfield, Bishton, Perry, G. Quilter, Howard Vaughton, W. Mills, George Tait. During the 1877/8 season, their captain was Harry Webster. Copley also played for Saltley College and later became Aston Villa's goalkeeper in 1879/80 just as they began to assemble their star team of the 1880s. Tait and Bishton also played together for the Excelsior club in Aston. I do get the feeling that this Birmingham club were a bit of a celebrity side, with most of the side coming from the ALG workforce, but with three or four top players from the Aston teams joining them for important matches. Remember, players were not tied to one club in those days before contracts and legal lost time payments. A star player was free to lend his skills to as many teams as he – or his stamina and availability – wished. His loyalty would only be put to the test if two teams for which he played were drawn against each other.

The team broke up as a direct result of the Aston Lower Grounds' cricket meadow being sold off for three streets of terraced houses which remain there to this day, the largest being Nelson Road.

To get a good idea of the size and location of the Aston Lower Grounds, walk to the top of the hill at Aston Hall by the Villa ground. Walk to the side of the Hall, and you will get a bird's-eye view by looking to the left of Villa Park at the three streets which were built over the ALG in 1889.

REFERENCES

Play Up Brammidge! Steven Carr, 2004
Sandwell Borough Archives Library, Smethwick
Birmingham Daily Post, 1870-1889
Walsall Observer
Staffordshire Sentinel, 1879

* Colours courtesy of Steve Carr from Charles Alcock annuals

Aston Lower Grounds

DANE.

ASTON LOWER GROUNDS.

BOATING on the improved and enlarg d Pool. The SKATING RINK open for Three Exercises Daily POUNTNEY'S BAND Every Evening.

Admission to Grounds, 3d. each. Admi sion to Rink, 6d. Use of Skates, 6d. Tickets for Rink to be had at he Entrance.

H. G. QUILT R, Managing Director.

Omnibuses leave Dale End every few minutes and Monmouth Street every half-hour to the Witton en rance. 225

ASTON LOWER GROUNDS.

GRAND FOOTBALL MATCH.

CALTHORPE v. SALTLEY COLLEGE

(BIRMINGHAM ASSOCIATION CUP TIE).

THIS DAY (SATURDAY), DECEMBER 7.

Kick-off 2.45 prompt. Admission 3d. 990

JOHN SANGER & SON'S NEW CIRQUE, Darling-

Aston Lower Grounds—Advert for 1883 Birmingham Cup Final

Birmingham Excelsior FC

Founded 1876-1888: the athletics club may have been founded in 1869

Colours

maroon and yellow hoops (1870s)
maroon and yellow stripes (mid-late 1880s)

Grounds

1. played at Witton Fields, Perry Barr during the early years 1876-1881 (see photo)
2. Aston Park (then important games at the Aston Lower Grounds) 1882-84 (see photo)
3. Fentham Road cricket and football ground, Aston (Birchfield) from 1885

'Witton Fields' was a large area of undeveloped meadowland between Aston and Perry Barr, the remains of which are now centred around Moor Green Lane Jewish cemetery almost underneath the M6 motorway as it passes over Witton. In 1860, part of the old manor was set aside as a cemetery, and the original high brick wall still survives. On the opposite side of Moor Green Lane are the extensive playing fields, now part of the Aston University recreational facility, but, for many years, known as the Joseph Lucas factory sports ground. Despite its slightly remote location, transport links were good, even 150 years ago. The Grand Junction railway was cut through Witton in the late 1840s, with a station at Witton. There was already the tame valley canal nearby, and George Kynoch set up a munitions factory near the railway in 1860. This was a large factory sprawling over some 20 acres, and until the end of the twentieth century, for the most part, still stood, only the entrance now surviving. The curious name 'Witton' derives from old English 'Wic turn', meaning dairy farm.

No records of their early games exist from the Witton Fields period, but as we come into the 1880s, there seems to be a connection between Excelsior men and athletics in general. Victorian sportsmen often excelled at several sports, such as athletics, bicycling, cricket, or rugby, and it was at a cross-country race promoted by Excelsior club at the Aston Lower Grounds in 1878 which led to the creation of the famous Birchfield Harriers Athletics club in the following year. The Excelsior club could be described as an all-round sports club, with its members entering competitions at paperchases, running, sprinting, cycling, athletics, cricket, and football. By

1881, the Excelsior clubs were known for their annual sports days which they put on at the Lower Grounds; competitors from all over the Midlands would compete in all sorts of athletics, bicycling races, etc., and there would be a mini-football cup with four invited teams, usually Walsall Swifts and West Bromwich Albion, and Wolverhampton Wanderers. Many well-known footballers would take part. Charles Alcock's 1900 annual says that Excelsior were still based at Witton in 1880/1 and confirms their formation year.

This 1877 team travelled to Walsall to play Bloxwich at the Little Bloxwich lane ground:

Mason (g); H. Dyass (back); Thornton and Hill (halfbacks); Longstaff, Chambers, Wilcox, Spriggs, Lawton, C. Dyoss, Wootton (forwards).

The majority of the side were attackers. Interestingly, Charles and Henry Dyoss** and Thomas and Joseph Spriggs were also playing for Walsall's Victoria Swifts at this time and also the Walsall Robin Hood club. Thomas Spriggs was a silver-plater, and Joe had a very specific occupation of a coach handle dresser. They were founder members of the Victoria Swifts from the Caldmore–Highgate district of Walsall.

An Excelsior line-up which played against Walsall Albion the same year was virtually a completely different eleven, featuring the Sprason brothers, Simkins, Bailey, Newey, Cooper, and George Tait. Presumably they had – like Rushall and Aston Unity – a large playing membership of perhaps forty-plus men, and either fielded just those eleven who were available, or they selected a team according to the strength of their opponents.

This fourteen-man Excelsior side played the Arcadian club in Calthorpe Park on Saturday, 10th February 1877, going down in a closely contested match by 2-1:

W. Sprason (goal); Smart, Tillotson (backs); Bailey, Wood (halfbacks); E. Rodgers, F. Sprason, W. Jones, W. Rodgers, J. Chapman, C. Baxter, Remington, A. Hill, Pank (forwards).

The Arcadians only used thirteen men (!): Robins, Johnson, Gosling, Wells, Bore, Evans, Grass, Powell, Fenn, Hands, Boucher, and Chambers. The Arcadians variously played at Calthorpe Park, Cannon Hill Park, Bristol Road, or Selly Hill Park. Interestingly, Archie Hunter says he played cricket for the Arcadians, and despite their Greek – mythology name, he said that they were founded from lads in a Birmingham warehouse!

An incident occurred in a friendly match against the Walsall Trinity club on 25th February 1878 at the Lower Grounds, when, with the score at 2-2, the Trinity men left the field en masse when two of their forwards had dribbled the ball past the entire Excelsior defence, rounded the goalkeeper, and scored. The home umpire – whose name is best omitted – disallowed the goal for offside! The Trinity men afterwards said that the umpire had 'next to no knowledge of the rules, and none concerning the offside laws'.

Internet research using sites such as Ancestry.com reveals that several of the Excelsior men* in the early 1880s seemed to have occupations associated with Birmingham's famous Jewellery Quarter, such as silversmith, tin-plater, jeweller, etc., although this does not necessarily mean that this was their source of origin.

In the 1880s, Excelsior had an enclosed cricket and football ground between Fentham Road and Trinity Road, Aston. Sadly, this is no longer there, and Arden Road is in its place. A small triangle of grass and playground is all that remains today of the 2.3-acre site (see photo). This ground was only a few hundred yards away from the Aston Unity ground on Trinity Road and not much further from the Aston Lower Grounds. There was also the old Aston Manor cricket ground on Trinity Road which is now occupied by the Broadway Community school.

By the end of 1881, Excelsior were said to be 'nearly the best team in Birmingham' (presumably they counted the Villa as not being in Birmingham then), with Riddell, Bushell, Tait, and Bishton being singled out for particular praise.

In late 1882, Exelsior had two closely fought friendly matches with West Bromwich Albion. The home game, a 2-2 draw on 21st October, was followed with a narrow 2-3 defeat at the Fours Acres on 2nd December.

In the mid-1880s, two of their best performances came in the Birmingham Cup. They won a thrilling game away to Handsworth at the Grove ground by 6-5 on Saturday 27th October 1883 and were one of the few teams to win at Long Eaton Rangers when they came away from the Recreation ground on Saturday 8 December, having scored the only goal of the match.

Interestingly, a team called St. George's FC played at the Fentham Road ground from about 1875 to 1886.

At first I thought this was the forerunner to Birmingham Excelsior, but as confirmed in Steven Carr's book *The History of the Birmingham Senior Cup*, both a St. George's team and the Excelsior were both playing at the same time after 1880, St. George's at Fentham Road and Excelsior at the Aston Lower Grounds. When the St. George's team ceased playing at Fentham Road, it seems that the Excelsior moved in there from 1885 until Arden Road was built over the cricket ground circa 1895. I have read erroneously that Mitchell St. George's were playing out of the Fentham Road ground, but this team was the original St. George's team.

They moved over to Cape Hill and amalgamated with the Mitchells brewery team to become Mitchell St. George's in 1886.

St. George's were clearly a strong team, especially at home, and reached the Birmingham Senior cup semi-final in 1883, trouncing Walsall Town 6-2 on the way. St. George's and Excelsior actually met in the 2nd round of the BSC in December 1881, with a 3-3 draw at Fentham Road being decided at Perry Barr (Wellington Road?) on Christmas Eve, when Excelsior ran out 3-1 winners. After the demise of Excelsior, the Packington team, which reached the final of the 1890 Birmingham Junior Cup, played from the Fentham Road ground.

During season 1884/5, Excelsior played 13, with 10 wins, 2 draws, and just 1 defeat all season, and scored nearly 50 goals, averaging 2.6 goals per game against good quality opposition.

Excelsior took part in the first ever Birmingham Junior Cup in 1888, being drawn away to Kings Norton United in round 1. They also hedged their bets by entering the Birmingham Senior Cup for each year of the 1880s decade, generally doing rather well, with the 3rd round being their usual exit point. Their heaviest competitive defeat came at the hands of the Wednesbury Old Athletics, who thrashed them 11-2 at the Aston Lower Grounds, despite being virtually at home, this being closely followed by a 0-10 defeat at the Chuckery away to Walsall Town two years later (1885). Generally, however, they must have been one of the best three or four Birmingham area sides in the early 1880s. The Wolves, for instance, needed three games to beat them in 1886, with the Football League status only two years away.

As to their demise, one can only speculate that, as with Aston Unity only two streets away, when the ground was sold off for new houses circa 1899, the team disbanded at the turn of the century, being homeless.

Famous players – George Tait 1 cap for England 1881

Wilbert Harrison went to B'ham St George's in 1886 as their star attacker.

Alf Farman (b. 1869) went to the Villa and ended his career with Newton Heath in 1895.

The Devey family – John, Edward, and Harry – went to Villa. John Devey was also a famous cricketer for Warwickshire, scoring over 6,500 career runs. He was two seasons at Excelsior club, previously having come from Aston Unity. He also had a spell at Mitchell St. George's in 1887.

Ted Devey went to Small Heath Alliance in 1888 as a wing-half, and thence on to Burton Wanderers. Harry was John's uncle, and he joined the Villa first, in 1888, then John followed him six months later. Wilf Devey was also the Excelsior club's vice-president.

Unfortunately, once the Devey brothers had been signed up by the Villa, and George Tait went to Albion, the quality of the team was much reduced, and they went into a rapid period of decline. George Tait died suddenly at the young age of 23. With the loss of Harrison to the new Mitchell St. George's, Excelsior's team going into the 1887 season would have been considerably weaker than in previous seasons.

Recent knowledge suggests that this amateur team is now thought to have been a works side from an Excelsior factory of the same name, which cannot be traced in the Aston area, although a metal-working company in Birmingham town centre (Vyse St.) had a factory called the Excelsior works. Interestingly, Excelsior suddenly moved its headquarters out of Aston to the Gaiety Palace music hall at 90 Coleshill Street in the city centre after a 0-5 defeat by local rivals Aston Shakespeare in the autumn of 1886 which dumped them out of the Birmingham Cup that year. The previous season, they went out by 7-1 to Burslem Port Vale in the 4th round. It could have been that they had run out of money for equipment; they certainly needed to approach the owner of the Gaiety Palace for his patronage, which was generously provided, and enabled the Excelsior to carry on a while longer. However, this does seem to tally with the year that they moved into the Fentham Road ground previously occupied by the St. George's team. Did Excelsior agree to merge with another Aston team after years of having to pay rents for the use of parks department pitches, typically a shilling a game?

In 1882, their best forward, Tom Pank, was snapped up by Aston Villa as part of their dastardly plan to nobble all the local teams by obtaining the services of the rivals' best players. Pank had been with the Excelsior for seven or eight seasons and had a younger brother with the unfortunate name of Frank Pank!

Other star players snapped up in Villa's plan included Eli Davis and Alf Harvey from the Wednesbury Strollers, Oliver Whately from Aston Florence, Albert Brown the ace Aston Unity centre forward and George Copley, the Saltley College goalie. Pank was a celebrated athlete who played halfback. He was a sprint runner, and very quick and strong on the ball, racing to the corner flag before lashing his crosses into the goalmouth, where no doubt a burly centre forward would charge the goalie into the net just as he was catching the ball. A recent discovery connected with the Aston Villa heritage trail from their *Claret & Blue* magazine reveals that before the cricketers from the Aston Villa Weslyian chapel formed a football team in the winter of 1874, the cricketers rented Fentham Road cricket ground in 1872, and it is thought that some early Villa matches were played there, before their move to Wellington Road. Additionally, Thomas Pank was revealed to have been the founder member of the Birchfield Harriers running club. This gives us a clear overview into the close association between the various sporting clubs in the Aston and Birchfield areas in the 1870s. Pank played for Excelsior and moved to the Villa, whilst founding Birchfield Harriers; Athersmith played for the Villa and ran for the Harriers; George Kynock was a Villa director and president of the Harriers, and William McGreggor also helped both Calthorpe FC in the 1870s, and later the Lozells FC in the 1890s. Several Aston Unity men – who were both cricketers and footballers – also turned out for the Villa too. So, despite an apparent rivalry of these close-knit sporting clubs, it looks like they shared not just players but benefactors too!

Excelsior's team which played Walsall Swifts in 1883 was: Brown (goal); Harris and Gee (backs); Bough and Gee (halfbacks); Simmonds, Tapper, Walker, Gwinnett, Sadler (forwards). Brown had replaced George Hubbard in goal from the previous season. At this time, they were playing a curious 5-3-1-1 formation with a fullback and a 3/4 back behind three halfbacks.

It was in this year, 1883, that Excelsior began a five-year adventure in the English FA Cup, but round 2 was the furthest they ever got, but still good for a small fry team.

In 1885, they were popular winners of the Wednesbury Charity Cup over the Old Athletics. Players were presented with silver-gilt chronometer watches by the committee of the Wednesbury Association at their annual dinner gala.

The 1884/5 team was: H. Meakin (goal); backs-F. Barlow and W. Dutton; halfbacks: A. Bailey and W. Farley; John Devey, J. Breese, E. Jevenen, G. Jenks, and A. Brown (forwards). They also had Harry Devey and Caesar Jenkins on the books. If you are a Villa fan reading this book, you will know the name Devey from their all-conquering team of the late 1890s. If you are ever in the vicinity of Fulham Road Sparkhill, have a look at No. 49. That's where Devey lived in the 1920s. It was said later that John Devey was regarded as a professional player by the age of 18, during his two years with the Excelsior club.

As you can see, the above eleven are completely different to the team of just two years before, illustrating how fluid the make-up of these teams were in those days. Maintaining the standard of the team's play with such a rapid turnaround of personnel whilst trying to keep hold of your best players must have been difficult. They were running two teams at this point, but the 1882 team which travelled to Walsall contained only Dutton and Coley from the following season's 1st team.

On 17th September 1887, Excelsior played the strong Walsall Swifts in the Walsall Cup, but an impressive crowd of 2,000 saw the Swifts have a comfortable 4-0 win.

Marston, Campbell, Owen from the 1887 team don't even appear in the team of the following season which was: Brown (goal); Gee and Harris (backs); Bough and Gee (halfbacks); Simmonds, Tapper, Walker, Guinnett, Sadler, and Ringwood (forwards). Excelsior lost another top player in 1888 when Charlie Short went to Small Heath but moved on to Unity Gas FC after only one year. Short ended his career with junior side Bloxwich Strollers in the mid-1890s. Gersham Cox moved on to have a football league career of 86 games with Aston Villa from 1888/9, having first spent a year with Walsall Town, and ended his days at Bloxwich too, via Willenhall Pickwick. The Excelsior 1887 team which thrashed Warwick County 5-0 on their own ground on 22nd October is again quite different to the team which faced Walsall Swifts as described above. The October team was:

Joynt (goal); S. Leonard, D. Leonard (backs); G. Hawley, F. Lee, G. Kendrick (halfbacks); A. Farneux, Genever, W. Siddons, J. Spittle, J. Devey (forwards). Only John Devey and Genever seem to be regulars around this time.

After 1888, the team seems to have fallen back from the front rank, as illustrated by their 0-6 defeat on 10th March to local rivals Aston Shakespeare. 'Bat' Garvey got 4, the other scorers being Solloway and Wilson, in match the *Birmingham Daily Post* described as one-sided.

I did come across a single-line match result in the *Birmingham Post* of a game played on Saturday 15th September 1900, wherein 'Aston Excelsior' lost 0-1 at home to Kings Heath.

Excelsior must have had either a large membership (Rushall Rovers for example in 1878 had sixty members), or drawn its team from a large factory workforce. This is all well for a purely amateur team so long as there is company or sponsor backing, but as the Villa had shown, speedy transition into embracing professionalism was the only way to guarantee a future. A population even of 60,000 Astonians was not enough to spread its support to the many aspiring Aston teams as the nineteenth century drew to a close.

To find the site of the old and much-used Fentham Road Excelsior ground today, drive to the junction of the A34 Walsall Road at Birchfield and Trinity Road (well known to Villa fans as the route to walk to Villa Park from the main road). Drive down Trinity Road 100 yards then go right into Hampton Road. The ground occupied all the area to your left between Freer Rd and Fentham Rd. Arden Road was built right in the middle of the cricket ground, but there's a small pathway which takes you to the Arden playing field, which is the only actual remnant left. If you now turn left and go to the bottom of Fentham Road, you will see a walled ground facing you. That was the old Aston Unity sports ground.

* Bishton, Coley, Angel, Riddel
** often given as Dyoss

Witton Fields

FA cup history	1st Round	2nd Round	3rd Round
1883/4	3-2 Small Heath Alliance (H)	1-2 Derby Midland (A)	
1884/5	2-0 Small Heath Alliance	0-2 Aston St. Georges	
1885/6	1-2 Derby Midland		
1886/7	3-3, 1-2 Derby Midland		
1887/8	5-0 Warwick County (A) (after 4-1 void game)	Bye	1-2 Gt. Bridge Unity (H)

References

Birmingham Daily Post 1880-90
Walsall Observer 1885
Wednesbury Free Press 1885

Fentham Road Ground Today

Bloxwich Strollers FC

f. 1893 (possibly earlier at 1875-1934)
reformed variously during 1952-1988

Headquarters:

1. Royal Exchange P.H, High Street (for W'ton Rd ground)
2. Red Lion P. H. Leamore

Status:
amateur, later semi-pro

Colours:
all white (1880s), 1890s – usually red shirt, white shorts; Amber and maroon stripes during 1940s. Red or red and white stripes during 1950s

Honours
Birmingham Junior Cup 1900/01 Birmingham Combination champions 1924/5

Grounds

1. Wolverhampton Rd (see text) 1877-1892
2. Little Bloxwich Lane 1893-1900
3. Red Lion Ground, Leamore 1901-1955

The Bloxwich team which played against the Wednesbury FC (later Strollers) in October 1879 was:

Evans (goal); Lindop (fullback); Beech, Steele, Lester, Westwood, Stokes, Collins, Hall, Partridge, and J. Vale (captain). James Lindop had a career in local politics; he owned three collieries in Bloxwich and later became a Justice of the Peace and was Walsall town mayor in 1887. Bloxwich would have been in all-white and Wednesbury in maroon shirts.

A team simply called Bloxwich entered the Birmingham Cup from 1880, and as there was but one football ground in the village, it is a strong possibility that this is the same team as the side which were known to be active from 1893. However, by the mid-1880s, Bloxwich were out of their depth in the Birmingham Cup, with severe defeats against West Bromwich Albion (0-15, 1884 – J. E. M. Bayliss scoring 6) and Walsall Town (0-17 in 1885) demonstrating the gap that was opening up. Fortunately, for teams like Bloxwich, the Birmingham FA started up a Junior Cup in 1887, and they were to play in that, along with the Walsall, Wednesbury, and Forester cups when they came long.

The original Bloxwich team played its early games on a field 'near to the railway station'. This was closed down at the end of the twentieth century and is now just a through line from Walsall to Cannock, with only a signal box and crossing gates remaining, but as a boy, I recall the cowshed style station with its blackened curved roof and platform which backed on to the Station Hotel pub which may have been used as their first headquarters. Having a pitch next to a railway station is a good move! As a football pitch was around 3 acres (their Little Bloxwich Lane ground was 3.68 acres), the 4-acre field between Station Street and Parkers Lane (once called Wolverhampton Road until renamed after a councillor) would be the probable location of early games. The field backed on to the Bloxwich brewery, and this, too, may have been where players worked when the team started out. Elmore Green J&I school now occupies the L-shaped field, and the old brewery was located at what is now the top of Signal Drive cul-de-sac.

Their first proper ground was a field on Little Bloxwich Lane from September 1893-1900, which they rented from a Mr Cartwright.* They developed the ground a little, with a perimeter railing, and a large pavilion along the western touchline, and laid a brick trackway from the main road. Until the 1910s, there were no houses along this main road to Lichfield, but today we see lovely Edwardian detached houses on both sides. The inaugural match was a game against a local side W'ton St. Chad's, resulting in a comfortable 5-1 home win. The original pitch is still there, behind houses on Lichfield Road, which was called Little Bloxwich Lane in Victorian times (see photo). At that time, however, Bloxwich was but a semi-rural village four miles north of Walsall along the main A34 route to Cannock. It retained its independence from Walsall until 1888 when Bloxwich and the surrounding areas were made into a new parliamentary ward. The new ward's first alderman was one James Lindop J.P., who had connections with the formation of Walsall Football Club in the 1870s. The population of Bloxwich was just under 9,000 when the football team started up and remained around 15,000 until the population trebled when several large housing estates were built on the north end of Bloxwich in the second half of the twentieth century. That original ground is still there today, I discovered, hidden at the back of Victorian and Edwardian detached houses on the Lichfield Road opposite the old T. P. Riley community school. It is enclosed on all four sides by tall trees and the touchline adjoins the town cemetery. It still evokes ghostly memories of Victorian footballing days although the wooden pavilion near the halfway line on the western side has long since gone.

The invitation card to the club's annual presentation evening for 1901/2 claims that they were winners of the Staffs, W'ton (1893), and Bilston cups; sadly, these were only the junior versions, but still, a modest success at local level. Ray Thomas, the club's president, was still proud of his little club 'Bloxidge'. During the 1880s, the club was run by President D. E. Parry, Honorary Secretary A. Taylor, and his assistant W. H. Bratt. They named their reserve side the Bloxwich Swifts.

Their second proper ground was the Red Lion ground at the back of the pub of same name in the Leamore district, on Green Lane. The Strollers played there from 1900/01 until their final demise in 1954/5. The club went insolvent in 1934 but was revived in 1950 when it spent a few seasons in the Birmingham & District League before withdrawing from the league at Christmas 1952.

The Red Lion Ground too is still there today, having been used by both Strollers for the first half of the twentieth century and latterly by Blakenhall FC, and Bloxwich United, although the pub itself was demolished at the start of 2000. Other minor local teams have also shared the ground in recent years. At the turn of the century (1901), ex-Bloxwich and Aston Villa star Charlie Athersmith was the licensee of the Red Lion, and he was instrumental in the Strollers setting up their new home there. Councillor Cartwright was to be the club's principal backer throughout the 1920s and 1930s.

Poor attendances plagued the Strollers, but this was little more than a large village until post-war when housing estates were built. Bloxwich's population had grown in the 1880s but was still only 14,000. Writing in the Walsall press, Club Secretary John Stokes laid the blame not on public apathy, but on the fact that Bloxwich people didn't get their pay packet until Saturday afternoon,** at which time, the matches were already under way, and the first port of call for hard-working and thirsty men was the nearest pub! Team captain Herbert Smith also added that the town's wealthiest citizens were too busy benefactoring cricket and other sports, with football a second thought.

Alternating between the Walsall and Birmingham leagues for most of their life, Bloxwich did have occasional local success.

Bloxwich Strollers were Birmingham League champion in 1896, and the 1890s was their best period. The years either side of the new (twentieth) century saw the Strollers reach their peak. They reached the Birmingham Junior cup final two years running; in 1900, they overcame Bournville, the Cadbury's works team 2-1, but then the same two sides appeared in the 1901 final, and this time the result was reversed.

Mostly the 1890s were spent in the strong Walsall and District League playing the principal local town teams such as Darlaston, Hednesford, Willenhall, Bilston United, and Cannock. They came 3rd in 1899/90 and went one better the next season, before finally winning the league title in 1902/03. Crowds were never much above 1,000, but their Staffordshire Junior cup semi-final against Wednesbury Old Athletic in 1905 at neutral Darlaston drew a large crowd of 5,000 but saw WOA crush Strollers by 5-1 and go on to beat Talke (Stoke) 1-0 in Stoke (Victoria ground).

In 1900, three Strollers men – Thompson, Cartwright, and Massey – were selected by the Birmingham FA to take part in an England Junior team trials match at Willenhall's ground, for a game against Scotland Juniors at the Small Heath ground on 7th April.

In 1905/06, the Strollers spoiled the Willenhall Swifts' day at the opening of their new Spring Bank stadium by winning 5-2 in the Walsall League fixture in front of a crowd of 1,500.

Curiously, in the final of the 1892 Wolverhampton Junior Cup, they lost 1-4 to Willenhall Pickwick, but exactly reversed the scoreline two years later against the same team in the same cup final.

Another good season in 1915/16 saw them finish runners-up to Darlaston, but their league match with neighbours Wednesbury drew only a crowd of 500.

Things were steadily improving, and by 1924/5, the Strollers were champions of the strong 18-club Birmingham Combination, above Hinkley, Halesowen,

Bromsgrove, Leamington, and Hereford, but only the matches against Walsall FC reserves drew a four-figure crowd. Despite occasional regional success, Bloxwich, little more than a large village, didn't have the population to support a professional team, and Strollers yo-yo'd between being amateurs and semi-pro, constantly losing its best players to bigger neighbours Walsall, Wolves, Albion, and the Birmingham sides. Strollers folded again when the Second World War came along but was started up again circa 1937 mainly, thanks to the efforts of local Councillor Cartwright who had been a long-time supporter. Their post-war record in the Birmingham District League was a story of constant struggles, both on and off the pitch. The year 1953/4 saw them at the bottom of 22 teams with a woeful 138 goals conceded in the 42 fixtures. The year 1954/5 was even worse, bottom again, but this time an embarrassing 162 goals conceded saw them finally call it a day, and they wound up and in 1955, halfway through their 2nd division (Bham Lge) fixtures. Even so, the Walsall press still gave them second billing on match reports after Walsall FC, and they were still seen as Walsall area's 2nd status club, mainly due to their long history, even though amateur sides like Walsall Amateurs, and Walsall Trinity were possibly better outfits.

A third attempt to revive the Strollers' name was made in the 1960s, but this team really had nothing to do with the club apart from keeping the name alive in the town. They entered minor cups, but they too folded before the decade was out (see photo).

Honours

Birmingham and District League title 1896
Birmingham Combination league title 1924/25
Birmingham County AFA Junior cup in 1899/90, beating Bournville (Cadburys) 2-1

Although Bloxwich never achieved much as a club, apart from the above, and the Walsall Senior Cup in 1951 (1-0 v Walsall Wood), they have had quite a few players who either moved on into League football, or ended up as a graveyard for ex-League players who were ending their careers:

Charlie Athersmith (1872-1910) joined Aston Villa after two seasons at Bloxwich (1888-90) and had 12 caps.

Arthur Stanton (1892-1917) joined Birmingham FC in 1913.

Jack Aston (1877-1934) went to Walsall, then to Woolwich Arsenal.

George Garratty (1888-?) moved to Wolves giving over 200 appearances.

Gersham Cox (1863-1940) came from Willenhall Picks and went on to play 86 games for the Villa.

Harry Lane (1909-77) came from Hednesford and went on to score over 70 goals for Birmingham FC.

George Robertson (1883-1921) joined Bloxwich in 1914 after years of playing for Glasgow Rangers.

Winston Crump, a relation to Sir Charles Crump from Wolverhampton, previous team Wednesfield Rovers, came from the Wolves in 1894, so too did Horace Bird in 1919.

Joe Cartwright (6'4" goalie) came from the 1920s

James Nicholls (1908-1984) was a goalkeeper in the 1920s, who went on to play for Manchester City in the 1930s.

The team of 1891 was: W. Perry, Johnson, Stackhouse, Emery, Athersmith, Gregory, Rowley, Aulton, Harrison.

The team of 1895was: Green (goal); Lyons and Proffit (backs); Hazelwood, Munn, Phillips (halfbacks); Dunston, Sadler, James, Aulton, and Harrison (forwards). Kendricks and Massey joined the team in 1899 from Willenhall Pickwick.

The team of 1927 was: Harold Guest (goal) Jack Martin, Howard Ford, Bill Thatcher, Sam Sumner, Jack Potter, Harold Deeley, Horace Marshall, and Bert Lane. Playing at this time was Isac Cope, who was an England Schoolboys International.

Most famous (subsequently) player was a young Charlie Athersmith who played for the Strollers as a teenager. He was really an athlete, said to be the fastest runner in the district when aged 11. Later he proved it by winning several quarter-mile events, including the famous Powderhall Sprint in Scotland as a Villa player – something the Villa management were not at all happy about as he didn't tell them he was risking his (by then, England) valuable legs in the event!

Bloxwich Strollers' finest hour, the final table for the Birmingham Combination 1924-25

	PL	W	D	L	F	A	Pts
Bloxwich Strollers	34	26	4	4	96	40	56
Walsall FC 2nds	34	20	8	6	93	27	48
Hinckley United	34	21	4	9	101	56	46
Halesowen	34	20	4	10	86	53	44
Leamington Town	34	17	10	7	71	44	44
Sunbeam Motors	34	16	8	10	83	68	40
Bromsgrove Rovers	34	17	5	12	74	58	39
Birmingham Corp Trams	34	14	8	12	61	51	36
Rugby Town	34	16	3	15	88	73	35
Bournville	34	13	7	14	74	75	33
Hereford United	34	12	8	14	71	70	32
Walsall Wood	34	13	6	15	64	74	32
Atherstone Town	34	11	7	16	68	90	29
Lichfield City United	34	13	1	20	45	86	27
Tamworth Castle	34	5	12	17	56	95	22
Foleshill Great Heath	34	7	6	21	53	95	20
Wolseley Athletic	34	7	1	26	50	105	15
Nuneaton Res./WOAC	34	4	6	24	40	114	14

In this year, Wednesbury Old Athletic finally folded and withdrew at Christmas, their remaining fixtures were take on by Nuneaton Towns' reserve side. Observe Hereford United halfway down the table. Presumably the Birmingham Council's trams team had no difficulty in getting to away matches! Even in this championship-winning season, Bloxwich crowds were poor. Their opening-day fixture against locals Wednesbury only attracted 500 to the Red Lion ground on 30 August.

Sadly, on my visits to the Red Lion ground in 2012, the present occupiers of the ground were oblivious to the history of Bloxwich Strollers, despite the fact that for most of the last hundred years, it was their ground. I do find it very sad that people and organisations become ignorant of their heritage like this.

References

Walsall Observer and *South Staffordshire Chronicle* 1880-99
Wolverhampton Express & Star
Walsall Local History Centre

* This may have been the same Cartwright family who supported the Strollers in the first third of the twentieth century.

** Walsall workers were by then being paid on the Friday night.

Bloxwich Strollers

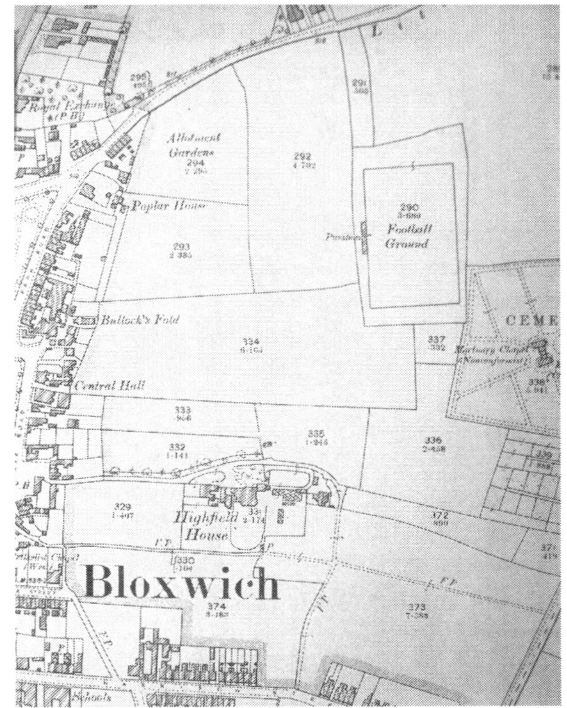

Bloxwich Strollers 1st Ground

Walsall Rugby Old Blox Strollers Stand

Burton Swifts FC

f. 1871-1901

Colours

1. blue and red stripes (1880s)
2. chocolate and pale blue halves (1888-89)
3. blue and white halves (1892-95)
4. maroon and amber halves/white (1895-97)
5. red and white quarters/blue (1897-1901)

As Burton United

6. blue and white quarters (1901/2)
7. maroon, black shorts (1902/3)
8. red, black shorts (1903/4)
9. green and pink quarters, white (1904/5)
10. maroon shirts (1905/6)
11. chocolate shirt, blue V (1906/7)

Grounds

1. Shobnall Street 1884-1891
2. Derby Turn 1889
3. Peel Croft 1891-1901 (now home to Burton R.U.F.C) on the Derby Road. The ground today looks very little changed from a hundred years ago.

They began life as Outward Star FC (1871-73); then as Burton Swifts (1873-1901); then as Burton United (1901-10) after they amalgamated with rivals Burton Wanderers. Early friendly opposition for Outward Star were Horninglow Victoria, Bass FC, Stapenhill, Burton Strollers, Alma, and Excelsior. After 1881, they began to compete for the Burton and District Challenge Cup, whose first winners were Burton Strollers and Burton Rangers. As the Swifts, they reached their peak in the early mid-1890s. Crowds were never big enough to sustain even a small club like Burton Swifts; the town had too many teams into which it divided its support; the rugby club, even then one of the country's top sides, outlived them all. Rivalling any other for the number of successive-season colour changes, it must have been well-nigh impossible for their fans to make up any rosettes or scarves, etc.!

Their 'Shobnall Street' ground turns out to be Outwards recreational ground on the west side of the canal at Horninglow, which used to be a separate village. The long path, leading from Shobnall Street to the canal footbridge and the old ground is still there. A site visit in November 2012 saw me follow signs to Horninglow from Burton and thence to the Shobnall Leisure centre. However, there was a profusion of football pitches near the car park, and it was a while before I met up with the groundsman. He said he had never heard of Burton Swifts; he started to tell me where Burton United used to play – I already knew – but when I asked him if he knew where the old canal footbridge was, he pointed into the distance. "See that old oak tree on the horizon? That's where the footbridge is," he said, obviously not for one minute believing that I was prepared to walk that far to look at a field.

However, we football researchers are a curious breed, and despite near-zero air temperatures and a descending fog, I set off. Half a mile later, I got to the field which I had decided that the Swifts used to play on, and I was greeted by a park sign proclaiming 'this is Shobnall Fields'. Bemused dog-walkers and hardened joggers are still wondering why a silver-haired man would want to take photos of a football pitch in such conditions at dusk. Despite less than ideal conditions, I was pleased to see that it is still used as a football pitch, but the one goal was rather close to the canal, so lost balls would have been a venue hazard, and although there were old trees around most of the ground, it was quite open to the elements. On a cold November day, the pitch was noticeably heavy and soft, and this is likely to have provided an obstacle to good passing football, despite a level surface. There was no banking, but ample room around the pitch for a crowd of perhaps eight rows deep – 3,000? To see this ground by car, look to your right as the A38 northbound at Burton crosses the B5017 at Shobnall. You should see some tall floodlights on your right-hand side. The Swifts' old ground is in the field just after the ground with the floodlights.

Derby Turn, their second proper ground, was on the Derby Road, and today, the new Burton Albion ground is but a few hundred yards away. It is also the name of the district. It was primarily the home ground of Burton Wanderers, situated 300 yards from the Derby Turn roundabout adjacent to the old Midland Railway good warehouse, which is still there. However, the Swifts were only there during 1889-90.

Peel Croft, the ground most associated with Burton Swifts, became the home to Burton Rugby Football Club after the demise of the Swifts in 1901, when they joined forces with Burton Wanderers to form Burton United. Compared with Victorian photographs, little seems to have changed at the old Peel Croft ground, and it still gives a good impression of what it was like 120 years ago.

The Swifts entered the Birmingham Senior Cup from 1885, a decade after its inception, twice reaching the semi-final. During this time (mid-1880s), they were playing home games at Shobnall Street. In 1889, they played some cup games at Derby Turn, the home of the Burton Wanderers. In the 1892 Birmingham Cup, they lost by 0-2 to the Wolves, who were in the First Division of the Football league by then, although the attendance was a disappointing 2,500. Then in 1896, it was the powerful Aston Villa, near their peak, who put them out by two clear goals in front of a paltry 1,000 crowd at the old Wellington Road ground. By this time, the Birmingham Cup was very much a second-tier event to the Football League and the FA Cup, and only crowds between league sides drew more than the low thousands.

During the 1880s, the Burton FA launched their own cup for teams in the town, and Swifts were successful in 1885/6 and 1888/9. They also took the Dudley Cup the same year. At this time, their large committee included Lord Burton, S. Evershed, the local MP, as vice-presidents, with W. Mathews as chair of the committee along with Messrs Walters, Grewcock, Cox, Fernyhough, Buxton, Clay, Goodwin, and Robinson. Club secretary was W. Barson, and the club treasurer J. Rushton declared a balance sheet of almost £200 for the 1888/9 season, but leaving the club with assets and funds of only £20.

At this time, Swifts were playing in rather colourful chocolate and pale blue halves.

They joined the Football Combination in 1890, and then joined the Football Alliance in 1891. They became members of Football League Div II 1892-1901. The year 1890/1 saw them finish a reasonable 4th in the nine-team Football Combination, and the following year saw them finish 5th in the 12-team Football Alliance, but still conceding 52 goals in 22 games. The years 1893 and 1894 saw them finish 6th in both seasons. After 1894, their time in the Football league's Division 2 was a struggle, never finishing higher than 11th out of 16 teams, or 13th when the League was increased to 18 teams. Defence seemed to be their main problem, as they generally conceded 70-80 goals a season.

Their 1892 team was: Horne (goal); backs-Berry and McDermid; Jones, West, Sutherland (halfbacks); Emery, Perry, Worrall, McBeth, and Edward May (forwards).

Highest-scoring victory was 8-5 v Walsall Town-Swifts in 1894, and their biggest ever defeat was a 0-9 drubbing by the newly named Manchester City (previously called Ardwick FC) in 1898. They were also thumped 9-2 when drawn away to mighty Preston North End in round 1 of the 1892 FA cup. Their 1897 narrow defeat by 3-4 to Liverpool would have been seen as an achievement for a little club at the time.

Early notable players were:

Lewis Campbell (f), ended his career at Swifts; he netted 13 goals for Burslem Port Vale in 1893/4 season.

George Kinsey (c/f): moved on to B'ham St. George's in 1887, then to Wolves, where he was capped 4 times for England.

Chas Satterthwaite (wf): was known for his powerful shot.

Tommy Leigh (c/f): moved on to Newton Heath in 1900 and scored a remarkable 46 goals in 43 games for them.

Arthur Chadwick (c/h): was capped twice for England in 1900.

Walter Perry (f): was bought from Warwick County FC in 1892.

Bob Crone: a tall six-footer, hard-tackling fullback.

Richard Gray (goal); Adrian Capes, George Elkins (winger); Charles Freeman (inside forward); Andrew Mitchell (fullback);

Hugh Walley (left-winger); Tommy Walker (right-winger); Jim Munroe (forward).

FA Cup History

1888/90	1-6 (3Q) Walsall Town-Swifts		
1892/93	3-2 4Q) Burton Wanderers	2-9 (A) PNE	
1895/96	2-0 (3Q) Singers (Coventry)	3-1 (4Q) Rockwardine	1-4 (A) Blackpool
1896/97	1-1 (4Q) Walsall TS 1-0 (H)	3-2 (5Q) Burslem Port Vale	3-4 (A) Liverpool

1898/99 0-0 (5Q) Heanor 0-1 (A)
1900/01 1-2 (5Q) Kettering (H)

Burton, famous of course for its brewery industries, had only 40,000 inhabitants, and with such a small population, it was surprising that the town's two soccer and top-class rugby side could entice enough followers to keep them going as professional teams as long as they did, and the only practical solution was to have but one club.

Swifts were always poor cousins to rivals Burton Wanderers, and always struggled in their years in both the Football Alliance and the Football league Division 2, never managing better than 6th place in 1894 when they scored a healthy 79 goals in 28 games. They amalgamated with rivals Wanderers to form Burton United in 1901.

REFERENCES

Derby Mercury
Staffordshire Sentinel
History of Burton Wanderers official web site

Shobnall Fields Ground Burton Swifts

Burton Swifts Home-Peel Croft

Burton Swifts Medals

Burton Wanderers FC

f.1871-1901

Colours:
Dark blue and white halves/black shorts

Honours:

Midland League champions 1893/4
Staffordshire Cup winners 1894/5

Ground:
Derby Turn, near the current Burton Albion new stadium on the Derby Road.

The site is now occupied by an old railway bonded warehouse, between the Derby Road and the Dixie railway sidings at the rear. Players used the Derby Inn across the road for facilities. A site visit in the autumn of 2012 revealed that the Derby Inn is still in business and that the land between the Derby Road and the railway lines was very flat and level, and so I would think that the ground would have been absent of the usual slope. No photos of the ground exist, but I am told it had an enclosing brick wall with two entrances.

They were member of the Midland League from 1889 to 1894. Generally, they were one of the best teams, finishing 4th, 6th, 5th, 2nd champions in those five seasons.

They won the Midland League in 1893/4, unbeaten in twenty games with a won 17, drew 3, lost 0 for 82-12 against record. The runners-up were Leicester Fosse.

Their usual opposition in the Midland League included Gainsborough Trinity, Lincoln, Derby Junction, Derby Midland, Staveley, Sheffield FC, and Notts Rangers.

Burton-upon-Trent, a small north-east Staffordshire brewery town right on the border with Derbyshire, holds a unique record of being the only town to have had four different clubs play in the Football League: Wanderers, Swifts, United, and now the Albion. And this from a town whose rugby club is better known in the Midlands than any of its football teams were! Visiting teams, whether football or rugby, would have been hit by the powerful smell of the pungent air produced by the many breweries and other factories which used brewing by-products such as Bovril and Marmite.

They were elected into Football League Division 2 in 1894 but failed re-election in 1897.

1895/96 was probably their best season when they finished 4th in the Football League Division 2 with a 19-4-7 69-40 performance. Wanderers surprisingly won the Staffordshire Senior Cup beating Wolves 2-0 in the 1894/5 season.

They also entered the Birmingham Senior Cup, but rarely made it past the first round, although they were exempt from the qualifying rounds which were introduced in 1888 to prevent ill-matched Football League and minor sides clashing with the inevitable double-figure win in front of a low crowd. This must have meant that at the time the Birmingham FA ranked Wanderers in the top sixteen sides in the Midlands. In the mid-1890s, the Wanderers drew Derby County out of the hat three years running. One remarkable Birmingham Cup tie was when they defeated Spital from Chesterfield by 7-3 on 18 October 1884. On the same day, rivals Burton Strollers beat Burton Pioneers 8-0 on the ground inside the Bass Brewery Co. Strollers were then in turn crushed 0-7 by Aston Villa in the 2nd round, whilst Wanderers were put out 1-6 by Walsall Swifts in round 3. The Pioneers' woe continued the following season – 1885 – when they were crushed 0-11 away to Derby Midland, and the Strollers too met a superior foe when Burslem Port Vale put six without reply past them on the same day. Wanderers' best effort was when they reached the semi-final of 1894, but they were thumped 8-2 by Wolverhampton Wanderers. They also got to the semi-final in 1898, but were well beaten 0-4 by Walsall at their new Hilary Street Ground.

Wanderers also entered in the Staffordshire Cup, but with little success, as it was beginning to be dominated by the likes of the Albion, Wolves, Villa, and Walsall. After meeting the Albion on 1st October 1887 at home, Wanderers, still a young team themselves, were thrashed 12-2 by a rampant Albion team where JEM Bayliss and Woodhall each bagged a hat-trick to send the 3,500 crowd home in shock. The reality was they were more at home competing for the Burton Cup with their hometown rivals: Swifts, Alma, Strollers, and the Bass Brewery side.

Their notable players included Moor, Horton, Dickens, Adrian Capes, Arthur Capes, T. Arkesden, Adam Heywood, Ben Garfield, and Bob Brown.

They obtained the services of the Devey brothers from Small Heath after they made their name as stars of the Birmingham Excelsior side from Aston in the early 1870s.

Many teams adopted the colours of more famous teams to which they hoped to be associated, sometimes after playing them, and Wanderers' navy and white halves were the colours of Oxford University, one of the most famous of the Old Boys' sides, who often went 'on tour' to promote the game both at home and abroad.

A huge gap had opened up by 1890 as shown by their 0-23 defeat to WBA in the Staffordshire Cup on 1st February 1890, although I suspect that the 1st team had a game on with better prospects of winning, and so Burton put out their 2nd team as lambs to the slaughter.

Their 1st team in 1890/1 which lost 0-8 away to Walsall in September included Waterson (goal); Tunnicliffe and Lowe (backs); Fellows, Chandler, Warrilow (half-backs); Joynes, Dooley, Richards, Mason, Hayes (forwards).

Midland League attendances were around 2,000-3,000.

The biggest attendance was of 6,000, who came to see their 2nd round FA Cup tie with Notts County in 1894, which just eclipsed the 5,500 for the local derby with Burton Swifts on Christmas Day 1896.

They entered the FA Cup for about ten years, but generally did not make it past the 1st round. They were, however, the last defunct team in this book to compete in the FA Cup and get through to the 1st round proper, as they did in 1896 when going out 2-5 to Everton, who went on to lose the final 2-3 to Aston Villa.

FA Cup history	1st Round	2nd Round	3rd Round
1888/89	Small Heath Alliance 0-9 (A)		
1892/93	Burton 2-3 (A)		
1893/94	Brierley Hill 2-1 (H)	Stockport County 1-0 (A)	Notts County 1-2 (H)
1894/95	Old Hill Wanderers 5-0 (H)	Blackburn Rovers 1-2 (H)	
1895/96	Sheffield United 1-1 (H) 0-1 (A)		
1896/97	Everton 2-5 (A)		
1897/98	Burslem Port Vale 1-2 (A)		

References

The History of the Birmingham Senior Cup, Steve Carr
Staffordshire Sentinel
Football League Club Database

Burton Wanderers

Calthorpe FC

Formed (1873-1898?) possibly until 1929

Colours

1. 1 navy blue and scarlet hoops (1876)
2. 2 dark blue shirt (1877)
3. 3 black and white hoops, navy knickers and stockings (1879)
4. 4 dark blue shirt (1880)
5. 5 black and white hoops (1881>)

They are recognised as one of the first football clubs in Birmingham.

Calthorpe began life as the Birmingham Clerks Association, being formed by clerks working in the city centre, possibly at the law courts. Calthorpe Estates owned large areas of what is now very expensive land in Edgbaston and Selly Oak, which, in the mid-1800s, were large parcels of grazing or meadowland. Much of it still remains, and from Five Ways Edgbaston all the way down to Birmingham University on the south of the city, there are large areas of manicured parks and private lawns, many of which are connected to the King Edward VI grammar school. They seemed to have become 'Calthorpe' around October or November of 1874, although the newspapers still used their old name for at least two more seasons. Along with Aston Unity, Calthorpe co-founded the Birmingham FA in 1875. In 1873, they would have found opponents few and thin on the ground, but with a membership of around fifty players, they would play internal matches, or games against other local sides, one half rugby rules, the other half association rules. By autumn 1875, they were playing the Wednesbury teams home and away, and probably the Moseley and Aston Unity clubs.

The Calthorpe club must have found opponents hard to come by before 1880, and so they turned their hand to cricket in the summer. A cricket match as early as 1859 at the Adderley Park in Saltley, east Birmingham, featuring a Calthorpe side, was reported in the *Birmingham Post*. It's not clear whether they are one and the same club, since Lord Calthorpes' estates covered several square miles to the south-west of the city, and the cricketers may have been estate workers or management.

The Calthorpe Estate had owned and managed most of Edgbaston and Selly Oak since 1717.

This early football team, still under their Birmingham Clerks Association FC title, played six matches in 1877.

Carson, Barker, Crosby, Lucas, Mason, Orr, Sutton, White, Millarde, Smart, Millman were the players. Carson and Campbell Orr were the team's founders. The club were wearing a plain navy blue shirt at this time. They chose to play the London FA Rules.

No positions were given, although no doubt everyone except a goalkeeper and one back were attackers. Orr was one James* Campbell Orr, the club's founder, captain, and secretary. It was he who wrote match reports and sent them to the editor of the *Birmingham Daily Post* from 1874 onwards. At that time and for decades later, it was down to the home teams' secretary to send in the match report to the press, and even then, they were lucky if it was published. No newspaper ever gave the slightest thought of sending a junior reporter to see the action for himself. If they had, we might actually get to find out what colours the early sides played in!

Whilst bemoaning a lack of football teams to play against in the *Birmingham Post* in November of 1873, Orr received a strange reply – an unknown gentleman claimed that a football team had been formed in Saltley of the previous year (1872), and gave an address of 'Hampden Cottage, Washwood Heath Road': whether such a team existed and which rules it played to, we shall never know. Possibly it could have been the beginnings of the Saltley College team ?

'Calthorpe Fields', around what was Pebble Mill TV studios, are largely now the King Edward VI school grounds (several locations between Bristol and Pershore roads). Even today, the whole area running between the Bristol and Pershore Roads, out to the south of the city, are largely greenbelt in private ownership, and a hundred years ago, even more so.

After leaving Calthorpe Park, other teams such as Birmingham Royal and Arcadians began to play there, and the park is heavily used today by around twenty clubs playing cricket, football, and other sports popular with the Asian community.

Grounds

1. Calthorpe Fields (whilst still known as Birmingham Clerks AFC)
2. Calthorpe Park (see photo**) during 1874 and 1875 rented from Lord Calthorpe, but he would not allow a gate fee to be charged.
3. Bristol Road: was next to the Gun Barrels public house, facing King Edward VI grammar school.
   The Gun Barrells pub was originally on the other corner of the road, being demolished and rebuilt as a result of the road-widening scheme with the Queen Elizabeth hospital expansion programme.
4. Bournbrook Hotel Grounds: from autumn 1876, Calthorpe played at the ground behind the Bournbrook Hotel (now the Old Varsity Tavern, Bristol Road).

When the Birmingham Football Association was set up in 1875, Calthorpe were at the forefront of the movement to organise the game. Their 7 guineas donation towards the purchase of the silver cup was a significant amount of money then to everyday folk. The annual salary to people such as the gardener, footman, teacher, servant, would be around £10 a year, so this would equate to around £1,000 today. This leads me to think that at least some of these 'clerks' must have had positions of authority at the town's new civic council.

The club's first three years were spent in and around Calthorpe Park, then in Edgbaston. By 1876, they had found a new home three miles down the Bristol Road (B384) at Selly Oak. The ground was directly behind the Bournbrook Hotel – still there today under a different name – and it had good facilities. It had a running track around the perimeter, a small pavilion, and standing room for perhaps 3,000 people. The ground had turnstiles, and the tram depot was right outside. There was also a small boating lake. Players refreshed themselves at the Bournbrook Hotel. It was a 13-acre site, hemmed in by the railway to the left, the Bristol Road to the right, and the little Bourn brook to the rear, across which was the rifle range! Athletics and cycling were the most popular events held there.

A rifle range for shooting competitions was established at the rear of the sports ground in 1860.

Usefully, the tram depot was right next to the hotel, giving very good transport links. Dale Road now occupies the site of the pitch. They were able to charge 3d entrance money for their game against West Bromwich

(Dartmouth) on 8/10/79. However, their game against the Dartmouth club from West Bromwich on 18 October 1879 only drew around 200 spectators, each paying 3d (1.5p). The ground was sold off and demolished in 1900 to make way for two streets of houses (North Street and Dale Street remains).

Calthorpe being one of the earliest teams in the Walsall-Birmingham region, found opposition hard to come by, and such teams would be very short-lived, and consequently results unrecorded. There were no match reports in the Birmingham press for the first half of the 1870s. However, they were one of the first to give a rivalry to Wednesbury Old Athletic and won 1-0 in Wednesbury on 20 March 1875. They hosted WOA three Saturdays later, result unknown.

By the early 1880s, Calthorpe had already missed the boat. Unable to charge a gate entry at both Calthorpe fields and Calthorpe Park, there was no income, only expense. I would think that the club members all had fairly well-paid jobs in the town hall and thus were able to keep the club going for some time. Bad luck had diverted at least one exceptional talent to the rival Aston Villa, and they had stood still or worse, during the late 1870s. By 1881, they were 10 goals inferior to unknown Spital FC from Chesterfield; Walsall Swifts trounced them 8-0 in the November of 1883, just after Birmingham St. George's had put 9 past them the month before. Their tenancy agreement with the owners of the Bournbrook Grounds did not allow the club to charge entrance money, and when it was used as the venue for the first ever Birmingham Cup final on 24th March 1877, an entrance fee of 3d (1p) was charged to the 1,500 spectators. Several authors have said that Calthorpe weren't allowed to charge a gate fee, and cite this as a reason for their demise, but clearly they did start charging 2d or 3d at the Bournbrook ground from 1876. I have seen several adverts where the forthcoming matches were advertised at a 3d entrance. The Bournbrook grounds had been in use for some time when Calthorpe set up base there, and many other sporting activities also took place, such as pedestrianism, cycling races, athletics meetings, and pleasure-boating. Nor were they the only football team to operate out of there – Selly Oak and Bournbrook did so too.

Injuries and accident were not confined to football. On Saturday 19th June 1880, a Northampton cyclist – John Gross – competing at the Bournbrook grounds, was thrown in front of his 36 inch wheeled penny-farthing and his left eye was pierced by some part of his machine, his eyeball being cut in two, making him blind.

Entering the Birmingham (Senior) Cup from its beginning in 1876, Calthorpe never made much headway, often going out at the first or second hurdle. They gave the Wednesbury Strollers a close game in 1879, going out 2-3 after extra-time. The following year, they recorded their biggest competitive win, with a 7-0 win over a young Perry Athletic side, oddly after a 2-2 in Perry Park. The 2nd round saw a repeat oddity. A 1-1 home draw with unknown Spital FC of Chesterfield was followed with a 0-10 drubbing in Derbyshire! Perhaps the best Calthorpe players didn't make the journey. We shall never know.

Calthorpe's 1st round meeting with a recently formed West Bromwich Albion caused sufficient interest for 1,000 people to turn out at the Bournbrook ground, only to see the visitors win 3-2 and progress all the way to the semi-finals.

It is not known for how long the Calthorpe team carried on. A Jeremiah Hare moved on to Birmingham (Small Heath) in 1895, but with the selling-off and demolition of the Bournbrook ground for private landlord housing in 1900, I suspect that, left without a ground, and parks' pitches forbidding the charging of gate money, it was here that Calthorpe met its demise.

An early team from 1878 was:

Carlton, Maddox, Elliot, (captain), J. C. Orr, Daniels, Maxon, Maddox, Greening, Rudford, Amphlet, J. Carson.

FA Cup history

1879/80	1-3 Maidenhead (A) scorer-Rushell
1880/81	1-2 Grantham (A)
1881/82	Scratched away to Nottingham FC
1882/83	1-5 Birmingham St. George's
1883/84	0-9 Walsall Town (A)

"They used to go to Glasgow and play the Queen's Park 2nd team," said Archie Hunter's autobiography. The original B'ham Clerks Association Club was founded by two Scots: James Campbell Orr and John Carson. Villa's William McGreggor is said to have helped Calthorpe during the 1870s.

Orr had been to St. Andrew's University, and Carson was a player for the Queen's Park 2nd team, so elements of both rugby and association codes were in their rules, but association won through. Orr went on to give long and great service with the Birmingham Football Association and for many years was its vice-president, working alongside Stafford Road's Charles Crump. Orr is recognised as one of the game's greatest administrators of the first fifty years.

As tenants of the Calthorpe estates however, the tenancy agreement meant that the club couldn't grow like the Villa and Small Heath did, and this was a major factor in their eventual demise. It could have been that the team members had good professional jobs in the city centre and were individually financially sufficient, but keeping a football club afloat is an expensive business.

Archie Hunter came down from Scotland to join Calthorpe, but after spending the whole afternoon strolling around what is now the Five Ways district, he couldn't find the Calthorpe ground. He ended in watching a cricket match in Addersley Park instead!Perhaps he was expecting to find a proper ground, with a fenced-off pitch and perhaps a banked terrace. This, of course, was not the case, since Calthorpe was a public park, although there was a pavilion used by the cricketers. George Ramsay suggested he'd be better off joining fellow Scots Will McGreggor and Ramsay at the fledgling Aston Villa club, which he did. Had those events not taken place, then the name of B'ham Calthorpe may well have been in the English Premiership today!

George Ramsay had come down to Birmingham in 1870 to join his brother Peter and set up a drapery business. He begun by being involved in the Calthorpe club, but one day, after a stroll past the ground of Aston Hall, he came upon a group of youths at football. Amused by their simple naivety of boot-it-and rush tactics, he gave then a demonstration of the Scottish style of dribbling, with colleagues backing up alongside should he be tackled. Immediately he was begged to join the lads of Aston Villa and made captain. Thus, the Scottish backbone of the rise to Villa's subsequent greatness robbed the Calthorpe club of a mighty future.

McGreggor (1847-1911), the father of the Football League, is buried in St. Mary's churchyard, Handsworth.

Leading players of course, moved on to the more successful clubs.

Charlie Simms (b 1859-1835)	went to Mitchell St. George's then Small Heath in 1884
Richard Adams	went to Birmingham in 1887 then returned later the same year
Harry Clayton	went to Birmingham in 1882
Edwin Fountain	went to St. George's in 1895

Jeremiah Hare	went to Birmingham in 1895 (this confirms that Calthorpe were still going in 1895)
William Jones (forward)	went to Birmingham in 1881
William Slater	went to Birmingham in 1880
Edward Stanley	went to Birmingham in 1881 (leading goalscorer)

Calthorpe continued to play in the Walsall, Birmingham, and Wednesbury cups and the B'ham Junior cup throughout the 1880s, often sustaining heavy defeats, such as their 0-9 English FA cup 1st round beating at the Chuckery in 1883 to Walsall Town. This suggests that they were a true blue amateur team who played with a 'carry on regardless' attitude, as they tried their best against professional teams who had leapfrogged Calthorpe into, as the papers of the day would say, 'front-rank position in the association game'.

The team of 1883 was: Meeling (goal); Taunton and Elliot (backs); Daniels and Hawkes (halfbacks); Cousins, Bingley, Amphlet, Walters, Addenbrooke, and Wheeler (forwards).

The second team that year was: Smith (goal); Taunton and Ebrdhardt (backs); Whitfield and English (halfbacks); Dennell, Daniel, Gibbs, Rossiter, and F. Taunton (forwards).

C. O. Addenbrooke and brother H. J. were often cited as Calthorpe's best players in the press reports, as too were the Gibbs brothers and Amphlett. Interestingly, one T. Addenbrooke was a key member of the Walsall Town side, at around 1878, and a leading member of the Walsall Cricket Club. I gain the impression that Calthorpe players would be described as middle class. The same year, the Calthorpe Athletics Club was founded, based at the Bournbrook Grounds.

By the 1882, Calthorpe, like many other Birmingham football teams, were also playing cricket in the summer, and often a game might take place between say Calthorpe and Aston Unity clubs at both sports!

Calthorpe FC continued to be reported in the Walsall and Birmingham papers until around 1900.

After several years of searching, I could find no record of their colours, but putting my Sherlock Holmes hat on whilst rubbing the crystal ball, I would have suggested that since Carson was a Queen's Park man, and he and Orr being obviously Scottish, they are likely to have worn black and white hoops. A second possibility is that James Campbell Orr adopted his old University colours from St. Andrew's, Fife, which were dark blue and light blue. Since the club was originally founded by the town hall clerks, they may have even used the colours on the town's coat of arms. There was no mention in any press reports on Calthorpe's colours. However, just before going to print, Steve Carr sent me a list of Birmingham area team which he'd gleaned from some 120-year-old books written by Charles Alcock, founder of the Football Association.

Finally I got to learn what Calthorpe's colours were! And my crystal ball had been right. Although Calthorpe began (1876) in navy and scarlet hoops, and then navy the following season, they did wear black and white hoops (with navy knickers) in 1879 and thereafter from 1881.

A sad advertisement appeared in the *Birmingham Daily Post* on 5 May 1891. Gray & Walker Co. were selling the fixtures and fittings of the Bournbrook ground on behalf of the brewery Inde, Coope & Co. The pavilion, seats, the bandstand, fourteen rowing boats and a canoe (!) were all up for auction. Even the four ornate cast-iron turnstiles made by Lowrie & Co. in Manchester were included. One wonders where these items ended up! (Now there's a real Sherlock Holmes investigation!). This event, of course, would have drawn a line under Calthorpe's further footballing activities from that moment: the club seems to have faded away after a few more years of perhaps nomadic existence at the turn of the century, at which time, it would have been nigh-on impossible to rent a ground anywhere in the city. There were probably ten teams to every park's pitch by then. The Birmingham FA handbook for 1927 to 1930 still lists Calthorpe as an active junior team until 1928, by which time they would be very small fry indeed.

To find Calthorpe Park today, simply take the Pershore Road (A441) out of Birmingham and after two miles, the park is on your left, just before the Edgbaston cricket stadium. The football was played in the centre and far side of the park, as the pavilion (no longer there) was in the centre. Incidentally, across the road from the park, there was another cricket ground, but I have been unable to discover who used it. The square site is now built over by Raglan Road and Constance Road. In the 1870s, Edward Road, now the boundary of the park, only came down the hill from the Moseley Road as far as Cheddar Road. I suggest you do not park in Cheddar Road if you are planning to find Calthorpe's pitch – it was a well-known red light district until recently!

To find the site of the Bournbrook Grounds, drive down the A38 Bristol Road out of Birmingham to Selly Oak, but not as far as the railway bridge.

Turn right into Grange Road by the Old Varsity pub (this says 'Bournbrook Hotel' on the front), and the new Victoria Hall building is the stadium site.

References

Birmingham Daily Post 1873-1899
Walsall Observer and *South Staffs Chronicle*
Wolverhampton Express & Star

Addendum

In the 1928 handbook of the Birmingham Football Association, a Calthorpe FC was registered as still active.

They had scratched when drawn away to Walsall Albion in the 3rd round of the 1928 Junior Cup.

There was no such entry for Calthorpe in 1929 or 1930.

* sometimes given as John – either way, he didn't use his first name, preferring to be known as Campbell Orr

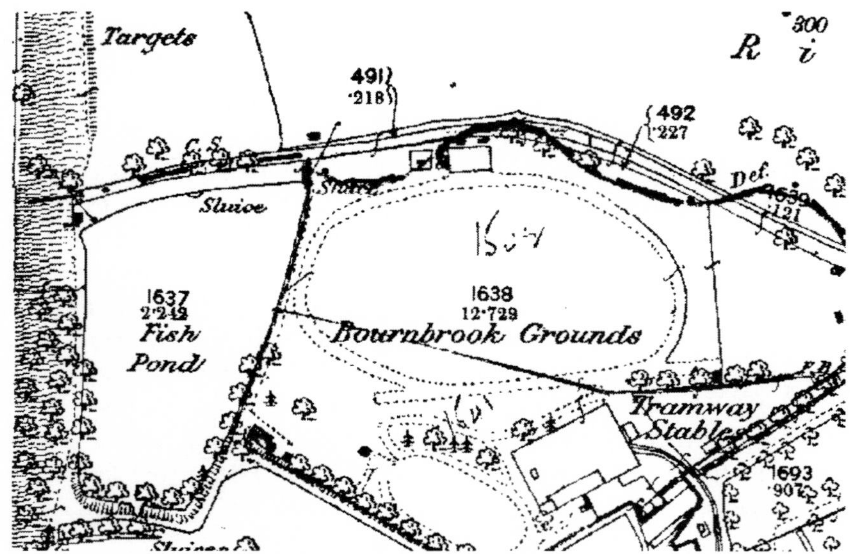

The Bournbrook Grounds—Calthorpe FC 1889

Calthorpe's Bournbrook Hotel HQ

Calthorpes' Bristol Rd Ground

Cannock FC

Founded: 1875*-1937

Colours

1. amber and black jerseys, black stockings (1877)
2. white shirts, navy black shorts (1890-1910)
3. all maroon, later with a yellow V (1930s)

Honours
Birmingham Combination champions 1920/1

Grounds

1. The Oak ground, Wolverhampton Road, Cannock
2. Simm Lane (now known as Park Road – at the rear of Cannock Chase College by the bus station
3. Cannock Athletic Grounds, Chadsmoor (now the Hardie Green estate)
4. Brookfields (from 1902->)-on the Walsall Road

Cannock, halfway between Walsall and Stafford is a coal-mining town, and no doubt the football team was comprised of miners and colliery workers, as it was even in the 1930s.

Charles Alcock's annuals of 1900 record Cannock's founding year as 1875. Their first ground was behind the Oak public house on Wolverhampton Road. Maps circa 1890 show that the original Wolverhampton Road had allotment fields behind it, and the ground was there, but today, the new ASDA car park and the youth centre occupy the spot. Their second ground was Sim or Simm Lane, now Park Road. Their ground became Cannock Park and is behind the college in the town centre.

Earliest records show a Cannock FC side travelling to Wednesbury's Oval to face the Old Athletics on Saturday 10 February of 1877 where they were soundly beaten 5-0 in a friendly fixture a decade before league football was invented. They didn't return to Wednesbury until Christmas 1882, when they fared even worse, going down 13-0 in a Walsall cup tie. Their biggest ever win was in 1892, when they beat Walsall Rangers 20-3 in a Walsall cup tie.

Their representative of the Walsall FA council was a Mr H. Thornton during the 1880s.

The team of 1888 was: Dawson (goal); G. Reeves, Hood (backs); H. Reeves, Best, B. Smith (halfbacks); S. Reeves, Whitehouse, Lukes, H. Smith, and Dutton (forwards). This team was soundly beaten 6-1 at home by Wednesbury Old Athletic in the 2nd round of the Staffordshire Cup. Their usual goalkeeper Summerton not being available may have contributed.

The team of 1892 was: S. Smith (goal); E. Reynold and B. Smith (backs); W. Wedges, R. Bates, W. Marshall (halfbacks); T. Wedge, W. H. Whitehouse, L. Evans, Hollingshead, C. Devey (forwards). Charles (Chas) Devey was one of the five Bloxwich Devey footballing brothers.

They lost the final of the Walsall Junior Cup in 1897/8 0-2 to Willenhall Pickwicks.

They entered the Birmingham, Staffordshire, Walsall, and Cannock Chase Foresters cups, and played in the Walsall and Birmingham District Leagues.

Crowds averaged between 400 and 2,000.

They were already organised enough to enter the Birmingham Cup from its inception in 1876. They were held goal less by St. George's from Aston but did well to win 2-0 the replay at the Bott Lane Mission ground* in Walsall. Eventual finalists Stafford Road beat them 3-0 in the 2nd round. In a repeat scenario the following year, Cannock were held goal less by Birmingham Royal but lost 3-0 in the replay, unrecorded, but probably at Wednesbury. Royal played at Edgbaston's Calthorpe Park after Calthorpe had moved out to the Bournbrook Grounds. Elwells FC put Cannock out at the first hurdle in 1878, and they stopped competing at senior level after 1880. Newspaper reports of the 1880s and 1890s show Cannock playing in the Walsall Cup and the Cannock Chase Forresters Cup, but by this time, they were in the lower order. Cannock may have folded and reformed in 1908 as some sources give this year as the club start date. The Cannock Town of 1908 may not have been the same earlier team from Victorian days.

Their new Brookfields ground had been built on the site of a farm of the same name and was opened on Monday 1 September 1902 by Club President Richard Grigg, when Willenhall Pickwicks were the first ever visitors and Cannock happily won by 2-1. It took me some months to locate this ground, but we now know that it faced the junction with St. Johns Road, and lay parallel to the main road, and close to it, with the railway at the far side. However, a measure of the poor support can be seen from the home and away Walsall League fixtures with Wednesbury Old Athletic, a small town of comparable size. Cannock's visit to Wednesbury's Lloyd Street ground on 9 September drew a 3,000 crowd. The return game a month later drew only 600 in Cannock, and no doubt a tenth of those were away fans. At their 1900 AGM, the treasurer reported a debt of £25. A typical weekly home game income would be around £5.

Around 1900, their top player was Sam Gray. One of their best players from the previous decade, William Marshall, was given a benefit collection in 1901 when it was realised he would never play again following an injury he sustained at the end of the previous season. They now moved their headquarters from the Crown Hotel in Cannock to the White Hart Inn during 1901, as a package which saw the outstanding debt of £25 ground rent on the old Sims Lane ground being settled by the publican.

Money was very much a problem after 1900, as Cannock's committee often thought long and hard about folding the club, only to be helped out from time to time and keep the club limping along. Like many football clubs, Cannock relied on a healthy injection of funds into the kitty from their annual sports day, designed to attract large crowds to watch local athletes compete in a wide range of activities from bicycle races to paper chases. Unfortunately, in 1901, a circus came to town at the same time and anticipated total receipts amounting to only £20 instead of the usual £70. Club treasurer W. Kent and Secretary W. H. Whitehouse appealed for backers in the local press. The 1902 team was captained by Arthur Belcher, with Thacker in goal and Charlie Devey up front celebrating a decade with the club, as Cannock struggled on.

On a high note, the splendidly named Basil Rhodes was selected for the England Junior team for a trial against the Scottish team. Around 1900-05, the local Cannock, Hednesford, and Brownhills clubs formed a small league of six clubs, the Cannock League, which was dominated by the Bridgetown Amateurs and Brownhills Albion. This certainly reduced match travelling costs, but only served to confirm that an under-funded and poorly supported Cannock FC weren't even the top team in the Cannock Chase area. Indeed, they were one of the weakest.

Their team of 1905/06 season was: Molyneux (goal), Stanley, Sheldon; Cooper, Smith, Hayes; Thorneycroft, Cope, Smith, Burden, Hutchins.

They spent over twenty years in the Walsall & District league during the period 1890-1910, never making the top half of the table, save for 1903 when they came 3rd. Usual opposition included the leading teams from the local Black Country towns of Wednesbury, Bilston, Darlaston, and nearby Hednesford. In 1909/10, they followed other local sides into the Birmingham Combination and surprisingly finished a respectable 9th out of 16 teams, but this was probably their peak position at this level. By 1911/12, they were back in the Walsall Combination, and by 1916, they were bottom. Cannock may have disbanded at this point, as it was the outbreak of the First World War, and many teams were broken apart as most of their players went to war in France, never to return. If Cannock did disband at the end of 1916, they also took part in another team's demise on the 29 April of that year. They beat Willenhall Pickwicks 3-2 at home in a Walsall league match. That was the Picks' last ever match before they too disbanded. The Picks, however, bounced back three years later and amalgamated with neighbours Swifts to form a new Willenhall FC.

In 1920, Cannock were back in form, and won the Birmingham Combination league. This was created for the top twenty junior sides in the Birmingham region and in the last decade of the Victorian era became dominated by the Bournbrook clubs. By 1921/22, they were back up in the Birmingham and District League, where they spent this decade playing higher level teams such as Shrewsbury, Kidderminster, Worcester, Nuneaton, and Stafford Rangers. Many of these went on to Conference or Fourth Division level in modern times. Cannock Town Council planning dept archives show that on 3 August 1921, Cannock Town FC submitted plans to build dressing rooms and bathrooms at their Brookfields ground, so seemed to be on the up. The previous year, in January 1920, the club had built a grandstand and erected new fencing. However, the 1930s proved to be a drop in fortunes, and the team fell into decline and back into the local leagues. This was mainly as a result of the national economic depression of the 1920s and 1930s, when miners lost their jobs and the public had no money to go to football games. Raising the gate fee from sixpence (2.5p) to a shilling in order to raise funds had exactly the opposite effect.

A Cannock or Cannock Town team of one sort or another was reformed several times in the first quarter of the twentieth century.

However, by the mid-1930s, their Brookfields ground, just off the Walsall Road was described as having 'a dilapidated pitch and facilities', and the club finally folded in 1937. The Brookfield Trading Estate off the Walsall Road is about 100 yards south of the spot of their old ground.

To find Cannock's old grounds today, simply go into Cannock Park and observe the area in front of you (Sims Lane ground); the Brookfield ground is at Bridgetown on the A34 by the trading estate of the same name.

Sources

A History of Cannock of My Lifetime, S. Belcher
Cannock Advertiser
Walsall Observer 1887-1910
Willenhall History Society
Dave Shaw, Hednesford FC
Cannock Town Council Records
Photos by Lee Morrall Photographic Services, Hednesford

* adjoining the bottom end of the Chuckery grounds, as used by the various Walsall teams

Cannock FC

Cannock's Simms Lane Ground Today

Coombs Wood FC

They were an amateur works team from the Coombs Wood Tube Works which represented the village in the Birmingham junior competitions.

Ground:
Tube Works sports ground, Coombs Lane, near Halesowen, Worcestershire

Colours
white shirts,* black shorts

Honours
Winners Birmingham Junior Cup 1899/90 and 1904/5

They generally played in the Birmingham Combination in the Edwardian era.

Coombs Wood is a small village near Halesowen, and, as such, it was a remarkable achievement to take the Birmingham Junior Cup twice. The main employer in the village was the Stuart & Lloyd steel pipeworks which became part of the British Steel empire.

The team would have been drawn from the steel tube mill workforce, with perhaps an interchange of players from the other nearby Cradley St. Luke's, Halesowen, and Cradley Heath teams. They also had a thriving cricket and bowls team which continues today. Here, there is a parallel with the Elwells FC team from Wednesbury.

The cricket ground amazingly is still there today, although there is a new housing development right next to it. The whole Old Hill-Halesowen-Cradley area is very steeply hilly, and it is a surprise to come across a level sports ground on the side of a steep hill. The hills were formed from industrial slag heaps in the mid-nineteenth century which were simply allowed to be grassed over. They were so large that you would take them for natural hills. A site visit in September 2012 revealed that a factory unit had been built on one of the two old sports grounds in recent times. I understand this was the football ground.

Protests over the slightest thing snowballed during the 1870s and 80s, and it seems to me that the authorities failed to do anything about it. Losing teams in cup ties would find all sorts of reasons against which to lodge an appeal and have the game replayed; ineligible players, darkness, pitch undersize, goalposts too high or too low. Funny how none of these things were appealed against before a match began! One such example involved Coombs Wood, when drawn to play Willenhall Pickwicks in the 5th round of the Birmingham Junior Cup on 12th February 1898. The Woods lost 1-2 at home and lodged a protest against a Picks' man on the grounds that he had previously played for his own amateur works side; amazingly the appeal was upheld by the Birmingham FA and the game ordered to be replayed at the Molyneux on 12 March. The Coombs lost again by 3-1, and so the whole thing was pointless, just wasting everyone's time. Both Pickwick and Coombs had the extra expense of travelling to Wolverhampton and give the twenty-two men another payday. I can't understand why the Birmingham FA stood for this nonsense, and, more so, why they didn't issue a ruling that any protests had to be given verbally at the start of the match, and in writing at the end.

In the 1900s decade, they were generally a mid-table team in the Birmingham Combination facing such opposition as Hednesford, Bilston, Cannock, Bromsgrove, Nuneaton, and Wednesbury Old Athletic. All of those sides came from much larger towns, and so they were the real tiddlers in the pond. Local rivals Cradley St. Luke's would have brought bumper crowds for the home and away league matches. For their home game against Wednesbury Old Athletic, a decent crowd of 800 turned out on 20th February 1909, only to see the Woods lose a 5-4 thriller. They finished a disappointing 13th that year, but still scored a remarkable 87 goals in 30 league games, only four fewer than rivals Cradley St. Luke's who were runners-up. In 1910, they came a creditable 5th in the Combination, behind Hednesford, St. Luke's, Wednesbury, and Darlaston.

Their best efforts came however in the Birmingham Junior Cup. They defeated fellow Birmingham League side Bournbrook 3-2 to win the 1899/90 trophy, and came back five years later to defeat Hoolbrook Olympic 2-1 in 1904/5 season.

Lowe, the Coombs Wood goalkeeper, and Westley, the fullback, were selected for the annual Birmingham AFA versus Scotland in a junior international game on 18th March 1895. No doubt, seen as the junior side in the area, Coombs Wood lost men to rivals Cradley St. Luke's and Halesowen, and one such man was Wally White (b 1864), their goalkeeper, who came to them from the Wolves in 1889.

Other well-known players:

Thomas Harrison (b 1867-1947) was an outside left who played in the 1880s and was signed by Aston Villa in 1888. He didn't make an impression there, and only played once for the first team, returning back to play for Halesowen.

Walter White (b 1864) played at the same time as Harrison. He was signed by the Wolves in 1888 but only spent one year there, scoring 2 goals in four first team games. He returned to the club in 1889 but later signed for Cradley St. Luke's with whom he played out his career.

Harry Parkes (b 1888-1947) was an outside right who played in the Edwardian era. He moved to Halesowen, and then on to West Bromwich Albion in 1906. Two years later, he signed for Coventry. After his playing career ended, he became a well-known manager at several clubs – Newport, Chesterfield, Lincoln, Mansfield, and Notts County.

Tommy Weston (b 1895-1973) was a left back who played briefly in the team as a young man before signing for Aston Villa in 1911 at the age of 16. He was there for over a decade, moving on the Stoke in 1922. He had also played for local junior sides Quarry Bank and Old Hill Comrades as a youth.

References

Birmingham FA centenary yearbook
The History of the Birmingham Combination

* possibly cream

Coombs Wood Sports Ground

Cradley St. Luke's FC

f.1896-1961

A church-based team from the St. Luke's Church at Four Ways, Cradley

Colours

1. red shirts, black trousers (until 1915) (1890s)
2. all white (as Cradley Heath) seasons 1926/7/8/9 (1920s)
3. red shirts, white shorts (1930s)
4. red and white hoops, white (1940s)

Grounds

the Victoria Hotel Ground (1890s)
Red Roses ground, Old Hill (1907-1917)
the old Dudley Wood Stadium (1920-1949)
Ash Tree Mound ground (1960-61)

Honours

Birmingham League champions 1926, 1931, 1932
Birmingham Junior Cup finalists 1906
Worcestershire Cup 1923, 1925, 1926, 1927
Birmingham Senior Cup 1927

It was founded by youths who attended St. Luke's Church in the town centre. Early founders were churchmen and businessmen led by the Siddaway family, Percy Bullas, and Doctor Deneen.

By 1900, there were at least ten football teams in the Cradley-Old Hill-Halesowen area. In the early days, St. Luke's used the old brewery as their changing rooms, and actually took a post-match bath in a large brewery vat! St. Luke's Church lies at the heart of the town, at Four Ways. There was an area of waste ground right behind St. Luke's, and it was probably here where the boys and youths first practised football, next to the present-day Bearmore playing fields. It was not really big enough for a regulation-sized pitch, but at around 80 x 80 yards, it was big enough to start with. Until they settled into their long-term home at Dudley Wood after the First World War was over, they had at least three grounds in the district, including the Red

Roses ground at the end of Pear Tree Lane, almost in Old Hill. The ground was in a large field between Peartree Street and the GWR railway line to Stourbridge. Although the ground had a poor reputation on account of its heavily sloping pitch, the club developed it with a small stand and erected an iron railing around the pitch. Crowds were up to 2,000. They were at this ground from 1907 until 1917, and when they vacated it, a small foundry was built on one half of the old football pitch. Presumably the nearby Blue Ball Inn was used for refreshments. There was also another ground opposite St. Barnabas Mission Church, on the western edge of the town, where the mineral railway crossed the Dudley Wood Road, in a 2.53-acre field. This was discovered on an O.S. map for 1890, which suggests that they played here at that date, which is some six years before their usually given formation date.

The Lukes played in local cups at first, then joined the Birmingham Combination as founder members along with sides such as Aston St. James, Bournbrook, Bournville, and Kings Heath. By around 1900, transport links into Cradley were improved when the tram arrived from Dudley. The whole area outside of the town was farmland, which was absolutely littered with mines, shafts, and collieries, with their associated slag heaps. This was, by any standard, the deepest heart of the Black Country. Chain-making and labour-intensive heavy industries were the lifeblood of the town; the numerous colliery and furnace chimneys and the smell of phosphorous and burning coal slack would have filled the air. Any visiting teams from a cleaner environment would have thought they were visiting the devil's backyard, and by being in the heart of the Victorian Black Country, no doubt any visitors would have had great difficulty in understanding the local accent! An 1882 map shows the earlier ground down by the Stourbridge extension of the Great Western railway lines on what is now Sutherland Road at the bottom end of the Bearmore playing fields. It is said that the home crowd would roar 'Ommer erm, Craaedley!' which, if you need a translation from Black Country to English means: 'Hit them hard, Cradley.'

In 1907, the Lukes moved to the ground to which they are most associated – the Dudley Wood Stadium behind the Victoria Inn owned by George Bridgewater. This was technically just 'over the border' in Netherton, and thus was actually outside Staffordshire and a few hundred yards inside Worcestershire. Bridgewater developed the land – an old fairground wake site –into a proper ground. Later, in 1938, an oval racing track was added, which became used for speedway and greyhound races, and it drew huge crowds of up to 14,000.

Anyone hoping to find the stadium which made the town famous through its speedway team of the 1940s, through to the 1960s, will be disappointed to learn it is now the site of a new small housing estate. Only the names Stadium Drive, The Lukes, and Raceway Crescent remain. With only Halesowen and Old Hill Wanderers nearby, the town could concentrate its support on one team, and crowds were pretty decent for a small town: their home match against Wednesbury Old Athletic in the 1909/10 Combination drew over 3,000 to see the battle between the sides who finished in 2nd and 3rd places. St. Luke's ran out 3-1 winners. The Lukes entered several local cups including the Dudley Guest, Wolverhampton, Wednesbury and Birmingham junior cup.

Unusually, as against all the other teams in this book, Cradley lasted right through until modern times: 1961, when the club was finally wound up. Over their eighty years, they had many good players who went on to better themselves by joining Football League sides. A list of their most well-known players is given.

Alf Bishop (b. 1902)	who played for them during 1927/8
Tom Evans (b. 1896)	who played in the 1910s
David Boxby	who played for seasons 1919/20
Jimmy Lee (1892-1955)	who played in goal in the 1910s and went on to a League career with Stoke and Aston Villa
Joe Smith (b. 1890)	who played with Jimmy Lee but went to Worcester City
Sid Wallington	who played for them in the early 1940s, having been with Birmingham and Bristol Rovers in the 1930s
Tom Fletcher (b. 1878)	who played for seasons 1900-1903 as an inside left
Wally White (b. 1864)	a forward who came from the Wolves in 1889, having started out with Coombs Wood
Sammy Stevens (b. 1890)	a forward who played during 1910-11 and had a career with Hull City and Notts County
Reg Hackett (b. 1899)	went on to have a long career with Southampton
Stan Hauser (1890-1958)	a goalkeeper who ended his career with Cradley after a 1930s spent at Small Heath
George Leyton (b. 1865)	played in the first team of 1896/7 and joined Small Heath, ending his career at Soho Villa
Tom Wooldridge (b. 1868)	joined Wednesbury Old Athletic but then became a well-known forward at the Wolves in 1900
Billy Morgan (b. 1891)	a left-winger who also had a League career with Coventry, Birmingham, and Crystal Palace
Harry Neath	an inside forward who was snapped up by Portsmouth just after the end of the War

Cradley's two most famous footballing sons were of course Steve Bloomer and Billy Wright. But of course, the legendary Bloomer never played for any of his birthplace sides; he started with the Derby Swifts before joining Derby Midlands, then Derby County. Billy Wright was sent to spend a few months with the Cradley team. After they signed him in order to build him up, as the Wolves manager, Major Buckley thought he was too skinny!

St. Luke's had a disappointment in 1906 when they were beaten 1-0 in the Birmingham Junior Cup final by, of all sides, the 1st Cheshire Regiment FC! who were based in Yardley, Birmingham.

The period from 1907 to 1910 was another good period for the Lukes; they finished 3rd in the Birmingham Junior League, with a whopping 102 goals in 30 games. The year 1908/9 was one step better, finishing as runners-up to Willlenhall Pickwick. The Junior League was now rebranded as the Combination, one level below the Birmingham League. They finished runners-up again in 1909/10 behind Hednesford Town, with the team below them 8 points adrift.

In 1909, the directors and backers of the team decided to turn the football club into a limited company and sold 1,000 shares, mostly to local businessmen. Prominent in this venture were George Bridgewater, brewer and licensee, his sister Adeline Bartlett, and early club founders Percy Bullas and Dr Deneen, the club's doctor. Mrs Bartlett held 110 of the 1000 shares. It should have led to the club growing steadily into a successful league side in the years to come, but it was not to be.

There was an amazing league match against Hednesford in the 1912/13 season. Cradley were leading 2-1 at halftime, but the 'Lillywhites' staged a remarkable second half comeback to win by 8-2!

The Cradley 1914 side which drew 1-1 away to Hednesford on 13 February was: Carradine (goal); Pearson, green (backs); Parkes, Cox, Reg Hackett (halfbacks); Dickens, Kendrick, Mole, Willetts, Glitheroe (forwards).

A freak accident occurred during a match against near neighbours Oldbury Town in 1915. On the 27th December, a gale blew the stand down, and one of Cradley's players, James Homer, was badly hurt and later died in hospital. A few years later, another old stand began to fall down due to lack of ground maintenance. Investment in the ground's infrastructure was a low priority in those days, and clubs only did something to improve the spectator's lot when they had to.

A peak period for St. Luke's was the 1920s. At this time, they were playing in an all-white strip. They won the Birmingham Combination in both 1919/20 and 1921/22, and went up into the Birmingham League from 1923. Crowds were around 2,000 to 3,500 at this time. Their trainer during this period was Arthur Hackett. Neighbours Halesowen were playing in the Birmingham League at this time – the next level up – but were a struggling side at this time, finishing bottom of that league in 1911. In the 1920s, Cradley St. Luke's had gone up one level and were playing in the Birmingham League, which Halesowen had dropped out of a couple of years before. By this time, they had dropped the 'St. Luke's' tag and were just known as Cradley Heath FC. Another successful period followed between the Wars, and Cradley Heath won the Birmingham League title in 1926, 1931, 1932. The Lukes had a wonderful 1920s decade in the Worcestershire Senior Cup, winning it no less than four times in a five-year period, only interrupted by a Stourbridge success in 1924. Crowds were now approaching the 5,000 mark, and the club should have been on a healthy footing, but a disaster occurred on 14th February 1933 when a fire destroyed the stand and the dressing rooms and it cost the club a £500 loan from which they never recovered. The bank now held the title deeds to the stadium and the lease of the football ground itself. The following season, they had to ask the players to take a ten shillings a week pay cut from their thirty shillings wages, and players started to leave the club and join Football league sides.

Their championship team of 1926, which scored 100 league goals, was: Langford, Gibbon, Albert Jones, Bridges, H. Johnson, David. Boxley, Morgan, Evans, S. Taylor, and Lowe. In the 1929/30 season, they scored 105 goals, but they only finished 3rd. After such a good spell in the late 1920s, they fell into a mid-table position after 1932 and never again finished higher than 5th (1950). In their final season before being wound-up, 1960/61, they conceded a terrible 143 goals in their 42 match fixtures.

In the mid-1930s, a new team of youths was started by the vicar of St. Luke's, in order to keep the name alive after the professional Cradley Heath team had left its roots behind, and they played in a chocolate and pale blue striped kit. Possibly confusingly, he named this boys' side Cradley St. Luke's too!

During the mid 1950s, the club was being steered through rocky times by the following men – chairman-Councillor Parkes, John Willetts, Dick Moore, Joe Amphlett, Norman Plant, and David Taylor, J.P.

The professional Cradley Heath entered the FA Cup from 1929, but it never got past the qualifying rounds, usually going out to bigger near neighbours such as Stourbridge, Bromsgrove, and Brierley Hill Alliance, one of the most exciting being their 5-3 defeat at Birmingham's top amateur side Moor Green in 1958.

In 1949, the Dudley Wood Stadium was sold off to become a greyhound and speedway stadium, and Cradley Heathens became famous nationally as one of speedways' greatest sides in the last half of the twentieth century. The old stadium, which had seen as many as 14,000 people cram in at the height of speedway popularity in the 1950s, was eventually closed down, and a housing estate now occupies the spot. This led to the end of football and speedway in the town.

As there is nothing to see of the Dudley Wood Stadium, the Red Rose ground is the best bet. Starting from the A4100 Upper High Street in Cradley Heath, take Plant Street and drive to the very end. This is now Bearmore Playing Fields. The old ground was to the left, at the junction with Plant Street and Bearmore Road. My site visit in the winter of 2012 revealed that the small Elim Pentecostal church building is on the site of the old pitch.

References

History of Cradley Heath Speedway team 'the Heathens'
Sandwell Borough Library Archives Department
Hednesford Town FC – 100 years – David Shaw
Trevor Siddaways Cradley Heath web site
The Black Country Bugle

Cradley St. Lukes 1900

Crosswells Brewery FC

f.1884-1889

Colours
– unknown

Ground
Vicarage Road, Langley (sports ground next to the brewery)

Birmingham FA representative:
Mr R. T. Holden

The team was formed by workmen at the Crosswells Brewery in Oldbury, a small town near West Bromwich, around 1884. The brewery had been built up by its founder Walter Showell. The Maltings' side of the brewery occupied most of Western road at the junction with Crosswells Road, across the road from the Langley Green railway station, but the main brewery premises were on Crosswells Road. At its peak, it was the largest brewery in terms of output in the West Midlands, selling some 80,000 gallons a week. Much like the Mitchells brewery at Cape Hill, it was self-sufficient, with its own fire brigade, blacksmiths, stables, and fleet of horse-drawn delivery vehicles. The manager at the time of their football period was William Thomas Davies. The brewery was eventually sold to Ind Coope Ltd in 1957 and then on to Wolverhampton Breweries of Banks's beer fame. Sadly the old Langley maltings building was badly damaged by fire in 2009, just as it was due to be transformed into apartments. The original brewery is now under the name of Alcohol Ltd and makes pure alcohol and derivatives for the alcohol, chemists, and chemical industries. Both parts of Crosswells are still there today (2012) although Alcohol Ltd suffered a large fire in November 2012, only a week after I went there to find their ground! The Maltings building in particular is steeped in Victorian atmosphere, with its old cobblestoned yards, dozens of drying windows and ventilation shafts, the whole factory being virtually blackened brickwork with an ornate black iron archway.

Today, Langley still has a dilapidated Victorian atmosphere about it, with new houses squashed in between rows of Victorian terraces, and there are many empty old brick factories, not the least Crosswells old maltings. A hundred years ago, it was still a sleepy village with almost no traffic, but today, it's right by a junction of the M5 and the Birmingham Road, and there is too much lorry traffic going through the village.

Walter Showell's Crosswells Brewery advertisements were a weekly front page feature of the *Midland Advertiser*. He is better known in modern times as the author of *Showells Directory of Birmingham*, a comprehensive 1885 book which lists all the businesses and occupations within the city. It was, in effect, the Victorian Yellow Pages.

Crosswells were an amateur works who side who entered local cups in West Bromwich, Walsall, and Birmingham, they once entered the English Cup. Their ground was next to the works on Crosswells Road, surrounded by Vicarage Road, and was known as Showells'Cricket Ground. Football, cricket and bowling clubs had their operations there until the mid-twentieth century. The cricket ground was built over about fifty years ago and Trident Drive now occupies the spot. The old workers' terraced cottages along the back of Vicarage Road are still there today. There was a pavilion on the right-hand side of the ground, which was also used by Langley cricket and bowls clubs. Visiting teams would have found the Langley Green railway station only a few hundred yards away.

After starting the 1886 season by competing in the by now popular 6-a-side football competition hosted by West Bromwich Albion at their Stoney Lane ground in the July of that year, Crosswells entered the Birmingham Cup in season 1886/7. But when drawn away to Calthorpe from south Birmingham, strangely found the home team had 'scratched' which gave them a walkover into the 2nd round where they faced a long journey to the Potteries. A pre-city Stoke side beat them 4-0. In 1886, the brewery-men entered the English FA Cup. They did very well to travel to Burton and beat the Swifts 1-0 on the 30 October; however they were brought down to earth when drawn away to mighty Wolverhampton Wanderers in round 2, and were hammered 14-0 on 13 November. The match, played at the Wolves' old Dudley Road ground, was played in heavy driving rain, which reduced the attendance to a few hundred. Wolves scored after five minutes (T. Hunter), and the goals just kept on coming. It was 5-0 after thirty minutes and 8-0 by half-time. The brewery-men actually rallied in the second half, in an attempt to put a score on the board, but Wolves were far too strong and added another six, Knight, Brodie, and Griffiths all netting hat-tricks.

Crosswells met West Bromwich Albion in the 1st round of the Walsall Senior Cup on 16th of October 1886 at Albion's new Stoney Lane ground, and the 2,500 crowd must have though Albion were playing their old-stars, as Crosswells trotted out no fewer than seven ex-Albion men onto the field.

No surprise then, when Albion won 5-2 with goals from Pearson, Holden, Horton (2), and to round off the misery and own goal by Crosswell's Moore.

After 1888, the Birmingham Cup, like the English FA Cup, was modified into regional knock-out to prevent costly long-distance journeys, but it seems that Crosswells either did not enter again, or they didn't make it past the qualifying rounds.

Crosswells were still playing local football though, into 1890s; they played Wednesbury Old Athletic in a friendly game during February of 1887 and went down by five clear goals, although this was no embarrassment against a leading club. Indeed, the brewery-men turned the tables a month later, when the return friendly fixture was played, and they scored the only goal of the game.

Their best player Tommy Horton went to the Wolves in 1885. Abel Frederick Bunn (1861-1921) worked at Salters Spring Works and played for West Bromwich Albion from 1879 to 1883 as a centre-half, and spent 1886 and 1887 with Crosswells. Jimmy Stanton (1860-1932) was a wing-half who came to Crosswells in 1886 from Newton Heath. Stanton too worked at Salters' and played for their works team, West Bromwich Strollers. Walter Brown (1867-1920) ended his football career when coming to Crosswells in 1891 after playing for several Aston area local teams.

FA Cup History –

Biggest defeat: lost 0-14 to Wolves and never entered again.

Biggest win: beat Dudley St. Edmund's by 23-0 on 6 December 1886 in the Dudley Charity Cup

Their 1885/6 team which trounced (Aston) Excelsior 7-0 was: Bradbury (goal); Moore, Hazelwood (backs); F. Bunn, Powell, Stanton (halfbacks); Bradley, W. Bunn, Neale, Southall, A. Bunn. Note the three Bunn brothers.

Two years later, the team was known as Oldbury Crosswells and the team now was: Mathews (goal); Riddle, Bradbury (backs); Hazelwood, Newby, Bunn (halfbacks); Aston, A. Bunn, Fairford, Neale, Southall (forwards). It was realised that Bradbury was no goalkeeper, and was put out as a back and Mathews brought in to keep goal. The story of Crosswells FC dries up in 1889, at a time when a new club from the same village sprang up; Langley Green Victoria. Using the Railway Tavern as their headquarters, they played in the newly formed Birmingham League from 1889 to 1892 and then they too, folded. It's quite possible that the brewery and the football team parted company around 1887. When Derby St. Luke's scratched to them in the Birmingham Cup, the brewery-men quickly contacted Small Heath Alliance, and went over to Coventry Road and played a friendly on 19th November 1887, which they won 2-0. At this period-1887, 1888-match reports were calling them Oldbury Town Crosswells, and by 1888, simply as Oldbury. Crosswells seem to have started adding players to their ranks from clubs from far and wide by 1886, and perhaps they felt that they no longer represented the brewery or indeed, the other way around, and that they needed to reform under a new name. Despite the current Oldbury Town FC unable to confirm or deny that they started out as Crosswells Brewery, it seems that is what happened. From 1888, Oldbury Town were playing from their new Birmingham Road ground, and, as Oldbury, results began to improve. In January 1888, the new team drew 4-4 in a thrilling local derby encounter with the high-riding Langley Green Vics in front of a bumper crowd. By the end of 1889, they were able to put Shrewsbury Town out of the Birmingham Cup by 4-0 in front of a 1,000 fans.

As Oldbury Town, they had a wonderful 1890s, winning the Worcestershire Cup in 1895,1897, and 1898.

To find the location of their old brewery ground, follow signs to Langley from West Bromwich or the M5, and Crosswells Road is at the junction of the B4182 and the B4169. Trident Drive is where the pitch used to be.

Crosswells Brewery Maltings, Langley

Derby Junction FC

f.1882-1895
Founded by Junction Street School old boys
Headquarters – the County Hotel, Station Street

Club President:
Mr Enos Bromage, the Hon. W. M. Jervis from 1888

Secretary:
Mr Draper

Nickname – 'The Junes' also 'the Brickyard Lads' in the 1870s

Grounds

1. the school ground*
2. the Vulcan Ground
3. the Arboretum Ground (1891)
4. Strutts Park, Duffield Road

Honours

Derbyshire Challenge Cup winners 1887/8, finalists 1888/9
FA Cup semi-finalists 1887

Colours
magenta and thin navy stripes, white knicks

Leading players
Malpass, Hopkins, Peach, S. Smith, Radford, Renshaw, Bromage

The team was started by older boys at the school in 1881/2 and at first played on the school's sports pitch. Well, that's what I understood until I made a site visit in December 2012 with my guide Terry, a local football referee and former player. Derby History Library assured us that there had only ever been one Junction Street, being just off the Uttoxeter Road (A516), but there was no school, and almost all the houses were Victorian, little having altered here in the last 115 years. We found the Junction Inn pub, which no doubt was used by both home and away teams for football matches, but no school. Searching an 1883 O.S. map drew us to the conclusion that the Baptist Chapel next door to the Junction Inn was the team's source. This was confirmed in 1924 when the Derbyshire Football Express ran a half-page article featuring the Bromage family of footballers who had founded the club half a century before. There was another pub, the Great Northern Inn on the opposite side of the road, directly facing the Chapel. I bet that led to many a heated discussion around religion versus the evils of drink!

The Bromages lived at 1 Olive Street at the time of the article, but, ironically, this was the very street which was built over the original Derby St. Luke's Peet Street school football ground just 500 yards away! The ninety-five-year-old Harry Bromage, interviewed in 1924, recalled of how all his five brothers played for the various Derby teams during the 1870s and 1880s, and he stated that the club sprang up from the Chapel Sunday school. In 1887, he recalled that the Junction played seventeen cup ties all told, and that "only West Bromwich Albion had beaten them that season (at Stoke's Victoria Athletics ground)."He further stated that they "started off playing at the Barracks Field, which is now the Rowditch Recreation ground*" and that "their early nickname was the 'brickyard lads'". That was before the papers began to call them the 'Junes'. Old Harry Bromage recalls the giant-killing 1887 cup team as:

Enos Bromage (goal), 'Togger' Hinds, George Potts, J. Walker, J. Siddons, Dick Smith, Jack Bromage, Jack Radford, Will Hopkins, Arthur Peach.

All the six Bromage family – George, Harry, William, Jack, Enos, and Harry Jnr. – went on to play for Derby County or Sheffield United.

The 'school ground', namely the Rowditch Rec, had a pitch size of 105 x 70 yards with a standing room around the perimeter for about 2,500 spectators. No shelter was provided apart from the umbrella of the old chestnut and beech trees lining the area behind the goals. Quite why the Junes would want to move away from seems like a nice enclosed decent-sized ground on their doorstep to use the Vulcan (Baseball Ground) and the Arboretum grounds is hard to fathom, unless it was simply the latter were within a short walk from the town centre railway station, making it easier for visiting teams to find, and in the hope that a more central location would attract a larger audience.

By 1885, they were being watched by 800 for the visit of Staveley. In 1884, they were using Siddals ground; in 1885, they played some games back on the school ground; in 1887/8, they were using 'the field by the Arboretum' (*Derby Mercury*). They kept the title Junction Street School until January 1886, when the words 'school and street' were dropped. The club, having the Junction Street School as its alma mater, had a continuing source of new players; by 1888, they had a membership of over sixty. Having seen the rise of both Derby Midland and Derby County as professional sides seemingly devouring all before them, the Junction FC committee stated at their 1888 A.G.M at the County Hotel that they were against the evils of professionalism and were proud to remain faithful to their amateur roots. They played most of the 1890s in the Derbyshire Senior League, although they were one of the struggling sides.

Both the Arboretum and Strutts Park are directly associated with Joseph Strutt. In the 1770s, his family developed Belper Mills, and he was a prominent cotton mill owner who also owned large areas of land mostly on the Darley Abbey side of town. In 1840, he gave land to the south of the town centre which became England's first Arboretum when he planted 1,000 trees and gave the parkland to the citizens for recreational and pleasure uses. He became the new Borough of Derby mayor. The other, much larger land, on the north of town by Darley Dale Abbey, became known as Strutt's Park. It stretched from both ends of the Belper Road (Duffield Rd) and was partly built over nearest to the main road, but much parkland still exists.

Their team of 1886 was:

E. Bromage (goal); A. Latham and Potts (backs); J. Siddons, Twigge, W. Hall (halfbacks); Radford, J. Bromage, J. Renshaw, S. Bradley, I. Renshaw (forwards) – yet again, two pairs of brothers making up the backbone of the side. George Potts was the team captain at this period.

FA Cup History

1884/5	1-7 W. B. Albion (H) (At Junction Street School – attendance 4,000!)
1885/6	2-2 (H), 0-4 (A) Darwen FC
1886/7	1-0 Wellington Town
	1-2 W. B. Albion
1887/8	3-2 Derby St. Luke's (A)
	3-2 Rotherham
	2-1 Lockwood Brothers
	Bye

	1-0 Chirk
	2-1 Blackburn R (6th round)
	0-3 W. Brom Albion (semi-final)
1888/9	0-1 Derby County

They entered the Birmingham Cup from 1885 season and had a good run in 1886/7. Beating the famous Wednesbury Old Athletics by 4-1 in the 3rd round the Arboretum, they lost 0-4 to Small Heath at the Coventry Road (Muntz St) ground, but like most teams that went there and experienced the worst senior pitch in the region, they lodged a protest with the Birmingham FA, and the game was replayed. Unfortunately, it was still at Coventry Road, but this time just one goal for the Heathens was enough.

The team started to enter the English FA Cup from 1884, and although they were trounced 1-7 at home to the powerful West Bromwich Albion, a tremendous 4,000 people turned out to see the historic match. This was an attendance figure Albion would have been pleased with back at their ground.

The year 1887/8 proved to be their peak season. They won the Derbyshire Cup by beating a tough Staveley 2-0 on Siddal's ground. Some folk adjudged Staveley to be more Yorkshire than Derbyshire as they were members of the Sheffield FA. There was even better to come.

A remarkable effort was produced in the 1887/8 season, when the school old boys' team actually reached the semi-finals (7th round) of the FA Cup itself. Beating Blackburn Rovers in the quarter-final makes amazing reading today, and must have done so then, as Rovers had won the FA Cup in 1884 and 1885 and thought that a semi-final clash with the Albion was a formality. Sadly, for the Junes, the Albion treated them as respectful opponents and ran out 3-0 winners, true to form book, and went on to win the cup, beating Preston North End at the London Oval in front of a modest 19,000. Derby Junction were the last small team to ever reach the cup semi-final stage, and so they deserve some recognition for this achievement. However, their great day at Stoke's Victoria ground on Saturday 18 February 1888 in front of 6,000 people was cut short with Albion goals by Bayliss, Wilson, and Woodhall. Their victory over Blackburn Rovers though, must surely rank as one of the all-time great FA Cup shocks.

The late 1880s's saw the Junes enjoy success in the Derbyshire Challenge Cup. They overcame Staveley 2-0 to win it in 1888, and the two sides met again in the final of the following year; this time, it was Staveley's turn to win by the only goal of the game. Reporters said that the Junes were very unlucky not to have scored as they had more of the game, and the greater chances.

The team of 1888/9 season was: Bromage (goal); Hind and Middleton (backs); Walker, Siddons, and Snelson (halfbacks); forwards: Wood and Kennerley (right wing), Housley (centre), Hopkins and Radford (left wing).

By 1891, things were going downhill. The *Birmingham Daily Post* said on 26 January, after their 2-6 defeat away to Warwick County, that Junction were a poor resemblance of the team of two seasons ago and that there was "a decided lack of that perfect understanding which hitherto characterised their efforts" That's Victorian speak for 'they were pants'.

From 1889 till 1893 then played in the Midland League but dropped down into the Derbyshire Senior League in 1893/4 when they folded rather dramatically on Christmas Day 1895. This was chiefly due to rise of Derby County who were professionals, and the Junction were amateurs who couldn't charge an admission fee since they often played on public grounds as well.

However, it appears that the Derby Junction ground is still there today, access via Coke Street, at the rear of the Uttoxeter Old Road. It is a reasonably level pitch, built up from the surrounding pathway, as the park is on quite a slope from east to west, with trees and old walls on all four sides. My visit here in December of 2012, on a frosty day, found me walking up the cobbled end of the short Coke Street, past a dilapidated Victorian nail-making factory into the entrance to the now called Rowditch Recreation ground. The old walls behind both goals were still there, as was the stone wall entrance, minus its wrought iron gates. This location is across the road from the end of Junction Street where it meets the Old Uttoxeter Road. One side of the pitch has a high grassy bank, and there is plenty of room behind where the goalpost stood to allow for spectators. The pitch is built up from street level, and the perimeter walls are some distance behind the goals, and thus it is quite open to winds and frost, and would have given a hardship to any spectators who huddled around the pitch. However, it was a delight to find an old ground virtually unchanged from 130 years ago, and as such, this is one of the best for the amateur football historian to visit.

As to the Vulcan Ground, there was no trace, but it is possibly we thought that there may have been a ground behind the Vulcan pub in the town centre. After some detective work by my Derby man Terry, we discovered that Sir

Francis Ley, who built the Baseball Ground as part of a sporting complex for his workforce, owned as foundry called – guess what – the Leys Malleable Iron Casting Vulcan works. It seems that until 1890 when American baseball was introduced, the Baseball Ground was previously known locally as the Vulcan ground. So another mystery solved! As we all know, it was Derby County who moved into what was the Vulcan ground, renamed it the Baseball Ground, and improved it with more terracing and stands, taking the capacity from 4,000 to over 20,000.

A view of the demolished Baseball Ground circa 2009 gives a good idea of what the old Vulcan ground looked like, because there was little else but a wooden fencing surround, about ten rows of earthen terracing, and a few wooden planking seats and barriers – all very basic, but at least it was near the town centre, and had the patronage of Francis Ley, whose large multi-gable roofed factory ran between the ground and the railway lines for some 300 yards. Previously, between their formation in 1884 and 1890, Derby County had used the Racecourse Ground (county cricket ground), but they frequently found that matches clashed with race meetings, and needed a new home, and so moved into the Vulcan ground, renaming it the Baseball ground.

Another ground which has not been identified with certainty is Siddals Ground, used by several of the Derby sides. The strong contender is Bass's Recreation ground by the River Derwent as it winds around Cock Pit roundabout. However, all my maps, going back to 1878, always call it as Bass's Rec. Siddall owned a lot of land here and there in Derby, and so 'Siddals Ground' remains a mystery for now.

As to the Arboretum Ground, the small Arboretum in Derby – the first in England – has one football pitch today, at the Rose Hill end of the park, by the entrance lodge. The lodge, and the old trees which form a rectangle around the well-kept field, help to evoke memories of the day when the Junes beat the mighty Blackburn Rovers here in December 1887. Six thousand Derbyites crammed into the Arboretum field ground, to see the Junes come from 0-1 down to take a famous win with late goals from Dick Smith and Will Hopkins. After their shock cup exit, Blackburn, who had won the cup twice that decade, protested about just about everything they could think of: 'snow-covered pitch having had cinders sprinkled over it', 'too much of a slope' (nonsense!), and that because the Junes had gone to Matlock Bath to train for several days, that the Junes must be considered as 'not being the amateur team which they claim'. All the protests were to no avail, and David had slain his giant.

The *Derby Evening Telegraph* ran an article on June 1983, all about that cup tie, and the reporter laid doubt as to the exact location of the 1887 cup tie. Was it the large flat meadow which today still has a football pitch, or the smaller field behind the bowling club, which today is a children's playground? Well, with the help of my Derby guide, Terry, we walked and measured both pieces of land. The smaller one, the playground was certainly wide enough for a pitch, but it didn't look quite long enough for us to have an FA regulation pitch on it, and Terry had a long experience of being a non-league referee – indeed several of his family played for Derby County and Burton Albion – so we came away with the conclusion that today's football pitch, between the tennis courts and the Lodge was the 1887 cup venue. An 1883 O.S. map illustrates that almost nothing had changed in Derby Arboretum in the last 130 years, apart from the playground, tennis courts, and a couple of changing rooms. All the pathways, as originally laid out, were still in their old positions, and so too, the trees on this side of the park. Today, the playground field is 80 yards wide x 98 yards long – OK for a Sunday parks' junior football team, but not up to FA regulation size, and there would be no room for spectators. However, there is a new path at the top end, which, if we turn the clock back to 1887, would have made the maximum available length at 113 yards. However, this still leaves no room for the 6,000 spectators, and the goalposts would have been almost in the trees! No, I think I'm sure that the bigger meadow was the one which was used. It has been claimed that today's football pitch was laid out as a flower bed. Well, if that was the case, it would have been ridiculously large, some 198 x 80 yards, and there is no depiction of any flower beds on my 1883 O.S. map which marks out every individual tree in the park. Also, the park was designed for that all-important Victorian Sunday pastime of promenading – parading endlessly up and down in your Sunday best with black parasols and big feathery hats, pushing junior in his perambulator, pretending that you are not trying to impress your neighbours with your display of wealth and social status! If that were the case, then there would have been pathways criss-crossing this gigantic flower bed, but no such paths show on the 1883 map of the park. There would have been room for both a large flower bed and a 120 yd x 75 yd football pitch.

The Junction Street Sunday school is no longer there (house numbers 8, 10 in its place) but would have been only a few hundred yards from the St. Luke's School, and so these two teams would have been very close neighbours and rivals. In fact, it is only 800 yards from Junction Street to St. Luke's Church. No doubt some boys knew each other from both schools and there was likely to have been a connection between the two. Indeed, the *Derby Mercury* of 1886 tells us that Twigge, Bromage, and Renshaw also turned out for Derby St. Luke's, and Ayre, the St. Luke's halfback, also turned out for Derby Midland during 1885/6.

Derby Junction football club disbanded suddenly at the end of 1895, another victim of the rise of professionalism, led by Derby County.

To find the old Junction ground today, drive to the A516 Uttoxeter Road which comes off the A38, and where the road splits into a Y shape, bear left down the Old Uttoxeter Rd. Go left at the 5-ways into Parcel terrace, then left into Coke Street. The old ground awaits, in all its entirety, unchanged in almost 130 years.

References

Derby Mercury 1884-1888 and 1924
Sheffield Evening Telegraph
Derby City Local History Centre
Derby Evening Telegraph 1983

Entrance to Junction Ground

Derby Junction Ground

Derby Midland FC

f.1881-1891

Grounds

1. said to have 'played on fields by the Midland railway station'
2. known to have played at Derby Arboretum (a football pitch still exists there)
3. Siddals Ground was their usual pitch in the mid-1880s.
4. The 'Midland' ground during last half of 1880s

Colours
thin black and white stripes/white shorts (john baines, bradford, football and rugby cards 1887)

Nickname: 'The Mids'

Honours
won Derbyshire Cup 1891

The team was founded by railway workers at the Derby Midland railway depot and Midland Hotel, built next to it, for railway travellers. They folded a decade later to amalgamate with the new Derby County team, but it fell at the right time as the railway had withdrawn its funding, and the club was in a poor financial state. Derby Midland also had a cricket team and often played during the 1880s at the Arboreum. Their attractive fixture against a Wednesbury Town team (that had just beaten Nottingham Forest to win the Wednesbury Cup) in November 1884 only drew 2,000 spectators for example.

Siddals Ground now seems to be known as Bass's recreation ground, and this is near Derby bus station and close to the railway station. It's hemmed in by the railway lines and the river Derwent and is used as a fairground. This location also fits the description of 'a field by the railway station', although no doubt there were several fields to choose from 130 years ago.

A site visit with my local football referee guide Terry in the winter of 2012 led me to view the Bass's Rec from a vantage point, and it is clear that there is only one way one could have a football pitch, and that is running parallel to the river. This is an important point as you will see in a moment. My guide then said if we walk on about a quarter of a mile, he will show me the 'old railway ground'. I was intrigued by this, because he didn't know that Derby Midland were a railway-based team and played 'on a field by the railway station'. As we emerged through the other side of a railway bridge which spanned the Derwent, known as Siddals Bridge (there's that name again), we came out to a very large but neglected field, populated only by a couple of donkeys. 'I used to play cricket and football over there forty years ago,' he said. I looked at the field, with its waist-high water reeds and bulrushes, and it seemed impossible that anyone could play cricket on such a lumpy and overgrown piece of land. He assured me that there used to be a fine flat and well-kept sports ground here and remembered the locations of the three pavilions and the bowling green on the far side. The triangular piece of scrubland was hemmed in by the railway branch which curved off to service the cattle yards and the river Derwent. All of a sudden, I said, 'I'm convinced that this is where Derby Midland used to play!' I had read some 1887 match reports wherein it stated that the Midland had 'kicked off towards the river'. This matched the position of the railway ground, as Terry called it, much more than the Bass's Rec. ground, where the goalposts would have been alongside the river instead. Here, at the 'railway ground', the pitch ran with the goals facing the river.

The nearly square ground today measures 140 x 130 yards, clear of the perimeter tree and hedge lines. A good view can be obtained by standing on the bridge on the A6 over the railway and river.

Terry also did some research and produced a photocopy of an 1860 newspaper report about a court case involving the sale of the land which was purchased by the Midland Railway Company from a Mr Bailey, where the value of the Old Meadows land was being challenged. Being enclosed by the river Derwent and the curving railway line, and being on low-lying pasture land, I would have expected that it would be prone to flooding, as suggested by the marshy reeds and bulrushes which thrive on the spot today. This would not help any team playing the passing game to any degree of success, and no doubt matches had to be switched to the other well-known Derby venues instead.

My new A–Z still optimistically shows this old field as a sports ground! But, ironically, the fork in the railway line from the station taking the Chaddesden Sidings at the cattle market is known as Derby Junction – the name of one of the team's rivals in the town! Nonetheless, by 1887, Derby newspapers were calling the Mids' home ground the 'Midland ground'. It was only 800 yards south of the County cricket ground, home of Derby Town, and later, to Derby County.

The Derby Arboretum – England's first – was donated to the townsfolk by Joseph Strutt in 1840. Leading player William Morley was a bank clerk at the Midland Railway, and it was he who was linked with three of Derby's clubs. He left the Derby Town team to found the Midland FC and then did the same to found Derby County in 1884. His father was secretary to the recently formed Derbyshire County cricket club (1871), which was going through hard times. They had lost all ten of their first-class cricket fixtures, crowds were poor, and they needed another source of income. A professional football team was their answer, and so Derby County FC were born. They wanted to use the name Derbyshire in the title, but the M.C.C objected to the FA, on the grounds that such a name would cause public confusion. And so it would. So the name was shortened, and the Rams began to 'do a Villa' and poach the top players from other Derby clubs, and within a few short years, they were ready to be admitted into the new Football League, much to the chagrin of much older clubs whose demises were attributable to the accelerated success of this new Derby County team.

Back to our team, the Derby Mids:

They played in the Midland League seasons 1889-0-1, and were one of the better teams. If it hadn't been for financial problems when Derby County came along, they could have been Derbyshire's other top team today. Opponents included Derby Junction, Gainsborough Trinity, Warwick County, Notts Rangers, and Staveley.

Their record in the Midland Lge:

1889/90 came 2nd:	PL20 W11-	D3-	L5	=25pts
1890/91 came 4th:	PL18 W8-	D4-	L6	=20pts

Best FA Cup: reached the 3rd round in 1883/84

They entered the Birmingham Senior Cup during the 1880s but never made much of an impact, a 2-4, 4th round defeat at the hands of Walsall Swifts played at the Aston Lower grounds on 4th March 1882 being their best effort.

The team of 1882 which travelled to play Walsall Town was: Haynes (goal); Winfield (back); Cooper, Latham, Wright (halfbacks); forwards: Gathers, Harrison (left wing) Cheetham and Evans (centres), Turner, Topham (right wing). Evans was captain.

In 1883/4, they got to the 3rd round of the FA Cup, but went out to the only goal of the game away to newly formed Wednesbury Town. They had beaten Birmingham's Excelsior FC in the previous round.

Their 1885/6 side which, with Derby County, was the leading team of the county was: Salt (goal); L. Wright and T. Hind (backs); Tarlton, Boak, Dan Ayre (halfbacks); Helliwell, Strutt, Scott, J. Selver, and W. Selver (forwards).

Probably the forward Strutt had family connections (possibly the grandson of Joseph Strutt who gave parkland to the town in 1840) with Strutts Park, used by several of the Derby town sides. The Mids were an ambitious team, and it was believed that their creation led to the demise of the old Derby Town team in 1881. Despite a newspaper article in the *Derby Daily Telegraph* in the July of 1881 by a Mr W. Shaw, the Derby Town secretary, scoffing any thought that old Derby Town had disbanded, nonetheless, at least three of Town's best players left to found the Midland side, including Harry Evans. Within a year of the Midland forming, the professional Derby County team had sprung up, aggressively poaching star players from other local teams.

By 1886, the sports newspapers were attempting to put some sort of order to the playing records of the leading teams of the day. The only basis on which they seemed to place any value was how many goals-per-match a team had scored during the season, quite without understanding that not every team's fixture card contained opponents of the same ability as another's. Thus, we see Derby Midland ranked 6th in Britain (Scotch and Welsh sides often included), above Renton and Rangers, with Villa, Preston, Albion, Forest, and Bolton being the top-ranked five clubs, based on goals per game. It is reasonable to say that the best teams are scoring the most goals, but it was not a level playing field, and the table was merely a guide to the curiosity to the reader. The other Derby teams, St. Luke's, Junction, were near the bottom of the twenty-one-team listing. Villa and Preston were averaging almost 5 goals per game over 21 matches!

George Holden, the star Wednesbury Old Athletic centre forward, spent one season with Derby Midland, but this was at the end of his long career, and by this time, his head-down and dribble selfish style was out of date, and the Midland fans didn't take to him. He returned to the 'Old Uns', much to the delight of the 'Wedgbury' faithful. He was a legend in the Black Country and gained 4 England caps. Charles Alcock described Holden as 'clever, useful, light but fast'.

In their last season, Derby Midland took an impressive scalp when they defeated neighbours Nottingham Forest 3-0 in the 1st round of the 1889 FA cup, but went out to Bootle 1-2 after a 1-1 draw in round 2.

Best Players were: W. Rose 1888; Steve Bloomer (1874-1938) played briefly during 1891/2 only – who became a legend at Derby County – had come from the schoolboys team Derby Swifts, with whom he had spent seasons 1888-91; and Jack Robinson – one cap for England. Bloomer* only stayed for one year, the final one before the club was amalgamated with Derby County. Harry Evans was their top scorer in 1883, and he had 'defected' from the old Derby Town side a year before, taking two others with him.

By 1885, the team were already showing a professional outlook, with local papers carrying adverts selling the team's colours on scarves and sashes and badges.

George Holden was capped for England when he was with Wednesbury Old Athletic, but he returned to the club where his heart lay after only one year; and George Daft was a Corinthians FC forward. George Bakewell, their star winger, was poached by the newly formed Derby County team when they started up in 1884/5. Whether he thought their gaudy colours of chocolate and amber halved shirt with sky blue sleeves was a more attractive proposition, it seemed that he was instrumental in the merging of the two teams, although the reality was that Midland had been absorbed in County and were no more.

These top two sides in the county clashed in round 1 of the Derbyshire cup in 1888, and this time it was County who came out on top 3-1 courtesy of second half goals from Needham and a brace from Bakewell cancelled out Daft's first half goal on fifteen minutes in front of a 3,000 crowd.

Mixed success came from the team's efforts in the Derbyshire Challenge Cup. The Mids were beaten in the finals of 1884 and 1885, both times by Staveley (2-1, 2-0). In the 1884 final, the crowd of 7,000 was a record for football in the county at that time.

The Derbyshire County Cup final of 1890 saw the Mids' revenge as they beat rivals Derby County 1-0, and again in 1891, they reached the final as holders, only to lose a close game with Long Eaton Rangers by 1-2. Derby County were now in the Football League, and it must have been at this point that the two clubs agreed to merge, although amalgamation had really been extinction.

FA cup history	1st Round	2nd Round	3rd Round
1883/84	Bye	2-1 B'ham Excelsior (Ward, Gignall)	0-1 Wednesbury Town (A)
1884/85	1-2 Weds. Old. Athletic		
1885/6	2-1 Birmingham Excelsior	1-3 Walsall Swifts	
1886/7	3-3, 2-1 B'ham Excelsior	0-14 Aston Villa	
1887/8	1-4 Ecclesfield		
1888/9	Didn't qualify for competition proper		
1889/90	3-0 Nottm Forest (Daft, Garden, Mills)	1-1, 1-2 Bootle	

*Writing in 1905, Steve Bloomer wrote – 'from the earliest days, when I commenced to play in a schoolboy team called the Derby Swifts, I was boiling over with enthusiasm for the game. Here, then, was a good beginning. My heart was in the game, and it was not long before I learned the glorious art of kicking goals, which has remained with me in some good measure since.' Most commentators of the association game in the 1950s, reflecting on the greatest forward of all time, chose Steve Bloomer as a close call over Billy Meredith. Bloomer left Derby Midland to join the recently (1884) created Derby County at the princely sum of 7/6d a week (38p). He went on to score a career total of over 350 League goals. He was said to appear as if uninterested in the game, standing about with hands on hips; when given the ball, he would start off like lightning, swerve past a couple of defenders, and unleash an unstoppable shot into the net.

To find the lost ground of Derby Midland today, follow St. Akmund's way off the A6, and do a complete circle left turn at the big roundabout and go down Meadow Road to the end. Park up at the *Derby Mercury* newspaper office car park and walk to the left along the river towpath. Make sure you go under the bridge with the river underneath and the railway overhead. When you come out the other side of the bridge, you will see large fields to your left. The marshy field 200 yards to the left, which is bounded by the curve of the railway, was the Midland ground.

References

Derby Mercury 1884-1888
Sheffield Telegraph
The History of Wednesbury Old Athletics, Cyril Willetts
The Story of Football, William Lowndes, London, 1952

Arboretum Ground

Derby Midlands' Railway Ground Today

Derby Midland's Steve Bloomer

Derby St. Luke's FC

f.1878-1891

They were a Church-based school team of amateur boys and young men, one of the first football teams in Derbyshire.

They eventually joined the Midland League in 1890 but didn't complete its fixtures, so its record was expunged.

Headquarters:
Parliament Street

Ground:
Peet Street, off New Uttoxeter Rd. Important matches were played on the County (Racecourse) Ground. The Racecourse Ground, as its name suggests, was a very large area, with cricket played in the one side within the horse-racing oval, and the football pitch was in one corner. Unfortunately, the grandstand, which was very ornate and multi-tiered, was set up for the horse-racing and cricket fans, over 250 yards away from the football pitch, so, in that respect, it was next to useless for watching any football match, unless one had one's binoculars!

Representative to the Birmingham FA:
Mr W. Walker

Club committee chairman:
Dr Moon

St. Luke's entered the Birmingham Cup from 1881 but rarely made it past the first hurdle, often scratching if a long distance was involved. They chiefly played friendlies or in the Derbyshire and Sheffield cups. By the mid-1880s, Derby had half a dozen useful teams against which they had to compete, and generally they were behind most of them. The Lukes weren't dazzled by the home team's lime green shirts when they recorded a remarkable 13-1 away win when they played Sawley Rangers in the 1st round of the 1884/5 Birmingham cup. However, they were put out in the next round when they travelled to Birchfield, Aston, and lost 0-3 to St. George's. They managed to beat 'Derby County' by 2-1 in the 1st round of the 1887/8 Birmingham Cup, but County had only sent their reserve team. Still, the record books show that they beat them. For unknown reasons, they scratched when drawn away to Oldbury Town in round 2 on Saturday 19 November. The expense of travelling the eighty-mile round trip, added to the fact that the team, a little more than grown-up boys, were no doubt leading factors. The following year, 1888, they were held 2-2 at home by Burton Wanderers in front of a 1,000 crowd, but lost by an amazing 3-8 in the replay at Derby Turn on 3 November. They did not enter again.

St. Luke's Church dominates Parliament Street with its curious imposing design, with its curved knaves and one of the tallest spires I have ever seen other than on a cathedral. The St. Luke's School was at the corner of Peet Street and Parliament Street, and indeed is still there today, but is now used by Harmony Interiors design company. An O.S. map for 1883 shows the 'school playground' at 90 degrees to Peet Street, with the California iron foundry at the top end. There was also another school in between the church and Parliament Street Rec, and these may have either been separate boys and girls schools, the junior and senior buildings, or two unconnected schools. The Lukes played its ordinary matches here, but a site visit in December 2012 revealed that circa 1900, it was built over by a short cul-de-sac, Oliver Street. Oliver Street, and thus the school ground, had a considerable slope from top to bottom, probably the most I have come across. The old foundry building is still there, and because all the surrounding streets are all of Victorian houses, loomed over by St. Luke's Church, it is easy to imagine a scene of street urchins in bare feet playing with spinning tops and jacks. Measuring the site of what was the old St. Luke's Peet Street ground – if you can call it that – it is well short of an official pitch, being just 90 × 45 yards, and that doesn't include any room for spectators!

At the other side of the church is the Stockbrook Rec, and as it is used for local football too, I would be surprised if St. Luke's didn't play there too, as there is a great deal of room for spectators, and it was only a hundred yards away in Parliament Street.

Their 1882 team which beat Sheffield's Hallam by 5-0 at Peet Street was: Wheatley (goal); Worthington (back); Wilton Harvey, Frank Harvey, Newbold (halfbacks); Watson, Renshaw, Mathers, Twigge, Selby, and Hall (forwards). This 6-3-1 formation would have been out of fashion at that time in Staffordshire. Harry Newbold (1861-1928) went on to play for the Sheffield Wednesday, later became Derby County's first manager in the year 1900, and later the manager of Manchester City in 1906.

This was the 1884 Team who took a famous scalp when they beat the Wolves 4-2 a.e.t in Derby on 22 November in a 1st round FA Cup replay. The first game had been a 1-1 draw at the Dudley Road ground, Goldthorn Hill in Wolverhampton in front of a 3,100 crowd.

Parsons, Harvey, Whamley, Wilson, Dolman, Twigge, Renshaw, Walker, Evans, Shipley, Wilde. Parsons was the club captain, and Frank Harvey was the team vice-captain.

A close game at home to Walsall in the 2nd round saw the Swifts go through by the only goal of the game on 6 December.

When the professional Derby County started up in 1884 after William Morley suggested that the county cricket club should start up a football team as a means of making an income for the near-bankrupt cricketers, amongst County's first signings were a couple of St. Luke's and Darley Abbey men. County's premier status was rapidly enhanced with key signings Benjamin Spilsbury and John Chevallier, veterans from the cup-winning Old Etonians team of the previous decade. Both Derby legends John Goodall (from PNE in 1889) and Steve Bloomer (from Derby Midland in 1892) enabled County to go from formation to Football League status within a decade. Unfortunately, County's success was at the expense of smaller, older sides like St. Luke's and Junction, not to mention old Derby Town, whose ground they nicked.

The year 1886 saw a fine FA Cup tussle with Walsall Town. The home game, played on the 30 October, was a 3-3 draw, with the home goals coming from Hawkesworth (2) and Wild. However, they were trounced 6-1 in the replay at the Chuckery ground on 13th November. On the same day, rivals Derby Midland were beating Birmingham Excelsior 2-1 in their cup replay to move into the 3rd round, only to be despatched 6-1 by Aston Villa. The Mids, by coincidence had also drawn their first game by 3-3 in Aston Park.

Their 1886 side retained only five of the 1884 side:

Parsons (goal); Raynor and Brentnall (backs); Twigge, Ayre, Shipley (halfbacks); Shannon, Hawsworth, Walker, Renshaw, Bromage (forwards).

Bromage, Renshaw, and Twigge also turned out for their Sunday school, Derby Junction. Ayre also played for the Derby Midland when they started up in 1885. It's possible that he had obtained a job working on the railways. Derby Midland and Derby County sounded the death knell for the older amateur derby sides such as Lukes, Junction, and the original Derby Town.

To find where Derby St. Luke's FC played today, take the Peet Street turn off the A516 Uttoxeter New Road at the old cemetary. The church is at the end of the road, with Stockbrook Rec facing you, and behind that high wall at the top of Peet Street was the old school. Olive Street was built on the football pitch.

FA Cup history	1st Round	2nd Round
1884/5	1-1, 4-2 Wolverhampton Wanderers	0-1 Walsall Swifts
1885/6	0-7 Wolverhampton Wanderers	
1886/7	3-3, 1-6 Walsall Town	
1887/8	2-3 Derby Junction	

Derby St. Luke's Arboretum Ground

Derby St. Luke's Stockbrook Ground

St. Lukes School Derby

Derby Town FC

f. 1876-1895?
folded 1881, reformed 1882

Ground
the old racecourse County ground, Nottingham Road

Honours
Champions, Midland Alliance 1892/3

Nothing to do with Derby County, which didn't form until this little team, bravely carrying the Town title, had folded.

Football became organised in Derby following a series of playing visits from the Sheffield FC in November of 1872. They came down to play local side St. Andrew's, and after cordial relationships were established, a Derbyshire FA was established adhering to the Sheffield FA rules. The Wednesday FC also came to Derby just before Christmas 1872 and played a Derbyshire representative side. In front of 500 curious spectators, the home side won by 1-0 in a 14-a-side game. Wednesday were beaten against on 3rd March 1877, this time by 6-0.

This first Derbyshire FA didn't last long, and the present organisation of that name was begun in 1883. Thus began a long-lasting allegiance with Derbyshire and Nottinghamshire teams to the Sheffield rules. Actually, the Sheffield FA were much more radical and advanced than even the London FA. Sheffield were pioneers of many of the game's modern rules, such as awarding a free kick on the spot for handling the ball, and a corner kick which was taken by the attacking side if the ball was put beyond the goal line by a defender. Until then (1870), a ball going out of play was returned to play by the side that got to the ball first, regardless of which side put the ball out! Sheffield rules also were advanced in that, under their code, offside only meant one defender was needed between the furthest forward and the goalposts. The London rules said three.

Derby Town were known to be playing at the County Ground in the early 1880s. The County Ground, also known as the Racecourse Ground, was also home to the newly formed Derby County until 1895 when they moved to the new Baseball Ground, and is better known as the home of Derbyshire County Cricket. A site visit which enabled me to see at close quarters the present layout of both the county cricket ground and the new development in front of the Nottingham Road, particularly the Virgin Active centre and the associated car park and Heritage Village, enabled me to work out what is there today compared to O.S. maps of Derby for 1882, 1891, and 1901. The southern part of the county ground bears little resemblance to 130 years ago. The county cricket pitch had been moved several times from its original position of much higher up. The centre part of the Racecourse was in fact a rifle-shooting range, and the portable small stands of the 1880s stood 50 yards to the north of the new stands of today. Stores Road, running north to south and parallel to the railway line, used to be a canal!

Today's Frank Whittle Way follows almost exactly the western and southern side of the racecourse, which came down to within a few yards of the Nottingham Rd. This is a helpful reference, since the football pitch was described as being: 'inside the racecourse, at the southern end, and to the west, with cricket ground stands some 300 yards to the right'. Various maps show that the cricket ground itself moved around a bit and took up its present position in 1936, after the stands were repositioned after the horse racing ceased. Comparing old maps of the ground with today's computer tool – Google Earth – my best guess is that the football pitch, which once hosted the replayed Cup Final between Blackburn and the Albion, was on what is now the Derventio Heritage Village at the side of the A61. The area is obviously flat and level and is easily big enough for a football pitch. None of the large trees which today outline the cricket ground were shown as existing on any of the pre-1914 O.S. maps.

Town were a strictly amateur side which entered the Wednesbury, Walsall, Sheffield, and Derbyshire cups in the days before League football. Little is known about this early Derbyshire team, although they did enter the Wednesbury Charity Cup for its first few years. They were beaten 6-2 at home in round 1 in 1880 by the strong Stafford Road (Wolverhampton) side who could be counted as being in the top 8 Midland sides at that time, so the result suggests a team who were able to compete, but not perhaps in the front rank.

They were possibly the first team in Derbyshire, certainly in Derby itself. They were founded at the end of 1876 by J. F. Tomlinson, Harry Evans, and W. Shaw. They were one of the first East Midlands teams to venture outside their own county. On 6th February 1877, they travelled to the Aston Lower Grounds and played a draw with Henry Quilters' Birmingham FC with this team.

J. F. Tomlinson,(captain), H. R. Wignall, R. Norton, L. Cubley, H. Johnson, A. Chaplin, J. Piggot, Taylor, and J. Newton. A couple of the Derby men couldn't find the Aston Lower Ground, and the home side supplied men to make up the numbers, as Birmingham usually played 12-a-side.

Derby entered the Birmingham Cup for the first time in 1879, and for some reason, local rivals St. Luke's scratched against them in round 1. In the second round, Derby were drawn at home to Shropshire club Oswestry, who were almost in Wales. As the two sides couldn't agree on a venue, the Birmingham FA told them to meet halfway at the Wednesbury Oval, where Derby triumphed 4-1 just five days before Christmas Day, probably on a near-frozen pitch. More luck followed, for Stoke's Burslem (Port Vale) also didn't fancy the long journey, and they too scratched to put Derby Town into the 4th round, which, due to the Birmingham FA's poor organising powers, was the last six teams. All these quarter-final ties were played at the Aston Lower Grounds during February of 1880. The other ties were Walsall Swifts v Wednesbury Strollers and Aston Villa v Aston Unity. Derby were drawn against perennial semi-finalists Saltley College. The college men, in their red and gold hoops, were beaten by 3-0 in front of a big crowd of 4,000 at the Aston Lower Grounds. This was the biggest crowd of the three quarter-final ties which were all played at the ALG. In the semi-final draw, still with an odd number of teams (3), Derby Town drew a bye out of the hat to put them (apparently) into the final, where they would meet Aston Villa. But wait, as was commonplace in the 1870s, Saltley College put in an appeal on the grounds that Derby fielded an ineligible player. The Birmingham FA investigated and found that not only was it true, but Derby had been warned about it previously, and for this deliberate breach of the rules, they were disqualified! Thus, Derby Town were denied their best ever chance to win the Birmingham Cup, which was, to all intents and purposes, the Midlands cup. In the final, Villa did beat Saltley 3-1, but the teachers had controlled the first half and had been unlucky to be held 1-1 at half-time. Since Derby beat Saltley by 3 goals in that void quarter-final game, one could speculate that they might possibly have beaten the Villa in that final, had they actually got there.

In 1880, a week before Christmas, they travelled to the Wednesbury Oval to play the Old Athletics in round 2 of the Birmingham Cup and were trounced 5-1 in front of a bumper 1,000 crowd at the Athletic Ground, now inside Brunswick Park. The previous month saw them beat Moseley-based cricket side, the Pickwick, 4-0 at the County Ground Derby in the 1st round.

In 1881/2, they again entered the Birmingham Cup, only to be beaten 2-0 at home to local rivals Derby Midland, again at the County Ground. Midland went on to reach the 4th round (Q/F), going down 2-4 in a good match with the Walsall Swifts at the Aston Lower Grounds. Derby Town did not enter the Birmingham cup after this year, but by which time, the other Derby teams had sprung up in competition: St. Luke's, Midland, Junction, and County.

In 1879, three Derby men were selected to play for the Birmingham AFA against the London FA: Gathers, Wignall, and Shaw.

The Harvey and the Wignall brothers were the backbone of the side, yet another example of sets of brothers forming a team.

This team travelled to play Walsall in 1882:

Smith (goal); Shaw and Johnson (backs); Morley, Latham, H. Wignall (halfbacks); Nutt, Ward, W. Harvey, F. Harvey, G. Wignall (forwards).

At the end of July 1881, rumours abound that a new team, Derby Midland, had started up, and they intended to draw away Derby Town's beat players. Shaw, the club secretary, wrote in the *Nottingham Evening Post* denying that Derby Town had folded; however, at least four Town men did join the Midland; Morley, the Chaplin brothers, and Harry Evans. Town briefly folded but were up and running again a few months later, and despite losing its top tag in town when all the other Derby sides started up, they kept going as an amateur club into the late 1890s.

The club were shown in a good light in 1882, when one of its players, who asked to remain anonymous, dived into the cold river Trent on 17 April and saved the life of a young girl. He had just left the Trent Bridge ground after playing for his team.

A revival of fortunes occurred in 1892/3 when Derby Town were Midland Alliance champions. They had won 16 of their 20 league matches with an impressive 69-13 goals tally. Several of the opposing sides were reserve sides of East Midland Football League sides. Other opponents included Notts Olympic, Sheffield, Long Eaton Rangers, Matlock, and Heanor Town. Another great season followed that, and they finished runners-up to Heanor Town, who had broken the league scoring record with 143 goals from just 26 games! The club at this time was steered by J. C. Bulmer (hon. sec) and C.

E. Birch-Thorpe. The club were using the Sitwell Arms at this time as their headquarters.

The Derby Town team for 1893/4 season which played in the Derbyshire League with neighbours Junction and Ilkeston was: C. F. Brentnall (goal); C. A. Gilbert and T. Stacey (fullbacks); W. Rose, J. Cox, T. Curtis (captain) (halfbacks); S. Mills, J. McLaughlin, H. Rose, G. Wright, H. Keel (forwards). They continued to play in the Derbyshire and Sheffield cup competitions. Strictly amateur, they gave away most of the gate revenue to charities, such as from their Grantham cup semi-final with Gainsborough Trinity in 1893.

References

Nottingham Evening Post 1880-1885
Nottingham Guardian 1882
Burnley Express 1882
Derby Daily Telegraph 1881
Sheffield Independent 1880
Sheffield Daily Telegraph 1877

Derby Town Played at the Racecourse County Ground

Elwells FC (Wednesbury)

Founded in 1869-1892 (reformed in 1883 and again briefly in 1890s)

A works team from the Elwells foundry by the Wednesbury Oval grounds. The company was later taken over by the Patent Shaft and Axletree Co (1840-1983) which had 3,000 employees at its Leabrook Road site.

Colours

1. scarlet shirts/white knicks as announced in the Wednesbury press to commence the 1881/2 season
2. light blue shirts after 1883

Team secretary – Frederick Allen

Elwells FC were predominantly at the team of the 1870s, who had the Wednesbury Oval as their home ground, which they leased out to the other Wednesbury clubs, and the B'ham FA for finals. They had a large workforce of several hundred to pick a team from, and later when the company moved into the town centre, and was taken over by Patent Shaft Co, had an even larger work pool to select from. At this early time, footballers were not tied either by contract or morals to one particular team, and although the other Wednesbury teams undoubtably shared players, Elwells team was only drawn from the company.

The Elwell family built the St. Paul's Church and created workers cottages for its mill workers. William Elwell was mayor of Wednesbury in 1787, and his family name was well-known in the town for generations.

Edward Elwells forge was famous in the district, with its huge chimney and procession of railway arches of the LNER railway spanning the two 25-acre pools upon which it was built in 1817 on leased land. Early advertisements in the Wednesbury newspapers show a mighty factory mill with several tall chimneys belching out black smoke. Edward later purchased the land outright in 1831 and developed the site into two mills fed by the little river Tame, a house, and thirteen workers' cottages.

The railway arches are still there today, spanning Elwells field (known as Wednesbury Oval), but across dry land since the pools were drained in the late 1860s. The two pools were very large, and were a well-known feature of the town, having been used for skating, fishing, and boating since 1804, and, again in 1855, when Elwell created his second pool around the foundry mill. Elwell moved his forge into the town centre in the 1860s, and the two large pools were drained, allowing the Wednesbury Oval to take shape as a large recreation area, although only the football and athletic ground were in any way developed, with a wide cinder running track around its very large (120 x 110 yards) football pitch which hugged the railway embankment and had an iron railing around its perimeter. The goal line at one end of the pitch ran parallel to the boundary wall on Forge Lane, and the touchline ran parallel to the railway embankment, still there today. Parts of the old wall still stand in 2012.

The ground was opened on 1 November 1880, and Elwells allowed it to be used (at a rent) by other football and athletic clubs. Wednesbury Old Athletic paid £15 a year to rent it. The running track, a later addition, was a 440-yard cinder oval, which was not banked.

Elwells subsequently became taken over by other larger companies, and their patented range of garden forks, shovels, and picks are known today under the Spear & Jackson brand, the remains of the large factory premises at the end of St. Paul's Lane* only being demolished circa 2007.

The team entered the Wednesbury, Birmingham, and Walsall cups, and generally gave a good account of themselves, only losing 1-2 to West Bromwich Albion in Dec 1881 at Four Acres in the Birmingham Cup, for example. They also beat a young Small Heath team 4-3 the following season so they were no mugs. Working in forges and steelworks would have made tough men of them.

They played in the B'ham senior Cup from 1877 to 1883 but never got past the 3rd round.

They came close to local success in reaching the final of the 1882 Walsall FA cup, but despite a spirited performance in front of 3,000 spectators, they were pipped 3-2 by Walsall's Swifts. The team that day was: Kenrick (goal); Davis and Nicholls (backs); T. Tonks, Frazier, Hayes (halfbacks); Kendrick, Styche, Cartwright, D. Tonks, and Waldron (forwards).

The team of 1879 was:

J. Addison (goal); backs: A. Tonks (captain) and J. Cooper; halfbacks: G. Nicholls and J. Doyle; Bailey, T. Tonks, J. Roberts, G. Kendrick, J. Banks, T. Gretton (forwards).

The above team defeated the West Bromwich Dartmouth by a record 12-1 on 1st March 1879. The same side also beat Tipton by 15-0 in the previous December, so, clearly, even as the town's '3rd' team, were a useful force. As can be seen, the Tonks and the Kenricks provided the mainstay of the side for some years, although the Tonks brothers also played for Wednesbury Old Athletic too.

The Tonks and Beasley families were also the mainstay of the Elwells cricket team in the 1870s.

For the away game with Walsall C. C. in August 1875, there were four Tonks brothers, two Kenricks, and three Bearsleys in the Elwells team.

Elwells trickled on throughout the 1880s in the Wednesbury cups, which, by then, had senior, junior, and school levels. They would sometimes play the big boys such as Walsall Town, but come off 6 or 8 goals to the worse. Elwells FC was quoted as having been disbanded in the Wednesbury press by 1885, but it seems they were restarted two years later but in a junior role; probably because all their best players had moved on or left the game due to being too old!

By 1887, Elwells were playing in the likes of the Walsall Junior Cup and other Junior Cups. They were playing these lesser games at the rather dilapidated Trapezium ground, as they no longer generated at crowd big enough to warrant using the Oval, which still belonged to them, but was rented out for the year to other teams.

In 1893, Elwells played the Old Athletic in a friendly on the 4th November and lost 0-3. This may have been a benefit game for a permanently 'crocked' player.

References

The Wednesbury Free Press
Walsall Observer
Fred Hackwood's *The History of Wednesbury*
Wednesbury and the Men Who Made It

* known as Forge Lane in Victorian times.

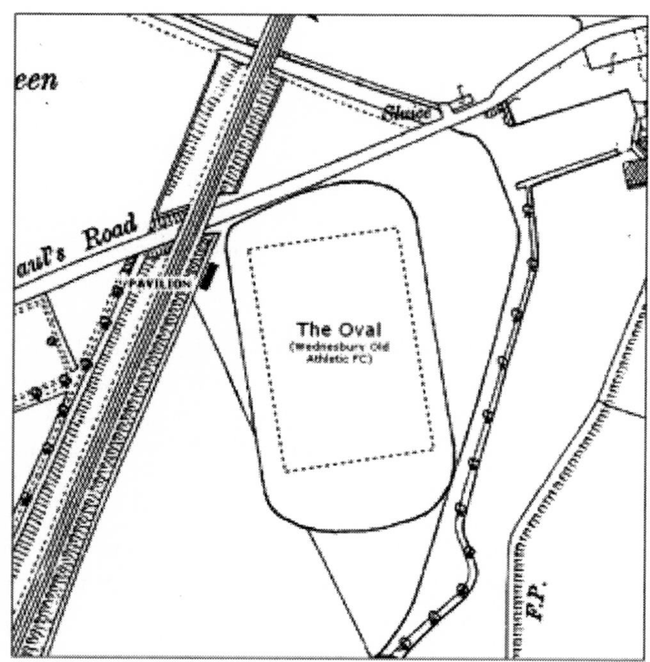

Wednesbury Oval-Home Of Birmingham Cup Finals

Great Bridge Unity FC

f.1878-1901 (at least)

Ground:
Horsley Football Ground, Railway Terrace, Horsely Fields*

Club Secretary:
Mr Doughty

Colours:

black and white hoops (1870s)
black and white stripes (1880s)

It was founded by workers from the Horsley Iron Company, which under one name or another had been there since 1789, occupying over 20 acres between Tipton Cemetery and Horseley Fields (road). The site had its own railway sidings, canal branch, and coal and timber yards and was virtually a self-contained community.

Famous throughout the world, they made iron bridges and girders for home and export to South America and Europe, including many of the world's most famous nineteenth century bridges, including much of the Suez Canal.

The Horseley Ironworks was in deepest Victorian Black Country, with collieries, open-cast mines, marl-pits, and heavy industry for neighbours, with the classic image of a sky full of smoke-belching chimneys for a backdrop to the constant noise from furnaces and steam hammers alongside the horse-drawn workings of the canal boats and railway sidings. It must have provided visiting teams from more salubrious areas quite a culture shock!

The football ground was at the side of the huge ironworks complex at Horseley Fields between Tipton and Great Bridge, which spanned both the Birmingham Canal Navigation (Dixon branch) and the junction of the Great Western and LNER railway tracks by Great Bridge station. Spacious, at 3.6 acres, the entrance was via Scott Street, which is still there today, although new houses were built exactly where the ground was, circa 2005. Workers in Railway Terrace would have had a free view into the ground. The old ground had been built over twice previously: firstly with the expansion factory of the

Ironworks, with a pipeworks factory of the site of one half of the pitch in 1934, then in modern times, a Railways distribution depot. Two other nearby grounds have been identified as possible grounds where football continued to be played at Horseley Fields/Great Bridge. At the rear of terraced houses on Clarks Grove, there used to be a sports ground** until the 1960s; there was also a football pitch just off Horseley Rd/Horseley Heath, which is now occupied by Dovecote Close. Another team, Horseley Heath Union Jacks, started up in the late 1890s and played until the First World War.

The 1878 Great Bridge side, which received Rushall Rovers on 19th October was:

Onions, Bolton, J. Turner, Bott, G. Turner, J. Powell, I. Powell, Edge, Lowry, A. Bolton. As you can see, they were a man short but still won by 1-0.

Very few records of anything to do with this team are to be found, although scant match reports against the various Walsall, West Bromwich, and Tipton teams continued to be sent to the Walsall newspapers throughout the 1880s. However, in 1887, they had their national claim to fame when they reached the 5th round of the English FA Cup, beating some useful local sides on the way before going down by just 0-2 to the strong Old Carthusians team which had been put on the reserve list for the invitations to the inaugural 1888 Football League by William McGreggor. As shown by their ability to defeat the strong Rushall Rovers team in 1878, the great Bridge side must have been very capable in their early days, but falling off the pace as we get to the 1890s. From results I have seen, they weren't very good away from home, suggesting that they weren't able to release men from work on Saturdays early enough to travel more than locally.

They entered the Birmingham Cup in 1883, having already played in the Wednesbury and Walsall cups. Sutton Coldfield put them out 3-0 after 2-2 at Horsley Fields in front of 300. They took a famous scalp in November 1885 when they beat Stafford Road by 1-0 but went out in the 3rd round 0-5 to Burslem Port Vale. Another good scalp was taken in the 2nd round of the 1877/8 competition when Derby Midland were dispatched 3-1. However, they found the Wolves too strong in the 3rd round and were trounced by 6-1. There was no disgrace in losing 3-6 to Wednesbury Old Athletic at the Oval in the 1st round of the 1888/9 cup as the Old Uns were having a revival of their old form. A long trip to Worcester in October 1889 proved well worth it as they beat the Rovers 4-1 to face another long trip to Kidderminster Harriers in round 2 at Aggborough. This time, however, they were soundly beaten by 8-2. Halesowen were beaten 3-1 to begin their

1890/1 Birmingham cup campaign, but it came to an abrupt end when Wednesbury Old Athletic put another six (without reply) past them in round 2. Great Bridge withdrew at the first hurdle of the cup in 1891, when drawn away to unknown Ladywood Conservatives; this must have been due to the fixture clashing with another cup tie on the same day, although Great Bridge could have done what several others had done before them and sent their reserve team, as they would probably have beaten them anyway.

Probably able to draw men from a large workforce at least ensured continuity of the side, but fielding the same side, week in and week out, is important too. Compare these two Unity team sheets for the same year – 1886 – the first side playing Derby Junction in February, and the second set of players meeting Cannock away in the October:

The February team was: Guest (goal); Rowley, Smith (backs); Millard, Clancey, Danks (halfbacks); White, Smith, Evans, Pittaway, Norman (forwards).

The October team was: Morris (goal); Styche, Lyons (backs); Burns, Beecham, Mason (halfbacks); Sowry, Colley, Worsey, Pittaway, Crabton (forwards). Only Pittaway appears in both matches. This almost random team line-up is one explanation for the inconsistent results of the smaller teams who stayed small for this very reason.

Unity's adventures in the FA Cup were short-lived, but 1887/8 saw them progress surprisingly far. They edged past Wolverhampton's fading pioneers, the Stafford Road, 2-1 in round 1 but had a convincing 5-2 win over Burton Swifts in the 2nd round, with goalkeeper Saunders in fine form. A close game with the useful Excelsior club from Aston saw Unity edge through 2-1, but the end of the road came when they were pipped by the same score at home to Bootle from Lancashire on 17th December 1887 in round 4. In 1888, Great Bridge Unity still had senior status, entering the West Bromwich and Walsall cups at that level. A measure of their ability was shown when they beat a useful – but not at their peak – Mitchell St. George's by 2-0 on Monday 30th April 1888, with the Unity defence gaining particular credit in the press report. Great Bridge became only one of the three teams to have stopped the Albion scoring against them in a match all season, when they played out a goal less draw at home on 16th May 1887. At a time when the football season was much shorter than it is today, the end of May seems rather late still to be playing ordinary matches; however, the Albion, with no cricket club to pester them for their ground back in the summer, went on playing until the third week of June!

Crowds ranged from two hundred to a thousand, depending on the attractiveness of the visitors, unlike today where the attendance varies according to the attractiveness of the home team!

By the early 1890s however, Great Bridge were a struggling team, finishing bottom of the Birmingham league despite scoring over 2 goals per game. The Walsall FA however were benevolent and still ranked them a senior team, according to their club representative, George Hughes, in 1887 (*Walsall Observer*). Most of their players worked and lived within a mile of the ground, on Horseley Road for example. Jem Bayliss' relatives were listed as living on Horsely Heath (road) and nearby Neptune Street and Providence Street.

Honours were few and far between, except minor local cups. They were beaten finalists in the 1888 Wednesbury Charity Cup when First Division West Bromwich Albion humiliated them 10-1 in front of 6,500 at the Stoney Lane ground on 21 May. Albion were at their peak by then and were one of the top four teams in England.

Great Bridge were founder members of the Birmingham & District League in 1889, and they spent most of the 1890s at that level.

They played in the Birmingham League from 1889 to 1892 but generally struggled in this company, and they were one of the biggest culprits in the League for failing to fulfil all their fixtures. Hawkins and Hill (both goalkeepers), Billingham, Roberts, White, Tomkiss, Surrell, and Stanford (centre) were their best players around 1890.

The club resigned from the League in 1892 and broke up. The team was resurrected the following year, as was commonplace with factory-based teams.

Their 1893 side was:

Brown (goal); Smith, Wilkes (backs); Gleeson, Burns, Colley (halfbacks); Horton, Smith, White, Holmes, Martin (forwards).

Their most famous players were: J. E. M. Bayliss (1863-1933) who came from Tipton, the Black Country's oldest team (f. 1872) and went to WBA as a centre forward.

George H. Cave went to West Bromwich Albion in 1896, aged 22, and was a popular fullback there, but, sadly, he died of pleurisy with pneumonia in 1901.

B. Styche went to Wednesbury Old Athletic in 1887.

Great Bridge lost several key players in 1891, and no doubt, the team went downhill with it. Danks and Norman went to Wednesbury Old Athletics, and Job White and Tom Hawkins (goalkeeper) went to Walsall Town-Swifts. White was apparently something of a bad boy, having just served a twelve-month ban from the Walsall FA for 'rough play' and turning out for both Great Bridge and the West Brom Albion – this at a time when the game was full of beaten teams appealing to the next month's regionals FA committee to have the game replayed due to ineligible players or short games due to bad light. Forward Martin too was suspended by the Walsall FA in 1890 for foul language and rough play, but it must be remembered these were hard, tough men whose football reflected their working life and conditions. Even 'clean' games from the 1890s would be considered as rough by today's standards, so rough play back then probably meant fisticuffs on the pitch!

FA cup history	1st Round	2nd Round	3rd Round	4th Round
1887/8	2-1 Stafford Road	5-2 Burton Swifts (A)	2-1 B'ham Excelsior (A)	Bootle 1-2

Scott Street, once a short cul-de-sac leading to a railway footbridge into the Horsley Ironworks, now occupies the spot of the ground.

Circa 1920, a new team called Great Bridge FC was started up based at the Seven Stars pub on Tame Road, and they played on a field behind it.

References

Walsall Observer
'The Old Uns' the story of Wednesbury Old Athletic, Steve Carr
Worcester Chronicle

* spelt as Horsley or Horseley
** also see Tipton FC

Great Bridge

Great Bridge FC came from Horsley Ironworks Co.

Hednesford Swifts FC

f.1897-1903

Ground:
Cross Keys Hotel

Hednesford is a small town just north of Cannock, surrounded by the famous Cannock Chase forest, and was predominantly a coal-mining town. These hard-working coal miners and colliers would live in rows of terraced houses built by their employers in the high part of town, and they would enjoy their few hours of free time, playing and improving their footballing skills on the many fields adjoining the Cannock Chase Forest.

Hednesford boasted two top teams for a decade – the Swifts and Town teams. As a teenager, I lived across the road from the Hednesford Town ground at the rear of the Cross Keys P. H. in the Old Hednesford district, so called because the original village was in the large dip between the villages of Heath Hayes and Rugeley. When mining became the villages' main business in mid-Victorian times, hundreds of miners' terraced houses were built on the Rugeley side on high ground, and thus, the village became a small town, and the town effectively moved half a mile north. I would go every Saturday to cheer on Hednesford because my father's business partner was Laurie Percival, their leading goalscorer. This was in the late 1960s. I always thought that Hednesford had played there since their foundation, 1880, as shown on the team shirts.

However, my new research shows that there was the Swifts' side playing at the Cross Keys ground, whilst rivals, the Town, played at the Anglesey ground in 'high town'. The Anglesey was a large Regency mansion house, later a hotel to the nearby railway station, with a football ground right behind it, just as did the Cross Keys, which was a sixteenth-century coaching inn on the Lichfield to Stafford route. The Anglesey had been built by one Edmund Peel of Fazeley near Tamworth. A wealthy landowner, he built it to house his many racehorses in the 1830s, since the Hednesford Hills were said to be the finest place on which to train racehorses in the Midlands. It became a hotel in 1864. The football ground was merely a patch of land fenced in with corrugated iron fencing, and thus the ground and the team took on the early nickname of 'the Tins'. The home crowd used to 'drum' the sheets with both hands and feet, creating a noisy wall of sound. Or as the local residents put it: a racket!

The Tin-men entered the Birmingham Cup from 1887 and played in the Birmingham Combination during the 1880s. In 1893, they got to the B'ham Cup semi-final, only to be thrashed 12-1 by Wolverhampton Wanderers. Their only honour then was in winning the Staffordshire Senior Cup in 1897/8.

Different sources disagree on football history in Hednesford; it is generally believed that two local sides, Hill Top FC who played on Reservoir Road (near the raceway), joined forces with Red & Whites FC from West Hill and formed Hednesford Anglesey. This would have been the 1880, which appears on the current Hednesford Towns' shirts. The team, sometimes known as Hednesford Anglesey instead of Town, was forced to move out at the end of 1903 due to a debt of £40 (£4,000 today) presumably to the hotel itself. A local councillor offered them a field behind his Cross Keys Inn, and so the team moved a mile across town.

The Cross Keys Inn was built in 1746 and was used as a staging post for horse-drawn mail and long-journey stagecoaches because it was on the original Holyhead to London stage route. It was reputed to have been used by Dick Turpin. But then again, where hasn't? In the early 1800s, it was notoriously known for cockfighting and bare-knuckle fighting, long after both had been made illegal in England. It was a place where large wagers were made and property and fortunes were won and lost. In 1860, the owner John Wilkins kept fine racehorses at Hednesford Hills, and in 1861, his horse 'Jealousy' won the Grand National.

Now a team called Hednesford Swifts were playing from at least as early as 1898, for they were playing in the Walsall and District League along with our Hednesford Town in that year. The year 1898/9 wasn't a bad year for the Swifts, finishing 5th behind champions Willenhall Pickwick, Bilston, Wednesbury, and rivals Hednesford Town. However, mostly, it was the Swifts who finished near the bottom, whilst the Town generally held a top 4 position. They entered the local Wednesbury, Wolverhampton, Cannock Forester, and Staffordshire cups. Swifts were already playing at the Cross Keys when their ousted rivals Town moved in by request. Since Hednesford Swifts left the Walsall League in 1903, not to be heard of again, this strongly points to Swifts amalgamating, or being absorbed by the 'Tin-men', and Hednesford Town became one team, briefly called simply Hednesford, later re-instating the 'Town' tag. The Town played in white, but no trace can be found for the Swift colours. Match reports from the 1890s often make reference to the fact that the Cross Keys ground was plagued by fog; several games had to be abandoned, or played short minutes. The ground was in a low dip between

Heath Hayes and high Hednesford, had a brook on two sides and there was a canal wharf close by. Players gave it the nickname of 'the Basin'.

Hednesford Swifts generally played in the Walsall and District league in the 1890s, never much making any impact. In fact, from 1898 till 1903, they always finished in the bottom three. In 1900/01 season, they had 2 points deducted for playing ineligible players, not the first time they had been in front of the authorities. Swifts were often in trouble with the football authorities, as their players had developed a reputation for bad language and fighting, or leaving the pitch in a sulk after contentious goals were given against them. On 10 January 1900, they had to scratch from an away fixture to Willenhall Pickwick because they couldn't afford to hire a brake to ferry the team there.

This team drew 1-1 with Stafford Rangers in the semi-finals of the Cannock Chase Foresters Cup on 3 March 1900 in front of a 1,200 crowd at the Cross Keys.

Heath (goal); Manley, Ferguson (backs); Smith, Amos, Bowen (halfbacks); Joesbury, Stone, McGrath, Ingram, Bridgart (forwards).

In a thrilling replay in Stafford, they went down 4-6, the following week. The Foresters Cup was a charity competition set up by the Ancient Order of Foresters, a sort of local masonic greenpeace organisation.

In 1901/2 season, they again finished bottom but one despite only conceding 5 more goals than they scored. The team was much changed, with several men moving between the two Hednesford teams and Cannock Town. The 1901/2 team generally comprised the following players:

Talbot (goal), Dave Morris, J. Spencer, W. Vickers, Bridgart, W. McGrath, G. Beard, E. Battle, Nicholls, and Evans.

Orlando Evans was their popular captain, and there is a picture of him in the Centenary of Hednesford book by Dave Shaw, showing Orlando Evans in the Town team of 1899/90 season, outside the Anglesey Hotel. This must have meant that he played for both Swifts and Town simultaneously. Evans later signed for Aston Villa and played with them during their golden era. The Swifts' manager at this time was a Thomas Stokes, and their team was under the sponsorship of a Mr Corbett. Battle and Evans were their best forwards. Due to their rivalry with the Town club up at the Anglesey ground, few players transferred between the two clubs, but one such man was centre half Jack Morris who went from Town to Swifts in 1901.

During 1901/02, both Hednesford teams and the Cannock teams got together to form a small Cannock League with Bridgetown Amateurs and Brownhills Albion.

The year 1903 seems to have been their last season. They had to seek re-election to the Walsall League but were turned down, which led to their demise. They had been in trouble more than once for poor discipline: in the match on 22nd November away to Willenhall Pickwicks, they lost 0-6, and two of the Hednesford Swifts players started fighting with Picks' men. The crowd joined in and a free-for-all ensued. Sounds like this Swifts team were a bit of a rough lot all round! According to the Hednesford Town Centenary handbook, when the Swifts disbanded in 1903, several of the old Swifts' men joined the Hednesford Town side at the Anglesey ground. The 1903 *Cannock Advertiser* lists these men as: Wilkes, Bird, Stone, Jukes, Bowers, Hayward, and R. Benn. This puts paid to the possibility that the two teams amalgamated, or that the Swifts were absorbed into the Tin-men. Despite the fact that the Swifts were no more by August 1903 – not reported or commented upon in the press – a Swifts' man, also called Corbett, was suspended for fourteen days with a fine by the Cannock FA for persistent violent conduct on 19 September, a common trait it seems, of the Swifts.

The Swifts had always been poor cousins to the Town club, and the newspapers treated them accordingly so. The *Cannock Advertiser* of the period gave equal top billing to Cannock and Hednesford Town, and the Swifts' reports were lumped in with other local sides such as Bridgetown Amateurs, Brownhills Albion, and Cheslyn Hay Village. In criticising the Swifts' side in 1902/3 season, the *Cannock Advertiser* said the team 'lacked combination and were erratic and selfish in front of goal' and 'that when will they learn that one man cannot beat a whole defence on his own when the pass is the better option', and concluded that the Swifts would 'fall to the lower ranks unless they obtained a better manager'.

A year later, councillor Noah Corbett cleared the debt incurred by the Town club at the Anglesey Hotel, on the condition that they moved to his Cross Keys Hotel ground, now left vacant by the demise of the Swifts team.* I would suggest that it was councillor Corbett who had disbanded the Swifts, with their bad record and crowds in the mid-hundreds, and realised that he would be financially better off if he switched his patronage to the better Town side who drew crowds of around 1500. He would benefit from the revenue generated by fans and players at the Cross Keys which he owned, unlike the Anglesey Hotel which he didn't. The Cross Keys ground, by the way, became known as the 'Basin', apparently because it was low down and prone to getting waterlogged. Entry was via two turnstiles built into a wall to the left of the rear of the hotel, and they were still there in the 1970s when I used to go there each Saturday as I only lived across the road. The exit point was through the old stables block on the right of the pub, which is now a restaurant.

As previously stated, the men of Hednesford and Cannock had hard lives down the pit and often didn't have time (or the money) to heat a bathtub of water and scrub up clean. Frequently they would turn out on the football pitch with black faces! They became known as 'Noah's Niggers'. I know it is no longer appropriate to the modern age to put into print, but, regrettably, that was their harmless nickname at the turn of the twentieth century. The men would also be prone to a high risk of serious injuries whilst at work, and often a team would be short of best players due to broken or injured limbs sustained at the coalface. One such example was when the two Hednesford clubs met in the local derby in 1897, Town man Palmer had to leave the field because he had severe knee pains which he sustained the previous day down the pit.

During the first quarter of the twentieth century, Hednesford FC enjoyed reasonable success in the Birmingham & District League, or the Walsall League, usually finishing in the top 5, playing teams such as Cannock, Rushall Olympic, and Wednesbury Old Athletic. However, all through this period, they suffered the same fate as all other second-tier clubs, in that all their best players were sold to the leading professional sides to keep the club's finances afloat. Jack Devey (one of the famous five Devey brothers), Steve Smith and Orlando Evans all went to the Villa, whilst Charlie Crossley went to Everton via Portsmouth. The barren decade of the 1930s saw the team's eventual demise; financial hardships were everywhere. Blackened coalface miners and pitmen, who used to work till 2 p.m. on a Saturday and turn out to watch or play for the team by 4 p.m., were now on short time or out of work. The club stuttered on until one day in 1938 when they couldn't find the £20 to fulfil an away fixture. They resigned from the Birmingham League and folded.

A year later in 1939, a new club was restarted at the Cross Keys, and this is the team which plays today at their new Keys Park ground, built on the site of the old Hednesford brickworks halfway between Hednesford and Heath Hayes. Sadly, the 120-year-old Cross Keys ground was sold off for new housing and demolished circa 2000, and Crossley Drive and Keys Close now occupy the spot where the pitch used to be. Crossley Drive virtually runs along the halfway line. Fortunately, the eighteenth century Cross Keys Inn is still there as it has listed building status.

References

Cannock Advertiser
Hednesford Town FC
Cross Keys Inn, Hednesford
David Shaw, Hednesford FC official historian

* August 1903. This would make it September or October when the Tin-men moved into the Cross Keys to start the new 1903/4 season.

Cross Keys Ground Hednesford Swifts

Hednesford's Cross Keys Inn Circa 1899

Kidderminster Olympic FC

f.1887-1890

Colours
red and white stripes

Ground
Chester Road cricket ground (still there today used by the Victoria C. C – see photo)

Started up in 1887 as a rival team to Kidderminster Harriers, who had been founded the year before them.

Olympic moved into the new Chester Road ground on 8th December 1888, which had been the town's cricketing ground for some years. The Harriers, who briefly played at the Chester Road cricket ground, being an offshoot of that club, moved into their new Aggborough ground.

Drawing crowds of around 2,000, the derby game drew upwards of 7,000 – a considerable percentage of the small town's population, famous of course for its carpets and mills. The opening game for the Aggborough ground saw football league neighbours Walsall Town-Swifts attract a 3,000 crowd. The stadium had a banked cinder athletics track around the oval perimeter, and a single wooden grandstand held about 700 of its claimed 15,000 capacity.

The Chester Road sports ground today is virtually unchanged from a century ago. The original high brick wall and lane to the pavilion is still there and reminds one of the Aston Unity ground near Villa park. The playing surface is near flat, and the grass is kept very short. If it was like that in the 1890s, it would have enhanced the Olympics' close passing game, making it easy to understand how a lesser team could be given the runaround on such a wonderful arena. On my visit there in August 2012, I found it tricky to find the ground, as the long high brick wall and the lack of any advertised entrance caused me to drive straight past and have to double back. I nearly had a day out at Stourport instead! A wooden painted board declares that this is the Victoria cricket club, and an unmade road leads to the clubhouse and car park. Tall pine trees surround the picturesque ground, which is altogether very well kept and neat. A walk on to the central area illustrated a firm well-drained ground, and this would have been key to Olympics' pretty passing game. It was hard to imagine the old banked cinder running track, as the whole enclosed field was grassed over, although there was ample room for spectators. The Olympic's claims for a 15,000 capacity seemed quite probable.

Olympic were accused of professionalism by the FA, but they made no attempt to hide it.

Impressively winning the inaugural Birmingham & District League, remaining unbeaten with 19 wins and 2 draws and a remarkable 85-9 goal tally, the Olympic were never actually awarded the trophy because many fixtures in that inaugural season went unplayed, although it wasn't possible for anyone to overtake them. They were so far ahead of the pack that they crushed second-placed Smethwick Carriage Works 8-0 in the home fixture! Technically, being in existence for only three seasons before their amalgamation, they could lay claim to have been unbeaten for all their existence!

In one of the biggest scores of all time in Midlands' senior football history, the Olympic annihilated a Hereford team by 25-0 in front of 2,000 at the Chester Road cricket ground in October of 1889. Hereford were playing in the Shropshire league at this time as there was no county set-up in Herefordshire back then. Olympic followed up this Birmingham Cup result with a 9-0 over another Shropshire League side Ludlow in the 2nd round, before bowing out to Walsall in the last eight.

Kidderminster Harriers folded briefly in 1888, and Olympic carried on through talks of a merger. They finally merged with Harriers in 1890. The new team combined the red stripes of the Olympic with the white shirts of Harriers for a red and white halves, black shorts kit. Oddly, the Harriers name was resurrected two years later, but it was the new Kidderminster FC which carried on to today.

In their last year, the Olympic took a famous scalp when they defeated the Casuals (London) by 5-0, only a week after the Casuals had made a draw at Derby County.

This team defeated Wednesbury Villa 8-1 on Saturday 27 April to bring the 1888/9 season to a close.

Tyler (goal); Oldershaw and Palmer (backs); Knowles, Robinson, J. Smith (halfbacks); Christmas, Griggin, H. Smith, Hodgetts, Scott (forwards).

The team of 1890/1 season was: Baynton (goal); Oldershaw and Palmer (backs); Baird, Benton, Lawson (halfbacks); Joynes, Dooley, Richards, Mason, Haynes (forwards).

Comparing the above two sides only a year apart, it can be seen that only the pair of backs remains in the club's final season before the amalgamation with Harriers.

Looking at the early results of matches just after the amalgamation, I would say that the new combined team did not gel very well, and they were not as good a combination as the Olympic were. The combined team started to lose matches, something which the Olympic contingent had never been used to.

To find the Olympic (and Harriers') old ground, take the A456 Birmingham Road out of Kidderminster. Turn right after half a mile on to the A449 Chester Rd North. The cricket ground is at the corner with Offmore Lane, an unadopted road which leads to the clubhouse and car park.

References

The history of the Birmingham League web site
Kidderminster Victoria cricket club
Worcestershire Chronicle 1891

Kidderminster Olympic's Chester Rd Ground

Leicester Fosse FC

f.1884-1919

Grounds

1. Field on the Fosse Road (Westleigh Avenue now occupies the pitch)
2. Victoria Park 1884-1887 and 1888-1889
3. Belgrave sports ground 1887-8
4. Mill Lane 1889-1891
5. County cricket ground, Aylestone Park, Grace Road 1890
6. Filbert Street – from 1891 (then called Walnut Street)

Colours

1. white shirts, navy (1884-1885)
2. black shirt with blue sash (1884-1886)
3. chocolate and blue halves (1886-1890)
4. white shirt, navy (1890-1899)
5. blue shirt, white except 1900/01 light blue,
6. dark blue, 1901/02
7. dark blue shirt with light blue sleeves (1899-1915)

Nickname – the 'Fossils' or the 'Filberts'

Founded in the spring of 1884 by a group of old boys from Wyggeston Grammar School, and boys who met at the Emmanuel Church in Park Street, they took the name of the Fosse Road into their title. Fosse means a group of trees or small wood, often at the edge of a bigger forest.

The youths agreed to each subscribe 1/6d (on shilling and sixpence = 7.5p) in order to purchase a football and a basic set of goalposts.

They began by playing in a field just off the Fosse Road,* but by November 1884, they had moved to Victoria Park (A6, London Road) which was their home for most of their first five years. Their earliest opponents were their old school team, Mill Hill House, Syston Fosse, St. Mary's, or Melbourne Hall. They only lost 2 games in the 1884/5 season, although they were forced to play some games under Rugby Rules in order to secure matches. Most of those teams all played in the park too. They thought they had found a better quality ground when they moved to the Belgrave bicycle and athletic ground in 1887 (now Cossington Rec), but found that they had to use the White Hart public house as their changing room, which was nearly a mile away! However, after one season, they found that their rivals, the Leicester Rugby Club, had outbid them for the tenancy, and so they had to return to the Victoria Park again. More wanderings found them spend two seasons at the Mill Lane ground, with some games played at the county cricket ground on Grace Road, Aylestone. Throughout this period, they were having a constant battle to draw the public away from the town's rugby team, which was drawing large crowds, usually ten times the numbers for football. However, what the Fosse boys had, which helped them through difficult early days, was a lot of ambition. They outlasted other town rivals such as Leicester Wanderers, Town and Association clubs. A clever move in 1888, in their last season playing at Victoria Park, they captured the services of a professional player, one Harry Webb (no relation to Sir Cliff Richard!) from Stafford Rangers for the princely sum of 2/6d (12.5p) a week, plus travelling costs. This small move was enough to pave the way forward and acted as a boost for the local boys, and no doubt a few dozen more locals turned out, curious to see what a professional football player looked like!

Leicester RFC, with their following in the thousands, had won the battle for the Belgrave sports ground, and they eventually settled in Welford Road in 1892. Even today, Leicester Tigers can outdraw Leicester City FC, as they are England's best attended rugby club with attendances often above 20,000, and the ground is frequently a sell-out.

The final resting place for the Fosse club, in Walnut Street, had been spotted several months previously, but the work being carried out to turn the field into a proper enclosed ground from which the team could charge an entrance gate meant the ground wasn't ready in time for the 1890 season. If you don't recognise the name of Walnut Street, it was soon renamed the Filbert Street ground, and when the new Leicester City club was launched in 1916 after the War had ended, they remained there for 111 years, until the move to the new Walker Stadium.

Fosse joined the Midland Counties League in 1891, became one of the better sides, and got elected up into the new Division 2 of the Football League in 1894. Promotion to the 1st Division followed in 1907/8, but they were relegated a year later. The year 1891 saw them play their first game at Filbert Street, against Melton Swifts.

James Thraves and Horace Bailey were Fosse's main goalkeepers throughout the 1890-1910 period, with 220 appearances between them. Bailey became Fosse's first international player. Several other players were long-served, and all the following men played over a hundred games for the Fosse:

Teddy King (236), George Swift (200), Bob Pollock (200), Walter Robinson (194), Billy Bannister (150), Jimmy Brown (153), Jimmy Durant (153), Shirley Hubbard (154), Arthur Randle (133), Johnny McMillan (131), Harry Bailey (125), James Blessington (118), Billy Dorrell (116), Richard Jones (113), and Fred Shinton (101).

McMillan, Brown, and Pollock were Scottish, and Richard Jones was Welsh, but all the others were Englishmen. Freddy Shinton (1883-1923) was a prolific goalscorer, with 58 league and cup goals in his 101 games, more than 1:2 ratio. He was sold to Bolton Wanderers for a massive £1,000 in 1910 but returned soon after. By the end of 1911, he was playing with Wednesbury Old Athletic in the Midland League! McMillan (1871-1941) with 48 and Dorrell with 47 were Fosse's next leading goal-getters. McMillan came from Derby County in 1896 and went on to help Small Heath gain promotion in 1901 by scoring 13 goals in their last 13 league games. Teddy King was fourteen years with the club, from 1914 to 1920.

In 1894, the Fosse recorded their biggest ever victory when they crushed Notts Olympic 13-0 in an FA Cup qualifying round. This was their first season in the Football League Division 2, and they finished a respectable 4th place. In 1898/9, they managed 3rd place, not quite enough for promotion. From 1900 to 1905, they fell back into mid-table positions, and it wasn't until the 1906/7 season, when a 3rd place finish gave them hope. The following year, they finished as runners-up and gained promotion into the First Division, but the glory was brief, as they came straight back down again, conceding 102 goals in their 38 matches, including a record 0-12 defeat to Nottingham Forest. They remained in the Second Division from 1909 until the end of the First World War, when they actually went insolvent and the club was wound up. At the resumption of national football after the end of the Great War, a new club, Leicester City, was formed, which leads us to the current team of today.

In the 1896/7 season, they entered the Birmingham Cup. By this time, however, virtually all the other clubs had been going for around twenty years and were more advanced than they. This was amply demonstrated when they were crushed 8-3 away to Walsall on Monday 7 December at the Saddlers' new Hilary Street ground (later to be renamed Fellows Park). Despite exemption to the competition proper, due to their league status, Fosse barely made it past the 2nd round; Wolves beat them 3-1 at home in the following season in front of 2,000, and Burslem Port Vale trounced them 5-0 in the 1st round of 1898/0. Just 500 people were at their Cobridge Athletic ground on Monday 19th December. Aston Villa ended their hopes in the 1899/1900 competition when they won 3-2 at Filbert Street on Monday 15th January. Just 2,500 turned out on a cold winter weekday night, but, by this time (1900), the Birmingham Cup had fallen from its high position, mainly due to the FA Cup and the Football League.

During all this time, they had of course been playing in the FA Cup, but until the 1909/10 season, had never got past the 2nd round, and indeed frequently not past the qualifying rounds. However, in 1910, Fosse got to the quarter-finals of the cup. They won solidly 4-1 away at Birmingham in round 1, had a narrow 3-2 home win over Bury (who were in the First Division then) in the 2nd round, and then another close game with Leyton (Orient) 1-0 in round 3. In the 4th round, they came up against the best team in the country, Newcastle United, and went out by 0-3. Newcastle went on to win the cup, beating Barnsley 2-0 in the replayed final at Crystal Palace, after the first game was a 1-1 draw.

The continued growth of Fosse from a schoolboy's team into a First Division club was predominantly down to a lack of competition from other clubs in the town. The rugby game, true, was more popular both then and now, but unlike elsewhere (notably Aston, Burton, Derby) where there were too many clubs clammering for a share of the public, Fosse had few rivals in a thriving and expanding town based on the lace and shoe industries. The public could concentrate on following one principal association and one principal rugby team. Having dropped the word *Fosse* from their title after the First World War, Leicester City are now, in the second decade of the twenty-first century, toying with the idea of re-instating the word which described their origins into their title once again.

Filbert Street stadium, once called the City Stadium, was demolished in 2003 and is now a residential accommodation for the university student population.

References

BBC Leicester Radio
Of Fossils and Foxes, Smith & Taylor, 2001
Football Club History Database

* possibly for only one game against other teams

Leicester Fosse

Long Eaton Rangers

f.1882-1899

Birmingham FA representatives:
Mr W. H. Watts

Colours
chocolate and blue (probably halves which became popular in the mid-1880s)

Grounds

1. pitch opposite side of road to Rec ground (Recreation Street)
2. Recreation ground (during 1884-1899) Station Street
3. Tythe Barn Lane during 1886

Honours
Derbyshire Challenge Cup winners 1891, finalists 1887, 1892

Rangers were founder members of the Football Combination in 1888, also founder members of the Football Alliance 1889.

They joined the Midland League in 1890 till 1899. Along with Derby St. Luke's and Derby Town, they co-founded the Derbyshire FA.

Usual opponents from their Midland League years included: Sheffield, Leek, Gainsborough Trinity, Derby Junction, Derby Midlands, Lincoln, Staveley, and Burton Wanderers.

They finished runners-up in 1889/90, two points behind Gainsborough Trinity. Sheffield United finished 4th!

Long Eaton played in the FA Cup from 1883 to 1898, but usually lost in the 1st round.

The Recreation ground was opened in 1884 and developed for use to everything from bicycle races, athletics, archery, football, cricket, and later, after the 1920s, for greyhound racing and speedway. It was remarkable for its very ornate two-tier ornate iron and wooden grandstand (see web site photo). The town railway station was only a few hundred yards along the same street, so ground access to visiting teams was good. Inevitably, Long Eaton Stadium was sold off for housing development, and in 2007, work started on a new housing estate. Grange Drive, once one of the stadium entrance points, is now overgrown at where it met the field, blocking any footway access. The long continuous brick wall all along Station Road is still mostly in situ at the time of writing.

Long Eaton went through 1882 and 1883 unbeaten at home, and their reputation went before them when they played Staffordshire sides, although due to the lower standard of sides in the East Midlands at that time, it may have been a false crown, for a Wolves team, who had only been formed virtually by schoolchildren five years previously, beat them 4-1 at Dudley Road. From 1883, they entered the Birmingham Cup as well as the Derbyshire and Leamington cups. They won 5-0 at Ashbourne in the 1st round of the B'ham Cup, but then were beaten 1-0 at home by the useful Excelsior FC from Aston. In 1885, they won 1-0 at Derby Junction and met the powerful Mitchell St. George's of Cape Hill Brewery in round 2. The first game at the Recreation ground was a 2-2 draw, but the Dragons were too strong in the replay and won another good game by 4-2 in front of a measly 500 crowd at the Aston Lower Grounds. In the 1886 competition, Rangers got past Derby Midland by 2-1 and were lucky enough to get a bye in round 2. The 3rd round saw two games against Aston Unity. After a 2-2 draw at home, the visitors refused to play extra time (probably due to bad light), so the replay took place in Aston a week later. It was 0-0 at full time, and the Rangers nicked an overtime goal to go into the 4th round for the first time. Drawn away to Darlaston, an old Black Country club founded in 1874 and still at their original heavily sloping ground, they won, but as usual, Darlaston, in all-white, claimed that Rangers played an ineligible player. A replay was ordered, back at Darlaston, and Rangers again won, by 2-0 to march in to semi-finals. They were drawn against Small Heath, and the venue – as with all matches after the quarter-final – was the Aston Lower Grounds. Small Heath must have felt they were almost playing at home, since their ground was only three miles away. A disappointing crowd of less than 700 saw a close game which ended 2-2. Yet another replay for Rangers nine days later on a Monday night of 21st March saw them beat the Heathens 2-0 to reach the final.

They would play West Bromwich Albion at Villa's Wellington Road ground, chosen for its capability to hold upwards of 10,000. A rather pathetic 500 turned out on 7th May 1887 to see a shock result, as Long Eaton's George Winfield scored the only goal of the game to stun the heavy favourite and their Albionite fans and win the Birmingham Cup. This triumph usually accorded the winners with the title of best team in the Midlands, but the formation of the new Football League was being discussed at the time, and Long Eaton were certainly not one of the Midland sides on the invitation list.

Rangers also tasted disappointment in the final of the Derbyshire Challenge Cup final of 1887, when Staveley beat them 2-0.

Back in the Birmingham Cup, they got to the 4th round in the following year (1888), before a disaster at Stoke saw them ship 7 goals. On Christmas Eve 1888, they did very well to win 2-1 at Cape Hill in front of a stunned 3,000 Mitchell St. George's crowd, with finalists Wolves putting them out 3-1 in the 3rd round, another decent showing against a League side.

They did well to reach the 1st round proper of the 1888/9 FA Cup where they narrowly lost 2-3 away to Alliance side Birmingham St. George's, who went on to the last 8.

The start of the 1890s saw Rangers reach the Derbyshire Challenge Cup final two years running. In 1891, they beat Derby Midland 2-1 to win the trophy and returned to defend it the following year but were beaten by the rapidly rising Derby County.

Their ten seasons in the Midland League was a set of inconsistent years. Finishing bottom the first year (1890), leaking in 73 goals in 22 games, they were runners-up the following season! Ninth followed by tenth, and then a reasonable sixth place came in 1894, although they lost more games than they won. The years from 1895 to 1897 were their best years, when they finished 4th and 3rd in their 28-game programme. The 1897/8 season saw them back in the bottom half again in 8th place, and when the League was expanded to 14 teams in 1898/9, Rangers finished bottom but one in 13th place.

The club went bankrupt at the end of 1899, and the ground was sold off and modified into an all-purpose sporting venue for greyhound and speedway racing.

Had they managed to remain solvent, and with modest growth, LER might have been perhaps another Nottingham Forest or Leicester City.

Long Eaton played in the FA Cup from 1888 until 1897, but by which time, the entries had grown so large that half the country's teams had to play off in a qualifying competition of up to 5 rounds, just to get to the 1st round proper. By 1890, the FA Cup was beginning to be dominated by the Football League sides. Their record is as follows:

1888/9	1st round proper	2-3	Birmingham St. George's (A)	
1890/1	4th Qualifying	2-1	Rotherham (H)	1st round proper 1-2 Wolverhampton Wand.
1894/5	4th Qualifying	1-1 0-3	Chesterfield (H) Chesterfield (A)	
1896/7	4th Qualifying	1-2	Ilkeston (A)	
1897/8	5th Qualifying	2-0	Ilkeston (H)	1st round proper 0-1 Gainsborough Trinity (H)

Their team of 1886/7 which confounded the experts and defeated the Albion 1-0 in the Birmingham Cup final on Villa's old Perry Barr ground was:

F. Start (goal); J. Wiseman and D. Smith (backs); J. Orchard, Plackett, B. Stevenson (halfbacks); forwards: G. Winfield,* W. Smith, T. Vesey, J. Smith, T. Hardy* (goalscorer).

To find the site of the old Long Eaton stadium, follow signs to the railway station, but continue along Station Road, under the bridge, and the site is all the land to the left, before Grange Primary School. It went all the way back to the A6005 Nottingham Road.

References

Derbyshire County FA web site
Long Eaton Library
The History of the Birmingham Senior Cup, Steve Carr, 2004
Charles Alcock football annuals 1905

Lozells FC (Birmingham)

f. unknown – possibly circa 1885

Honours

Birmingham Combination champions 1894/5
Birmingham Junior Cup winners 1894/5

Ground
the Grove Hotel ground, Oxhill Road, Handsworth

Birmingham FA representatives:
Messrs J. Tillotson and A. G. Homer

Lozells FC, a short-lived amateur team from the north Birmingham district of the same name, rose to prominence briefly in the mid-1890s. They are not to be confused with Lozells Villa who were a different club.* I cannot trace the founding year for the team, but football was certainly being played at the Grove Ground by 1884. They reached the Birmingham Junior Cup final in three out of four years during 1894-97. They also won the Birmingham Combination in its third year of existence, 1895. Another rival team, Soho Villa, had taken the inaugural title; no doubt these two sides shared players. Aston Villa founding figure William McGreggor worshipped for forty years at the St. Andrew's congregation church in Lozells, directly facing the ground on the Oxhill Road. It is known that he helped the Lozells FC become established. Of their two representatives to the Birmingham FA, Tillotson went on to become the vice-president of the Association in 1887. Their first ever Junior cup tie, in 1887, was against Packington, a team who would later reach two finals. In February 1891, their forwards, C. Harley and Arthur Allen, were chosen to play for the Birmingham FA team against Leicestershire FA at Coventry.

They beat unknown Park Mills (a junior team from Aston Manor) 2-1 in 1894 to wrest the Junior trophy from the fast rising Singers FC from Coventry, who were also riding the crest at the time. They had beaten Willenhall Pickwicks in the semi-final 1-0 in a replay after the first game was drawn 2-2 at Molyneux. They came close to retaining the trophy in 1895, but Willenhall Pickwicks beat them 4-1 after a drawn first final. Two years later, they were back in the final again, but narrowly lost 1-2 to Bilston United.

The Lozells–Handsworth district, being close to the football-mad Aston Manor, was also a flourishing footballing district. Most churches in the area had their own football teams by 1890. St. Paul's in Lozells, alone had five teams, no less.

Their ground was said to have been the Grove Tavern ground. There is a pub on the corner of Grove Lane and Oxhill Road, which was built in 1891, called the Grove Tavern, so ties in nicely with the rise of the football team. Yet again, we come across the pattern of a corner pub having a football or cricket ground on land behind it. No doubt, when the pub was being built, perhaps in the 1870s, the wasteland was so cheap, it was sold as a 5-acre parcel.

Most people would call this location the Handsworth Wood area. Even today, there is a large area behind the pub where the football ground was. Another telling factor is that St. Andrew's Church is across the road. This is the church which William McGreggor worshipped at for over forty years; McGreggor helped to launch the Lozells club. This seems enough to me to say that this is where Lozells FC did play. The O.S. map for 1913 confirms my investigation; that behind the Grove Hotel, as it was then called, there were a cricket ground and a football ground, separated by a narrow lane, Laurel Grove. Each field had its own pavilion. The Grove ground was also used by other local minor teams, including rivals Lozells Villa and Handsworth. Transport was excellent: the tram stopped right outside, from both the city centre and West Bromwich. The horse-drawn tram from the city had been installed in 1885 and was electrified by 1906. My site visit to the old Lozells FC ground reveals that it is now the site of the Lozells Community Sports Centre, run by Birmingham City Council's Leisure Department. The top end of what was the pitch is now a bowling green; the bottom end is a five-a-side football and basketball area, and the whole is watched over by St. Andrew's Church.

In 1892, one Hugh McIntyre, formerly a twice cup winner with Blackburn Rovers, took over the tenancy of the Bell Inn on Lozells Road. He may have been instrumental too in helping the Lozells team become established. In this year, Lozells had probably their biggest competitive win, when they steamrollered Aston Brook St. Mary's by 19-0 on 24th November in the Birmingham Junior Cup. St. Mary's, little more than a schoolboys' church team, had been one of the earliest teams in the Aston area, playing both rugby and association rules, and cricket too in the summer, and are well-known as being the first recorded opponents of the fledgling Aston Villa.

Their team at this time (1893) was as follows: Ross (goal); Chattaway and Hodgetts (backs); Williams, Salt, Beach (halfbacks); C. E. Harley, Edwards, C. Harley, C. Staite, and Saunders (forwards).

For a short time, in 1894, Lozells had Billy Garraty of Aston Shakespeare and Aston Villa fame in their team; this may have coincided with the time that Lozells reached three Birmingham Junior cup finals.

By 1895/6, they were improved when Skelton and Johnson joined the ranks, and they, along with Chattaway, were chosen to represent England at Junior International level in 1896. Perhaps the fullback Hodgetts was a brother of the famous Dennis Hodgetts of Albion, Villa, St. George's and England fame. Although by 1893, Dennis Hodgetts would have been 30 or 31, and it may have been the great man himself, adding his huge experience in the twilight of his career.

Arthur Griffiths (b. 1879) played for Lozells as a fullback in his youth and went on to have a football career with Bristol Rovers (1897-1904) and Notts County (1904-11). The move to the Bristol side may be explained that, at the time, the Rovers were playing in the Birmingham & District League, which was next down to the Football Alliance, the equivalent of the old Third Division.

To find the old Lozells ground today, take the A4040 from the A41 by the Albion ground, signposted to Perry Barr, and after two miles, you will see the St. Andrew's Church on your left, just before the crossroads with College Road. Turn into Laurel Grove facing the church, and the sports area is on the right. Alternatively, take the A4040 Wellington Road from Perry Barr circus, and it's about two miles along the road on the left, just past the Grove Pub.

References

www.midlandspubs.co.uk
Aston Chronicle
The Grove Tavern P.H.

* as pointed out by the *Birmingham Daily Post* on 19 May 1893 when it had erroneously reported that the Junior Cup had been presented to Lozells Villa by mistake

Grove Ground Lozells FC

Grove Tavern, HQ for Lozells FC

Mitchell St. George's F.C.

f.1882-1892

THE PROFESSIONAL WORKS TEAM OF the Mitchells Brewery at Cape Hill, Smethwick.

Just as West Bromwich citizens refute that they are in any way part of Birmingham (as the national media often say), then Smethwick folk will tell you the same. Smethwick is its' own place, so when this brewery team added the word *Birmingham* as a prefix, this may have alienated many of its followers.

The team drew its name from the name of the amalgamation of two teams who operated some five miles apart; St. George's who had been based at their Fentham Road ground in Birchfield (Aston), and the brewery's own side, Mitchells FC, named after the managing director of the brewery who founded them, Harry Mitchell. They were known as Mitchell's St. George's until 1888 when, as football went national (with the Football League founded), they called themselves Birmingham St. George's FC. By then, there were several other St. George's teams around the country, notably in Bristol, and Wellington.

Harry Mitchell had a full life, being heavily involved with all aspects of the huge brewery and its large workforce (1,000+), the local Smethwick fire brigade and other civic duties. Sadly he died in 1894 from typhoid when aged only 32. His father Henry created the Harry Mitchell Park (now Leisure Centre) to the public as a memorial to his son. This subsequently passed into Corporation hands. Mitchell senior began open sports days from 1894 for his workforce, but also for the public to compete in, and attendances would be up to 2,500.

The Cape Hill Brewery was for a hundred years, the largest employer in the district, and was a small village within itself. It had a fleet of 200 vehicles, of course horse-drawn in those days, a hospital, fire station, railway network, and numerous buildings for the purposes of brewing, and an extensive sports and social network, with cricket, tennis, bowls, swimming all encouraged by the pioneering socialism of the Mitchells. There was a parallel here with the Bournville factory and village ten miles to the south, although the chocolate was known nationally, but the beer (M&B) stayed in the Midlands. As with the footballers of the Cadbury works at Bournville, the Cape Hill football team had a wonderful ground to play on, after Harry Mitchell had built the cricket and football sports ground at the bottom of the works estate near the bend in Shenstone Road. It was a large Oval, with proper wooden seats laid out as terracing all around, a concrete track, and several pavilions and small stands. The playing surface was as level and flat as a billiard table, so claimed the team secretary, Will Stansby, in his 1887/8 yearbook in the possession of Roy Burford, where he invites clubs such as Glasgow Celtic, Preston, Villa etc to 'experience the best playing surface in all England'. With a ready-made audience of the huge workforce and their families to support them, it was no surprise to see crowds of between 3,000 and 8,000 gather for attractive visiting teams. Deadly rivals Albion of course drew the biggest crowds! They were well patronised too, by leading public and civic figures. Joseph Chamberlain MP and later Prime Minister, was the Dragons' Patron. The *Birmingham Post*, in May 1888, looking forward to the next season, declared that the top 4 clubs in the West Midlands were Aston Villa, West Bromwich Albion, Wolves . . . and Birmingham St. George's. Not Stoke, not Small Heath, or Walsall Swifts; a team even most Brummies haven't heard of today, was in the top four.

Colours

1. white shirts with a black St. George's cross on the left breast/black shorts (through the 1880s)
2. light and dark blue stripes
3. dark blue with light blue hoop around chest

Grounds

1. a field at the rear of Yorkshire Grey Pub on Dudley Road*
2. 1885: the Belle Field, Winson Street, Smethwick (originally was G. K. Nettlefold Co. sports ground (at a time when Nettlefold FC had Dennis Hodgetts and Frank Coulton in their team) GKN went to the Thimblemill ground, Smethwick. Bellefield originally ran from Cape Street to Cuthbert Road by St. Cuthbert's Church and extended for 9 acres. This is a really large area, and you could get a cricket pitch and two football pitches on this sized land. Remaining on the site from the 1880s are the pair of junior and infants schools which stand on the corner with Winson Green Road. Sadly, I have to point out that if you intend to search out the Bellefield ground today, do take care, as this is not a very safe area, so either stay near your car or have someone with you.

The land was begun to be built over around 1898, and Heath Green Road, Chiswell Road, and Bellefield Roads built on the football side. The Bellefield pub stands ready to be demolished as of 2011. The ground was described as 'an enclosure', so, presumably, it was fenced or walled in, although no records of it being developed exist. To the south of Bellefield stood the lovely wooded 5-acre grounds of Bellefield House, occupying what is now the centre of Bellefield Road.
The land probably belonged to the brewery.
3. The Oval Cricket Ground, Portland Road, Rotton Park, Edgbaston (now George Dixon school fields)
4. The M&B sports ground within the brewery by bend in Shenstone Road from 1887 (see photo)

* this location is so close to the Bellfield, that they are probably one and the same.

Nickname: 'The Dragons'

Headquarters/changing rooms:

1. Cape of Good Hope Public House, Birmingham Road, Cape Hill
2. The Blue Gate Public House, Smethwick (from 1888, sponsor: Mr Sam White) (this is still there today, next to Smethwick Library, facing the 300-year-old octagonal toll house)

Players

Charlie Simm (from Calthorpe, went to Small Heath)

Tom Green (who came from Worcester)

James Welford, who went to Villa in 1893 when the club folded

Albert Brown (1862-1930) went to Villa in 1888 and bagged 37 goals in 86 games. Arthur Brown (from Villa)

Dennis Hodgetts (1863-1945) was a key forward who was sold to Villa in 1888 and scored 62 goals in 178 games for them over 11 years, gaining 6 England caps whilst he was there. He ended up as a Villa vice-president.

Bert Harrison (b. 1867) was MSG's star centre forward. He came from the Excelsior club in 1882.

By 1882, the Dragons had already got their two star centre forwards in place; Bert Harrison, and Dennis Hodgetts who had been playing for Nettlefolds works side and Dreadnought FC.

Their first team of 1882 under the new name* was: Will Stansby (goal); Eagle (back); Jones (3/4 back); Barton, Cheatham, Baker (halfbacks); Harrison, Hodgetts, Stevenson, Tonkinson, and Milton (forwards). Stansby was also the club's hard-working secretary. Dennis Hodgetts and Bert Harrison would be the Dragon's star attackers in the late 1880s. Harrison had come from the Excelsior club in Aston, which had a ground in the next street to the old St. George's club before the move. No doubt, as the team was being assembled in 1882, that Harry Mitchell was enticing players with offers of brewery employment, but very quickly he had made a team capable of competing on equal terms with the leading Midland professional sides, Villa and Albion.

In 1883, the team secured their major silverware to date when they defeated arch-rivals – to-be West Bromwich Albion by 2-1 at Stoke's Victoria Ground to take the Staffordshire Senior Cup. It was another five years before their next silverware went into the cabinet when they added the Derbyshire Cup, to make their name known throughout Midland football circles. Before 1888, of course, cup ties and friendlies against the leading clubs were the order of the day, and another well-known scalp was added to the Dragon's list with the visit of former FA Cup winners, Oxford University. The two clubs' fortunes were in opposing directions at this time, with the Oxonians in their dark blue and white halves, had their best days behind them, and the Dragons were too strong this time and won by 5-0.

The team of 1886 which beat Oxford University was: Hadley (goal); Bradbury and Castle (backs); Blackham, Richards, and Thorpe (halfbacks); forwards: Davis and Marshall (right wing), Devey (centre forward), Shaw and Harrison (left wing) – the classic 2-3-5 line-up. Sammy Bradbury came from Walsall Town at the end of his career and was now a back, having been centre forward at Walsall. Jack Devey went to the Aston Villa at the start of the 1891/2 season.

Their new Cape Hill ground was opened on 24th September 1887, with the visit of Lockwood Brothers from Nottinghamshire resulting in an easy 6-0 win for the Dragons. An interview I had with Roy Burford at Cape Hill, Smethwick proved most interesting. Roy had been for many years the M&B FC secretary and former player, and was able to give me first-hand experience of playing on the Cape Hill Oval ground itself in the 1950s and

1960s. He said that the surface was kept immaculately well and that the grass was kept very short, even though it was primarily a cricket ground.

They missed out on being elected to the new Football league in 1888 by 2 votes. Teams such as Notts County (10-0), Wolves (5-1), and Stoke (5-1), which the Dragons had all beaten that year, were chosen instead, much to the dismay of the Mitchell family. It was a surprise that Notts County were elected instead into the League. William McGreggor, founder of the idea of the Football League, admitted some years later that his twelve clubs selected were based on best average attendances, rather than their playing records! Without any further ground enhancements, i.e. stands, the capacity of Cape Hill was probably 8,000, and this would have held them back. However, the darkest cloud was the fact that West Bromwich Albion – only three miles away – had risen to become one of the top three or four teams in the country by the mid-1980s.

They then spent three years in the Football Alliance, playing against teams who would all become well-known members of the Football League, such as Nottm Forest, Stoke, Darwen, Newton Heath (Man Utd). The Dragon's best year was 1890/1 when they finished 4th with a PL 22 W12-D2-L 8 For 64-Against 22 =26pts record and a pleasing 5-2 defeat of champions Stoke at home. The Alliance was widely regarded as the second-tier to the Football League, and the newspapers of the day would print the Alliance results and league table below the Football League table. The Dragons were regularly playing clubs such as Sheffield Wednesday, Newton Heath (Man Utd), Sunderland Albion, Stoke, Walsall Swifts, Grimsby, etc., and in English or Staffordshire cup ties, any games against West Bromwich Albion, Wolves, or Villa would attract crowds of between 5,000 and 9,000 to their excellent Cape Hill ground. Trouble was, as elsewhere, their top men were continually being drained away to the likes of West Bromwich Albion and Aston Villa. They were at the top for only a short while, perhaps six years.

Their team for 1891/2 was usually: Kenyon or Morgan (goal); backs: Coulton, Roberts or Thorpe; halfbacks: McGuffle, Richards, Phillips; forwards: Davis, Mathews, Bond, Harrison, Shaw.

Bert Harrison, an ex-Excelsior player, and one of the original St. George's men who relocated from Birchfield, was their 'star' attacker.

Harry Mitchell Jnr. had provided his new 'pet' team with easy jobs as beer sales reps or publicans of local alehouses, in order to disguise the fact that they were really all paid professionals.

By June of 1891, however, the Dragons were in deep trouble. A general meeting of all players, members, and officials was called by the father and son owners, Harry and Henry Mitchell. At the Yorkshire Grey Inn on Dudley Road, they informed a stunned gathering of nearly a hundred men, on 20th July, that the brewery had severed its connection with the football team, and that from now on, they had to pay their own way, and, furthermore, there was no money in the kitty. By way of atonement, Mitchell let them have free in-perpetuity use of the Cape Hill ground, and both he and his father each promised them £50 a year sponsorship funds. Will Stansbie stepped down as club secretary and was replaced by Mr Hobson. It was the end of the road of what was supposed to be the start of the history of a famous club . . . The committee, led by Job White and Ed Underhill, reported a playing record for the previous season of played 42, won 18, lost 19, with 5 drawn and a goal tally of 101-106. It was a sad day, marking the real end of Birmingham St. George's as Cape Hill's professional side, who came so close to Football League status. On the same day, 130 miles away in London, the Football Association had lost a motion by 67-76, proposed by N. L. Jackson, that professional players – and thus professionalism – be banned from English cup ties. The way was clear for the above-the-counter paid by the week player, re-inforced by the professional teams who created the Football League, to lead the way into the new century.

When the team unexpectedly broke up at the end of the 1892 season, its players were sold to almost every club in the region. Bradbury, Bailey, Kinsey went to the Wolves; John Devey to the Villa after Dennis Hodgetts had gone there four years previously. James Welford went to the Villa in 1893, just as Albert Brown (1862-1930) had done so in 1888, and became one of Villa's top goalscorers with 37 goals from 86 games. This must have come as quite a shock to the Dragons' supporters, who no doubt turned mostly to the Albion, who were only three miles away, for their transferred loyalty.

At their peak, this Birmingham St. George's team must have been ranked in the best dozen teams in the whole country. One can only imagine what might have been . . .

Their 7-2 thrashing of a very capable Walsall Town side in 1886 indicative of their abilities.

Trophies won: Derbyshire County Cup 1888/Staffordshire Cup 1883 (2-1 over WBA in front of 5,500 at Stoke FC)

Ground attendance record (Cape Hill) 7,805 in 1887 FA Cup 2nd round V. WBA

Entered the English FA Cup from 1881/2 until 1891/2:

	1st Round	2nd Round	3rd Round	4th Round
1881/2	0-9 Weds Old Athletic (A)			
1882/3	5-1 Calthorpe (H)	0-3 Aston Unity		
1883/4	0-5 Weds Old Athletic (A)			
1884/5	5-0 Aston Unity (H)	2-0 B'ham Excelsior (H)	2-3 Walsall Swifts (A)	
1885/6	0-3 Derby County			
1886/7	3-1 Small Heath Alliance	2-1 Derby County	7-2 Walsall Town	0-1 West Brom Albion
1887/8	2-1 Walsall Town (a)	0-1 West Brom Albion		
1888/9	3-2 Long Eaton Rangers	3-2 Halliwell (A)	0-2 Preston N. End (unbeaten cup winners)	
1889/0	4-4, 2-6 Notts County			
1890/1	2-0 Crusaders (A)	0-3 (H) West Brom Albion		
1891/2	2-1 Sunderland Albion (A) ** replayed as 0-4 (H)			

However, Sunderland appealed to the FA due to an ineligible player, which they lost 0-4 at home after having won the away game. The same year, they were deducted 2 points for the same offence in the Football Alliance league, which contributed to the Dragons finishing last in 12th place. These were the two events which made the club's founder Mitchell decide to fold the team, much to everyone's surprise. He had thought for some time that the FA were somehow against him or his team; denied a place in the original 12 to found the Football League, even though William McGreggor had got them (along with Old Carthusians and Halliwell) on his invitation list; and then, when the Alliance was embraced as one into the Football League as its 2nd Division, the Dragons were left out again. His personal misery was complete just a couple of years later, when the poor chap died aged only 32.

If ever a team that was meant to succeed and survive until today, it was this one: professional almost from the start, a good 3,000 or 4,000 following, sponsored by and encompassed within the massive Mitchell (later M&B) brewery works, led by Harry Mitchell himself, and with the crest of England's St. George on their shirts. Had things taken a natural course of evolution, there would today be Albion, Villa, Wolves, and Birmingham St. George's in the Premiership.

So what went wrong?

Well, like most clubs, they had ambition (lots), a superb ground (claimed by their secretary in letters to the likes of Celtic, Sunderland Albion, and Football League clubs to be the best surface in all England), and a decent support plus commercial backing. Mind you, they had a bit of a reputation for rough play, and more than once, they had to be escorted away from the away team's ground by the police, in order to avoid the angry home fans waiting for them after the game!

However, they had West Bromwich Albion as near-neighbours, and the Aston Villa weren't too far away either. So, as Charles Darwin proved time and again, only the strongest survive in close competition and the weakest will fall to the wayside. And so did MSG. Their best players were drawn time and again to the Albion; visitor incentives (cash promises), wage bills, and ground maintenance all took their toll, and by the 1890s, the team was financially struggling, even with, no doubt, the enigmatic Mr Mitchell frequently putting his hand in his own pocket to keep them afloat.

Sadly, the club disbanded at the end of 1892 due to financial difficulties. The brewery had withdrawn its backing, and the team's playing record had steadily gone downhill after a continual drain of its best players to the WBA, and crowds falling back to around 2000 were not enough to keep a professional club afloat. The team had at least two revival attempts, but as a shadow of its former self – the team that never was' – and spent the most of the twentieth century in the Birmingham works leagues, with minor successes. The revivals were not of the professional team, rather, the original brewery works' side, which it seems continued on and off throughout and beyond the Birmingham St. George's years.

The *Birmingham Post* in 1896 mentions a game played by Mitchells Brewery FC, but four years later in April 1900, a result is given for Birmingham St. George's. It seems that the name was kept going throughout the Edwardian era, by the brewery team, although at a much lower level than in its heady heyday of the late 1880s.

The works team were still playing annual matches against West Bromwich Albion in the 1940s and 1950s, and they were still good enough to beat an Albion 3rd team by 5-2 in 1947. Playing now as M&B FC, the now junior level works team played the second half of the twentieth century in Birmingham league works football, at first in black and white stripes, then in an all-white kit after the 1940s, finally reverting to light blue with navy trim in the last decades of the 20th century. The final blow came in 2002, when, to the shock of generations of people in the district (and further afield), the huge M&B works was demolished and sold off to become the inevitable housing estate.

To get an idea of the location of their lovely old Cape Hill ground, take the B4149 Rotton Park Road off the A457 Dudley Road, turn right to the top of Southfield Road, and you would be looking at it, as Maynard Road now occupies the spot.

Biggest competitive win: 16-1 v Aston Clifton – Saturday 8th October 1887, Birmingham Cup 1st round

ACKNOWLEDGEMENTS

Roy Burford (M&B FC secretary/historian, Cape Hill)
Smethwick Library, *The Deerstalker* magazine (M&B brewery)
Birmingham Daily Post 1876-1892
Smethwick Telephone newspaper

* see St. George's FC

Albert Brown

Mitchell St.Georges' HQ-the Blue Gates Inn

Notts Olympic FC

f.1884-1896 at least

Ground
Churchville fields, Radford also the Gregory Ground, Lenton.

Headquarters
the Queen Inn, Old Radford

Colours

1. light and dark blue (1886)
2. red and black stripes, black (1890s)

Very little is known about this Nottinghamshire team, as it rarely ventured outside the county FA competitions. They entered cups in Derbyshire and the Sheffield FA and minor cups such as the Chesterfield, Grantham, Newark, and Notts Junior cups. Like most north Midland clubs, they used the Sheffield Rules. In the 1880s, they entered the Birmingham Cup, but as this was predominantly for senior teams, they withdrew after a few years. One particularly thrilling match was their 4-6 home defeat to Walsall Town-Swifts at the 3rd round stage on December 1888. In the 1890/1 Birmingham Cup, they got through the qualifying rounds only to be thrashed 8-0 when they travelled to face Wednesbury Old Athletic on the 7th February. Olympic were probably the weakest of the Nottingham teams, behind Rangers, Forest, and County. The 1884 founding date is confirmed by Charles Alcock's FA records.

The team played in the Midlands Alliance in 1892/3 but finished only 9th out of 11 teams. Two years previously, they finished bottom but one. Regular opponents included Matlock, Heanor, the Sheffield Club, Forest Swifts, Newark, Mansfield, and Sheffield Strollers. The Midland Alliance was a level below the Midland League. They were a step behind the main Nottingham clubs, Forest and County. County were simply known as the Notts Club until the 1890s. Olympic were playing at the Churchville ground during 1885-88, but they also used the Gregory ground in Lenton when it became waterlogged.

Their most famous player was Harry Daft, who later went to Notts Forest and got capped for England in 1890s. He was also a Corinthian and a cricketer.

Other notable players include:

Herbert Kilpin (1870-1916), who went out to Italy in the 1890s and co-founded the famous A. C. Milano football in 1898 with his friend Alfred Edwards. This is why A. C. Milan play in red and black stripes today. Herbert played for the Olympic for twelve years, from 1884 to 1896. A. G. Hines, the club's honorary secretary, became vice-president of the Football Association itself.

This Olympic side drew 1-1 with Rotherham Swifts on Saturday 23 March 1889,:

Smedley (goal); Hayes, Brothers (backs); Mountney, Harvey, Jackson (halfbacks); Ackroyd, Carter, Atkins, Wolley, Hepenstall (forwards).

Not knowing Olympic's colours, I made a leap of faith and thought that it was possible that Kilpin borrowed his old club colours when founding AC. Milan, which would give us red and black stripes. This proved to be correct. Quite often, men who went to the continent and South America and founded football teams clung on to their old schools and colleges' colours in an attempt to remind themselves of dear old blighty and bring their alma mater colours to their new-founded side. I discovered an old team picture from around 1892 in their red and black stripes, but according to Charles Alcock's annuals, they team were playing in light and dark blue in the first half of the 1880s. Again, probably stripes.

This was their side in 1893 against Notts Rangers which was played on the Gregory Ground at Linton: Pilkington (goal); Mallett and Thompson (backs); Cookson, Towers, Mountenay (halfbacks); Mann, Buck, Britain, Newton, Greary (forwards).

The Gregory Ground was a large square of land defined by the Derby Road, the Ilkeston Road and Lenton Road, and was next to the gasworks. It was also home to the then amateur Nottingham Forest team during 1886-90 seasons. The pitch area was 115 × 75 yards. At the time, Forest were getting poor crowds of around 500 when Notts County were getting around 5,000 at their popular Trent Bridge ground. It seems that the Gregory Ground was too far away from the town centre to draw people there in numbers. During Forest's tenancy, they had levelled it off and put an iron railing all around the pitch. Forest had also spent £400 on ground improvements, including bringing their old pavilion with them from their previous ground called Parkside, and had erected a grandstand capable of holding 2,500. They also erected a refreshment hut, a press office hut, and caused the local trains on the Midland line to stop at Lenton on match days. The largest attendance at the Gregory Ground was the 10,000 who assembled in October 1887 to see Forest v Notts County in round 2 of the FA Cup, Forest winning 2-1. It is now owned by Notts Local Education Authority and is used by schoolchildren for football and sports days, and the Notts Unity Casuals cricket team.

By the end of the 1890s, the club was in trouble, both financially and with the Notts FA. Both in October 1894 and in 1896, the club had failed to properly maintain their ground, specifically not having marked it out in readiness for the oncoming season, and also for the pitch being 13 yards too short of the minimum length. During 1892 and 1896, the club had been in trouble with the Nottinghamshire County FA several times for fielding ineligible players, meaning that they had recently turned out for other teams, and had points deducted by the league committee. There were also reported incidents of fights breaking out at more than one match involving Olympic men. The last newspaper report I could find was that of December 1896.

The team resurfaced when a team photo appeared in the 1902 Nottingham Telegraph and showed the red and black stripes I had predicted; much later in 1936, another article appeared when the old club was being reformed for about the third time.

Biggest defeat was 0-13 to Leicester Fosse in an FA Cup qualifying round match, 1894.

References

Nottingham Evening Post 1886-1898

Notts Olympic used the Gregory ground at Lenton

Herbert Kilpin of Notts Olympic

Notts Olympic

Nottingham Rangers FC

f.1868-1896

Colours

1. all white (1881)
2. pale blue and cardinal red (1884)
3. black and white (1888)

Ground
Meadow Lane, also Arkwright Street ground

Honours

Nottinghamshire Senior Cup 1887, 1888
Wednesbury Charity Cup 1882/3

Rangers were of the strongest sides in the county in the late 1880s, along with the old Notts Club (County), and Forest.

They were founder members of the Midland League in 1889 and entered the English FA Cup from 1885 to 1889.

They entered the Birmingham, Derby, Mansfield, Newark and Notts County junior cups and ended their days in the Notts Amateur league. They spent the 1890s in the Midland League or the Midland Alliance. Their ground, Meadow Lane, was taken on by Notts County in 1910 after the Rangers had gone. It was an undeveloped open ground, next to the cattle market. The Arkwright Street ground, next to the river, was used by Nottingham Forest, before moving across the river in 1893. Notts County – a club leading a nomadic existence despite its 1862 formation, but never having its own ground – also used the Arkwright Street (Town Ground) during April 1895 to April 1897. The Town Ground was next door to the County cricket ground, Trent Bridge, which Notts County rented from 1883 until they permanently settled into the old Meadow Lane ground in 1910 and spent £10,000 developing it with stands and terracing. They actually floated their old stand from Trent Bridge across the river and re-erected it on the Meadow Lane ground! How I would have loved to have seen that event!

Notts County, by the way, did not appear in their well-known black and white colours until 1891, having spent the 1880s in chocolate and blue halves, and the 1870s in a range of amber and black outfits.

In 1882/3 season, Notts Rangers won the Wednesbury Charity cup when they defeated West Bromwich Albion 5-3 in a thrilling game in front of a 4,000 crowd at the Oval. Albion scorers were Aston (2), Bisseker, but the local press did not give the Rangers scorers' names! Only the previous December, Rangers had just beaten Albion 3-2 at home in a friendly, so the two teams must have been closely matched at this time.

From 1882, Nottm Rangers entered the Birmingham Cup, and not without making a mark, often reaching the 4th round, and by 1888/9 season, when the entrants were so many that they had to have a qualifying competition, Nottingham Rangers were given an exemption into the competition proper with other well-known sides such as Walsall Swifts, Aston Villa, and other Midland sides who were now playing in the new Football League. Rangers were playing in an all-white strip at this time.

Notts Rangers reached round 4 for three consecutive seasons – 1882, 3, 4 – and were only eliminated on each occasion by one of the top sides; 1-4 to West Brom Albion in 1882, 1-2 to Walsall Swifts in 1883, and Albion again 1-1, 1-5 in 1884/85 season. They chose to play their 2nd round game with Stafford Road at the Castle Grounds, a site now occupied by the council's County Hall on Loughborough Road.

Rangers had beaten Wolverhampton Wanderers in the 3rd round, 3-2 at the Arkwright Street ground, which was right on the riverbank. The Town Ground at the end of Arkwright Street was used by Nottm Forest from 1890 to 1893, after the club had endured the dreadful Parkside Ground before moving to the much better Lenton Gregory ground. Forest spent £1,000 developing the ground – purchased from Councillor Woodward – improving the pitch and creating spectator facilities. The Gregory ground had a wonderful playing surface, but little or no spectator facilities, such as grandstands, and as it was primarily used by Linton cricket club, who didn't want the ground to be turned into a football stadium, Forest moved to the riverside location of Arkwright Street. They renamed it the 'Town Ground', and although no signs of it exist, it is exactly opposite to the current City Ground on the other side of the river Trent. The Town Ground proved a good omen for the Forest, as they went on to win the Midland Alliance in 1892/3 and subsequently got elected up into the Football League.

The Town Ground, albeit fine in all other respects, could not hold the ever-growing numbers who flocked to see Forest play, and as the turn of the century approached, Forest moved out and built a new, much bigger ground directly across the river – the City Ground.

In the 1886 Birmingham Cup, Rangers went out in the 3rd round again to the Albion, this time, by 2-7 at home, but Albion went on to win it. Another 4th round exit occurred in 1887 to a team that went on to win the cup, this time losing 1-4 to Aston Villa. At this point, the selection of the country's top 12 sides to make up the inaugural Football League was only months away, so even these defeats show that Rangers weren't far off the mark and could be ranked in the top ten or twelve sides in the Midlands. A bumper crowd of 3,000 at Meadow Lane saw them go out in the 1st round proper, again to the Albion in 1890/1 season, the last time the Rangers entered the Birmingham Cup at senior level. During the 1880s, Charlie Shelton was the team representative at the Birmingham FA committee meetings.

They had success in the district, winning the Nottinghamshire County cup two years in a row, 1887 and 1888. In the 1888 Nottm Final, they were due to play Notts County, but because the club had been recently suspended by the Notts FA, they were replaced in the final by Ruddington, a minor club. Rangers, not even fielding their strongest side, had little trouble beating them 4-2 in front of a small crowd. They were one of the few teams other than Forest or County to win it before 1900. However, after helping found the Midland League in 1889, they were expelled a year later for failing to fulfil their fixtures, and they ended bottom with 1 win, 4 draws, and 10 defeats and an 11-36 goal difference. Typical league opposition included Gainsborough Trinity, Warwick County, Derby Junction, Leek, Burton Wanderers, and Derby Midland. At the end of the 1880s, Rangers were playing in a black and white strip, probably stripes or halves, as hoops had gone out of fashion by then.

Rangers hit a high note when they thrashed the claret shirted Nottm Jardines FC by 10-1 in the 1st round of the 1887/8 English FA Cup; they defeated Grantham in round 2, had a bye in round 3 before losing 1-3 away to Darwen in Lancashire on 17th December.

A novel event took place in March 1889 at the Gregory Ground, Lenton. The home side – the then amateur Nottingham Forest – played the Rangers in a floodlit evening match, supposedly under the equivalent of a dozen 14,000 candlepower lights on towers. It attracted 5,000 people (ten times the usual Forest gate) but was said to have been a bit of a flop, as the lights cast so many strong shadows on the pitch, it was hard to tell what was going on, especially ball-handling, elbows being used, and offsides. Rangers won the game 2-0.

In 1889, Rangers provided Sheffield United's first ever opposition from their creation that year, when they met in an FA cup-tie at Bramall Lane.

After Christmas 1896, no reports could be found in the Nottingham press, at which point the club seems to have disbanded. They reformed some years later, perhaps after the end of the First World War, since they were active again in the 1920s.

Their team from 1881 was:

J. Mundle (goal); J. Linekar, C. Smith (backs); H. Winfield, H. Harrison, C. Comery; A. Brown, Winfield, H. Harrison, H. Shelton, C. Guy (forwards).

Their 1884 side which went to play Wednesbury Town was:

Bull (goal); Knight, Alf Shelton (backs); Saddler, Liver, Charlie Shelton (halfbacks); forwards: Archer, Parker (right wing), Hodder (centre), Gandy, Hickling (left wing). The wing men would operate in pairs, down each flank, and one would support or back up the other, their sole aim was to 'middle' (Victorian phrase for centring) the ball to the centre forward, who would shoot, head, or just bustle the ball (complete with goalie if needs be!) over the line.

The team of 1886 was:

W. Gandy (goal); H. Knight and H. Newborough (backs); Mack, Charlie Shelton, Alf Shelton; (halfbacks); Gilbert, Archer, Fred Geary, Cook, Hodder.

A point of interest is that William Gandy is now in goal, having been the inside left the previous season. Specialist goalkeepers, such as we have in the modern game, were not developed as such in Victorian times; a 'crocked' forward might be asked to try out in goal, in order to remain in the team, and make a decent job of it. In one Wednesbury Strollers' match, the captain was so angered at his forward's lacklustre performance that he ordered the wretched fellow to go in goal for the rest of the game!

Entering the 1885/6 FA Cup, Rangers went out at the first hurdle to local rivals Notts County by 3-0. Both the Shelton brothers also played for Notts County, so I wonder where their loyalties lay for that Rangers v County cup-tie. Alf Shelton was capped six times for England in the 1880s.

Halfback Charlie Shelton was capped for England in 1888 and didn't die until 1951. He may have been spotted in their two games against League side Sheffield Wednesday in the 1st round of the 1888/9 FA Cup. A 1-1 draw at home saw the Rangers travel to the Olive Grove ground and lose 0-3. It was still a good performance to get that far because the FA had introduced a separate qualifying competition in that year.

REFERENCES

Sheffield Independent
Nottingham Evening Telegraph
The History of Notts County FC
Nottingham Guardian 1889
Charles Alcock's 1905 annual

Fred Geary Notts Rangers

Racecourse Ground, Nottingham 1888

Old Hill Wanderers FC

f. unknown-suggest circa 1889

Ground

1. Old Hill cricket ground
2. Halesowen Road

They were a semi-professional team from the Black Country, based between Dudley and Halesowen.

They competed in the high standard Birmingham and District League from 1892 to 1895.

Colours
black and amber stripes, black

Old Hill is a village near Halesowen and Cradley Heath and was involved in heavy industry, and the local area is full of mineral mines, collieries, and a network of canals and railways which connected the collieries and mines to the mainline railway goods depot. There were also several brickworks, timber yards, iron works, and chain-making factories in the district. One would expect that local employment was high in the Victorian days, which all means that more people can afford to go to football matches.

They were Birmingham League champions in 1893/4 season but surprisingly withdrew and folded in 1895. Regular league opposition included Berwick Rangers, Worcester Rovers, Stafford Rangers, Halesowen, Stourbridge, Smethwick Carriage Works, and the reserve sides of the Black Country Football League sides. In their three seasons in the Birmingham League, they finished in 6th, 1st, and 10th places. Only 18 league games were played in 1892/3, but this rose to 26 in 1894/5 as extra teams joined the league. Their championship-winning side netted 70 league goals in 26 games in 1893/4 but conceded almost as many in the following season in a dramatic loss of form.

They entered the Birmingham Cup from 1892 but went out at the first hurdle against nearby rivals Halesowen in front of an impressive 2,000 crowd. The following season, they beat Shrewsbury Town, who were only in the Walsall League at the time, by 3-0, before bowing out by the same score to Brierley Hill Alliance in the 2nd round. This time, there was an even better crowd of 3,000 at the Halesowen Road ground. The year 1894 saw Old Hill go out in the 1st round again, this time away in Shropshire to Wellington St. George's, who were Shropshire League champions that year. That was the last time they competed at that level. They are likely to have begun playing at the Old Hill cricket ground which is on Timbertree Road. The cricket club are also called Wanderers, suggesting a common root. In 1894, they entered the FA Cup and got to the Fourth Qualifying Round before being eliminated 5-0 by Burton Wanderers.

A large 5-acre field at the oddly named district of Mouse Sweet opposite the Cookseys Hotel pub continued to remain shown as a field on several O.S. maps from 1880 through to 1939, and this is thought to be their ground. It is still used today by Sandwell sports college. The only other possibilities are a football ground marked as such on a 1919 O.S. map at the end of Pear Tree Lane, opposite the Blue Ball Inn. This ground had a drop-forge works built over one end of it around 1930, but this ground was shown only as a field on the 1909 O.S. map. A third ground, a mile due west which was in Cradley Heath, off the Dudley Road by St. John's Church, was probably that of either Cradley Heath St. Luke's or Cradley Town.

This ground, which was featured on a 1939 O.S. map, was not there at all twenty years previously. Confusingly, a 1909 map, just after Old Hill's peak period, showed no football ground at all in either Old Hill or nearby Cradley!

Their players of note were: William A. Smith (b. 1882), a forward, went on to play for several teams around the West Midlands, including Coventry, Birmingham, West Bromwich, and several local sides.

Alex Leake (1871-1938), a halfback known for his great stamina, was with Wanderers when they won the Birmingham League title. He was spotted by Small Heath scouts, who signed him up in 1894. He played nearly 200 games for the Heathens before moving to the Villa in 1902 and then Burnley in 1907. He ended his playing days at Wednesbury Old Athletics in 1910. He was capped five times for England in the 1904/5 season. Writing in 1901, C. B. Fry described Leake as one of the best halfbacks of the day.

Isiah Turner (1876-1936) had a short football league career with Stoke and ended his days at Old Hill as their goalkeeper.

Billy Williams (1876-1929) was the team's fullback. Smethwick-born, he played for West Bromwich Albion. When he lost his place in the team, he moved to West Smethwick FC then Hawthorn Villa, two local sides, before neding his career at Old Hill Wanderers for seasons 1892-1894.

Charles Izon (1870-1920) was a forward who also played at Smethwick with Williams. He left in 1893 to join Small Heath.

George Timmins (b. 1858) was one of the famous Albion side who had all come up together from working at George Salter's Springs factory in West Bromwich. He'd played in three consecutive FA Cup finals with the Throstles. He finished his career at Old Hill in 1890, by which time he was 42!

Harold Green (1860-1900): Harry was another old Albion man from the Salter's works; he had had a wonderful career, being in at the beginning of the Albion football club, and went on to gain three FA Cup final medals in the 1880s whilst at W.B.A. He joined Old Hill in 1891 but died only nine years later at the age of 40.

John Lee (b. 1869) was a forward who came to Old Hill from Small Heath in 1895, spending two years with Wanderers. His footballing career started with top local amateur side Walsall Unity who played on the Mellish Road, Rushall. He moved on in 1897 to local semi-professional sides Bilston and Darlaston who played in the Walsall & District League.

From the above key players, it seems that Old Hill received several men from W.B.A who were at the end of their careers, and this was probably their successful period of the 1890s. Naturally, all careers come to an end, and it was probably the retirement of those old experienced hands and the drain of their best young players which led to the club pulling out of the Birmingham League and dropping back into junior level, before folding altogether around 1900.

To find the Old Hill grounds today, take the A456 exit to Halesowen from J3 of the M5. Turn right into the B459 Dudley Road. Continue on the A459 Halesowen Road for three miles until you reach Old Hill, a mile short of Netherton. Turn right into Bluebell Road. The ground is in front of you. The Old Hill cricket ground is back down the hill two miles to the crossroads with Barrs Road. Turn into Barrs Road, and the cricket ground is just past Haden Hill Leisure Centre.

References

Old Hall Library
Cradley Heath Local History Centre
The History of the Birmingham Senior Cup, Steve Carr

Old Hill Wanderers

Old Hill Wanderers Ground

Old Salopians FC

f. unknown

Very little is known or recorded about this early pioneering Shropshire team, as it was not a permanent club, but re-formed on bank holidays when old boys returned to Shrewsbury to play against the grammar school.

Salop is the old name for the county of Shropshire, which, as it borders mid-Wales, is predominantly rural, even today, and apart from Shrewsbury, Market Drayton, and Wellington (now Telford) offered little scope for football teams to develop. However, Old Boys from the Shrewsbury Grammar School had since the 1860s played football in one form or another as a cock-house system, similar to at Harrow. Playing fields were spacious and many along the acres of meadows which lay alongside the river which ran through the town centre. Leading scholars would go to Oxbridge and gain professional positions in the City of London, or in Birmingham law firms, for example. J. G. Wylie and H. Wace were two such young men who, upon returns to their alma mater, would form teams to play the school team, perhaps at Christmas and Easter. Wylie and Wace were better known as forwards for the London Wanderers, who won the FA Cup five times in their short twelve-year history. Former Old Salopians had for some time, in the 1860s, been in the habit of forming ad hoc Old Salopian teams for Christmas matches, but this was not yet a club in the proper sense; even when the club was set up on a proper footing at the start of the century (1902), it was still based in London.

Shrewsbury Grammar School was an eminent public school in the Victorian era (as it still is today of course) and holds an important place in the history of football. Throughout the formative years – 1850s – 1860s, the school played an active role in the development and publication of Shrewsbury, Cambridge, and Football Association rules of the game. Shrewsbury school representatives E. L. Horne and H. M. Lubbock (a Wanderers player) signed the 1856 Cambridge Rules for the University Football Club, which paved the way for public schools and universities to play against each other with a common set of laws of the game. The schools were also involved in the earlier still 1848 Cambridge Rules document. Mind you, it was said that Shrewsbury clung on to one of their peculiarities – dowling – for some years afterwards! The Douling game permitted a high or bouncing ball to be brought under control with the hand and also permitted hacking, that is, kicking the shins of the opponent. Knowing public schools, no doubt they weren't too fussy whose shins they kept on kicking! Forward passes were of course not permitted until after 1876.

COLOURS
white shirt/blue trousers in the 1870s.

Reformed in 1902 as a proper club, but in London, colours being – royal blue shirt, gold lion rampant feature on chest, white shorts.

In 1902, the club was set up again on a more formal basis and competed against other Old Boys team with considerable success in the twentieth century, particularly in the Arthur Dunn cup for amateur sides, having won the trophy five times in the 1920s and 1930s.

Most famous players include:

J. C. H. Bowdler (Wales international) W. Oakley (11 England caps)

M. Morgan-Owen (16 caps for Wales) J.Brockbank (1 England cap)

J. G. Wylie (Wanderers cup winner)

Hubert Wace (Wanderers cup winner)

Also, J. C. Thring and the Reverend Burn who gave much thought to the formalisation of a universal set of association football rules whilst at Uppingham School were Old Salopian men.

FA Cup History-

1876/7 Scratched when drawn away to Oxford University
1877/8 withdrew after submitting their entry form

ACKNOWLEDGEMENTS

Shrewsbury Grammar School
Shrewsbury Library Archives Department
Old Salopians web site

Old Salopians' Alma Mater-Shrewsbury old Grammar School

Oswestry FC

f.1860-1993

This team was founded 1860, making them one of the world's oldest football teams.

Dissolved (insolvent) 2003

Grounds

1. Victoria Park cricket ground
2. Park Hall (capacity 2,000) after 1992

Founder members of the Welsh FA in 1876

Colours

1. navy blue and white stripes (circa 1877)
2. navy shirts with white diagonal sash, white knickers (1879)
3. all blue (1880)
4. red shirts (1885)
5. navy and white halves (1900)

Won Cheshire County League 1872

Played in Welsh Premier League 1995-2003

Oswestry is a small town in Shropshire, only a few miles from the Welsh border. During the 1870s and 1980s, they were a pioneering club in both Shropshire and the North Wales football scene.

The first team in Oswestry were called St. Oswald's, and there was also the White Stars team. At a meeting on 4th September 1875, it was decided that a stronger team could be put together if a team representing the town could be assembled from the best two or three teams. This combined side was called Oswestry United.

Playing at the local cricket ground on Victoria Road, early opponents included Chirk, Wrexham, and the Ruabon Druids. When clubs in the north-west of England (counties either side of Cheshire) set up the

Combination League, Oswestry, Wrexham, and the Druids joined this league, as only north Wales had any established football clubs in the early years. With only a handful of Shropshire clubs within forty miles, this was a sound move.

Oswestry took part in the first ever Welsh Cup competition, and despite they were technically in Shropshire, and therefore England, the club nonetheless preferred to compete in Welsh FA competitions and indeed registered themselves with the Welsh FA and not the English FA, based in London.

Oswestry supplied no less than nine players for Wales' first ever international (against England) in 1879, played at the Kennington Oval.

By 1879, Oswestry were looking further and further afield for opponents since Shropshire and north Wales held only a few teams. One such opponent was the Wednesbury Old Athletics from Staffordshire, and on Saturday 27th December 1879, they travelled to the 'Wedgbury Oval' only to be beaten 4-0 in front of just 400 spectators. By 1879, Wednesbury matches were attracting 2, 000 to 3,000 people. A return friendly game was played on Saturday 13th March 1880, but this time Oswestry went down by 1-7. From the start of 1880, other teams from Shropshire and north Wales were travelling to the Black Country in search of new opposition, and Oswestry were soon followed to the Oval by Newtown White Star and Ruabon Druids.

Oswestry even entered the Birmingham Cup at the start of the 1879/80 season, following on from several Shrewsbury sides, no doubt encouraged by Shrewsbury FC's cup success of 1878.

Drawn at home to Burton Lily in the 1st round, their opponents scratched on account of the long distance. Round 2 saw Oswestry drawn against the Derby Town club, who as first out of the hat, had choice of venue. On the advice of the Birmingham FA, it was played at the Wednesbury Oval on Saturday 20th December 1879, but Derby were too strong and ran out 4-1 winners. Oswestry did not enter the Birmingham cup again, but several other Salop clubs – Shrewsbury Castle Blues, Wellington St. George's, Wellington Town, and Ironbridge – began to enter from the mid-1880s.

The 1883 team was: R. T. Gough (goal); J. H. Williams, S. Powell (backs); W. T. Foulkes, M. Evans, S. Smith (halfbacks); J. Evans, E. G. Shaw (left wing), W. H. Davies (centre), G. Farmer, J. Roach (right wing) (forwards).

The club won the Welsh Cup several times, including in 1884, 1901, and 1907.

In 1884, they narrowly beat the Druids by 3-2 to take the Welsh Cup for the first time, only for Druids to come back and beat them 2-0 the following year. Druids appeared in eight of the first nine Welsh Cup finals, winning five of them, and by the end of the century had acquired legendary status. Oswestry weren't finished yet, and they overcame perennial Welsh Cup winners, the Druids, in the 1901 final by 1-0 in front of 5,000 crowd at Wrexham Racecourse.

The winning side comprised:

John Morgan, James Edwards, Henry Jones, George Richards, Fred Butterton, Will Jarman, E. Hodnett, Martin Watkins, George Storey, S. H. Goodrich, Tom Parry (captain).

The winning goal was accredited to an own goal from the Druids goalkeeper, W. Roose, who diverted a corner kick into his own net. It was an all-Shropshire Welsh Cup final in 1907 as Oswestry triumphed 2-0 over Whitchurch.

The Edwardian era was mostly spent playing in the Lancashire Combination and when the First World War began, most of their players – just like all over England – went off to serve in the trenches, so the club closed down until 1920.

At this point, they added the title 'Town' to their name and began to play in the new North Wales Alliance. When they became that league's champions in 1924, they joined the strong Birmingham & District League. This had most of the leading clubs from the Midlands counties within its ranks, including Hereford, Kidderminster, Worcester City, Stourbridge, Wellington and, albeit on its last legs, the famous old Wednesbury Old Athletics.

The 1950s were relatively successful, with Oswestry becoming Birmingham League champions in 1953. After a relegation season, they bounced back with the Division 2 title in 1958. The 1960s saw the club move back into the Cheshire League, meeting teams like Rhyl, Northwich, Wigan, Bangor, and Macclesfield. The Southern League was their home during the 1970s, but the club was heading into insolvency by the time the 1980s came around. Matters came to a head when they reluctantly had to sell off the old Victoria Road ground to the developers, and it looked like it was the end of the road for the club after nearly 130 years.

Eventually, after five years of difficulty, both financial and administrative, the club 'resurfaced' again in 1993 and joined the Welsh national League at 1st Division level. An inaugural match against old foes Shrewsbury saw 1,000 spectators assemble at the club's new Park Hall ground, formerly an army training facility.

After a very successful 1990s decade in which they did the league and cup double several times, rising to the level of the League of Wales, they were denied promotion on the grounds that the stadium was not up to the premier standard required, mainly from a lack of floodlights. After another few years of hard work by the club and its followers, the ground was brought up to standard, but once again, finances were less, and it needed the rescue plan and amalgamation into the T.N.S football club to keep the game alive in the town in the twenty-first century.

Some of Oswestry's early pioneering footballers include:

William Davies (1855-1916) played either forward or halfback and has the claim to fame of being the scorer of Wales' first ever international goal in that 1879 away to England. A good cricketer, he represented Shropshire at cricket. He also played for the Druids, who, because during 1878/9 found themselves without a ground, lent several players to the Oswestry club, so they could get a game.

John Jones (b. 1856) was known as 'Dirty Jack' due to his uncompromising style of play, with no quarter given or asked! He worked as a coal miner at Gwersyllt, near Wrexham. He too played for the Druids, as from 1875, and was capped for Wales.

William Williams – 'Little Billy' – was the third Druids player to spend 1878 with Oswestry. He was noted for his great stamina and 'could run all day'. He was a noted strong tackler. He was with Druids for fifteen years and was capped eleven times for Wales.

George Beare (1885-1970) was a 'wing dribbler' who ended his playing days at Oswestry after a long career throughout the 1920s and 1930s with Blackpool, Everton, Cardiff, and Bristol City.

Arthur Foster (b. 1869) was a fullback who ended his career with Oswestry after playing throughout the 1890s in the Potteries, with Hanley and Stoke.

Jack Hallam (1869-1949) was a right-winger who spent 1888/9/90 at Oswestry before having a long career with Small Heath, where he scored 54 goals in 133 games during the 1890s. He was a speedy winger and created many of what we would call 'assists' in the modern game. He was capped once.

Jack Hampson (1887-1960) started out as a youth with Oswestry and went on to have a Football League career, mainly with Port Vale, before a serious injury in 1924 ended his career as a halfback.

Seth Powell (1862-1945) was a fullback who played for Oswestry White Star in 1884/5 and for Oswestry Town for 1885-1890, before departing for two seasons with West Bromwich Albion, where it was said he was on £2 per game. He was capped seven times for Wales. After a spell with Burton and Chester, he returned to Oswestry to the United side in 1895/6.

Isaac Lea (1911-72) was a right-half who started his career at Oswestry at the end of the 1920s before spending twelve Football league seasons with Birmingham and Millwall.

Tom Parry played for Oswestry at the turn of the twentieth century and gained seven Welsh caps during 1900-1902. He played with his brother Maurice on four of those internationals.

George Davies (1927-) started his playing career at Oswestry in 1946, and after five seasons, went to Sheffield Wednesday (1950-56) with nearly 100 appearances, ending up at Chester and Telford.

Oswestry had effectively shut down as a club at the end of the twentieth century, but an answer to keep football alive in the town came when they were merged with Total Network Solutions in 2005 (T.N.S) from Llansantffraid eight miles away in Wales. T.N.S was the sponsored name of Llansantffraid FC.T.N.S – for short. They were sponsored by the company of that name in 2000, but when they were brought out by British Telecom in 2005, that arrangement came to an end, and T.N.S renamed themselves 'The New Saints' and went on to dominate the Welsh Premier with titles in 2005, 2006, 2007, plus a Welsh Cup success.

Football in Oswestry is now played in green and white hoops, instead of navy blue of yesteryear.

Rudge FC (Coventry)

f.1889-1898 reformed in the Edwardina era
The works team of Coventry Whitworth Company Ltd.

Colours
red shirts, white shorts

Ground
The Red House ground, Stoney Stanton; sometimes the Coventry cricket ground (1890/1)

Honours

won Birmingham Junior Cup 1897
Leamington Cup 1895
Midland Advertiser Charity Cup

Coventry, like Birmingham, was at the forefront of the bicycle, motorbike, and motor vehicle industries across the decades in Victorian times. On the back of the bicycle boom of the 1890s, when up to 10,000 people would gather at the Aston Lower Grounds to watch professional bicycle races, Coventry's two leading football clubs arose from companies that manufactured bicycles during this period. Actually, the Rudge bicycle company had merged with the Whitworth Bicycle company of Birmingham in 1894, and later, during 1911-1946 made the Rudge Four motorbike. They had works in Crow Lane and Spon Lane, and at their peak in 1896, they produced 75,000 bikes in a year. Later, in pre-war times, the name Rudge was more associated with raced motorbikes.

By the early 1890s, the Coventry papers were all behind its two rising star teams, Singers and Rudge (Whitworth). In 1891, the long-awaited clash came when Rudge met Singers in a cup tie, which Singers won 6-1 on 23rd November to claim top-dog status. However, Rudge continued to improve, and Coventry district had two of the Midland's best junior sides. This was the Rudge team which comfortably beat Walsall Olympic 5-0 in April 1891, and thus put an end to Olympic's 23 games unbeaten season-long run.

Greaves (goal); Hatton, Morris (backs); Gandy, Salisbury, Bates (halfbacks); Hands, Perry, Middleton, Chatfield, and Hinds (forwards).

Singers were the established side, but by 1893/4, Rudge were up to Singers' standard, and the town enjoyed several seasons in which these two sides were very successful. By 1892, Rudge were seeing off all local junior sides, sometimes by double-figure victories. Despite the intense rivalry between Rudge and Singers, Rudge actually played at least one 'home' match on Singers' ground! On 26th January 1892, Rudge defeated Southfield of Birmingham by 5-1 in a game limited to one hour due to the waterlogged state of the pitch. Perhaps they wanted the Birds' fans to see what they could do!

Rudge FC entered the Birmingham and Walsall and Leamington cups, and 1893/4 was said to be their peak season. They also entered the Wednesbury Cup back in 1880 but didn't make any impact until the 1890s, when they were seen as annual contenders. The team used the Lord Nelson P.H in the early 1890s as headquarters, later the Market Vaults Inn.

Running the team were T. G. Price (secretary) and E. G. Ward (hon. sec) along with Johnny Round and club captain Harry Hands, who became the club legend. At some point in the late 1890s, Rudge added the word *United* to their title, although the Coventry and Leamington papers didn't always use it.

Saturday 15 April 1895 saw Rudge get through to the final of the Leamington Cup where they were successful against the Willenhall Pickwicks by 4-2. A large crowd was boosted by a train full of Picks' supporters. Ironically, it was reputed that groups of people left Willenhall for Coventry on bicycles, some of which would have been made by Rudge!

Herbert Chapman, the famous Arsenal manager of the 1930s, and his father William were connected with Rudge from its formation year.

At their AGM of 1896, the committee bemoaned its 20-game season – won only 5, drew, 3 and lost 12, although with a goals tally of 81-40, suggests close defeats and some hefty victories against lesser opposition.

This team of 1897 defeated Warwick United 3-0 to take the B'ham Junior Cup.

Ball (goal); Hatton and Reeves (backs); Bates, Gandy, Salisbury (halfbacks); Sam Weston, Holmes, Harry Hands, Holden, Lewis (forwards).

The Warwick United side included a trio of men who had signed from Saltley Gas in 1895: Cooke, McKenzie, and Thorne.

Sadly, however, just as the rivalry between Rudge and Singers was at its height, the Rudge team disbanded without warning at the end of 1898, although the Birmingham papers were talking about Rudge's rapid decline in 1897 just after they had finally won the Birmingham Junior cup. This can only have been because key players left the team.

As with any works' side, the opportunity for revival is always there, and this must have occurred in Edwardian times as the 1928 yearbook of the Birmingham Football Association lists one Rudge – Whitworth FC as an active junior club member. In the 1930s, the two factories used to play each other at football, and even the individual works departments had their own football teams. The inter-department football cup was a popular feature throughout the 1920 and 1930s in the Rudge empire social scene.

References

Birmingham Daily Post
Midland Daily Telegraph 1892
Coventry Evening Telegraph 1892-1898
Lichfield Mercury 1899

Rushall Rovers FC

f. 1868 (claimed) known as 1874- 1880 re-formed as a minor team 1882

They were probably the earliest team in the Walsall district. Rushall is a village three miles north of Walsall on the route to Lichfield, and next to the ancient village of Pelsall, known for its 1,000-year-old common. The population of Rushall before 1890 would have been about 500 as the whole area for a mile in each direction was farmland and fields towards both Aldridge and Bloxwich. Spectators would have been drawn in from the neighbouring villages of Pelsall, Aldridge, and Bloxwich, since the limited local support would not have been sufficient on its own. Headquarters were very probably the Miners Arms which until 2011 was on the corner of the Lichfield Road and Rowley Place. As one of the earliest sides in Staffordshire, they were instrumental in the founding of the Walsall and Staffordshire Associations and were one of the first teams on many new clubs' fixture lists in the 1870s.

Grounds

1. a field some 500 yards behind the Miners' Arms P.H. on the Lichfield Road, Rushall (now Rowley Place Recreation ground). This was christened 'Rovers Field' by the club, and had a changing room and gymnasium.
2. a field on the Lichfield Road opposite the old schoolhouse facing Cartbridge Lane

Colours
all white, large blue Staffordshire knot across chest, blue pill-box caps, black stockings

Club President:
Major Strongitharm; Vice-President: Mr R. Shut; Secretary: T. Bott

An appeal for men to form a football team in Rushall circa 1870 drew nearly fifty men. The club continued to keep a playing strength of around thirty players in its team as they ventured out to play other early sides in the Walsall district such as Wednesbury Strollers and Walsall Victoria Swifts. With Major Strongitharm from Rushall Manor (famous for its week-long siege in the English Civil War) at the helm, it seems that the Rovers were well connected. It was probably his land which ran from the Lichfield Road almost back to Aldridge, on which they formed a playing ground (see web site photo).

By the early mid-1870s, Rushall were selectively playing newly formed teams in the Bloxwich, Walsall, and Wednesbury areas.

What became noticeable from research done by Walsall football expert Kevin Powell, was the fact that Rushall Rovers were, in plain speaking, a 'posh' team, and refused to play any other unless of the same social standing. Their leading players were comprised of Walsall's wealthy gentleman new middle-class, several of whom were leading town council officials.

In 1874, Rushall Rovers were the first visiting team to play at Walsall Town's new Chuckery ground. The match was 15-a-side, which was not unusual at that time; even up until 1880, some teams hadn't settled into the familiar 11-a-side yet, and some clubs were still experimenting with Rugby and Sheffield rules. The remains of Rovers' old ground are still there behind the houses on Lichfield Road near the village Labour Club.

During the mid-1870s, any new team would find opponents few and far between, and Rushall Rovers would have been many teams' first opponents. On New Year's Day 1876, they travelled to Wednesbury but lost 0-1 to the Old Athletics on Wells Field. They also lost by the only goal of the game when they went to West Bromwich FC (Dartmouth) on 25th November later that same year and played the Dartmouth team at Four Acres. The only other teams operating locally in the first half of the 1870s were Stafford Road, Wednesbury, Birmingham, Calthorpe, Aston Unity, Tipton, and Saltley College.

Having lived near Rushall during the 1970s, I was quite familiar with the Miners Arms football ground and played on it many times without realising I would be writing about it thirty years later!

Rovers didn't enter the Birmingham Cup until 1878 when after beating B'ham St. Luke's 7-0 they went out to Wednesbury Old Athletic 1-3 at the Oval; at least the 1,500 crowd would have been the biggest Rushall had experienced. The principles of the club precluded them from entering cup competitions, just in case they had to play a 'working-class' team! The following year, they returned to the Oval, to be trounced 6-1 by works side Elwells FC. Travelling must have been a bad experience for they never entered the Birmingham Cup again, limiting themselves to the Walsall and Wednesbury cups. However, at the end of the 1870s, opponents were thin on the ground, and Rovers found themselves meeting the various Wednesbury teams nearly ten times during 1878 to 1880.

The team of 1877 which played the Stafford Road team was:

Newbold (capt.), E, Goodwin, S. Oerton, H. Oerton, Cotterill, Fellows, Parkes, Pepper, Parker, Roberts, Nicklin, Moss, Bott. There were two Roberts brothers, Henry and Edwin.

Note there are fifteen men in this team, yet they still lost to the twelve-man Stafford Roadsters! The Oerton brothers' family home – Highgate House – was on Folly Lane, right by the Walsall Swifts' ground.

This eleven-man side travelled to play Wednesbury Strollers in 1878: Roberts, Newman, Greatorex, A. Dewry, E. Dewry, Newbold, Adams, Ludlow, Angel, Cross, Tidsell.

Arthur Greatorex was the same man as the one who helped found the Walsall FC team in 1874 and played cricket for Walsall C. C.

In 1879, Rushall added the large Staffordshire knot design across the white team shirts, which had previously been plain.

At the end of the 1880 season, Rushall Rovers announced that they were going to amalgamate with Walsall Town, and the last match the original team ever played was against Elwells FC of Wednesbury. Newman, Greatorex, Cozens, and Newbold were already associated with the Walsall club. This Rovers side lost 0-7 to Elwells at the Wednesbury Oval.

Cotterell (captain), Goodwin, Cress, Thompson, Sheldon, T. Bott (goal), S. Bott, Newman, J. Leckie, J. Marsden, Cozens.

The Rushall team seem to have been resurrected two years later as they were playing friendly games again.

Their team of 1882 playing a 1-3-6 formation was: Fereday (goal); Hollwood (back); Yates, Harrison, Orme (halfbacks); Middlebrook, Hollowood, Jebbit, Meek, Owen, Clare (forwards). As you can see, it is an entirely new eleven. These men are probably from the old Rovers 2nd and 3rd teams from before 1880.

In 1893, the Rushall Olympic came on the scene, playing on the ground behind the Miners Arms pub on the Lichfield Road, which was the Rovers' ground. It is not known whether this was a new team, or the old Rovers revived. This common land is still in use today as Rushall Park, with two football pitches and some recent changing rooms. The ground is generally hilly and bumpy, and unlike some other grounds (especially used also for cricket), it doesn't look like it was ever levelled off much. After the houses were built all down the Lichfield Road towards Walsall in the late 1920s/ early 1930s, a sports ground was developed behind the houses facing Cartbridge Lane. There were tennis courts, a bowling green, a clubhouse, and a football and cricket pitch, accessed by a bridle path which is still there today. It is likely that the new Olympic team used it at some point before their current Bosty Lane ground.

They played junior level local football in the Walsall Amateur league and continue to this day very successfully in the West Midland League.

REFERENCES

Walsall Observer 1870-1880
Walsall Advertiser 1870-1880
'The Old Uns' – Steve Carr, Groty Dick Publishing, Tipton

Rushall Rovers 1879

Rushall Rovers pitch still in use

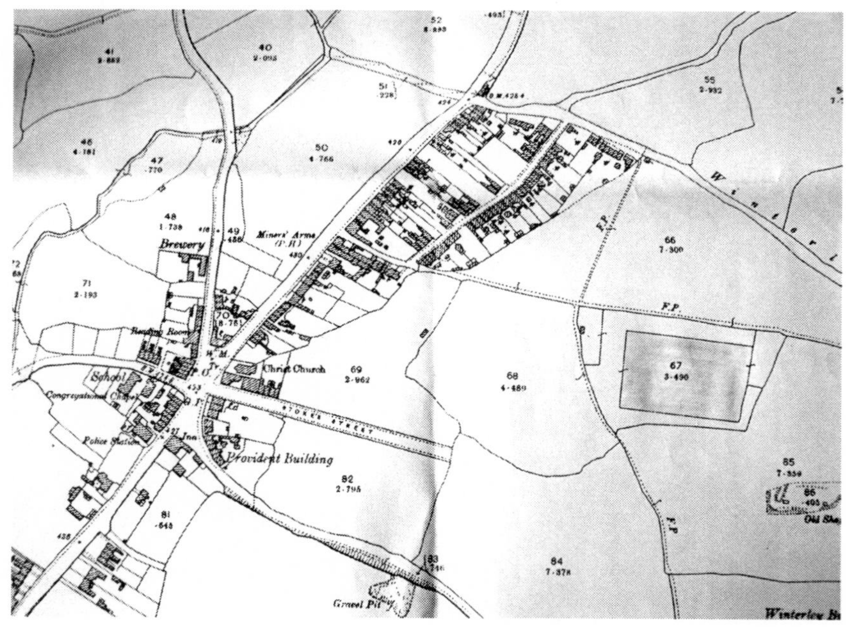

Rushall Rovers

Salters FC (West Bromwich)

f.1879

This club was formed as the works team from Salter's Springs Company, West Bromwich. In the autumn of 1879, the cricket club, who were using Dartmouth Park, formed a football team. The actual date is often cited as 20th September 1879, but I have seen no documented evidence for this.

Salters was one of West Bromwich's largest employers and manufactured springs, weighing scales, and measuring equipment. The company dates back to around 1770, when the two brothers, Richard and William, set up a small business at Bilston, before soon moving to West Bromwich. The company expanded and soon became the town's largest employer. They later produced bayonets, coin-operated weighing machines (including the famous ones for Cadbury chocolate found on railway stations everywhere) and in 1895 made England's first typewriter.

George Salter was keen on sport and promoted various activities to his large workforce, especially cricket and football. He was one of West Bromwich's most important men of the period. He attained high public office (Mayor and W. B. A Chairman) and was a social reformer through his sporting patronage. In 1860, Thomas Bache Salter purchased Springfield, a large house on Roebuck Lane, and this became the Salter family's residence for over a century. By 1970, it was used as the social club for Salter's employees.

Their first ground was Springfields sports ground, off the Roebuck Lane (now by the metro tram station). The Deveraux Road estate now occupies some of what was Spring Fields. Clearly, the name refers to (Salter's) Springsfields, and indeed, there is the appropriately named Salter's Vale nearby. In the 1940s, all of this area was just undeveloped grassland, and Google Earth tells us that there was a sports ground either side of what is now the metro line at Kenrick Park halt. There was an oval running track and a football pitch in Kenrick Park itself, although this was not accessible from Roebuck Lane, only from Contance Avenue, and so, less likely fits the description of 'being at the bottom of Roebuck Lane'. There was also a football ground at the rear of the Vine Inn, a celebrated Indian curry-house pub, favoured by Baggies fans today. However, further investigation, courtesy of British History Online maps, tells us that the whole area on the western side of Roebuck Lane was known as Springfields. There were four main fields, which ran from the junction with the Birmingham Road, all the way down to the railway (now the Metroline). The cricket field was a 6.38-acre field, and there was a pavilion, several pleasure benches, and rows of trees defining the walkways to each part of the grounds. Studying carefully an overlay of a present-day view from Google Earth, I adjudge that the path from the metro station to Devereux Road, and that part of Devereux Road which leads to Salisbury Road, was the site of the cricket pitch. I assume that football was played on the same pitch. If not, then the field to its left, field number 827, being 4.8 acres in size, could have been used, although much of that field still exists today and the ground is a bit rough. A third large field, some 6.7 acres, at the corner of what is now Salisbury and Burlington roads was available. 'Springfields House' itself was at the top end of Roebuck Lane, and the house and its lawns were where Salter's Vale is today. A lane or track ran from near no. 27 Roebuck Lane (today) to the pavilion. After the death of George Salter in 1902, Springfields was turned into the sports and social club for Salter Springs Co. employees, right up until about 1970. Many ex-Salter employees still alive have good memories of the Salter Social Club in the post-war years.

Cricket had been played on Roebuck Lane from at least 1860, for on 12 July of that year, West Bromwich cricket club played an England XI there, and two years later, Salters cricket club also played the England United XI. The cricketers left there after 1893.

The footballers are also recorded as playing on 'Bagots Field ' during 1887, defeating Oldbury Town Crosswells by 2-0 on 21st November. Salters FC also defeated Smethwick Carriage Works FC by 3-1 on 23rd October 1886, so it is possible that Bagots Field and the Springfields ground are one and the same, or an adjacent field. Both of those two opponents competed in the Birmingham Senior Cup or Birmingham League, and so it can be judged that a full strength Salters' team would be very a competent one, comprised as it was of several men who were now playing for the Albion. Salters' colours are not recorded, but it is very likely that the shirt incorporated a Staffordshire knot with an arrow through it, as this was the company's trademark, and this was copied on to early Albion shirts too.

There were no less than seven Salters' employees in the 1886 West Bromwich Albion cup-winning side. It is unclear whether the West Bromwich Strollers was a team formed by workers from Salters as an outside club, or whether the Strollers were actually the Salters' works team itself. Whichever way, after the Strollers evolved into the Albion, workmen annually assembled a Salters football team which played Albion and other works teams. To this day, there is a close bond between the two organisations, since Salters was the mother-figure which spawned the West Bromwich Albion club and gave employment to footballers for generations afterwards. George Salter himself, in addition to turning out at cricket for Salters and West Bromwich Dartmouth, also played a key role in the West Bromwich FC, the footballing off-shoot of the Dartmouth club. He regularly played in goal, or wherever else he could be of use, from 1876 to 1881.

Early key players included:

Amos Adams (1880-1941), a defender, played over 200 games for the Albion, after starting out with Salters in the mid-1880s.

Harry Bell (1862-1948), also a defender, played with Albion from 1879 whilst at Salter's but was forced to retire early in 1887.

George Timmins (b. 1858), Harry Green (1869-1900) both fullbacks, enjoyed three Cup Finals whilst with the Albion; Harry Green, Bob Roberts, Charlie Perry, George Woodhall, and Ezra Horton were all still working at Salters when Albion lost the 1886 FA Cup Final to Blackburn Rovers at the Derby Racecourse ground.

Salters and West Bromwich Albion became synonymous; with Salters men on the board, training team, and management. There was also a separate part of the grandstand at the Hawthorn ground for important Salters' men.

Thomas Wilbury, of the Mayers Green Congregational Church, which they attended each Sunday, brought them their first football. Wilbury was also, with George Salter, on the committee for the Albion.

So having launched the Albion from its nest, the Salters works team carried on just being a small-time amateur works' side, but for some years, Albion men continued to work at the Salter's Spring factory. Salters FC made their one and only appearance in the Birmingham Cup in 1882/3 season, but on Saturday 28th October 1882, they lost 2-3 away to minor side Grove and didn't enter again.

Salters were still a capable side, especially towards the end of the 1880s. They beat Smethwick Carriage Works 3-1 on Saturday 23rd October 1886 and Oldbury Town Crosswells by 2-0 on 21st November 1887, at Bagot's Field, West Bromwich.

Salters football team continued to play friendlies and minor cup competitions (e.g. Walsall Junior Cup, West Bromwich Junior Cup) for some years, until the turn of the new century. They also launched their own Salters Cup for minor teams in the area, such as West Bromwich Trinity Victoria and the Tipton Lancers.

An entry in the Birmingham Football Association yearbook for 1929 still listed Salters FC as an active club, with their club secretary being one George P. Wilson of 22 Bernard Street, West Bromwich.

References

Whittakers' Guide 1914
Birmingham Post 1886/7
Play Up Brammidge! Steve Carr, 2004
Cricket Archive Oracles
Salters cricket club

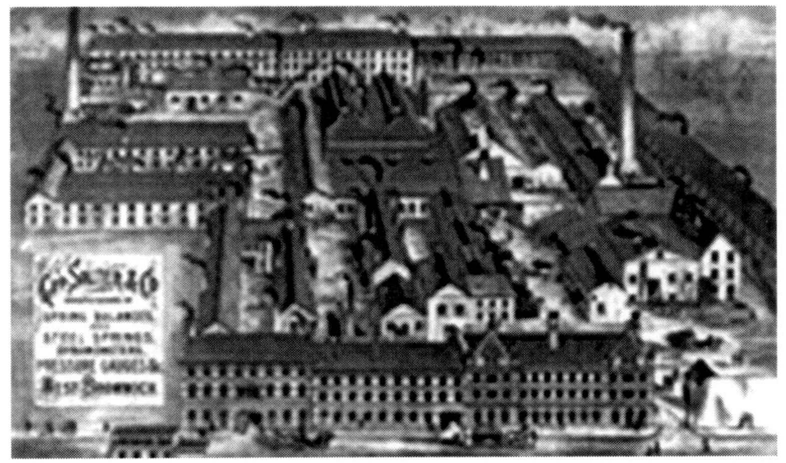

Salters Factory

Salters, and Albion Goalie Bob Roberts

Saltley College FC

f. 1870 full name: St. Peter's College, Saltley
It is believed to be the oldest football team in the Birmingham district.

Nickname: 'The Old Salts'

Colours

1. red and gold hoops (1870s)
2. medium blue shirt with gold yoke, red socks (circa 1880-1900)
3. red and gold quarter shirts (1940s/1950s)

Birmingham FA representatives:
G. Copley and J. A. Toy

'Star' players:
Teddy Johnson, James Egin, George Copley

The young men from Saltley teachers college in east Birmingham were a good early team who did well in the local cup competitions. The college was a Christian-faith training college, and its players were lean and fit, both physically and mentally. They were likely to have been teetotallers.

They chiefly played the rugger game and still have a rugby team today (see web site). The well-kept sports ground cannot be seen from the road, and the ground still has a meadow-like atmosphere, the pitch being used also for athletic events until the college was closed down from its purpose in 1978. It is now almshouses and local government offices. It once stood alone in fields but is now hemmed in by council houses.

In 1875, they were instrumental in the development of the Birmingham AFA and sent Messrs Swallow and Thompson as their representatives to the meetings, and so hold an important position in the history of Birmingham football.

In 1876, the *Birmingham Post* began to print local football results, proclaiming that the people of Aston had taken up 'football exercise' in a big way and that there were several clubs already in existence. Amongst several low-scoring games, the one which leaps out is the Saltley College 5-0 Aston Villa scoreline. Villa were only in their 2nd season, and Saltley College had been playing a version of football-cum-rugby for at least five years by this time. Soon, the rugby team – which still plays today as the Old Salts RFC – split off as the two codes made their separate way.

In 1877, they had the dubious pleasure of being the first visiting team to Small Heath's new Coventry Rd (Muntz Street) ground on 11th September 1877. They were beaten 5-0 and blamed, as most visiting teams did for the next twenty years, that the terrible pitch would allow them to play their usual passing game.

However, they were crushed 10-3 by Wednesbury Old Athletics at Wednesbury Oval on 26th September 1878, which highlighted the plight of a college-based football team where its best men might leave every two years.

The Collegians reached the first ever Birmingham Senior Cup final, losing 1-3 to Aston Villa in 1879/80 with this side: Copley, Barnett, Hollyhead, Mathinson, Chattell, Sumner, Johnson, Cornes, Dodsworth, Richards, Morley. But they came back for another three consecutive semi-finals, a testimony to their capability as a useful side.

The team of 1880 was: George Copley (goal); backs: D. Rutherford and W. Dodsworth; halfbacks: T. Mattinson and H. Beesley; forwards: W. Sumner, A. W. Rickards, Teddy Johnson, F. W. Cook, D. Williams, and J. Egin, Johnson and Egin being their best two men. The many changes were down to the fact that men studied at the college for a minimum of two years, and so the team was at the mercy of availability more than most; it's a credit to their organisation that they continued to compete at this level for over a decade.

George Copley was pinched by Aston Villa in 1882 and was their goalkeeper for some years after. Before coming to Saltley College, Copley had been goalkeeper at Quilter's Birmingham C&FC at the Aston Lower Grounds. Villa's plan was to snap up all the best players from all the surrounding clubs and make an instant super team, which is exactly what they did, and this moved the Villa on leaps and bounds until they stood head and shoulders above teams within a ten-mile radius, with only the Albion, Wolves, and Walsall able to give them a good game after about 1881.

The College was built in 1852 by Lord Norton as a Christian teachers' training college, 'for the theological education of lay Christians' and is still there today in the Saltley district of Birmingham near Adderley Park station. It was closed as a training college only in 1978 and is now run as a Christian trust foundation with headquarters in Edgbaston. With the help of my Birmingham guide John Green, who had business links with Saltley College, we were able to enter the college building and go through to the sports field at the back. The last thing he expected to be revealed was the well-kept ground, not much used for that purpose these days, as much of the college was now inhabited by elderly or at-risk people who were in effect living in a protected almshouse setting, maintained by the St. Peter's College Trustees.

Adderley Park itself was the first municipal park in Birmingham.

By the 1880s, the college had trained 300 students. Importantly, they had their own sports field within the college grounds. They played their home games there and importantly had the benefit of being able to practise and train daily if they wanted, on their doorstep. This mirrors the earthen parade ground of the Royal Engineers FC at Chatham, who also benefitted from regular practice, without having to walk long distances to the pitch.

In 1885, the College men entered the Birmingham Cup again after a few years' absence, but a long trip to face the Castle Blues at Shrewsbury proved fruitless as they were beaten 4-0 at Monkmoor. They had a double Darlaston visit in 1886 when they won 2-1 at Darlo Town in round 1 but then were beaten there when they returned in the November to play the All-Saints who beat them 3-1. The year 1887 saw them go out to Sutton Coldfield at the first hurdle, and 1888 was no better as they were beaten by the Handsworth team called Southfield.

Edward 'Teddy' Johnson (1860-1901) was a speedy right-winger who played for Saltley College from 1878 to 1881. He was born in Stoke, so, fittingly, he joined Stoke FC where he gained 2 England caps in 1884, scoring 2 goals in England's huge 8-1 away win in Ireland.

Jack Addenbrook had more football fame as an administrator. He joined the Wolves in 1883 and was a regular in their 2nd team. He was from a large family of Addenbrookes who played for several teams across Wolverhampton, Walsall, and Birmingham.

After a short spell as secretary, he became Wolves' longest serving manager, of some thirty-seven years.

To get a view of the Saltley College ground today is almost impossible I'm afraid without special permission from the Trust, as I did in 2010. Walk into the college car park and bear right and go the end, right around the back. You will get a glimpse of the sports ground through the chain-link fence.

ACKNOWLEDGEMENTS

Tony Mathews, *Complete Record of the Wolves*, ISBN 978-1-85983-632-3
Ian Jones, Trust Director, St. Peter's College, Saltley
Birmingham Daily Post
The Old Salt's Association

Saltley College

Saltley College Football Ground

Saltley College

Shrewsbury Engineers FC

f.1875 ?

They were a short-lived club formed by some royal engineers based in Shropshire, probably at the Copthorne Barracks

Colours
unrecorded, my best guess is red and blue hoops

The recorded history of Association football in and around Shrewsbury between 1860 and 1880 is very scant; a whole day spent at the town's Archives Library at the fifteenth century Old Shrewsbury Grammar School proved frustrating. Apart from a well-produced book on the history of Shrewsbury School, there was almost no documented history on file or in the newspapers. It is likely that they played at the Barracks ground at Copthorne, which is still there today.

We do know that a succession of young men went through Shrewsbury school and on to the universities and professional careers in London, or they came back to Shrewsbury, Wellington, and Birmingham to set up their businesses. These men would return perhaps for a short while to Shrewsbury and set up short-lived football teams. Often we find the same names in these teams, who probably weren't football clubs in the proper sense. What we do know is that the Shrewsbury Engineers won the Shropshire county cup when it was first begun around 1876. This was probably their debut season.

Much ado was made in the press when Shrewsbury Engineers met the Wednesbury Strollers in the 1st round of the 1878 Birmingham Cup competition. The Midland Athlete newspaper thought that whoever won this tie would surely go on to win the cup. With no reputation outside of Shropshire to call on, I can't see what this claim was founded on, apart from the knowledge that the Salop team contained one or two well-known individuals. As it was, the Strollers ran out 3-1 winners and went on to progress to the 3rd round (last 7). The Midland Athlete said the Engineers were a fast and pressing team, but they were behind the better teams of the day with respect to their lack of passing, with old-fashioned long dribbling by the man in possession of the ball. This sounds like classic London Wanderers' playing style. However, in October 1878, Shrewsbury Engineers played a home-friendly match with the Wednesbury Old Athletic, who had built up a reputation as being one of the top three or four sides in the Midlands.

The Engineers won 3-2 and thus must have rapidly put themselves near the top of the footballing tree in the West Midlands, having beaten both the Wednesbury clubs, six months apart. In the following year, Engineers entered the Birmingham Cup and comfortably beat the little Christ Church team of West Bromwich by 4-0 at Four Acres, in round 1, at the West Bromwich Dartmouth ground, which was in the field next to the school. Christ Church School had been the foundling school for Dartmouth and also the Albion. However, in round 2, Engineers found a strong Shropshire foe in a Newport side and were beaten 2-1 at the little Victoria Hotel ground before a big crowd of over 500. My family once lived in Newport, and I doubt that was nothing less than the entire population of that village! Newport entered the following year but were steamrollered 6-0 at home by the young Aston Villa; Engineers did not enter the Birmingham competition again.

Entering the Welsh FAW cup in 1880/81, for the one and only time, they went out 0-1 to Newtown White Star in the 1st round.

The Shrewsbury Engineers team of 1878 was: Morris, Williams, Lane, Stanley, Davies, Tyrer, T. Ward, Wilson, Dodson, Holbrook, E. Davies.

Wilson and the strangely named Tyrer both also played for Wellington St. George's, and Thomas Ward was actually a Newport FC man, and so he would have played against them in the 1879 game.

If they played at the Barrack ground, Copthorne, then Copthorne Drive is the street which now occupies the location of the ground, on the other side of the road to the impressive castellated barracks.

References

History of the Birmingham Cup, Steve Carr
Shrewsbury Local History Library

Old Salopians' Alma Mater-Shrewsbury Old Grammar School

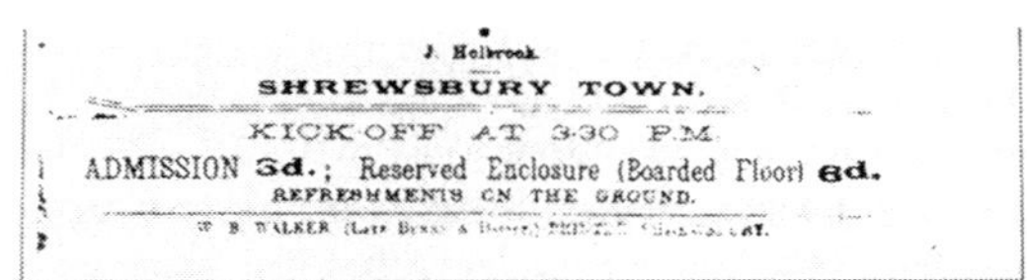

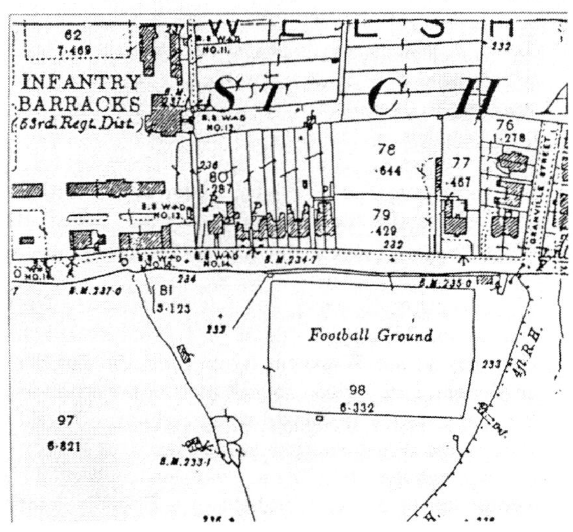

Shrewsbury Engineers' Barracks Ground

Shrewsbury FC

f. 1874-79
No connection with present-day Shrewsbury Town

Honours
Birmingham Senior Cup 1877

Colours
all white (1879/80)

Grounds

1. played at Monkmoor Lane and the Parade ground in 1877-1879
2. Armory Field
3. Cotton Hill Fields
4. Also at the Shrewsbury Racecourse ground
5. Amblers field circa 1889 (as the new Shrewsbury Town)

The old racecourse ground was demolished in 1920 and partly built over. The Shrewsbury Hospital now occupies the spot. All the above grounds were used by various Shrewsbury teams in the nineteenth century.

The history of football in Shrewsbury is very random and largely unreported in the local press, and several teams claiming to represent the town or the county were formed and disbanded during the 1870s.

Boys from Shrewsbury grammar school (see photo) have long since played football in one version or another on the many meadows along the riverbanks, and in-house games were developed similar to at Harrow in early years (1860s). Shrewsbury School, one of England's oldest, has a long history of playing football and was playing up to ten matches a year against other schools and colleges throughout the 1860s. Because of the promotion of athletic sport by the headmaster, football was compulsory three times a week by 1870. This would nurture and provide the schoolboys with a platform on which to develop their football skills. Old boys would come home from their new bases, often London, and provide the school team with annual matches. This went on all through the 1870s into the twentieth century. A day spent in the Archives library of Shrewsbury Old Grammar School in May 2012 produced frustratingly very little.

The first team called Shrewsbury was started in 1874 but only lasted a year. It was reformed in 1875 but only played a few games between its own members for the first year or so. Shrewsbury grammar school has a long and famous football history; many of the game's early rules were formulated with the help of Old Salopians, and the school's first ever match against an outside team was in February 1877 when they met the Uppingham school, also famous for its connection with the early rules through assistant headmaster, J. C. Thring. The school had, of course, all through the 1850s and 1860s, been playing in-house games to their own version of the rules, in the same way that Harrow, Eton, Charterhouse et al had been doing in the south.

The oldest set of the rules of football (the 1848 Cambridge University Rules) now reside in the school's Moser Library.

John Hawley Edwards was known to have captained the Shrewsbury FC side from 1876 to 1880. He was a top-class all-round athlete in the true Victorian manner and was a county cricketer for Salop. He also played for Shropshire Wanderers and the Wanderers in London. He is believed to be the club's founder, along with C. E. Wace, a fellow professional colleague.

The team won both the Shropshire Cup and the Birmingham Cups in 1877/78. This was a surprise to the football establishments of Wednesbury and Aston, as Shrewsbury were an unknown factor. They beat the favourite Wednesbury Strollers in the final of the Birmingham cup at Villa's old Wellington Road ground by 2-1, with Ward and Sprott scoring for Shrewsbury and Tom Bryan replying for the Strollers. They had also beaten the other Wednesbury side, the Old Athletic, by 2-1 in the 3rd round, the winning goal coming in the eighty-fifth minute after a Strollers man had headed the ball into his own net to give Salop a twenty-ninth-minute lead. This result should have sent out a warning bell to the Strollers. Well at least somebody from the huge 6,000 crowd should have told the Strollers what to expect! Opponents were not to know that Shrewsbury had three London Wanderers men in their ranks! Edwards and the Wace brothers had already got cup-final medals from early FA Cup finals at London's Oval. In the inaugural Shropshire County cup final, they beat the Wellington Institute* by 1-0.

The Copthorne Parade Ground was on the opposite side of the road to the impressive barracks and was long ago built over. Its 6-acre site is now mainly Copthorne Drive and the surrounding cul-de-sacs.

The 1877 Shrewsbury team was: C. E. Wace (goal); E. J. Jones (back); B. Hallam and B. A. Salt (halfbacks); forwards: H. S. Chapman, A. T. Ward, W. E. Sprott, Hubert Wace (a London Wanderers' player), J. H. Edwards (also of the Druids and Wanderers), F. E. Salt, S. H. Sprott.

A year later, the team saw only three changes: W. Henry, W. Holt, and Edward Locke in place of B. Hallam and the Wace brothers, who were presumably detained in London.

A friendly match was played on Wednesday 14th March 1877, when Shrewsbury hosted the Stafford Road club from Wolverhampton. The 'Roadsters', having reached the final of the Birmingham Cup, and yet to meet their adversary, Wednesbury Old Athletic, were surprised to be outplayed by a strong home team who won 2-0 with goals from J. H. Edwards, the two Salopian backs, Ward and Wace being singled out for merit in the newspaper reports of the Birmingham press.

After Shrewsbury had won the 1878 Birmingham Cup final, the Wednesbury Strollers' men rather unsportingly claimed that several of the Shrewsbury players should be declared ineligible on the ground that they didn't reside in Shrewsbury. The first claim, involving A. T. Ward from Newport, Salop, about fifteen miles from Shrewsbury was thrown out by the smallest of margins, and the second claim against Hubert Wace was on the grounds that he resided in London! It was illustrated that he did in fact reside in London, but he was studying at The Bar to become a solicitor, that they were merely his rooms whilst he qualified; he did in fact own a large house on the outskirts of the town. The Midland Athlete newspaper said of the Shrewsbury team that 'their forwards were together, fast, smart, and unselfish with the ball' but added that 'their combination passing play was poor'. The two cup finalists at least shared a convivial supper together afterwards at Nocks Hotel in Wednesbury.

Strangely, they didn't return the following season to defend their trophy; rather a team called Shrewsbury Engineers competed for the rest of the decade. That team was beaten 3-1 at home in the 1st round of the 1878 competition. The Salop Engineers team was no doubt connected with the famous Royal Engineers side from Chatham, Kent, as both Shrewsbury clubs contained Engineers and Wanderers men. The Shropshire Engineers also went on to win the Shropshire County cup.

The Shrewsbury FC side which overcame Wednesbury Strollers on Saturday 6th April 1878 to win the Birmingham Cup at the Aston Lower Grounds was:

C. E. Wace (goal); E. J. Jones (back); B. A. Salt, A. T. Ward, H. V. Chapman (halfbacks); S. H. Sprott, W. E. Sprott, H. Wace, J. H. Edwards, F. E. Salt, G. H. Lock (forwards). These names differ slightly from Steve Carr's excellent 'The History of the Birmingham Cup', but I have taken my names directly from the Cup Final programme published by the Birmingham FA on the day. The Shrewsbury formation then was a 1-3-6, whereas Strollers, in maroon shirts, played a 2-2-6 formation.

In 1879, the first incarnation of the first team to use the Shrewsbury Town team name began but folded after a year.

In 1879/80, another team sprang up called the Shrewsbury Castle Blues. They joined the Welsh FA and entered the Wednesbury Charity cup without making any impact. They eventually gained a reputation for rough play and bad discipline, and following yet another game where fighting broke out and the football authorities fined the club, they decided to disband in 1886. Their most famous player was the oddly named Clopton Lloyd Jones, formerly of the London cup winning team Clapham Rovers. Lloyd Jones was born in Salop, at Hanwood House, played as an inside right, and later served on the Shropshire AFA committee in the 1890s. He was a keen bowler, rower, and played cricket for both Shropshire and Herefordshire.

On Saturday 11th January 1879, a team called Shrewsbury Athletic failed to turn up as arranged at Wednesbury to play the Old Athletic side, and the game never took place.

The present-day Shrewsbury Town weren't formed until 20th May 1886, believed to be as a resurrection of the old original Shrewsbury club from the 1870s. Castle Blues, themselves founded by grammar school old boys, were effectively forced to disband after a succession of rough-house matches and badly behaved players at their matches. Blues, as their title suggests, played in blue and white halved shirts, with white knicks. The Blues had beaten Wellington Town 2-1 to win the Shropshire Challenge Cup in 1884, but news reports described the game as more like a medieval battle than a football match between so-called gentlemen! Two years later, when the Castle Blues had been knocked out of the same cup competition by Wellington Town, the Blues players all turned up at the Ditherington ground of Castle Rovers, whom Wellington were playing in the next round. All through the game, the Blues' men hurled insults and threats of bodily harm to the Wellington players, and a fight broke out at the end of the game (won by Wellington) in which Bradshaw, their centre, was literally stripped naked and thrown into the canal next to the pitch! Three castle Blues men later appeared in court, and when the Birmingham FA got to hear about it, they ordered the Blues to disband, and they did so at the end of April 1887. There was now a void in Shrewsbury for a principal team, and so a meeting was called at the Turf Hotel on 20th May 1886 with a view to restart the old Shrewsbury club. Surprisingly, a few Castle Blues men were admitted into the ranks of the new organisation, which became the start of the present-day Shrewsbury Town club.

Most Shrewsbury teams incorporated the royal blue colour from the town's crest. The original Shrewsbury team played in all white, and a decade later, the new Shrewsbury Town began in all white too, but soon changed to royal blue shirts and blue stripes during the 1890s.

After 1886, the new Shrewsbury had started to play friendlies with teams which were emerging from mid-Wales. A Montgomery newspaper report from 27th March 1888 names this Shrewsbury side which played against Newport: Roberts, Jones, Long, Steadman, Morris, Davies, Prosser, Pearson, Ellis, Day, Carson.

The *Shropshire Star* reported that Shrewsbury only went with eight men and had to borrow three players from Newport. The match was played at the field behind the Victoria Hotel, the bottom part of which is now the town park. This then was the beginning of the present-day Shrewsbury Town side. Newport FC played in rather garish colours at their Victoria Park ground, behind the hotel of the same name by the medieval village church. Their shirts in the 1880s were scarlet, black, and blue stripes. Before that, they were just scarlet and black stripes when they were at their Chetwyn End ground in the 1870s.

The Shrewsbury team entered the Welsh FAW cup in 1886, began with a resounding 10-0 win away to neighbours Wem, but were brought down to earth when one of Wales' strongest sides Newtown beat Shrewsbury 1-0 at home in round 2. Now calling themselves Shrewsbury Town, they went down 2-0 at home to Oswestry in the 1st round of the 1887. In 1889/90 season, they got through to the 4th round, which was the last 8; they hammered Aberdare 15-0 in round 1 but met their match when once again, Newtown beat them 4-0. Scoring an average of 5 goals per game, Shrewsbury Town won the 1890/1 Welsh Cup, beating Wrexham 5-2 in the final. The year 1892 saw them robbed of a place in the final when it seemed that they had comfortably beaten Westminster Rovers by 4-0. However, as was all too commonplace in those days, Rovers protested after losing, about the state of the pitch, and the Welsh FA ordered a replay which Rovers duly won 3-1. An interesting game took place earlier, in the 1st round when Shrewsbury travelled and eliminated neighbours Wellington St. George's by 3-2. Season 1893/4 saw an interesting match in round 2 of the Welsh Cup when Shrewsbury, who seemed to have dropped the 'Town' tag again, comfortably beat neighbours Wellington St. George's again, by 6-1. The Shrews went on to round 4 where Oswestry put them out 2-0. Season 1894/5 Welsh Cup campaign started off in sensational style: the Shrews annihilated Mold Allyn Stars by 21-0! And that was on their ground! Normality returned in round 2 as they were put out 4-0 by the famous Druids of Cefn Mawr near Wrecsam (Wrexham). This last version of a Shrewsbury team went on to become the present-day Shrewsbury Town.

References

Shrewsbury Old Grammar School
The History of Shrewsbury Town FC
Charles Alcock annuals 1900-05
Welsh FA Football Database
The Wednesbury Herald
Shrewsbury Archive Library
The Shropshire Star

* This may have been the first name that Wellington Town used.

Shrewsbury Football

Shropshire Wanderers FC

f. 1872-1880

The club was founded by two London Wanderers men who had been through Shrewsbury and Ruabon grammar schools, John Hawley Edwards and Llewellyn Kendrick.

Importantly, Shropshire Wanderers were the first team from the Midlands to enter (1873) and compete (1874) in the FA Cup.

John Hawley Edwards (1850-93) was a London Wanderers player; he also was founder and captain of the Shrewsbury FC team which existed from 1886 to 1880. That Shrewsbury team were not connected with the present-day Football League side.

He was a regular in the side from 1873 to 1880 when he returned to his native county from the capital. Strangely, he was capped for England in 1874 and then played for the Welsh national side in 1876. Edwards scored for the London Wanderers in the 1876 Cup final at the London Oval. Llewellyn Kendrick qualified at the Bar in London and became a city solicitor, but his family home was Wynn Hall in Ruabon, near Wrexham. He was a prominent footballer with the Wanderers of London and played in four cup finals in the 1870s. In 1876, he, along with some other businessmen, formed the Cambria Football Association; within a year, it had changed its name to the Welsh Football Association.

The Salopian version of the Wanderers were the only team in the history of the FA Cup to have won a game on the toss of a coin after its home-and-away games with the famous Sheffield Club were goal-less draws. Team colours are unrecorded, but the London Wanderers began in an all-white uniform when they were known as Forest FC playing at Snaresbrook, before changing to their vivid hoops of orange, mauve, and black, although most early Shrewsbury teams incorporated the royal blue and gold of the town crest. Many early sides simply played in a white shirt and black or navy trousers cut off on the knee, sporting velvet caps with tassels!

In 1874/5 season, they entered the English FA Cup and remarkably reached the semi-finals; admittedly they didn't actually play their 1st round opponents, but a 1-0 win over the Civil Service team in round 2 followed by two games to get past Woodford Wells (1-1, 2-0) put them up against the wealthy old boys of the Old Etonians.

The Old Etonians were already the most famous team in the land – perhaps with the exception of the Wanderers – and they arrived in carriages wearing top hats and canes, and their pale blue – green and white halved shirts were made of silk, a stark reminder of the gulf of the Victorian class system.

They acquitted themselves well and only lost by the solitary goal of the game. Crowds were said to be around 700 for each of the three cup games. Coincidentally, the Salop Wanderers' last appearance in the FA Cup was a 1-0 defeat at the hands of Wales' top side, the Druids. Druids played at Plas Madoc park (now a housing estate) in Ruabon, which is where Kendrick resided and practiced. They later moved to a ground on Llewellyn's estate at Wynnstay in 1879. He had a hand in starting the Druids up too. They were formed in 1872 out of the amalgamation of Ruabon Rovers and Ruabon Volunteers. Their famous white and black colours went on the win the early Welsh Cup several times, sharing top billing with Wrexham, with Llewellyn as the Druid's captain. Llewellyn is now regarded as the father of Welsh football; both he and Hawley Edwards, a fellow solicitor, founded the Welsh FA at the Wynnstay Hotel. In a glittering professional career, he became Coroner for Denbeighshire in 1906, retiring from football in 1887, having represented both England and Wales.

In 1876, Wales played their first ever international against Scotland, and the Salop Wanderers' goalkeeper, David Thompson (also of Druids) was capped for Wales. Sadly, he conceded 4 goals in their defeat.

An interesting FA cup tie with the Royal Engineers on 9 December 1876 took place, for the match report in the *Birmingham Daily Post* reveals that the Shropshire Wanderers had both London Wanderers and locally based Royal Engineers men in its ranks! The Royal Engineers (Chatham) won 3-0 in front of a 2, 112 crowd. In the previous round 1, Shropshire Wanderers had been drawn to play the Druids! Since the two clubs shared several key players, it is likely that had a discussion to see which one would scratch, as the game was never played. In the end, it was the Salop club who went through. It was said, that by 1876, the Shropshire Wanderers were the first team in the Midlands to be playing the combination-passing game; this is very likely to have come from their association with the Chatham Royal Engineers team, who along with Queens Park (Glasgow), and Cambridge University were demonstrating the superiority of these new tactics, compared to the kick-and-rush game.

There was also a Shrewsbury Engineers FC around 1880, and it sounds as though they shared players with each other.

The Salop Wanderers team which met the Royal Engineers in that FA Cup tie in 1876 was:

Gilkes (goal)*

G. Mason and L. Kendrick** (backs);

Mason and H. V. Chapman (halfbacks);

Kenyon-Slaney,*** J. E. Denning, J. G. Wylie,** Hawley, A. T. Ward,† B. V. Randle, and Edwards.‡

The Engineers only turned up at the ground on the stroke of 2.30 p.m., the advertised kick-off time, and departed back to Chatham directly. It was goalless at halftime, but the Royal Engineers stamina told in the second half and they scored 3 goals. The home side put Randle in goal after the second goal went in. The *Staffordshire Sentinel* of 1876 said that 'despite an admission being charged, an immense number of persons assembled to witness the match'.

FA cup history	**1st Round**	**2nd Round**	**3rd Round**	**4th Round (semi-final)**
1874	Sheffield Club 0-0, 0-0 #	Civil Service Club walkover	2-0 Woodford Wells	0-1 Old Etonians
1875	Sheffield Club (A) Scratched			
1876	Ruabon Druids	Walkover	0-3 Royal Engineers (A)	
1877	Druids	0-1 (A)		

won on toss of a coin after nearly four hours of goal-less play

In summary, they were an ad-hoc team for when Kendrick and Edwards returned to Shrewsbury, as Shrewsbury School archives library produced no recorded information.

+ A. T. Ward played for several clubs across Shropshire – Old Salopians, Shropshire Wanderers, Newport

++probably J. H. Edwards

* Gilkes replaced by Randall after injury

** Wanderers men

***a Royal Engineer

Singers FC (Coventry)

f. 1883-1898
became Coventry in 1898, later Coventry City

Honours
Birmingham Junior Cup 1891, 1-0 v Willenhall Pickwick
1892, 2-1 v Willenhall Pickwick

Formed by Willie Stanley and workmates from the Singer Cycles factory at the Alma Street works, in the Hillfields district of the Coventry. A previous attempt at a football club, called the Coventry Association FC had been short-lived. A local man, J. Sidney Clarke had been trying to organise some football activity on Stoke Green since 1870, but this was a mixture of rugby and Sheffield rules, and it led to the formation of the town's rugby club. According to Lionel Bird's comprehensive book on the *History of Singers FC*, Stanley called a meeting on 13 August 1883 at the Lord Aylesford Inn (sadly lost in the blitz bombing) in Aylesford Street, and the football club was begun. They used the White Lion public house at Gosford Green as their headquarters. William was the manager and secretary as well as team centre forward for the first few years!

Their first ground was the huge 8-acre field at the edge of town known as Dowell's Field, or the Far Glade, at Gosford Green. For the most part, it is still there today, although some of it was built over in the 1920s. Gosford Park Junior School and playground now occupies about one half of what was the pitch. The second, much better ground, was at Stoke Road by the Britannia Mill, and was naturally enclosed with tall trees and hedges, which made it feel like a private ground. There was a pavilion and fencing and entrance was from 2d (<1p). Crowds were ever increasing, and their final match at Stoke Road, against Nottingham Forest, attracted 5,000. This is now built over by Britannia Road, Mowbray and King Richard Streets. As it ended up, their most well-known ground, Highfield Road (which wasn't on Highfield Rd!), which the Sky Blues occupied until the end of the twentieth century, was almost in the next field directly north by 500 yards.

The team subsequently gained the early nickname of the 'Vocalists' circa 1887, although some Birmingham papers were calling them the 'Birds'.

Colours

1. blue and white stripes (1888)
2. pink and blue halves (1889)
3. all black, with orange 'S' on chest (1890)
4. light blue shirt, dark blue shorts (1891)
5. red and black halves (1892-1898)

Grounds

1. Dowells Field (a.k.a the far Glade) St. George's road off Binley Road (1883-1887)*see web site photo
2. Britannia Street (1887)
3. Stoke Road (1887-1889)-now occupied by Mowbray and King Richard Streets
4. Highfield Road stadium (1899-2005)

Early near-success came when they entered the first Birmingham Junior cup in 1888/9 and got to the semi-finals. Their opening round 1 match was away to the young Small Heath Alliance team.

They played in the Birmingham League from 1894, then the Southern league until 1919.

Their league record was nothing to write home about, finishing 13th for three consecutive seasons (1894-5-6). Seventh in 1897 was their best year. In their first league season under the banner of Coventry, they came 16th and conceded 100 goals in 30 matches. Thus a pattern of strugglers was set which modern-day Sky Blues fans will have empathy with! At this time, their main local rivals were the emerging Whitworth works side known as Rudge, who won the Birmingham Junior cup in 1896/7. Rudge was another cycle-making company which prospered during the cycling boom of the 1890s, of which Dunlop's pneumatic tyres were a key element for ladies taking up the pastime. The two clubs vied for the king-of-the-town status during this period, and it was no surprise when Singers FC applied to the Birmingham AFA for permission to change their name to Coventry City FC in May of 1898. A surprise objection came though, from the town's long-standing rugby club, Coventry RFC, on the grounds that the public might get confused. The FA in London, however, had no such worries, and Sir Frederick Wall sent Singers a letter on 12 August 1898 to confirm they were now known as Coventry City.

Best Players: Harry Edwards – went to Small Heath

The Singers' side of 1893 was: Kirk or Casey (goal) Alldrick, Weston, or Bates (backs); Simms, Edmonds, J. Mason or Brigg, Law, Bird (halfbacks); Dorrell, Wilson, Bodley, Fletcher, W. Mason, Roberts, Harry Edwards (forwards).

The Singers' best years were between 1887 and 1892. They won the Birmingham Junior Cup in 1891 and 1892, defeating unlucky Willenhall Pickwick on both occasions. They also picked up the Walsall Junior Cup in 1892 by beating Bloxwich Strollers 3-1 at Villa's Perry Barr ground. However, they were thumped 6-2 by Wednesbury Old Athletic in the 1892 Wednesbury Charity cup final.

Despite the frequent shirt colour changes as listed above, by 1894, they were being called 'the reds' by the Coventry press, so presumably they had dropped the black from their shirts.

Their 1891 side which beat Willenhall Pickwick 2-1 on 18th April, to retain the Birmingham Junior cup was:

Kirk (goal); Glew, Cashmore (backs); Howell, Cannings, Edmonds (halfbacks); Dorrell, Bird (captain), Mobley, Pretty, Banks (forwards).

To find Dowells Field today, it's by the large roundabout at the junction of the A444 and the A428 at Binley. In fact, all four of Singers'/Coventry's grounds lie alongside the northbound A444.

ACKNOWLEDGEMENTS

The Vocalists, *History of Singers FC*, Lionel Bird, from Coventry City FC web site
Coventry Evening Telegraph 1892
Coventry Herald 1893

Small Heath Alliance

f.1875

Colours

1. dark blue shirt, with a white sash, white shorts (to 1882)
2. royal blue shirt (1886-1893) except – 1885/6 black and gold stripes 1889/90 black shirt with gold trim
3. pale blue shirt with dark blue trim (1893-1900)

Nickname: 'the Heathens'

Small Heath began life as a winter football team of the Holy Trinity Cricket Club in autumn 1875. The first pitch was waste ground on Arthur Street directly opposite St. Andrew's today (to become the bus depot building still there). This would have been a terrible pitch, as Arthur Street slopes noticeably, both top to bottom and side to side. The principal young men who founded the club were: W. H. Edmunds, the James brothers, and the three Edden brothers: Will, Tom, and George. The James brothers stayed loyally with the team for over ten years. They agreed to turn out in any dark blue shirt which each man could purchase or possessed.

They then moved to an enclosed field on Ladypool Road, Sparkhill, for one season, with a roped-off perimeter and some palings, which enabled them to charge a 3d (1p) admission. No one has been able to locate this ground, but I suspect it was the ground in St. Paul's Road just off Ladypool Road in Highgate district, which was used by the Pickwick cricket club and later by Havelock FC (who became the famous Moseley rugby club). This is now a small public park.

They then moved into the Muntz Street ground (now the exact site of Muntz School) in September 1877. The rent was £5 p.a., and the first gate receipts= 6/-(30p). This was known as the Coventry Road ground at the time.

Such was the interest in football in Birmingham that Small Heath had a 22-match fixture list by 1878. In 1878, they entered the Birmingham Cup. This was a bold move, only three years after their inception. They were drawn at home to the strong Calthorpe club, who won by the only goal of the game at Coventry Road. The following year, they were given no chance when they were drawn away to mighty Wednesbury Old Athletic, the cup holders. In one of the biggest cup shocks of early West Midlands' football, they came away 2-1 victors from the Oval, and the stunned 2,000 Wedgburians trudged off home. Another thrilling tie saw the Heathens clash with Aston Unity in the next round. A 1-1 draw at home in front of almost 1,000 brummies saw an 8-goal thriller at Aston Lane, with Unity coming out 5-3 winners. The year 1880/1 season saw the Heathens reach the 4th round. They cruised past Stoke (then a junior team) by 6-1 and were lucky enough to get a bye in round 2. The 3rd round saw them get their own back on Aston Unity, for they beat them 6-4 in another high-scoring match. Due to the odd numbers of entrants, and the fact that the Birmingham FA didn't seem to be able to understand that knockout cups work best with multiples of eight teams (32, 64, etc.), there remained 6 sides in the 4th round. There were some big names there in the draw, viz. Albion, Villa, Walsall Swifts, WOA. All games were played at the Aston Lower Grounds, and they drew the Swifts out of the hat, and they proved too strong for the young Heathens, winning by 4-0. The Swifts went on to beat Villa in the final, so Heathens fans would have been happy to hear the news! The Old Athletics got their own back in round 2 of the 1881/2 competition when they crushed Small Heath by 7-2 at Coventry Road. An unknown side called Small Heath Swifts managed to get to the 3rd round in 1882 but wish they hadn't when Aston Villa annihilated them by 21-0 in front of just 500 people. That works out to 1 goal per 25 people! A curious match in round 2 of the 1884/5 competition saw them apparently beat Excelsior 2-1 at home, only for the match to be ordered to be replayed after an appeal. The replayed game saw Excelsior stun a huge 3,500 crowd by winning 5-3. In this year, 1885, the team turned professional.

There were goals galore when they met Sandwell in round 1 of the following year. A 3-3 draw at their Trinity Road ground saw the Heathen crush them by 10-3 in the home replay. Another 3-3 draw in round 2, this time with Wednesbury Old Athletic, saw the Heathens go out by 3-1 in the replay at the Oval on 28 November. Season 1886/7 saw them get past Stafford Road (7-0) and a schoolboy side Coseley (13-0) plus a bye to get them into the 4th round again. A measure of the improvement of the team was shown when they beat Derby Junction by 4-0 to reach the semi-finals where they faced Long Eaton Rangers from Derbyshire. At this point, the Rangers were nearing their peak and went on to win the cup, beating West Bromwich Albion in the final. It took them two games to get past Small Heath; a 2-2 draw at the Lower Grounds was replayed on 21st March 1887, and the Heathens went out 0-2. After 1888/9, Small Heath were considered strong enough to be one of the eight teams exempt until the competition proper (4th round), and from then on, they often reached the semi-finals. The first time was in 1893, but they won't want to remember that Aston Villa trounced them 5-0 in front of the competition's biggest attendance yet: 15,000. They lost the 1895 semi-final by 3-2 in extra time when the Albion beat them at the Molyneux Grounds, Wolverhampton. The Villa put them out in both 1903 and 1904, but finally Small Heath* got their own back on 26th September 1905 when they won 3-1 at the Lower Grounds. Better than that, they then got past Stourbridge (6-1) to meet the Albion in the final on 20 February. Small Heath* by this time were in League Division One, having made steady progress through the turn of the century. On a bitterly cold day in front of a paltry 1,500 crowd, they overwhelmed the Albion by 7-2 and thus won the Birmingham Cup for the first time. A few months later, they added the Staffordshire Cup to the trophy cabinet to complete a wonderful season. The Villa were beginning to look over their shoulders . . .

Their first silverware came back in 1882 when they defeated the famous Wednesbury Old Athletic in the Walsall cup final.

Muntz Street ground had a hump at one end, and a line of trees next to the road, which came almost up to the touchline and was in effect a three-sided ground. It was too easy for spectators to get into the ground without paying from Gesseys Fields. Even twenty years later, the pitch was famously terrible, known locally as the 'celery patch'. Visiting teams, in cup ties, would offer financial inducements to switch the venue back to their own ground, because they knew the lumpy, bumpy pitch would wreck any playing skills they possessed. On the plus side, the team were steadily improving and began attracting the star players from the smaller local teams. Being on a main 'A' road, there were good tram and train services to the ground.

The club set about improving the ground over the years, erected a stand at the Coventry Road side, and later (1897) bought the old stand from Villa's Wellington Road ground for the princely sum of £90, dismantled it, transported it to Muntz Street, and reassembled it again. In 1889, they joined the Football Alliance, which was the unofficial division below the new Football League, and by 1892, Small Heath were crowned champions of the newly formed Second Division at the first attempt. They could now join the ranks of the big three, Wolves, Villa, Albion, in the First Division with heads held high. By 1900, crowds were peaking up to 30,000; houses had been built over Gessey's Fields and had hemmed in the ground, which was bursting at the seams for cup ties and derby games, and a new home was urgently needed.

An old brickworks site was identified only half a mile away and was developed into the St. Andrew's ground at a time when Small Heath evolved into Birmingham City Limited, with shareholders, and the chrysalis that was

Small Heath Alliance had become the Birmingham City butterfly. The chief reason for the success of Small Heath lay in the fact that Aston was its own town, albeit only three miles away, but the inhabitants there had all gathered around the Villa, displaying a tribal fervour within their own community, and Aston people were separate from Birmingham people. Small Heath, mainly due to the inability of any of the other junior local teams to make anything of themselves, i.e. Calthorpe or Warwick County in the 1890s, ended up without rival in the city, and their club and grounds were in a high-density population area. Even today, in the twenty-first century, in a city of over a million inhabitants, there is no third senior club with the demise of famous amateur side Moor Green.

Today, the Muntz Street school and community centre occupies the exact spot where the football ground used to be, albeit at 90 degrees to the ground, which had its goal behind Muntz Street (then a lane, ending at the fields just past the pitch), and its touchlines ran parallel to the Coventry Road. The name 'Muntz Street' was not used until St. Andrew's was built, as they are both effectively on the Coventry Road.

By 1884, Small Heath had strengthened themselves to be able to defeat the long-established Wednesbury Strollers by 8-2. This result was an illustration of one old era ending and another on the up. The Strollers were fast fading from the scene, with Small Heath's time yet to come. The 1880s and 1890s saw steady progress both on the pitch and in terms of stadium and facilities described above, and it was on the cusp of 1890 that the Heathens rattled in their club record scores. They defeated Nottingham Forest 10-0, Ruabon Druids 10-0, and Walsall Swifts 12-0 (twice), all during 1899. However, 1895 saw them take their biggest defeats, losing 9-1 to Blackburn Rovers and 8-0 to Derby County, both in the First Division.

This team of 1885 defeated Aston Unity 3-0 in the Walsall Cup, oddly played at the Aston Lower Grounds, Bodenham (goal); Gossey (back); T. James, Summers, F. James (halfbacks); forwards: T. Whitehead & A. James (left wing), W. Slater and Teychenne (centres), Hards and Rotherham (right wing).

This 2-2-6 was a bit behind the new thinking of the 2-3-5 formation that Cambridge University and others were now playing at the time. Two years later, they fell in line as this 1887 line-up against Walsall Swifts shows: Charsley (goal); Gittings and Spiller (backs); Morris, Caesar Jenkins and Ed Devey (halfbacks); forwards: Short and Walton (right wing), W. Devey (centre), Stanley and Heath (left wing).

In 1888/9 season, they entered the Birmingham Junior Cup in its opening year, and their opening game was a tough draw against the Singers FC of Coventry, who went on to win it twice at the start of the 1890s. Around 1895, the founding James brothers were turning out for the Lozells FC side, at the end of their footballing days.

In 1888, the club dropped the Alliance tag and fourteen years after that became plain Birmingham FC.

On Monday night of 30th April 1888, Small Heath staged a charity match, attended by 700 spectators. All three James brothers played for Small Heath Past v Present.

During the 1890s, Small Heath had steadily established themselves as one of the top twenty sides in the country. They were champions of the new Division 2 of the Football League in 1892/3, and runners-up to unbeaten Liverpool the following year, when they finally got promotion. They found life in the top flight a struggle, finishing 12th in 1894/5. However, the next year, they finished 15th out of 16 teams and got relegated back to the 2nd Division, where for the rest of the decade, they generally finished in the top six. Their reserve side was doing well in the Birmingham League, and they were runners-up in 1895/6, with 100 league goals, and came 3rd the following season.

At the club's AGM held at the Jenkins Street Board School (!) on 16th February 1895, the committee of Alf Jones (sec.), W. Hart, H. Willmott, Councillors Eli Bloor and J. Wilkinson, reported that despite modest success as a second division club, finances were poor and local support was well below expectation and needs. On the same day, Aston Villa were making plans to accommodate an expected 40,000 for the visit of Sunderland for their 2nd v top 1st Division league clash the following day.

The intense modern-day rivalry between Birmingham City and Aston Villa is well known nationally and is set to continue until the spiralling madness of footballers costing tens of millions of pounds, combined with the steady decline of attendances at all levels of the modern game force clubs into insolvency, and their eventual demise. Exactly like in the 1890s when small clubs tried to exist as amateurs, hoping to compete for crowds with the professional league sides. The home economics of living within one's means still has not been learnt!

As to the two club's rivalry in Victorian times, well, unlike today where we think of the Blues and the Villa as being from the same city, back in the last quarter of the nineteenth century, Aston and Birmingham were two nearby towns, and each had their own separate high-density communities from which to draw their following from. Today, in the north of the city, in areas like Kingstanding and Perry Barr or Sutton, there are an equal mix of 'Blue-noses' and 'Villains', a scenario which was unheard of a century previously. The Villa had, of course raced away by the late 1880s from Small Heath; as the Heathens improved into the 1890s, Villa roared away again with a golden decade of FA Cups and Championship titles into the Edwardian era. It was another fifty years before the rivalry was on an equal footing.

A Complete Record of Birmingham City – Tony Mathews 1995

FA Cup history as Small Heath-

1882/83	1st round	2-6	Stafford Road (Wton)
1883/84	1st round	2-3	Birmingham Excelsior

ACKNOWLEDGEMENTS

British History Online: A History of the County of Warwick (vol. 7)
Birmingham Daily Post

* As it is well known that Small Heath became Birmingham City in 1905, there are several large books which provide an extensive history of this team, far beyond the scope of this book. Suggested reading includes:

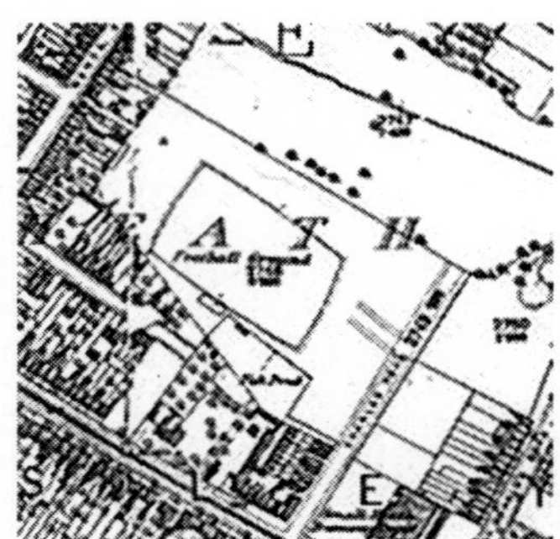

Small Heath's Muntz St. Ground

Smethwick Carriage Works FC

f. unknown – suggest circa 1887

Ground

1. Lewisham Park
2. Brasshouse Lane 1889/90
3. Middlemore Road sports ground, Smethwick (from 1890)

Team colours

1. red shirts, black shorts
2. red and white stripes after the 1930s

Honours

Birmingham Junior Cup winners 1890 (v Packington)
finalists 1891 Staffordshire Junior Cup (v Stoke Swifts)

Nickname – The Carriage-men

Lewisham Park had been leased to the townsfolk for recreational purposes by Lord Dartmouth in the 1860s, and the team began playing there until their own recreational ground had been made. It is still there today on Dartmouth Road near the Rolfe Street station.

Smethwick Carriage and Railway works was built in the 1870s when the London factory was moved to the Black Country. It became a huge factory employing around 2,000 people until 1963 when it was split up and sold off as separate industrial units. Many are still there today. A visit to the site of the grounds and factory in October 2012 revealed that even though two factory estates were built on the old sports ground, a view from the railway bridge by the infants' school allowed one a good overview of the size of the 15-acre ground.

They were fundamentally a works' team, but the factory was huge, some 60 acres, stretching from the A41 Holyhead Road down to Mornington Road, with a workforce of over 800 men to chose from. The locomotive and carriage works, with its network of internal railway lines, was only a quarter of a mile from the Albion ground, the Hawthorns.

They played in the Birmingham & District League and Birmingham Combination League. They were founder members of the Birmingham & District League in 1889 but fell back into works' league football after the start of the twentieth century (see 1940s photo). Their representative on the league management committee was Mr M. J. Round.

The team's greatest success came in the 1889/90 season, when they triumphed in the final of the Birmingham Junior Cup, defeating unknown village side Packington FC by 2-0. The match was played at the Coventry cricket ground on Saturday 5th April, and thanks to a special excursion train from Smethwick, they had the majority of the crowd on their side. The carriage-men edged the first half and held a 1-goal lead at halftime from Bond. Packington had the better of the second period, but the carriage-men broke away and scored a second decisive goal. They were clearly the best works side in the Birmingham district, and there would have been hundreds of such teams by then.

Their biggest win in the Birmingham League was when they thrashed the Willenhall Pickwick by 12-0.

The Carriage Works' team which beat Aston Victoria 5-1 on 11 November 1890 was:

Martin (goal), Turley, E. Sheldon (backs) Price, Bostock, Reeves (halfbacks), Gregory, Whittles, Mobley (centre forward) Wharton, Newhall.

This was only two months after their new ground inside the works' sports field was opened, on 22nd September, 1889, previously having played in Lewisham Park. I suspect that the football team were given their own sports ground by the company management as recognition for winning the Birmingham Junior Cup five months before.

It came to light just before publication that the team played on 'Brasshouse Lane' for a while, prior to getting their own sports ground inside the works. Brasshouse Lane turns out to be an old name for Halfords Lane, which runs down the side of the Hawthorns, and I would say they used the area which is now the Albion Community Sports Hall, next to the railway line, as the whole of that side of Halfords Lane was fields up until modern times, with two farms occupying the whole of the Hawthorns side.

In their five years on the B&DL, Smethwick gave a good account of themselves, never finishing below the halfway mark. They finished 4th on two occasions, in 1890 and 1891, and drew crowds of around 500 to 1,000 to their sports ground, which was accessed from an entrance at the end of Paddington Road, off the Holyhead Road (A41) just past the WBA ground. Kentish Road's terraced houses ran at the back end of the ground.

A site visit in the summer of 2012 reveals that the old entrance is now blocked when someone erected a wooden car garage across it. The site of the recreation ground can be seen from the nearby railway bridge on Wattville Road by the infants' school. It is now the rear end of an industrial estate, which itself has known better days. Smethwick Carriage Works resigned from the Birmingham League at the end of the 1894/5 season, by which time they were known simply as Smethwick FC. The reason is unknown, but perhaps the parent company stopped subsidising the team with its playing expenses, or it may have been that the company suddenly started to ask for a weekly rent on the sports ground. In April 1890, four Smethwick Carriage players were selected to play in the representative match, Birmingham Association v Leicester Association at Coventry: E. Sheldon at fullback, A. Bostock at halfback, B. Whittles at forward, and F. Mobley at centre forward.

Their own recreational ground was within the works complex, a huge 15-acre site near the junction of Hollyhead Road and Middlemore Lane, and only 500 yards from the West Bromwich Albion's Hawthorns ground. These two clubs were indeed very close neighbours, although Albion were the successful professional team with FA cup wins to their name, and SRCW were the lowly amateur works team, they could still give them a decent game until the turn of the century.

Their large sports ground was used for many different sports and activities; football, cricket, archery, tennis, bowls, athletics, and fun-fairs and carnivals. The pavilions, band stand, and bowling green lay at the corner where Belmont and Kentish roads join today. The tennis courts were at the top-most corner off Middlemore Lane, but access to the grounds appears to be limited to a single pathway coming off Paddington Road. The sports ground altogether measured 315× 135 yards and had cricket, football, tennis, and bowls all side by side. The football pitch had the athletics track around it. On wakes weekends, pavilions, and marquees would be erected and thousands would go there for a day's pleasure. When the factory was built from 1878, the land all around was just fields or wasteland, but by 1880, it had all been built upon with terraced housing. All the houses on the Watville Rd side of the ground still remain today as they were, the Watville School arriving in the early 1900s.

The factory had been moved up from London to take advantage of the rapidly expanding iron and steel, making heavy industries of the Black Country and its network of extensive canal and railway lines. The Smethwick works naturally encompassing its own network of an internal railway system linked to the adjacent Handsworth and Smethwick goods depot, for here they made railway wagons of every description and coaches for home and abroad; later, in wartime, tanks, aircraft, and even buses were manufactured.

The works even had its own fire brigade, and here, there may be a link to B'ham St. George's FC, as Harry Mitchell was a fireman with the Smethwick fire brigade in 1879. There may also be a yet to be discovered link to West Bromwich Albion, as their grounds were only hundreds of yards apart.

The *Worcester Chronicle* complained that on 20th April 1895, when Worcester Rovers went up to play the 'Carriagemen', that the Smethwick ground was the only one in the Birmingham League which did not have any goal nets and that the league committee ought to quickly do something about it.

Their best player was probably Teddy Sandford (1910-1995) who played for them in the late 1920s, but then signed professional with WBA as an inside forward in 1929.

References

Smethwick Telephone newspaper
Smethwick Local History Library

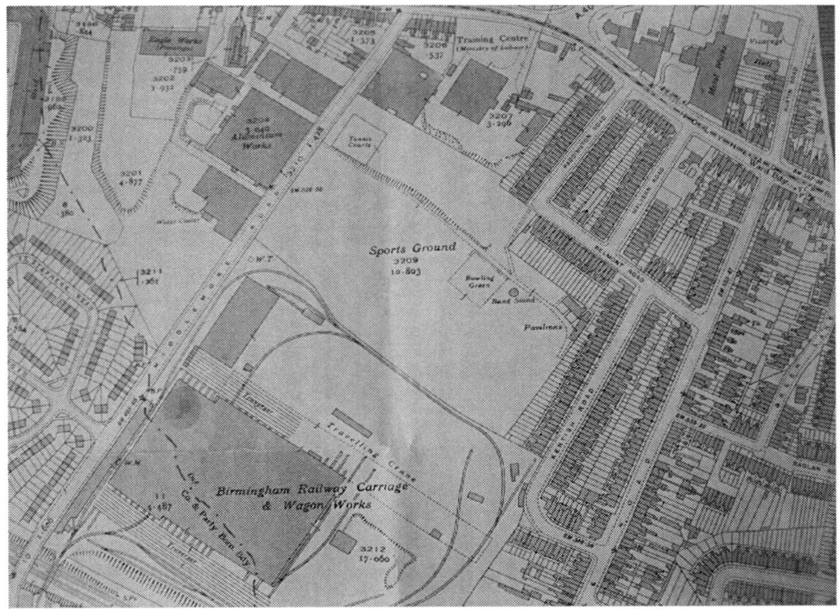

Smethwick Carriage Sports Ground

Smethwick CW Ground

St. George's FC (Birchfield, Aston)

f. 1875-(1885)†

Grounds

1. Aston Park 1876-1880
2. 1881-1885 Fentham Road cricket and football ground, Aston

Colours

black shirt with a white dragon on chest
black and white stripes

Hon. Secretary:
Mr T. Merrick

Nickname: 'The Dragons'

By 1876, a team called St. George's were playing friendly games against local opposition such as the early Wednesbury and Aston teams. In January 1876, they travelled to the Oval to play the Old Athletics, score unknown. They entered the Birmingham Cup from 1876/7 season going out to Cannock after a replay, at the first hurdle. Aston Villa, themselves a fledgling side, put them out in 1877/8 by 2-0 at Wellington Road, but after that, St. George's usually had a good Birmingham Cup run, peaking in the 1882/3 season when, after defeating Stafford Road 2-1, Walsall Town 6-2, Nechells Royal Oak 7-2 and Walsall Alma 7-1, they got to the semi-finals, where once again, Aston Villa beat them by 4-1 at the Aston Lower Grounds in front of 2,000.

There are no churches in the vicinity called St. George's, so their origins are probably a local factory. Their name is most likely to have come from the St. George's parish of Edgbaston in which they lived. There was also another team playing from the Fentham Road ground in 1879 called St. George's Claremont, but I cannot trace who they were, possibly the St. George's second team, or another minor local youth side. The only reference to Claremont I can find is a street of that name over in Soho, a mile out of Birmingham on the Smethwick side. Birmingham football historian Lee Gauntlett thinks that St. George's FC had 'Claremont' at the end of their name when they were formed, and they dropped it soon afterwards. If correct, this would move their origin two miles west to the Soho district of Handsworth.

However, Steve Carr's History of the Birmingham Cup tells us that both St. George's and Claremont St. George's entered the 1879/80 Birmingham Cup competition, and both teams played home games at Fentham Road. Perhaps 'Claremont' were St. George's second team.

The St. George's usual 1878/9 side was:

Cattell, Lockley, Brittain, Wigley, Pallet, Smith, Jones, Pallet, Horton, Arrowsmith, Evans. The newspapers sometimes called them St. George's Claremont during their early days when they played on Aston Park (as did most Aston teams when they started out).

The Pallet brothers, if not others, were also playing for Aston Unity at the same time, which doesn't come as a surprise since their two grounds were only a street apart. The heavy 1-9 home defeat by Unity in 1879 may have been because Unity had first call on those dual-club players. A year later, their side which travelled to play Bloxwich was entirely different:

Eagles; Stephens, Pritchard, Midgley, Tovey, Brinsford, Edwards, Appleby, Spokes, Lingard, Edkins (captain). The Palletts were turning out for Aston Unity, but Eagles, their goalkeeper, had joined them, and he was to stay at the club until the move to Cape Hill.*

On 22nd September 1881, St. George's ran out winners against West Bromwich Albion by the impressive score of 7-1 at Fentham Rd. Albion got some honour back in the following January when they won the home friendly fixture by 3-0 at Four Acres.

Season 1883/84 saw the clubs's silverware cabinet used for the first time, when they won the Staffordshire Cup, following on from Walsall Town the previous year's winners.

Season 1884/5 saw them hammer a young Coseley side 15-0, then beat Derby St. Luke's 3-0 before meeting the, by now, powerful West Bromwich Albion in the 3rd round, away at their Four Acres ground on Seagar Street. Football league status was only three years away for the Albion, yet St.

George's triumphed there by 3-2, a great performance. The Albion fans, already unaccustomed to defeats from local teams, went home stunned. Sadly, in the 4th round, they met a much-improved Walsall Town team whom they had thrashed 6-2 only a couple of years previously and went out by 4-1. The Dragons' star players in the early 1880s were Manton, Harrison, and Green.

The team were reported in the *Midland Advertiser* that they were still at Fentham Road in the February of 1885. At the same time, the Mitchells Brewery FC are reported as playing on the Cape Hill pitch.

The Mitchells Brewery football team in November 1884 was:

Wheeler; Richards, Grimley; Guest, Dudley, Gough; Bannister, Kimberley, Perks, Mallett, Allen.

None of those names appear against any Mitchell St. George's side of that or the previous year. This is clearly the works' own team, which seemed to have been replaced wholesale by the St. George's team from Fentham Road. As the 'Birmingham St. George's' team appear in photographs and football cards throughout the 1890s into the 1900s decade, and shown to be playing in light and dark blue hoops and stripes, this is clearly the brewery's own works team continuing to play after the professional B'ham St. George's were disbanded in 1892 by Harry Mitchell. We now know that about five years after the professional 'Birmingham St. Georges' folded in 1892, the brewery team re-introduced that name for about a decade.

Now, after June 1885, there seems to be no trace of this Fentham Road St. George's team, and this is where a mystery begins. Mitchell's St. George's had begun from the Cape Hill brewery in 1882 and entered the Birmingham Cup the year after we last hear of the St. George's from Aston, leading to a speculation that they were the same team. Wednesbury Old Athletic played both St. George's in 1885, the Aston team in the Wednesbury Cup at the start of May (1-1, 0-2), and the brewery boys in both the Staffordshire and Birmingham cups in December. It would appear that the Birchfield St. George's amalgamated with the brewery side over at Smethwick and the new team became Mitchell St. George's (later Birmingham St. George's). This must have been in the autumn of 1885, as Mitchell St. George's were recorded as playing at the Bellefield ground, Smethwick by that date. Since it is recorded that the brewery side existed from 1882 to 1892, then from 1882 until 1885, that must have been the Mitchells FC were in existence prior to the amalgamation. It would also make no sense for a team like St. George's who had their own sports ground to move to a pitch on a shoddy field five miles away. I think the bait attraction came when the brewery had the excellent oval sports ground built at the top end of the brewery village. The reason for St. George's leaving their own ground and moving to the next town is not known, but brewery jobs were part of the package.

Now a team called (Birmingham) Excelsior played at the same Fentham Road grounds after 1885, having previously played on the Aston Lower Grounds' nice Meadows pitch for about five years. So, at the end of the 1885 season, in the summer, it appears that the quite useful St. George's team moved out. Excelsior, who must have been one of their local rivals, moved into their Fentham Road ground.

So the St. George's mystery unravels thus: the (Birchfield) St. George's received an offer from Harry Mitchell circa summer 1885 to move wholesale across town to Smethwick to replace the brewery's amateur works' side to become their new professional representative team. They would play at nearby Bellefield ground, until the new cricket and football ground was built at the bottom of the works, and change their name to Mitchell St. George's, in exchange for his personal sponsorship. The rest of the story continues under the title of the new team name. When they vacated Fentham Road, the Excelsior team moved in. After the demise of the professional St. George's in 1892, the works team carried on representing the Mitchells and Butler's brewery.

References

Birmingham Daily Post
Charles Alcock's football annuals 1875-1899
Walsall Observer and *South Staffordshire Chronicle*
Tony Mathews, History of West Bromwich Albion, 2005
Mitchells & Butlers brewery

* + also see Birmingham St. George's FC

Birmingham St. Georges' Dennis Hodgetts (Far Right)
In Villa Team of 1892

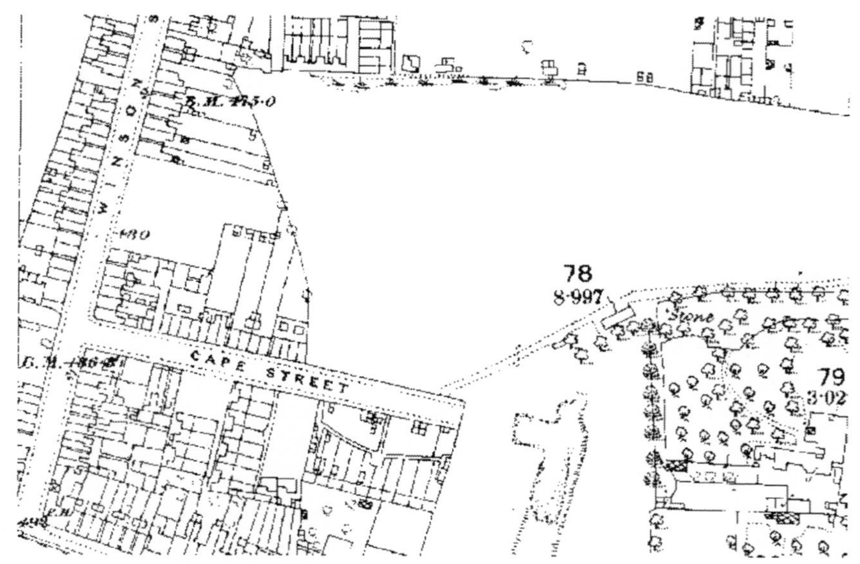

St. Georges' Ground at Bellefield, Winson Green

Stafford Road FC (Wolverhampton)

f.1867-1888

The Great Western and LNER railways converged half a mile north of Wolverhampton's two railway stations (high and low) in the district of Bushbury, and it was here that a sprawling loco repair and maintenance depot had been built. It is well-known to railway buffs as the Bushbury Shed. Nearly 1,500 men were employed there, and the progressive management had set up a workers' institute in 1855 to provide its poorly educated workforce with schooling and recreational facilities, as many had never been to school at all, or just for three or four years.

There was a library, gymnasium, railway seaside trips, a billiards room, and a fishing pool created on the first field by the canal bridge at the end of Foxes Lane (still there today as a sunken grass circle). A few years after the football ground was made, the institute also built a general sports ground near to the Gas Works, just under the multi-span viaduct. Buildings such as Cashmores warehouse and the NHS Independent Living centre now occupy the site.

Institute membership grew rapidly until there were over 800 members.

The Institute remained for over 100 years and was finally demolished in 1964. The huge Stafford Road railway depot works is now a trading estate near Goodrich (ex-Goodyear) Tyres company.

In the same year, a cricket, fishing, and athletics club had been formed, and in the winter of 1872, the football team was started by the enigmatic Charles Crump MBE. Crump was the leading name in Wolverhampton and held several high offices in civic and church life. He became mayor of Wolverhampton and was the Birmingham FA's first president. He became vice-president of the Football Association and from 1883 to 1923 was a member of the FA Council. Born in Leominster in 1840, he came to Wolverhampton in 1857 to take a position as a railway clerk at the Bushbury works on Stafford Road. A brilliant engineer, he rose to become chief clerk from 1868 until 1905. In his monocle and full grandee beard, Crump was the wise man of the Birmingham football scene, known for being an authority of every point of association football regulations.

He had seen what could be done when he saw the Stoke FC team born out of the LNER railway depot there. He set up the town's first football team with men drawn from the thousand workforce of the extensive Bushbury loco depot, which was almost a small village in itself. Crump loved the Christian muscularity of the game and played upfront whenever possible until he was in his early forties. By this time, his business and civic responsibilities caused him to move away from playing the game into becoming one of its greatest administrators. Crump was a deeply religious man and held the position of superintendent at the Darlington Street Methodist Sunday School.

He must have had a reputation as a fair and just man, for he was in great demand as a referee for cup finals; most of the Wednesbury, Walsall, and Birmingham cup finals were refereed by him, including the honour of refereeing the 1883 English Cup final between Blackburn Olympic and Old Etonians, which in itself marked the end of the Amateur Era. On his eightieth birthday, the FA presented him with mementos and a gift of £4000 in gold sovereigns as a mark of a lifetime service to football. He had been a staunch supporter of the amateur game in pre-professional days but had grown to accept the way that the game had developed by the end of the century.

Team Colours

1. navy blue and white hoops in 1877
2. all white in 1879
3. white with black hoops in 1881
4. cardinal red and black halves, white knicks in 1890s (see photo)
5. red shirts, white shorts in 1920s
6. post-war red shirt, white sleeves

Grounds

1. Fox Lane recreation ground (now near the city refuse Incinerator plant)
2. Molyneux grounds (before the Wolves moved in) during 1884-5
3. Tettenhall Road: one of the four possible sites which include W'ton cricket club, Newbridge Park, and Lower Green village. The pitch was heavily criticised as being boggy with long grass, and the latter site fits the bill, with its pronounced slope, both from top to bottom, and left to right. It's also in a dip, not far from the canal and brook. There's also a village green pub, and that is usually a good pointer! However, a short-lived club called the Wolverhampton Association FC played at Newbridge Park in the 1870s, and this could be to where they moved in the 1890s.
4. Bushbury Lane grounds (Star Motor Company ground) post-war period

In 1879, they drew 2,000 spectators for a game with the Walsall Swifts. This would have been the largest attendance in the area at the time, although facilities were basic, with players having to change in a pumping shed by the canal. On the 11th November 1876, Stafford Road met West Bromwich in a Birmingham cup tie: a dozen spectators amongst the crowd were from St. Luke's School in the town and had just resolved the day before to form a football team. They were impressed and learnt much of how to play the game properly, subsequently becoming the Wolverhampton Wanderers, the team that contributed much to the demise of Stafford Road within a decade.

Stafford Road developed a reputation as a bit of a strong-arm and enthusiastic team by the late 1879s and had a good following; it was said that when they travelled to Wednesbury to play the Strollers on 23 rd March 1878, more than half of the 450 crowd were from Wolverhampton. They lost 3-2 but had the temerity to claim the game since it was stopped three minutes short of the ninety due to darkness, but this was a result of them turning up late themselves! On 19 March 1881, a crowd of over 3,000 assembled on Fowlers Field at the end of Fox Lane for the visit of the famous Old Etonians for the 5th round tie of the English FA Cup. Stafford Road gave a good account of themselves before going down 1-2 to the previous cup winners, but one can only imagine the culture shock of the upper-class university men in their top hats and silks at their visit to the grimy and smelly Black Country, surrounded by collieries and belching chimneys! The Old Etonians had been to nearby West Bromwich in 1877 to play a friendly against the new Dartmouth FC, but even West Bromwich would have been a better place to play compared to the Fox Lane ground, it being surrounded by a canal, three railway lines, a sewerage plant and a sky full of tall chimneys. Although the concept of a club 'owning' a player buy purchasing his services was a long way off, and their players were free to play for however many teams they wished, it was still rather underhand when Stafford Road borrowed Wednesbury Old Athletic's two centre forwards for a Birmingham cup tie with the fast-rising Aston Villa in 1879/80 season. It did them no credit, for they still lost at home. On a return visit to the Fox Lane ground two years after my original photograph session, I walked from the canal bridge to the top, by the railway line foot crossing to gain a more panoramic view. I could now see that the large field, some 5 acres, had a hump all across the centre, and the pitch would not have been as level as I first thought. Drainage would have been poor, much as it is today, with a nearby brook often flooding adjacent rough fields, only occupied by tethered gypsy horses, and so I expect that rainy days made the pitch churn up quite quickly.

Sadly, as an early club, their best days were in the 1870s and early 1880s.

They had twice reached the final, and another semi-final in the first three years of the Birmingham Association Cup, but entry to the National FA cup came almost too late for them although the wonderful year of 1881 would have been their crest. As the 1880s and 1890s came, their best players would go to the Wolves, who were professional, and no doubt paid better terms than Stafford Road finances would permit. As an independent football club, the Wolves could import and export players; the Stafford Road FC, being a company side, could only draw from their own ranks, or lose top men to the Wolves or Walsall.

In 1879, they, along with Aston Villa became the second and third teams from the Midlands ever to enter the English FA Cup, with the agony of being matched against each other! However, the following season in 1880/81, Stafford Road FC got to the 5th round (last 6), only to lose 1-2 to the most famous amateur team in the country: the Old Etonians. The Eton old boys had such famous leading amateurs as Hon Lord Arthur Kinnaird, H. C. Goodhart, H. Whitfield, and J. B. Chevallier in their ranks. The pale blues found Stafford Road a tough opponent. Had Stafford Road won that game, they would have drawn the bye into the final against the Old Carthusians.

The club limped on, reformed once (1910) or twice, and ended its days in the lowly Wolverhampton Friendly League with other parks teams until 1930. The team was reformed yet again after the Second World War and enjoyed local success, twice reaching the final of the J. W. Hunt Cup (for amateur teams around the black country, though latterly won by Willenhall Town), beating Oxley 4-2 in the 1950 final, and now wearing an Arsenal-style kit of red shirts with white sleeves, the post-war playing years being spent at the ground behind the Star Motor Company plant in Bushbury Lane. The team finally ceased at the demolition of the works in 1964, putting the 1,500 workforce on the dole.

Players

E. Ray, J. Whitehead, G. Sellman were all selected to represent the Birmingham AFA against the Sheffield, London, and Scottish FA representative sides, games which were very popular in the nineteenth century. With the growth of the Wolves outpacing all other Black Country teams, it was inevitable that many of the club's best players were poached by Wolves, players like Arthur Blackham in 1882, Richard Baugh Snr 1886, and

Walter Annis 1898, Jack Smith 1902, Ernie James 1904, Richard Baugh Jnr 1918, and Alf Cannon in 1925, although Alf Pearson came to them from the Wolves in 1884. Edwin Reay, their goalkeeper, was more than once selected to play for the Birmingham FA, and, in 1880, was said to be the finest goalkeeper that could be found within the West Midlands.

James Treen Fullwood, who played for them in the 1880s, having come from Wednesbury Old Park FC, was from a famous Wolverhampton family of civic notability, and for several generations, the Fullwoods held high civic office in the town, including that of mayor. The Fullwoods also started the Staffordshire Motor Tyre Company in 1908, which, in modern times, became Goodyear Tyre Company.

By the late 1870s, Stafford Road were fielding up to three teams, but of course they had a huge social and athletic institute of nearly a thousand strong men to pick from. Stafford Road were one of the top teams in the region until about 1883 when they fell out of the leading ranks.

Their 1876 side which lines up to play West Bromwich (Dartmouth) was: R. Gowland, L. Gowland, G. Sellman, T. Whitehead, W. Grant, T. Wardle, C. Crump, J. Whitehead, E. Jones, E. Davis, J. Ludham, and the Reverend Lightfoot.

John Lightfoot was the local vicar in Heath Town and promoted the Christian virtues of football to his congregation. He later was instrumental in setting up both the Heath FC and Heath Town clubs.

The SRW won the Wednesbury Charity Cup in 1880 after wins against Derby 6-2, Wednesbury Old Athletic 3-1, and Elwells FC by 3-0 in the final, on what was effectively Elwells' own ground, the Oval. Gold medals were presented to the team members by the Wednesbury Association, and the cup was shown to the Stafford Road club at its annual dinner gala at the Coach and Horses Hotel in Wolverhampton's Snow Hill. This was probably their zenith year, as they were a club of the 1870s; by 1883, they were losing 8-1 to Walsall Swifts and other sides like Wolves, Walsall, Villa were leaving them in their wake. Nonetheless, they carried on, just playing and enjoying football as an amateur works team, although it was rumoured that two or three star forwards were being paid around 5/ – a week (25p).

Stafford Road Works entered all the local cups: Wednesbury, Walsall, Wolverhampton, and Birmingham.

In the Birmingham Senior Cup, they had great success in the 1870s; losing finalists to Wednesbury Old Athletic 2-3 in 1876/7, they beat 2-1 by Wednesbury Strollers in the 1877/8 semi-final, and beat the Walsall Swifts in the 1878/9 semi-final by 7-2 after a 1-1 game was ordered to be replayed, as it was a 'short' game not of the correct ninety minutes' duration. History repeated itself in the 1879 final as the Old Athletic once more triumphed by 3-2.

SRW were no strangers to a good-sized crowd. A crowd of 7,500 were at that Swifts v SRW semi-final, and a crowd of 5,000 was there at the Wednesbury Strollers tie in the previous round. Even early games against the Wolves would draw 1,000 to 2,000 numbers. Their brief tenure of the Molyneux ground and their home Fox Lane ground were both spacious arenas.

The team of 1883 was: Caddick, Richards, Sheldon, Morgan, Turton, Chataway, Jones, Baugh, Baker, Foster, Danks.

The team of 1884 was: Caddick, Riley, Durrance, Nicholls, Turton, Scott, Griffiths, Yates, Thomas, Baker, Fisher.

The team of 1887 was: Ray (goal); Durrance and Stanford (backs); Jones and Richards (halfbacks); Gowland, Baker, Daken, Lane, Charles Crump, Jackson (forwards). Thus, it can be seen that Charles Crump was still playing upfront in the attack even when he was nearly forty! He truly saw the team as his own creation and personal 'pet'.

After the end of the 1880s, now playing in a cardinal red and black halved shirt with white knicks and black socks, Stafford Road were well off the pace and a long way behind their old rivals, the Wanderers, who were moving up into the new Football League. Stafford Road fell back into the world of parks and works football.

When the football team was wound up for the first time, players who hadn't joined the Wolves split off and formed three minor local teams: Heath Town, the Heath FC, and Loco & Railway FC. Only Heath Town still exist. In 1910, institute members reformed the club, but many of them went off to the Great War in France just five years later.

The club was reformed more than once after the Great War, and this version was still going in 1933 (see photo web site). They played on the old Star Motor Company sports ground, on the Bushbury Road up until the 1960s. This is also still there, now a public park (Bushbury Park) facing the junction of Fordhouses Lane and Bushbury Lane. A site visit revealed how Google Earth misleads – from the air, it seems to be a boomerang-shaped field with room for more than one football pitch, but when I got there, it was nothing of the sort. The side coming off Bushbury Lane rises steeply until past the small playground; the centre portion is broadly level, although very uneven, and the far side is again a steep hill. Thus, there was only one place to play football, and that would have been across the middle section. Again, the ground was heavy with poor drainage, and it would have made even a bad park's team pitch.

To view the old Foxes Lane ground – the site of their best matches – drive to the centre of Wolverhampton and follow signs to Bushbury, along the Stafford Road. After only a few hundred yards, turn right into Fox Lane off the A449. This old lane is only driveable until the canal bridge. Walk over the old canal bridge, pausing to look to your left, where the huge railway works lay, beyond the railway tracks. Continue for a couple of hundred yards along the new path (you're now inside the park). Ignore the tempting shape of a cricket oval set in a bowl to your right (this is post 1950s) and continue past the new lake. The football pitch is the topmost field, some 228 yards square. An easier route is to turn into Prosser Street off the A460 Cannock Road, which takes you to the park, but you miss out on the Victorian canalside walk which the visiting teams would have done 140 years ago.

FA cup history	1st Round	2nd Round	3rd Round	4th Round	5th Round
1879/80	2-1 Wednesbury Strollers	1-3 Aston Villa			
1880/1	7-0 Spilsbury	7-1 Granthan	Bye	Aston Villa 3-2 (Away)	Old Etonians 1-2 (W'ton)
1881/2	1-3 Wednesbury Strollers				
1882/3	6-2 Small Heath Alliance	1-4 Walsall Town (A)			
1883/4	5-1 Aston Unity	0-5 Aston Villa (A)			
1884/5	0-2 Walsall Swifts				

1885/6	7-0 Matlock Town	2-4 Wolverhampton W anderers (A)
1886/7	Didn't qualify	
1887/8	1-2 Great Bridge Unity (H)	

References

Wolverhampton Express and Star
Great Western Railway Magazine
Birmingham Daily Post
Walsall Observer 1880-1885

Stafford Road FC

Stafford Road's Fullwood Circa 1885

Dickie Baugh-Stafford Road FC

Bushbury Lane, Stafford Road's Last Ground

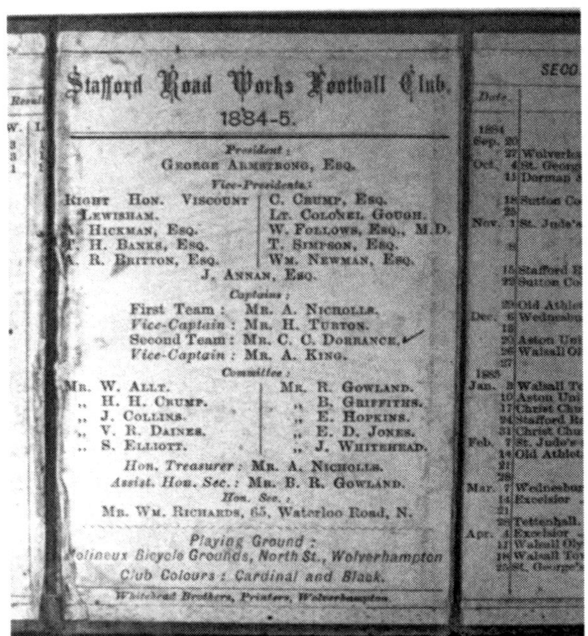

Stafford Road Works Football Club.

1884-5.

President:
George Armstrong, Esq.

Vice-Presidents:

Right Hon. Viscount Lewisham.	C. Crump, Esq.
Hickman, Esq.	Lt. Colonel Gough.
H. Banks, Esq.	W. Follows, Esq., M.D.
R. Britton, Esq.	T. Simpson, Esq.
	Wm. Newman, Esq.

J. Annan, Esq.

Captains:
First Team: Mr. A. Nicholls.
Vice-Captain: Mr. H. Turton.
Second Team: Mr. C. C. Dorrance.
Vice-Captain: Mr. A. King.

Committee:

Mr. W. Allt.	Mr. R. Gowland.
,, H. H. Crump.	,, B. Griffiths.
,, J. Collins.	,, E. Hopkins.
,, V. R. Daines.	,, E. D. Jones.
,, S. Elliott.	,, J. Whitehead.

Hon. Treasurer: Mr. A. Nicholls.
Assist. Hon. Sec.: Mr. B. R. Gowland.
Hon. Sec.:
Mr. Wm. Richards, 65, Waterloo Road, N.

Playing Ground:
olineux Bicycle Grounds, North St., Wolverhampton
Club Colours: Cardinal and Black.

Whitehead Brothers, Printers, Wolverhampton

Stafford Road Fc Fixture Card for 1884-5

Stafford Road's Home Ground Was the Molyneux in 1884-5

Stafford Road's home ground-Foxes Lane

Staveley FC

f.1875-1892
Staveley is a Derbyshire mining and steel-making village near Chesterfield.

Honours

Derbyshire Challenge Cup winners: 1883/4, 1884/5, 1886/7, 1888/9.
Finalists: 1885/6, 1887/8
Sheffield and Hallam Senior Cup winner 1879/80; finalists 1888/9
Derbyshire charity cup 1886

Grounds

1. the Elm Tree ground
2. Staveley recreation ground, off Inkersall Road

Colours

1. amber and black hoops (1870s)
2. navy blue shirt from 1881

The team was disbanded when the formation of Sheffield United led to almost half the Staveley team being signed up by United.

They were an amateur Derbyshire village team, active during the 1880s and 1890s. They were one of the first four clubs in Derbyshire and helped in the formation of the Derbyshire County Association. Friendlies and local cup ties in the 1880s brought them up against teams such as Matlock, Derby Town, Derby Junction, Derby St. Luke's, and the Notts and Sheffield teams. They were founded by workers at the steelworks and were said to be 'a tough and ambitious outfit'. Their amber and black hoops outfit must have looked very eye-catching in the early years, possibly being influenced by Notts County who also played in those colours at the start of the 1870s. Their matches against Sheffield Wednesday later became infamous; an 1882 Wharncliffe Charity cup tie saw a late opening goal for the Wednesday, at which Staveley appealed to the referee, J. C. Clegg, for offside. As he was at the other end of the field, he awarded a goal, at which point the whole Staveley team walked off the pitch. Clegg, the giant founder of the Sheffield FA and FA committee man, managed to get them to return and play out the last ten minutes. Later matches between the two sides were marred by foul language emanating from the Staveley men.

Their first ever game was played on 21st October 1876 when they beat Renishaw FC by 1-0. They only played three games that year, and only five in 1877, losing 0-7 to Sheffield Exchange on 20th January, but replying with a 9-1 win over Sheffield Albion in October of 1880. Regular opponents at this time were Mexborough, Lockwoods, Spital and Heeley.

They once reached the 5th round of the FA cup in 1886. Players used the Elm Tree public house on the High Street as a changing room. As many pubs, for some reason, had a football field behind their premises, it would appear that the site of the old ground is now occupied by Morrisons superstore. It is thought that they also used the Crown Inn as their headquarters.

Their team announced for the 1887 season in the *Derby Mercury* was as follows:

F. Wagstaffe (goal); W. Young, H. A. Peel (backs); J. Rice, Hay, Marshall (halfbacks); W. Needham, L. Potter (reserve goalkeeper), Wilshaw, R. Meakin, W. Madin (forwards). First and second reserves: J. Hay and J. Blaydon (1876 team captain). Reference was made to the attempts of Derby County to poach their best players.

They were founder members of the Midland Counties League in 1890; however, they finished bottom of the ten clubs league with only 2 wins in their 18 matches and resigned before the start of the following season. League opposition included Gainsborough Trinity (champions), Long Eaton, Derby Midland, Burton Wanderers, and Rotherham. This (1891) was also the final season for Derby Midland, who were absorbed into the new Derby County.

Well-known players included:

William Cropper (1862-89): He tragically died whilst playing against Grimsby on the 12 January 1889 after being kneed in the stomach. At the time, he was only thought to be winded and wasn't taken to hospital until the following afternoon where he died, possibly from a ruptured spleen. He was better known as a medium pace bowler and batsman for Derbyshire CC. He scored over 1,600 runs in 60 matches and took 171 wickets. Also in the team at this time with Cropper were Thomas and William Mycroft and father and sons, Joseph, Frank, and George Davidson, all of whom came from Bridlington, where Cropper is buried. There was a large turnout of both cricketers and footballers from all over the region to the funeral.

George Hay (1851-1913) was Staveley's goalkeeper in the early years. He too was more famous as a cricketer, with nearly 700 runs and 148 wickets for Derbyshire CC. He became a cricket umpire in the 1890s when he retired. The Hays were a family of footballing brothers who served the club well, but two of them ended up being signed by Sheffield United.

Harry Lilley (1868-1900) was a left back, who went on to have a Football League career with Sheffield United from 1890 to 1894. He played for Staveley from 1887 to 1890. He was capped for England 1892 v Wales.

William Lilley was a goalkeeper who played during 1887-90 with Staveley. He was one of the group of players who went to Sheffield United in 1890, staying there until 1894. He then moved to Rotherham for the 1894/95 season. Remarkably, he scored 3 goals whilst at Sheffield. He moved from club to club with his brother Harry, although he nearly signed for the Wednesday instead before his brother persuaded him to go to the Blades.

Ernest Needham was a famous cricketer as well as an international footballer. He is said to be a wonderful defensive halfback who had great accuracy of passing to feed his forwards, a man of great stamina and balance, who made it look easy. He too signed for the new Sheffield United team and went on to score 50 goals for them from 1891 to 1909, scoring 3 goals in sixteen England appearances from 1894 to 1902. He won the League Championships at Sheff Utd in 1897-98 and FA Cup winners medals in 1899 and 1902. He was a top cricketer too and scored over 6,500 first-class runs at county and test cricket.

With the loss of the above five key men, it is easy to see how Staveley lost its football team by 1892.

Entering the English FA Cup, between 1881 and 1888, Staveley played a total of 20 FA cup ties.

They were beaten 5-1 by Sheffield Wednesday in the 3rd round of the 1881/2 competition, but not until after three epic games, and lost 4-1 to Walsall Town in the 1st round of the next season. Blackburn Rovers put them out by 5-1 in the 4th round of the 1883/4 season, whilst Notts County beat them 2-0 at home in 1884. Once again in 1885/6, it was Blackburn who put them out, but this time by 7-1 in the 5th round. Staveley had eliminated Mexborough, Long Eaton (4-1 A), and Nottingham Forest (2-1 H) en route. Notts County again were their undoing by 0-3 in the 1886/7 competition, at the 3rd round stage on 11th December, whilst their last ever FA Cup year saw Derby County win 2-1 at Staveley in the 1st round of 1887. One of their most remarkable ties was a qualifying round match in 1890 against Sheffield Walkley, where they won by the huge score of 19-0. Needham, at this time was playing as a forward; he gradually moved back down the team by the time he joined Sheffield United as a centre half a few months later.

In 1879/80 season, Staveley secured its first silverware when they defeated Hallam by 3-1 at Bramall Lane to lift the Sheffield & Hallamshire Senior Cup. Hallam were founded at the Plough Inn, Sandygate Lane, Sheffield in 1860* and are thus recognised as the world's second oldest club after Sheffield FC. Hallam played in blue shirts, white knicks, and their founder and captain, John Shaw, was instrumental in the formalisation, along with Charles Alcock of the Wanderers of the national playing rules in the early 1870s. In 1890, Staveley had another good run in the Sheffield Cup and were beaten 2-0 in the semi-final by the new Sheffield United, who themselves were beaten 1-0 by Rotherham in the final after a goal-less drawn first game. Rotherham wore a fetching chocolate and navy hooped shirt at this time, but were wound up in 1896 and resurfaced in 1900 as United, having merged with Rotherham County.

A decade later, they again reached the final but were narrowly beaten 2-1 by Rotherham, now in blue and yellow stripes, again played at Bramall Lane.

During the 1880s, Staveley had great success in the Derbyshire Challenge Cup. They got to no less than six finals, winning 4 times, losing 2. Their cup final opponents were usually either Derby Midland (2-1 1884, 2-0 1885) Derby Junction (0-2 1888, 1-0 1889) or Heeley (0-1 1886) and Long Eaton Rangers (2-0 1887). This gave them a reputation in the county as a great cup team, although their 1889 final against 'the Junos' was a very close affair and could have gone either way, the Junes being very unlucky not to have scored (*Sheffield Independent*). Rollinson scored that winner at the County Ground in front of 4,000 spectators. The crowd of 7,000 who witnessed the 1884 Derbyshire cup final against the Midland was the biggest attendance for a football match in the county at that time.

In the 1880s, as well as competing in the Derbyshire, Nottinghamshire, and Hallamshire cups, Staveley also entered the Birmingham Association cup.

On Saturday 27th October 1883, they travelled the short distance to Chesterfield, where they defeated Spital at the Spital Vale ground by 2-0, and followed this up with a 5-1 win against Black Country side Oldbury in the following December. To reach the 3rd round at the first attempt was no mean feat for a village side, but they had the misfortune to be drawn away to Aston Villa in round 3. A modest crowd of 2,000 at Villa's old Wellington Road ground saw Staveley go out by a respectable 3-0. The following year, 1884, they overcame Derby Junction in round 1 and then were drawn against Wolverhampton in round 2. Fortunately, it wasn't the Wanderers, but Wolverhampton Rangers, and in an amazing 11-goal thriller at the Recreation Ground, Staveley won by 8-3. The 3rd round beckoned again, and this time they had to travel to Aston again, but not to face the Villa, but their across-the-road neighbours, Aston Unity. Strangely, the game was arranged between the two clubs to be played on Monday 29th of December, and this time Staveley came away from Trinity Road with a 3-2 away win. The 4th round draw was unkind to them as they were drawn against Aston Villa again. This time however, the game was to be played at the Aston Lower Grounds, this being the 'neutral' venue for all the quarter-final ties. A heroic performance on Saturday 24 January, probably on a frozen pitch, saw Staveley come away with a great 1-1 draw in front of 2,000 fans. The replay, back at the ALG once more, was played on Monday 2nd February 1885, but, this time, the Villa made no mistake, with a clear 5-0 victory. The only other east Midlands side to reach the quarter-finals with them were Nottingham Rangers. They too had a 1-1 draw, with Wednesbury Old Athletic, but lost the replay heavily by 5-1.

Encouraged by this achievement, they once again entered in 1885 and played a neighbouring village side, Darley Abbey, running up a huge 11-1 scoreline at the Rec. Round 2 saw them drawn away in Birmingham again, to the Excelsior club from Fentham Road. For some unknown reason, Staveley scratched from their 14th November fixture, and despite all the Nottinghamshire and Derbyshire teams being drawn together in the new 'Northern Section' to reduce travel costs in 1886, Staveley never entered the Birmingham cup again. November 1886 also saw Staveley rattle up a double-figure score, when they thrashed neighbour Chesterfield 10-0.

Although Sheffield United had been assembled by the committee of the Sheffield FA in order to produce a super team, using players drawn from all the Sheffield clubs, Staveley's demise really came about when United nicked their best men. Salt was rubbed into the wound when United beat Staveley 2-0 in the semi-final of the Sheffield Cup in the spring of 1889. Staveley were gone within three years.

References

Sheffield Telegraph
Football in Sheffield, Percy M. Young
The History of the Birmingham Senior Cup, Steve Carr
Charles Alcock's football annuals 1875-1899

* Percy Young gives 1857

Ernest Needham Staveley

Stoke Swifts FC

Colours
red and white stripes/white

Honours

Staffordshire Junior Cup 1891, 1892
Birmingham League 1910

Ground
Victoria Athletic Ground

Playing in the Combination league in the 1890s, they were one of the top sides, finishing 4th in 1891/2, 2nd in both 1892/3 and 1893/4, before joining the Midlands Counties League and finishing 2nd to Loughborough Town in 1894/5. Returning to the Combination in 1897/8, they finished a respectable 5th. Usual opponents included Chester, Buxton, Leek, Nantwich, Chirk, Dresden, Stockport, and Wrexham.

Believing at first that this was an independent team, I began research. There was also a Hanley Swifts team to consider, and I found a good team photo of them in their red and white hoops. Also, Stoke City were previously simply Stoke FC and began life as Stoke Ramblers wearing blue and black hoops in the 1860s. However, I quickly discovered that Stoke Swifts was the name that First Division Stoke FC gave to their reserve team which played in the Football Combination League!

Starting out as Stoke Ramblers in 1868, they played at the Victoria cricket ground (no connection) until 1875, when they moved briefly to Sweetings Field, which was opposite the Victoria Ground.

Swifts played in cup competitions as if they were a separate team from their senior side and won the county junior cup in 1891. The final was played at the County cricket ground, and their opponents were the Smethwick Carriage Works team, whose ground was about 500 yards from that of West Bromwich Albion. Stoke Swifts retained the Staffordshire Junior Cup in 1892, when they eventually overcame a determined Willenhall Pickwick side after no less than three games. Willenhall had beaten another Stoke area team, Newcastle Swifts, at home in the semi-final by 3-1 on 2nd of January. The first final, which was a 0-0 draw, took place at the Molyneux,

Wolverhampton on Monday 28 March in front of a 2,000 crowd. The first replay, a 1-1 draw again at Molyneux saw Stoke score a late equaliser to take the final into a third game. This time, the Cobridge Athletic ground was the nominated venue, which was the home ground of Burslem Port Vale. On Thursday 21st April, before 1,500, Stoke made no mistake and won 4-2 to retain the cup.

The Stoke Swifts team of 1888 was: Worthington (goal); Timmins and Ginnton (backs); Meakin, Kemp, Bates (halfbacks); Morrell, Rowley, Broadhurst, Bardell, Ryder (forwards).

No doubt, when the Swifts had an important cup tie, such as the county junior final, several players would be drafted in to strengthen the team from the 1st team pool. This is the concept which I find unsporting, to say the least. All the other sides trying to win the county junior cup would have been fielding their best eleven, playing at the limit of their capabilities. They did not have the luxury of borrowing two or three star players to artificially boost their chances of silverware. Admittedly, clubs like Stafford Road or Derby Midland borrowed men from neighbouring teams on occasion, but they did not borrow men from, say, Aston Villa or West Bromwich Albion to win cup finals.

The old Stoke City Victoria Ground was of course demolished at the turn of the century (1997), but its still vacant site can be glimpsed from the A500 dual carriageway which the locals call the 'D' road.

The ground had been used by Stoke FC since 1878 when local side Talke FC were the first visitors. However, the ground had already been in use for a few years as an athletics ground, being named after the nearby Victoria Hotel. Originally oval, it had a small 1,000-seater stand at the Boothen Road end and a bigger 4,000 capacity stand on the opposite side. The ground remained undeveloped like this until the First World War. The players changed in a small hut in the corner of the ground which had the luxury of a stove to keep them warm!

Tipton FC

f.1872-1880

Ground
the Shrubbery Ground, Horseley Road

Colours
navy blue plain shirts (1877)

Headquarters
The Spring Cottage pub, Horseley Road

Tipton is a small town between Dudley and West Bromwich in the heart of the Black Country and has a rich industrial heritage.

The grounds of neighbours Great Bridge Unity, Wednesbury Strollers, and Old Athletic would have been less than half an hour's walk away.

The Shrubbery ground was by the town cemetery near the junction of Horseley Road and Alexandra Road. The original Horseley House was between Horseley Road and Clarkes Grove and was the residence of Joseph Amphlett, a partner of the Horseley Iron Company.* What is now Gordon Drive used to be the tree-lined avenue leading up to Horseley House, which stood at what is now the end of Clarkes Grove. The grounds were behind the mansion house. The present-day Shrubbery pub, built in 1936, is a reference to Amphlett's wooded grounds.

Amphlett may well have helped both the Tipton and Great Bridge Unity clubs, as there was an Amphlett who played for Calthorpe in Edgbaston in 1878. The sports ground at the rear of Clarkes Grove became the Horseley Ironworks' ground, and later it was the Triplex-Lloyd cricket ground in the mid-twentieth century. It was lost to posterity when houses were built over it in 1974. Galton Drive now occupied the spot where the ground was.

The present-day Tipton Town were only formed in 1948 as Ocker Hill, a Sunday parks' team, and has no connection with this very early team. Almost nothing about this first team is known, and as they only lasted from about 1872 to 1878, it was at a time when newspaper coverage of even important games was at a premium. It's also unclear whether Tipton Providence were a separate team or evolved from this Tipton side.

The first mention of a Tipton football club dates back to 1872, and thus they were the earliest of the Black Country teams. This puts them even earlier than the Wednesbury teams (Strollers/Town 1873, WOA 1874). Until the Birmingham Cup came along in 1876, the only diet for the early teams in Staffordshire and Warwickshire was friendly or challenge games, or matches played in-house between two sides drawn from the pool of players within the same club, that is, reds v blues, or captains XI v major smiths XI, etc.

On 8th December 1875, the Birmingham Association came into existence following the Aston Unity and Calthorpe clubs of that town calling a meeting at the Mason's Hotel in the town centre with a view to form an association, and thus representatives of around a dozen clubs went along. Messrs Leach and Peacock went along to represent the Tipton club. Just two weeks later, it was agreed that a cup competition should be started in order to find the best team in the Birmingham area, an idea which had been proposed by the *Birmingham Daily Post* newspaper. As it was too late into what was then considered to be the football season (October–March), they decided to wait until the start of the following season to start the competition properly, but, in the meanwhile, the Birmingham FA decided to put on an exhibition game to see what public interest there would be. Accordingly, the Aston Villa and Tipton clubs were invited to play this 'exhibition final' at Wednesbury town's Crankhall Farm ground. Tipton won the game (score unrecorded but possibly 1-0), but some newspapers recorded it as the first Birmingham cup final, which it plainly wasn't. Even the Birmingham FA's own centenary yearbook on 1975 gives it as the first final! Gate receipts were said to be only 2s 4d. That's a tiny 12p in today's currency! Even for allowing for a minimum gate fee of one penny (more likely 2 or 3d), then the paying 'crowd' would have been less than thirty souls. So despite a disappointing public turnout, the watching committee decided it was a good thing and proceeded to make plans for the organising of the first competition in 1876. Quite why the Birmingham FA selected a Tipton team which had never particularly made itself noticed on the football field is anyone's guess, when either Calthorpe, Rushall Rovers, Stafford Road, or Wednesbury Old Athletic were much more likely to give a demonstration of the art of football in 1875.

By 1876, Tipton were certainly playing the Wednesbury and West Bromwich teams. A match on the 4th November at the Four Acres ground of the West Bromwich Dartmouth club was returned the following February when 'Brammidge' went over to Tipton's Shrubbery ground and won by the only goal of the game. On the 8th December 1877, Tipton travelled the short distance to the Athletic grounds in Brunswick Park to play Wednesbury Old Athletic but were beaten by 5-0.

When the Birmingham Cup competition began properly in the October of 1876, as luck would have it, Tipton were drawn to play . . . Aston Villa, this time at Villa's undeveloped Wellington Road ground, which was just a field at that point, as they had only just moved into it from messing about in Aston Park. At this time, 1876/7, Tipton were playing in a navy blue shirt, and the Villa were in 'scarlet and royal blue striped jersey, royal blue cap and stockings, and white knicks' to quote from an 1893 article recalling Villa's earliest history. The Villa team would have included George Ramsay and other founder members in that game. Tipton again won 1-0 to progress to round 2 where they met a club that was even older than themselves, the students of Saltley College. Saltley or St. Peter's, to give it its proper name, was a Christian-faith teachers' training college in east Birmingham, and they had their own sports ground within the college buildings. The score is unrecorded, but on Saturday 2nd December 1876, it was the college men who went through to the semi-final, only to be put out 2-0 by Wednesbury Old Athletic, the first ever winners.

1877 saw Tipton try again, but they were drawn away to the Shrewsbury Club. At this time, first out of the hat did not mean you were drawn at home; club secretaries had to negotiate where to play the game. Travelling to Shropshire was out of the question for little Tipton, whose players were no doubt employed in strenuous labour-intensive heavy industry, with no spare money for train fares, and so they scratched. As it was, the Shrews went on to win the cup in the following April.

1878 saw Tipton make a little more headway in the cup. They squeezed past the Arcadians FC from Selly Park by 2-1 on the 9th November at their own Shrubbery ground and were drawn at home again in round 2. They edged past Walsall St. Mathew's FC in Christmas week by 3-2 to reach the 3rd round. However, they had the misfortune to be drawn away to the strongest team in the competition, Wednesbury Old Athletic. Eleven-to-nil was the final score, and what effect this had on Tipton is hard to say, but they never again entered the Birmingham Cup, although other small clubs like the Arcadians and Saltley College carried on to the end of the 1880s. To put this score into context, I should say that the Old Athletics – the 'Old Uns – had only been defeated twice in the previous three years, only by one goal in each case.

Another huge defeat occurred in December 1878, when they were thrashed 15-0 by Elwells FC, the small Wednesbury team. Almost nothing is heard about Tipton as we move towards 1880, and it seems that they had called it a day after barely a decade in existence.

REFERENCES

The History of the Birmingham Senior Cup, Steve Carr
Charles Alcock's annuals 1875-1899
The Centenary Book of the Birmingham Football Association 1975
The History of the Horsley Iron Works Company
Great Bridge Library

* see Great Bridge Unity FC
Note: Horseley was often spelt Horsley in the mid-Victorian period.

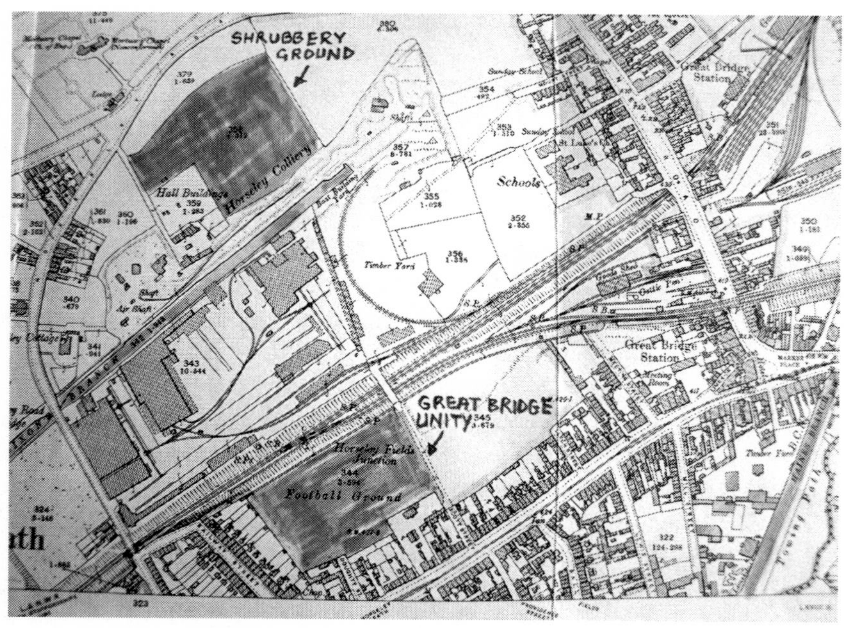

Tipton & Great Bridge Unity Grounds

Unity Gas Works FC

A works team based in the Saltley district of Birmingham
f.1885-1893

Grounds

1. Rupert Street
2. Green Lane, Bordesley 1889 (also Bellefield the same year)

Honours

Birmingham Junior Cup finalists 1888
winners 1891 Walsall Junior Cup

Representative on the Birmingham FA:
Mr S. Meunier

The club was formed by players who worked at the Unity Gasworks in Saltley, Birmingham. The site is still there today, although it was decommissioned about ten years ago. There is a football pitch there today in adjacent Rupert Street, but this cannot be verified that it was their ground. However, the whole of one side of Rupert Street (facing the Cromwell School) was vacant land during the late 1880s and early 1890s. The likeliest site is where the large goods depot was built in the first quarter of the twentieth century. A Birmingham cup tie against Lozells in December 1886 was played at Green Lanes ground. Later, in 1889, we find them playing at far-off Showell Green Lane (now Sparkhill park) some three miles away from their origin (see photo). In 1887, they also played at a ground on Green Lane, Bordesley, near the present-day St. Andrew's ground of Birmingham City. It's possible that the playing field by First Avenue in Bordesley Green was used by Unity Gas, as it has been there as a recreation area for at least the last seventy years.

Site visits throughout 2010 and comparisons with early twentieth-century maps shows the whole Duddeston–Saltley area to be heavily industrialised, with hundreds of factories huge and small, which used to be interconnected with a network of railway sidings and canals, with almost no open ground or fields available or suitable for football matches. The nearest public space is Adderley Park, Birmingham's oldest park, half a mile to the east. It seems improbable that Unity Gas didn't play in Adderley Park at some time or another. The Aston Cross ground was also only three streets away, but I cannot find any mention of them playing there, probably because Aston Shakespeare FC and Aston Victoria FC were using that ground at the time.

Unity Gas were defeated in the 1st final of the 1887/8 Birmingham County Junior cup to Aston Victoria, and many thought they would return eventually to take the trophy, as by then, they were one of the leading Birmingham amateur sides. This side overcame Langley Green Vics 2-0 in the semi-final of that year:

Webb (goal); Glew, Elkington (backs); Morgan, Jenkins, Munier (halfbacks); Shaw, Cotterill, Lowe, Howell, Watson (forwards).

By 1888, the Birmingham newspapers were assessing the prominent clubs of the region and said that the best three junior sides in the Midlands were Aston Victoria, Unity Gas, and Langley Green Vics, although I would have added Singers or Rudge to that list.

Saltley Gas FC were a separate side, from the nearby municipal gasworks.

Unity Gas were co-founders of the Birmingham FA and the Birmingham and District League. Like several other Birmingham teams, they entered the Warwickshire cup, as of course in those days the town was in that county, and Walsall and north Birmingham was in Staffordshire. Handsworth, previously an independent village, was incorporated into the city of Birmingham in 1911, and Perry Barr was in Staffordshire until 1928, when it, too, was 'given' to the ever-expanding Birmingham.

For the season 1889/90, it seems that the Gasmen were forced to play at the Bellefield ground, five miles due west, over at Cape Hill, Smethwick, for reasons unknown. Perhaps their own pitch had now been sold off and built over with houses. Bellefield was simply a large 9-acre open space near the junction of Winson Green Road and Birmingham Road, used by several teams until, eventually, it, too, was built over by 1900. See the page on Mitchell St. George's for more details about the Bellefield.

Season 1889/90 saw them finish 9th (of 12) in the Birmingham and District League; by this time, their days as a force on the Birmingham football scene were over. A factor would have been if key players were unwilling to carry on turning out for the team when their 'home' ground was miles away from the workplace. A thrilling encounter with Warwick County on 6th March

1889 saw them win by 6-4. They only entered junior cups in the 1890s. They resigned from the Birmingham League in 1890 when the club was surrounded with rumours that it was on the brink of folding. 1890 saw one of Unity's biggest cup scores when they defeated Coleshill by 13-0 in a Birmingham Junior cup tie.

The *Coventry Evening Telegraph* of 1893, when reviewing the possible winners of the Birmingham Junior Cup, said that a couple of years previously, in 1890, the Unity Gas team were 'the best junior team in the county', but a trophy had yet to come to them. In 1891, their luck changed, and they overcame the well-known Wednesbury Old Athletics to lift the Walsall Junior cup. The Coventry press seemed to view the old Unity Gas team with some affection and had hoped that they would get a revival of fortunes, but it was not to be. Key players had left the team, and they were no comparison of previous years.

Famous top player was Charlie Athersmith who left them in 1891 to join the Aston Villa team just in time for their magnificent decade of the 1890s which was trophy-laden. Athersmith, upon investigation, was a bit of an enigma, for no one born under that name could be traced in the Birmingham area. It turns out that his real name was one William Harper. As a boy, he was a remarkable talent. He played for Bloxwich Wanderers at the tender age of 12, moving to Bloxwich Strollers and then Unity Gas FC. He was a speedy winger who went on to play for England. He was known for his fast play and uncanny close control with the ball at speed. Not everybody was keen to see Athersmith line up against them. Willenhall Pickwick lodged a complaint to the Birmingham FA, saying that as Athersmith was a nationally known professional player with Aston Villa and that he was not eligible to take part in local cup ties. The complaint was rejected when the Birmingham FA met on 2 April 1891 at the Midland Hotel in the city centre, on the technicality that the Football League did not interfere with cups run by the Birmingham FA!

This side won 3-2 at the County ground against Warwick County on 13 April 1888,

Benton (goal); Cotterill, Francis (backs); Skidmore, Summerhill, Jones (halfbacks); Wilkinson, Hill, Forcett, Young, Timmins (forwards).

In 1890, Unity took a big name when they beat Wolverhampton Wanderers 2-1 in the Wednesbury Cup and went on to lose the semi-final 3-2 after a replay against Hednesford. However, by 1893, Unity Gas had folded, due to lack of money. They ended their days in the Birmingham Junior League, but as ever, the club had no money to fulfil away fixtures and struggled to keep a team together. The gasmen were becoming an unreliable opponent; they failed to turn up at an away match with Causeway Green on 24 November 1892, and they were fined by the Birmingham FA, money they could have done with. Dare I say the obvious pun that their 'flame was going out'?

The Birmingham press, in February 1894, thought that the fortunes of the gasmen might be on the way up, following a good display against the powerful Coventry Rudge side, who only beat them 3-2. However, only the goalkeeper and centre half Matt Summerfield were singled out for praise, with the Unity forwards said to be below the level of yesteryear, and it was not to be.

A new team, which went on to do well on the junior scene, arose from their ashes, building its side around the best of the old Unity team: Windsor Street Gas FC. A quick look at an 1890 map for the area reveals that the same gasworks were known at Windsor Street gasworks at that time.

The remarkably named Caesar Jenkyns (1866-1941) had a couple of seasons with Unity Gas, coming from Walsall Swifts in 1886, moving on to greater things with a career that took him via Small Heath Alliance in 1888, to Newton Heath and Woolwich Arsenal in the 1890s. His career ended in 1896, when he returned to his native Wales after becoming a pub landlord in Birmingham. He was said to be a strong-tackling 'hard nut', strong if not exceptional, but good enough to have been capped for Wales. However, he was known for his temper and was sent off four times in his career, not an easy feat in those days of crunching tackles and shoulder charging!

George Short (1866-19?) went to Small Heath Alliance in 1887; it was a classic case of a small club losing its star players to the new professional sides.

The Unity Gas team of the early 1890s included: Albert Young, Wilkinson, Thorne, Reynolds, Lucas, Humber, Wally Walters, Phillips (their goalie of 1890/1), and these, along with Athersmith, were their best remaining men.

In February 1891, Mathew Somerfield was selected to play for Birmingham FA v Leicester FA at Coventry, to partner Edmunds of Singers FC and Allen of the Lozells FC in the halfback line.

References

Coventry Evening Telegraph 1893
Birmingham Daily Post 1892

Unity Gas & Walsall man Caesar Jenkins

Unity Gas ground

Walsall Swifts FC

f. September 1875-1888*

They were founded as Victoria Swifts (1875-78) then as Walsall Swifts (1878-88), and then as Walsall Town-Swifts (1888-1895).

Colours

1. amber and black hoops (1875-1879)
2. maroon shirt, white knicks (1879/80)
3. all Maroon (1881-1888)

Grounds

1. Lammasland 1875/6 part
2. Birmingham Road 1875/6 season
3. Follyhouse Lane 1877-1881
4. Chuckery Ground 1881-1893

Honours

Birmingham Cup 1880/1 and finalists 1884, 1886
Also Walsall Cup several times
Finalists Staffordshire Cup 1881, 1882, 1887

Grounds

1. They first played on Lammasland, which is now the goods yard of the Midlands Railway (LMS), Midland Road, near to the War Memorial known as the Cenotaph locally. This land was the site of the original Walsall racecourse in the eighteenth century and was hampered by the Walsall brook running through it. The football pitch needed planks and turves laid over the brook in order to commence the game! The Jerome Retail Park and Midland Road now occupy the spot. Jerome K Jerome, the author of *Three Men In a Boat*, having been born at the house on the corner of Caldmore Road and Wednesbury Road. I, too, incidentally was born in the same street.
2. They played on a rented field at the middle of Follyhouse Lane in the district of Highgate, although it was known as the Windmill district in the 1880s. This was rented from the licencee of the Windmill

Tavern, the Walsall Albion club having started the season there, but were ejected. Follyhouse Lane was known simply as Folly Lane in the 1870s and extended up to near the bend on present-day Highgate Drive. My on-foot research of this forgotten old road (it is now merely a dirt-road alley running at the back of large houses almost from Caldmore green to the ring-road, the Broadway) leads me to strongly suspect that the ground is now the site of the present-day Highgate Drive near the Walsall Rugby Club ground, now built on with 1930s style houses. The first two-thirds of Follyhouse Lane rise then fall steeply out of Walsall and don't level out almost until the Broadway, where there are several sports pitches today, including the Highgate junior school, the rugby ground, and a sports ground of the university. It is only the Broadway end of Follyhouse Lane which is anywhere near level, the lane rising steeply back towards town.

3. In season 1875/6 they played on a pitch at the rear of the present Moathouse Hotel (cricket close), now site of Walsall Tennis Club. A site visit shows the Cricket Close cul-de-sac behind the pub had room for a cricket or football pitch. There is also a small brook at the back of the houses, which seems to put the pitch, where now resides the private Walsall tennis club, accessed only from the golf club with its keypad entry.

Swifts then moved to Follyhouse Lane in autumn 1877. Headquarters at Follyhouse ground were the Windmill Tavern, Bath Street (then known as the West Bromwich Road). Later, when they moved out to the Chuckery grounds, they were the Royal Exchange public house (recently demolished) on Ablewell Street. This would have been a fair walk, so presumably they went by horse-drawn transport from Ablewell Street to the end of Sutton Road. There were no roads at all on this southern edge of town, it being nothing but fields all the way up and beyond what is now the Scott Arms district of Great Barr. Maps of the area from the period give little clue as to why the Swifts called it their 'beloved ground'. The whole of the south side of the town towards Birmingham was just miles of fields, only two or three farms between the West Bromwich and Birmingham Roads. Today, the Broadway defines the south side of Walsall, but this was not built until the early 1940s. In the 1870s, Folly Lane led south out of town to nowhere except fields near the Maw Green Farm, now Tame Road East. Assuming a field was rented of around 3 acres, and the fact that only the fields at what is now the Rugby Club were anywhere near on level ground, the 'best fit' was a 4.2-acre field near Maw Green Farm at what is now the rear gardens of the houses on the bend of Highgate Drive, or a 3 acre field at the present day junction of Highgate Drive and Road. No maps from the period show any facilities, such as a pavilion, shelter, or even running water, and, unlike today, the only way to the pitch was a quarter-mile walk down the whole length of Folly Lane, so I can only think that the players got changed and washed in one of the farm buildings by arrangement. After a while, Swifts erected a tiny stand as crowds grew to over 2,000.

The origins of the team have never been established, although clearly they came from the Highgate/Caldmore/Windmill districts of the town. In 1882, the club called a special meeting of its members and arranged this to be at the Windmill Tavern public house on Bath Street, Windmill. The Victoria Swifts had also used the same tavern to entertain the players of the Sheffield Providence club which paid a winning visit to the town on 29 December 1877 when the first 1,000 crowd in the district assembled at Follyhouse Lane to see the Blades win by 2-1. The tavern was owned by Joe Abnett at that time. This was their registered headquarters in 1877 before using the Royal Exchange on Ablewell Street, which is on the main road out of town to Birmingham. A study of an O.S. map circa 1880 draws one to the Highgate brewery, which is in the heart of Swifts' roots, but, unfortunately, the brewery didn't start up until a decade after the Swifts did. Interestingly, after they joined forces with the Town club in 1888, they built up and moved to a ground on the West Bromwich Road in 1893. This lay on the corner with Highgate Road and thus was only a stone's throw from their favourite Follyhouse Lane field; indeed the two fields lay within sight of each other. Having lived my childhood in Bath Street in the 1950s, I have a good knowledge of the area: two other possible sources for the team's origin are the Bath Street Iron Foundry which dates back to 1800, and St. Michael's Church directly opposite. They may also have separately worked in the small workshops dotted along Bath Street and Caldmore Road (which had over half of its addresses listed as saddlery businesses in the 1880s) and simply all met in the Windmill Tavern which was on the corner of Bath Street. A final possibility for the source of the Victoria Swifts was a leather factory at the bottom of Caldmore Road which was called the Victoria Works of E. Stanley & Co.

Long since demolished, I'm sure I can remember a pub being there when I used to play in Bath Street as a child in the late 1950s. I find it fateful to discover that a pub of which I took no notice for half my life turns out to have been the headquarters of Walsall Swifts!

No author of the several books on the history of Walsall Football Club have made any attempt to discover the origins of either the Swifts or Town teams;

indeed, one book goes from the 1870s to the 1930s in its first four pages! I have established that the Town emerged from the Walsall cricket club at the Chuckery, as the football and cricket clubs shared officials, players, and ground. A day spent reading through the *Walsall Observer* for the whole of 1873 and 1874 brought to light the fact that the Town put in an advert on 12th September 1874 for players to form a football team. This indicated that not enough cricketers wanted to make up a football team and extra men needed to be recruited. There is no such advertisement in either 1874 or 1873 for the Victoria Swifts; this also indicates that the group of young men who started the team were already sufficient in number. This suggests that they all worked together, attended the same church, or drank together at the same pub, as did the men of Willenhall Pickwick. The Red Book Directory of Walsall businesses for 1876 lists few factories in the Windmill district, and those which are listed are small buckle-makers and horse bits manufacturers, etc., so the iron foundry on Bath Street looks a strong contender, if they all worked together. The obvious contender the Highate Brewery wasn't there before 1890, and if they originated from the church, I think they would have incorporated the St. Michael's name in their title, as did Barnsley St. Peter's and Southampton St. Mary's. The other possibility is that men from the iron foundry met with other workers in the Windmill Tavern and agreed to form a football team together.

Elijah Stanley & Co had a leather goods and horse ironmongers factory at 31 Mountrath Street, Caldmore; the item of interest here is the fact that the factory was called the Victoria Works; if the Victoria Swifts lads used their factory name in the title, then this business would rise to the front as a source candidate. I have discovered the occupations of each of the players of the first Victoria Swifts side; most of them were employed in occupations linked with Walsall's famous leather and horse industry: saddle-stichers, horse-bit makers, silver-platers, leather curriers, etc.

Throughout the history of football, the town of Walsall was of course famous for its leather goods and still is, despite overseas competition from places like Italy, Jabez Cliff & Co, at their Globe Works were making footballs in the town almost as soon as they set up business in 1873 and went on to supply the FA Cup final ball for many years. No doubt they made the balls used by the early Walsall Swifts and Town teams. Sadly, their 140-year-old five-storey factory in Lower Forster Street went up in flames in 2011 and they relocated to Aldridge.

During the 1880s, several of the Swifts' players were also turning out for other teams: Harry and Charles Dyoss and one of the Spriggs brothers also played for Aston Shakespeare, some ten miles away. Additionally, Elijah Stanley & Co was only 200 yards from the old Lammas ground (old Walsall Racecourse) upon which the new team began their life, and across the road from the Swift's first headquarters, the Vine Inn on Caldmore Road.

In 1876, Walsall Victoria Swifts entered the Birmingham Cup, but they were narrowly beaten by nearby Wednesbury (Strollers) at the 1st hurdle, at their Crankhall Lane ground. West Bromwich Dartmouth put them out by 2-0 the following year. They returned the favour in November 1878 by putting Dartmouth out 4-1 at Folly Lane, but by the time they met the unknown St. Thomas's FC of Pershore Road, Birmingham, on Saturday 14th December, they had altered their name to Walsall Swifts.

As I mentioned earlier, The Swifts were the team of the people, with the Town being regarded as the 'toffs' side, being formed by businessmen, with local politicians on their committee. Swifts were not without their own patronage; their president was the Alderman Evans. After moving to the Chuckery grounds, the headquarters were the Royal Exchange public house, Ablewell Street (no longer there) and the players changed there, walking several hundred yards to the pitch, sharing a meal there with their opponents afterwards.

In March 1880, such was the local interest that between 7,000 and 10,000 people flocked to the Wednesbury Oval for their Birmingham cup semi-final tie with Stafford Road (W'ton). The crowd kept spilling on to the playing area, and eventually the game had to be abandoned with less than an hour played without a score. This was thought to have been the biggest crowd ever to assemble for a football match in England up until then (8/3/79). The English Cup final drew less at the London Oval. Swifts turned out in maroon shirts, and Stafford Road, led by the bearded Charles Crump, in all white.

The replay at Witton Lane (Aston Unity's ground) attracted only 3,000, but they saw a one-sided 7-2 victory for the Swifts.

Swifts reached both the 1884 and 1885 Birmingham Cup finals, but Villa were too good on both occasions, winning 4-0 and 2-0. A third consecutive cup final defeat in 1886 after a replay saw the cup go to the rapidly rising West Bromwich Albion. The first game was 1-1 with Jones (Swifts) and JEM Bayliss scoring for Albion. The replay, again at the Lower Grounds, saw Albion's Woodhall score the only goal of the game in front of a huge 10,000 crowd.

The Swifts finally had their glory day in 1897, when they beat the Wolves by 2-1 at Villa's old Wellington Road ground in front of a rather disappointing 5,000 crowd. Clearly, the locals were not very interested in watching two Black Country sides battle out the final of a Birmingham cup! By this time of course, they were the Town Swifts and were just moving into their new Fellows Park ground, which was to be their home for almost a hundred years.

From 1881, the Swifts played at a pitch on the Chuckery grounds on the hilly south side of the town, on the way to Birmingham and Sutton Coldfield. This heavily sloping area of undeveloped fields levelled out opposite to the later Arboretum extension pleasure parks, and it was here that Walsall cricket club had made a base in 1832. Swifts' long-serving trainer, James 'Grab' Ashwell, was a former player and was with them throughout the Chuckery days. At this time, Swifts were getting crowds of around 3,000 and of course double that for the derby game against the Town. Their first big success came at the end of the 1881/2 season when they beat the fancied Aston Villa by 1-0 to win the Birmingham FA Cup in front of 7,000 at the Aston Lower Grounds. The Villa team by this time had risen to the front rank and included the formidable Archie Hunter, Olly Vaughton, Arthur Brown, and Eli Davis in attack. The Walsall press were not best pleased with the Villa, because they had a habit of paying for Hunter to come down by train from Glasgow, where he had business links, just to come down to play in important matches for them. There was a general rule that a player must live within nine miles of his club ground, and clearly Glasgow was not! Many had been the times that the Walsall, Wednesbury, and Birmingham FA committees had met to decide on the issue of appeals from (beaten) teams concerning the eligibility of opponents' players; in one mildly absurd case, that of a player in Shropshire who upon investigation found that he lived 300 yards inside this boundary limit and that the appeal was thrown out.

The early 1880s were good years for the Swifts, for they also reached the finals of the Staffordshire Cup in both 1882 and 1884. As would be expected, they frequently won the Walsall Cup, usually meeting rivals the Town in the final.

The Chuckery ground had been set aside by Lord Bradford in 1832 for public use, for recreational and sporting use, and had been used by Walsall Cricket Club who were there for seventy years until 1908. They developed the ground, with iron railings defining the cricket area and built two pavilions, the earliest one of brick, a wooden one, and a third wooden structure, being the refreshment room. This possibly allowed the home and visiting team to have separate changing rooms, although if the cricketers were playing, they would have had the first call on what were, after all, their club's facilities. The cricketers charged the footballers a shilling for using the pavilions, through which they had to walk to get to the football pitches, which were otherwise fenced off by a long hedgerow. Although the Chuckery ground was a large area, about the size of a dozen pitches, much of it was on a steep slope on the town side, and only the 'summit' was used for best matches. Other local sides also played there, including Walsall Athletic, White Star, Shannons and Queen Mary's school. A large house known as the Shrubbery, belonging to the Wheway family, who later built a school in the town, was at the edge of the ground, and this still stands today as a private retirement home.

Eventually, as football fans got used to the mile walk to the Chuckery, the area began to be built over with cheap terraced housing. However, the middle-class residents of Sutton Road and Crescent began to protest about the noise and rowdyism and managed to get both the Swifts and the Town forced out of the ground at the end of 1893.

One day in November 1884, two crowds of less than 1,000 on each adjacent pitch saw the Swifts score 19 without reply against local side Nettlefolds whilst the Town were hammering Willenhall Swifts 17-0! However, generally, attendances were poor for one of the larger towns in the Black Country, the Swifts getting 3,000 on a good day, but the Town were the poor relations, sometimes with less than a thousand around the touchlines. As the novelty of 1870s football as a spectacle had worn off, it was all about winning cup ties and attracting famous opposition in the 1880s, in the days before the Football League. The Swifts were amongst the top three or four sides within twenty miles of Birmingham, and their tussles with Aston Villa and Walsall Town were eagerly anticipated, but as the 1890s came along, the combined Town–Swifts side, now playing higher national opposition in the Second Division, found they were always going to struggle on the national scene, and crowds got smaller and smaller.

The present-day Chuckery is a hilly district of the town on the Birmingham (south) side. The three streets called Florence, Walsingham, and Montcrieff were built on the two pitches that the Swifts and the Town played on. Nothing remains to give any clue to the fact that this location was the premier footballing and cricket venue for the town for over thirty years, save a small section of cobbled pathway near the Chuckery primary school, and a tiny alleyway coming off the Crescent. Both the Swifts and the Town were given their eviction notices at the end of the 1893 season after a series of complaints to Lord Bradford's agent about noise and troublemakers. Ironically, a council notice at the entrance to Montcrieff St. today proclaims 'no ball games'!

Going back in time to the beginning, their early fifteen-man team of 1874 was:

W. Robinson, J. Robinson, T. Spriggs, J. Spriggs, Tapper, Stokes, Hawley, Wallace, D. Bray, Careless, Mason, Dallard, Draper, G. Bray, Taylor.

Note the three sets of brothers, a common feature of early teams. As many as five brothers could be found in some teams, e.g. Aston Unity. The Ruabon Druids, the famous Welsh team, had seven Davies brothers at one time!

In November 1879, Swifts had one of their biggest ever wins when they crushed a youthful Perry Athletic by 14-0 at the Follyhouse Lane ground, but even this was eclipsed a year later when they hammered Harbourne by 16-0 in front of a 700 crowd.

The 1880/1 team was as follows: Davies (goal), Dyoss, Howls (backs), Jones, Sheldon (halfbacks), forward line: Tapper, Meek, Stokes, Ashwell, Brandrick.

The above side played B'ham Excelsior on 24th January 1880 at the Follyhouse Lane ground, Little London district of Walsall. Admission was 2d, reserved paddock 4d (1.5p). Tapper, Meek, Stokes and Sheldon stayed in the team for most of the 1880s. The Swifts had the double-edged sword of having its best players chosen to represent either Staffordshire or Birmingham FA's in representative matches. At the time, it was thought of as quite an honour to be chosen for these representative games, but the problem was that clubs were without their best men, often on the same date as a cup tie. George Tapper was said to be particularly fast with the ball.

Consequently, investigation into some of the more surprise cup tie results, or giant-killings, reveal that a team like the Swifts were three or four men down and had to field reserve team men. This practice went on even into the Football League and Alliance days of the 1890s. Players thought it a great honour too, though, and were in the habit of proudly wearing their representative medals not only in team photographs, but actually whilst playing too! Some wore them on their shirts, while others had them on leather belts.

A long-awaited clash came in 1882 when Swifts met Town in the 3rd round of the Birmingham Cup. Technically 'at home', Town were beaten 2-1 in front of Walsall's largest crowd yet – 4,000 – with Brandrick netting both Swifts' goals with a late reply from Town's Roberts. Because of their social aloofness, the Town club had avoided playing any other clubs in Walsall, especially if they were working-class.

At this time, the club's officials were: Thomas Dixon (vice-president), William Smith (hon secretary), Alderman Evans (president), Charles Taylor (vice-president), Dennis Bray (dep. secretary), and Harry Dallard (team umpire). At this time, umpires were provided by the two teams, not as now, by the relevant FA.

Star player Harry Wood (1868-1951) joined the Wolves in 1885 and was capped once for England. He was nicknamed 'The Wolf', renowned for his powerful daisy cutter shot.

During the 1880s, Walsall Swifts, and to a lesser extent, Walsall Town were making a name for themselves, and, just like today, they were almost on a par with the Villa, Albion, and Wolves, and able to run them close. However, when it mattered, they were put into their place in three Staffordshire Cup finals. They lost heavily 1-5 to Villa in the 1881 final, returned as favourites the following year but were beaten 4-1 by rivals Walsall Town, losing heavily again to West Bromwich Albion 0-4 in the 1887 Staffs final, with Bayliss (2), Woodhall, and Paddock getting the Albion goals in front of a modest 4,000 at the Stoke Victoria ground. Swifts also lost three consecutive Birmingham Cup finals in the mid-1880s to the same teams: 0-4 to Villa in the 1884 final, 0-2 to Villa in the 1885 final, and 0-1 to the Albion in 1886. The title of 4th best team in the West Midlands seemed to be their true status, although by 1880, they were only second best to Aston Villa in the entire Midlands.

The Swifts and the Town amalgamated in 1888 and were called the Town – Swifts, then simply as Walsall at the turn of the century. The new colours were meant to be a rather splendid blue and maroon stripes joint affair, but as the 1888/9 season started, they switched to simple red and white stripes, later red and white halves, and eventually copying Villa's claret and blue. Although several Swifts men were chosen to represent Staffordshire and Birmingham, only two men were called up by England; Alf Jones was capped twice in 1882, Bert Aldridge in 1889, just after the amalgamation year. The new combined Walsall team won the Birmingham Cup two seasons running (1897, 98) and beat First Division Wolves on both occasions.

Founder member Henry Dallard (1858-1940) continued in football in later life: he joined the Wolves in 1892 as their reserve team manager and became a vice-president of the Birmingham Football Association in the 1920s. He could probably be described as the leading football pioneer of all time in the town of Walsall.

To find the Follyhouse Lane ground today – or where I think it was – follow signs to Walsall Rugby Club on the Broadway near the A34 Walsall Road. Turn up Delves Road with the school on your right, then first right into Highgate Drive. See how steep Highgate Drive is, but 140 years ago, the bend marked the end of Folly (house) Lane. I believe the ground lay at the rear of the houses between Delves Road and the 1930s house on Highgate Drive, towards the junction with Highgate Road. The whole area back in the 1870s was just farmland, and remained so until the 1920s.

FA cup history	**1st Round**	**2nd Round**	**3rd Round**	**4th Round**
1882/3	1-4 (A) Aston Villa			
1883/4	1-5 (A) Aston Villa			
1884/5	2-0 Stafford Road	1-0 Derby St. Luke's (A)	3-2 Mitchell St. George's	1-4 Notts Club
1885/6	Bye	3-1 Derby Midland	1-2 Wolverhampton W	
1886/7	didn't enter			
1887/8	Wolverhampton W 1-2 (H)			
1888/9	5-1 Sheffield Heeley	1-6 Wolves (A)as Town Swifts		

Biggest competitive wins

19-0 v Nettlefolds	(GKN)-Saturday 25th October	1884 Birmingham Cup 1st round
18-1 v Bourneville-	Saturday 19th September	1885 Birmingham Cup
16-0 v Harbourne-	Saturday 23rd October	1880 Birmingham Cup
15-1 v Aston Clifton-	Saturday 16th December	1883 Birmingham Cup

Sources

Walsall Observer & South Staffs Chronicle 1870-1900
Walsall Local History Library, Bloxwich Centre
The Red Book of Walsall 1876/1877
The Caldmore District of Walsall 1861-1871, Mary Lowndes M.A.
Steve Carr, author, Birmingham
Charles Alcock's annuals 1875-1899
The Birth of the Saddlers – Bradbury & Powell, England,2014

* Acknowledgements to Geoff Allman's book *The Story of Walsall FC*, 2000, ISBN 0 7524 2091 7.

WALSALL TOWN FC

f. 1874-1888

COLOURS

1. white shirt bearing town coat of arms (1870s)

GROUND
the Chuckery sports ground

PRESIDENT:
William Coath (1870s) later S. Russell

VICE-PRESIDENT:
Mayor J. Newman, J. P

SECRETARY:
F Keay

HEADQUARTERS:

The Dragon Hotel, High Street (also known as the Green Dragon)
The Royal Exchange (circa 1882-88)

HONOURS
Staffordshire Cup winners 1881/2, 1884/5 Wednesbury Charity Cup 1886

THE TEAM WAS SET UP in September 1874 by prominent members of the town. It was a winter off-shoot of the Chuckery-based Walsall Cricket Club, with William Coath and Arthur Greatrex spearheading the football team.

The Town were considered by the Walsall public to be the 'Toffs' club, whereas the Swifts were the team of the townsfolk. Early headquarters were at the (Green) Dragon Hotel on Walsall's market hill at the foot of St. Mathew's Church, although both clubs later shared the Royal Exchange (now Hotel) on Ablewell Street as it lies on the main route out of town which led to the Chuckery district. The Dragon Hotel was also the HQ of Walsall Cricket Club, another link between the two sporting clubs. Mark, then William, Parker was the licensee of the Dragon during the 1860s and 1880s; by 1840, the Dragon had become the town's most influential social and political meeting place. The mayor and town council held its meetings on an upper floor, and there were facilities for bowls and theatre plays.

Walsall Cricket Club had been playing at the Chuckery ground for over forty years previously; since two of its leading players and officials were A. C. Greatrex and T. Addenbrooke, who co-founded the Town football team, added to the fact that the football team immediately began by using the Chuckery as their home ground, all points to the fact that it was the cricketers who founded Walsall Town FC. The cricket club was decidedly new middle-class; Greatrex owned a saddlery ironmongers business in Lower Forster Street in the town and had formed the town's first version of the Rotary club, the Walsall Constitutional Association, along with one J. F. Crump, a solicitor, who was brother to the famous Charles Crump, president of the Birmingham FA. Additionally, one William Coath was club president to both the town's cricket and football clubs. In Benjamin Evans' History of Walsall Cricket Club (1904), he states quite clearly that four leading cricketers – Cottam, Addenbrooke, Powell and Newman – all played also for Walsall Football Club in the beginning (1874). Additionally, the man who put the advert in the Walsall press asking for footballing men was Robert Leighton, the cricket club secretary. Calling themselves simply Walsall Football Club at the beginning, they were clearly a middle-class club, whereas their rivals, the Swifts, were founded by workmen from the saddlery and horse furniture industry.

Thomas Addenbrooke was from a large family of footballers. Both he and his two brothers, J. H and H. G, all played for the short-lived Wolverhampton FC club during 1880-83, also for the fledgling Wolverhampton Wanderers. J. H became manager of the Moyneux Hotel in 1896 and stayed as a loyal servant to the Wolves for many years. H. G. Addenbrooke also was a leading figure at the Calthorpe club at Edgbaston with another brother Charles. Yet another Addenbrooke, Hubert, played for the Sutton Coldfield team, who played at the exotically named Crystal Palace ground, which was in fact by the town gate entrance to Sutton Park.

Five years after their formation, Walsall Football Club (as they were known then), still hadn't got an official kit. This was ratified at their AGM on 22nd September 1879 when Eb Cozens, who was also the cricket team president, declared that for the forthcoming season they would play in 'white shirts with the Walsall coat of arms on the chest and a blue ribbon on the left sleeve' and that the club 'would adhere to the Sheffield Rules'. They added the name Town when the Victoria Swifts dropped the Victoria and added the Walsall to their name, but in the papers, the Town were always seen as the senior club, not justified after 1880 when the two teams were fairly equal.

The Town club refused to join any association from the start, particularly the newly founded Walsall Association, to which belonged all the town's other (many) clubs. This aloofness continued for many years, until they came to their senses and realised that they no longer could call themselves the team which represented the town.

Town played at the Chuckery ground from the off and were joined there by the working-class Swifts in 1881, after Swifts had had a fairly nomadic 1870s at, at least three other sites around town. Early local opposition came from the nearby village team of Rushall Rovers, who played the 15-a-side match in all-white with a large blue Staffordshire knot across the chest.

The Chuckery ground was a large piece of land on an elevated position on the south side of the town, towards Great Barr.

Walsall cricket club, who'd been there since the 1830s, had developed the Chuckery ground by enclosing it with iron railings and a wicket fence and erected two pavilions. So, on one site, we had the town's leading cricket and football teams all playing virtually side by side. The pavilions were in the middle of the land, separating the cricket field from the football fields. Players would get changed in the brick pavilion and walk through the other side to the football pitches. These football and cricketers were clearly middle or upper middle class and shared the highest social connections in the town. When the land was sold at the end of the 1890s for housing development, a road named Chuckery Road was built facing the home of a Walsall mayor, Mr Wheeway, with the other end going right through the site of the cricket pavilions. Town and Swifts pitches were side by side, now occupied by Florence and Lumley Streets. I chuckled when, on my site visit to Florence Street in August 2012, a street sign read: 'No football games to be played here.' Following poor results in the 1890s from the Town-Swifts side, many fans would have agreed with that!

Football was said to be so popular in Walsall that by 1882, there were around thirty teams in the town, led by names such as Walsall Alma, Albion, White Star, Locomotive Albion, Trinity, Athletic, and Unity.

The first match for the Town at the Chuckery was against Rushall Rovers on 3rd October 1874, the game being only noted for 'a great many examples of rough play from both sides' (*Walsall Observer*). Fifteen-a-side was the order of the day for that Rushall match, with Walsall FC lending the visitors five men because nearly twenty home players had turned out, all expecting a game. Curiously, the Rushall goals were scored by the borrowed men!

Two years later, in 1877, Henry Quilter's Birmingham FC came to the Chuckery. This time, the match was 12-a-side and Walsall fielded the following men:

Cottam (C); J. Russell, Greatrex, F. Brace, F. Lawrence, F. Wood, G. Brawn, J. Adams, J. Addenbrooke, E. Cozens, A. B. Lindop, T. A. Russell. That would have been a match of some importance at the time. Most of this team were wealthy factory owners or town councillors.

Addison Russell was team secretary at this time. By a curious coincidence, A. B. Lindop was my family doctor's grandfather, and Addenbrooke was chair of governors at my old school, Queen Mary's Grammar School – not when I was there, may I add!

The Walsall Town side of 1879/80 was:

W. Keay (goal); E. J. Newman (captain and back); J. Keay, H. Taylor, H. Stone (halfbacks); Smallwood, Adams, A. Harvey, Withers, Tonks, and F. Keay (forwards). This is an unusual 1-3-6 formation, more defensive that other sides at that time, but note the three Keay brothers. Matches were keenly reported in the Walsall press, who analysed the performance or lack of it, of every single team player on the pitch, and they weren't reticent about making suggestions as to which players needed to be got rid of! Rivals the Swifts had been quick to enter the Birmingham Cup, but the Town didn't compete until 1880/81 season, and it was the Swifts who put them out, and not for the last time. Town weren't even the 2nd Walsall side to enter this competition; in 1879, three local sides called Walsall Albion, Athletic, and White Star entered. In middle age, the Keay brothers continued to play local junior football with the St. Mathews-based Walsall Brotherhood club during the early 1890s.

At the end of 1880, Town benefitted from an influx of players when neighbours Rushall Rovers decided to call it a day, and after they folded, all their best players joined the ranks of Walsall Town. Many leading Rovers' men also belonged to the Walsall club in the late 1870s.

In 1882, Walsall newspapers were exalted to report to the citizens of the town that the team had toppled the leading club in the country and at their ground too! This refers to Town's wonderful 3-2 win at Blackburn Rovers who were at their peak around the mid-1880s, winning the English Cup three times. At this time, both Walsall teams had the habit of undertaking tours to play the principal Lancashire clubs. Keay, the goalie, was singled out for special merit. It was said to be Walsall Town's greatest ever result. A few months later, Town and Swifts met in the replayed final of the 1882 Staffordshire Cup to cement both these two sides' leading positions in Midlands football. Swifts would have been slight favourites, but Town surprised them with a clear 4-1 victory. In 1884, the Town had their record away win, when they travelled to Stourbridge in a Birmingham Cup tie. They hammered the Standard FC 11-0 at their Wood Street ground and followed this up by scoring 9 past Aston Shakespeare, then 10 past Excelsior before going out to the Swifts in the semi-final. The early mid-1980s saw Town at their peak. The 1884/5 season also saw the Town successful again in the Staffordshire Cup, which by then was 3rd in line of importance to West Midland teams after the English FA and Birmingham Cups. They beat the Wolverhampton Wanderers by 2-1, in a match where they were seen as the underdogs. During that season, 1884/5, Walsall Town scored 103 goals in 22 cup and friendly matches against varying opposition, with only 1 defeat all season. It's a puzzlement why crowds did not improve on their below-3,000 average.

The Town usually entered the Birmingham, Wednesbury, and Staffordshire cups with a reasonable degree of success. They first entered the Birmingham Senior cup in 1880/1 season, only to put out by rivals Walsall Swifts by 3-0 in the 3rd round at Folly House Lane. There was a repeat performance the following year, this time by 2-1 at home before 4,000. In 1884, an all-Walsall final was a possibility in the BSC, but the Town were edged out 2-1 by Aston Villa who were virtually playing at home at the 'neutral' Aston Lower grounds, whilst the Swifts beat WBA 1-0 to reach the final, where Villa were too strong. Four goals too strong! The year 1885/6 saw another all-Walsall BSC semi-final, with Swifts again emerging victorious, where yet again Villa were triumphant in the final. By the mid-1880s, there were so many entrants for the Birmingham Senior Cup that the draw was regionalised. This meant that Town and Swifts were extremely likely to keep on meeting in the quarter-final stages, and this may have been a factor in their decision to join forces.

Walsall folk have always been fickle fans, no more so in modern times with the Saddler's fanbase dropping from an average of 14,000 to 4,000 in my lifetime, and so it was in the 1880s Walsall. Sometimes crowds would drop below a thousand, and when the Town were doing badly, the low hundreds who trudged the near two miles uphill out of town to see the team lose yet again at the Chuckery were not bringing in enough revenue to keep the club going, and several meetings were held to awaken the general apathy of the townsfolk during 1887 and 1888.

Walsall Town entered the FA Cup in 1883, almost a decade after their formation. At this time, they were playing in a white kit. They were put out at the first hurdle by the newly formed Wednesbury Town, who had created a strong but short-lived side from the exiles of Wednesbury Old Athletic and some Elwells' players. They didn't reach the 3rd round until 1886 but found the Mitchell St. George's side too good and went out by 2-7 at Cape Hill, Smethwick. By 1888, Town had amalgamated with the Swifts, and so the FA Cup story continues with that side.

The Town team of 1885 was: W. Keay (goal); Newman (captain) and Tonks (backs); Collington, Taylor, Evans (halfbacks); Roberts, Stone, Bradbury, Bird, Dodsworth (forwards).

Samuel Bradbury, my ancestor, was sold to Birmingham St. George's, and then he moved to the Wolves in 1892. Note that four players were still there from the 1880 side. Keay had been the Walsall goalkeeper for over seven years, and the captain E. J. Newman was presented with a ten-year-long service medal at the club's annual general meeting at the Royal Hotel in 1886. Despite Walsall's fame for world-class leatherwork of every description, it surprised me to read in *The Walsall Red Book* for 1889 that there appeared to be but one maker of footballs and cricket balls in the town, one C&R Hartley Co. Ltd, of Butts Road.

On the 21st November 1887, old pioneers Stafford Road (W'ton) wished they hadn't gone to the Chuckery ground when Walsall Town embarrassed them with a 16-0 scoreline in the Staffordshire Cup, with Shaw netting six of them.

Amalgamation with Walsall Swifts in 1888 was not only an economic but a footballing necessity if the town was to keep up with soar-away teams like Aston Villa and West Bromwich Albion. Town were on the verge of disbanding due to paltry crowds of a few hundred for league games against less attractive opposition. The two Walsall teams met for the final time on 12th March 1888 in the semi-finals of the Walsall Cup in front of 3,000 at the Chuckery.

This was Town's last team: Osbourne (goalie); Jones, Brettle (backs); Beech, Lea, Barnett (halfbacks); Somerfield, Cope, Shaw, Wykes, Hicklin (forwards).

It was not a lucky day, with Swifts' Tapper putting the ball through the posts just as the final whistle was being blown!

The new Town Swifts side only selected five Town men, suggesting the Swifts men were superior, which was generally borne out in the two teams' achievement statistics.

For the combined Walsall Town – Swifts, the first game of importance was the final of the Birmingham Cup in 1888. A surprise 0-0 draw against the higher ranked Aston Villa at Muntz St saw the B'ham FA committee choose Aston Lower grounds for the replay venue.

Walsall protested as they though the neutral Wednesbury Oval was more like it, so they refused to play a replay.

B'ham FA at first awarded the trophy to Villa, but three weeks later changed their minds and declared the cup to be shared. The Town Swifts moved into a new ground after being expelled from the Chuckery at the end of the nineteenth century, and this was on the West Bromwich road out of town in the Fullbrook district, and this was what the ground became known as. They only spent a few years there, despite building a large grandstand down one touchline, and a changing room, since the ground was low-lying and was subject to frequent flooding. The Whitehall junior school faces this location today, as it did then, and with Haskell Street occupying exactly where the pitch stood.

Biggest competitive wins:

17-0 v Bloxwich Saturday 14th November 1885 Birmingham Cup 1st round

References

The *Walsall Observer* 1870-1900
The Walsall Red Book

** *Source*: *Walsall Observer* 1882. Several other sources quote 1877 as their formation date. Geoff Allman in his *History of Walsall Football Club* book (ISBN 0 7524 2091 7) gives 1874.

* previously called Victoria Swifts

Walsall Town with Staffordshire Cup

Walsall Swifts in All Maroon Kit

Walsall Swifts' Follyhouse Lane site

Harry Allen of Walsall Swifts 1886

WALSALL TOWN-SWIFTS FC

f. 1888-1895 then as Walsall FC

THEY WERE FORMED IN 1888 when the town's leading two sides, Swifts and Town, decided to amalgamate in order to save both clubs from extinction, as they were both financially in a bad situation, struggling to attract any more than a few hundred spectators by this time. They believed that by making a new team out of each side's best players, they could better challenge their main – and more successful – rivals Aston Villa, who had often been their stumbling block in winning the Birmingham cup in the past.

The *Walsall Observer* carried articles about both teams thinking of winding up. Only five years before, both Town and Swifts were riding the crest of a wave, both within the Black Country and at national level.

GROUNDS

1. The Chuckery (now Lumley Road and Montcrieff St) 1888-1893
2. Wednesbury Oval, Maw Green (sometimes if the West Bromwich Rd ground was waterlogged) 1893 only
3. West Bromwich Road – known as the Fullbrook ground (1893-1896)
4. Fellows Park – known as Hillary Street ground (1896-1990)

COLOURS

1. red and white vertical stripes, navy knicks (1888)
2. red and white halves, navy shorts (1893/4)
3. all red (probably the maroon kit as below)
4. maroon
5. claret and blue stripes (1895)
6. white and red (1896)
7. claret and blue halves, black shorts (1900)
8. amber and navy (1909)

When the Swifts and the Town held a meeting where amalgamation was agreed, they intended to play in gaudy maroon and blue stripes but switched to the red and white stripes on the eve of the 1888/9 season. I would love to have seen that maroon and blue stripes kit!

As the new combined team, they continued to enter the FA Cup where previously they had entered as two separate teams. They got through to the 1st round proper in 1888 and beat Sheffield Heeley 5-1 to meet the Wolves in round 4. Wolves proved too strong as they had just been chosen to play in the newly created Football League, and the Saddlers went out by 1-6 at Dudley Road. The Town Swifts did not make it through to the competition proper again until 1897, by which time they were known simply as 'Walsall', and on that occasion, Newton Heath put them out by 1-0. Indeed, during the early 1890s, the FA Cup was beginning to be monopolised by northern sides, with only Albion, Villa, Wolves, and Stoke getting into the last 16 on any regular basis.

Even when the two sets of supporters were combined, crowds were never spectacular; they only drew 5,500 for their League Division II game v. Small Heath Alliance on 2/9/1893, and that was one of the best attendances of the season. Earlier, in 1888, they played a 2-2 draw with West Bromwich Albion, which drew a healthy 7,000 crowd to the Chuckery ground, although the visitors probably brought a tenth of the crowd.

The first combined team of 1888/9 season was:

Jack Tracey (goal) (Swifts)

Alf Jones (Town) Sam Reynolds (Town)

Jack Morley (Swifts) Bill Lee (Town) George Morris (Swifts)

David Wykes (Swifts) Tom Athersmith (Swifts)

George Cope (Town) Shiner Shaw (Town) George Tapper (Swifts)

Alf Jones, a fullback, left the club and joined Great Lever, and was almost immediately given his first England cap to play against Scotland. He holds a unique place in Walsall football: he is the only man to have played for Swifts, Town, and Town Swifts.

The Chuckery grounds have their own chapter elsewhere in this book; the Wednesbury Oval was used as an emergency ground for a few weeks at the start of the club's League Division Two season of 1893 because their new Fellows Park ground wasn't entirely ready and passed inspection for League action.

The West Bromwich Road ground was improved with a perimeter running track, a pavilion on the halfway line near the main road, and a wooden grandstand running for a third-pitch length down the touchline. But the club were only there for three years, as it suffered from being waterlogged as it lay at the bottom of a slope. Occupying the site today are – Grange, Haskell, and East streets. Haskell Street lies where the pitch used to be. A visit to the area reveals that the Fullbrook ground was almost back-to-back with the original Swifts' Folly House lane ground of the 1870s. There is even the possibility, since all around this area was just meadow fields until the 1900s, that they were both two sides of the same large field. Folly House Lane marked the perimeter of Walsall's road and lane system on the south (B'ham) side of the town until the start of the twentieth century, with only the Birmingham Road between the Fullbrook district and Great Barr, now the most north-westerly suburb of Birmingham. There was a further two miles of open farmland to the south of Great Barr until the town of Aston.

A strange thing happened on Saturday 27th April 1889. Walsall Town-Swifts were due to meet Small Heath in the final of the Walsall Cup. Small Heath were due to play Aston Shakespeare in the semi-final of the Warwickshire cup at the same time, and they thus failed to turn up for the Walsall final! As Small Heath easily won 6-0, it could be proposed that they should have fielded their 2nd team against the Shakers and sent its 1st team to play Walsall.

Players used during the 1890s included :-

goalkeepers: Warner, Edge, and Benwell

backs: Robertson, Proffot, Withington, Pinches, Hawkins, Bailey, Smellie, Stokes, Reynolds

halfbacks: Tonks, Morley, Stokes, Holmes, Brettle, Hodson, Cook, Forsyth, Ball

forwards: Shaw, Holmes, Hunter, Whittock, Lofthouse, Copeland, McWhinnie, J. O'Brien, Hartley, Gee, Wilson, Gray

Modest success came during the 1890s, with Second Division League football played at West Bromwich Road and the new Fellows Park ground, but by the end of the 1890s, Walsall were at their lowest point again. Poor results, an inconsistent team, and low crowds led to having to apply for re-election several seasons in succession. In the winter of 1895, the Town

Swifts were actually wound up in court, but they soon relaunched themselves, this time simply as Walsall Football Club, the name which the cricketers chose in 1875 when they began to play football.

They were voted out of the League in 1895 but regained their League status a year later. Eventually, in 1901, they were thrown out of the Football League, and two decades of non-descript lower level football followed. Firstly in the Midland League, and then the 1910s were spent languishing in the Birmingham & District League with local sides like Wednesbury, Kidderminster, Worcester, and Willenhall.

At the outbreak of the First World War in 1914, Walsall spent 1914/15 playing in the newly formed Walsall Combination League. Attendances at this difficult time were very low; their home game against old local rivals Wednesbury Old Athletic drew only 400 people to Fellows Park. Many people at this time did not think it was proper for football to continue, let alone go and watch it. The town's premier side did not recover until the other side of the 1920s. After losing their Football league status, Walsall supporters had to watch their fallen team struggle to beat local sides like Stourbridge, Worcester, Brierley Hill, Dudley, Kidderminster, and Wellington Town, and the reserve sides of the big four black country clubs: Villa, Albion, Wolves, and Stoke. It would be 1921 before League status was restored.

Walsall Town-Swifts dropped all its tags, and with it, its references to its own history, in 1895, and reverted simply to Walsall Football Club. This, ironically, was Walsall Town's earliest monicker at the Chuckery two decades before.

Interestingly, a year after the Swifts–Town amalgamation, several members of the original Walsall Town club, Messrs H. Cozens, J. Cottram, H. G. Greatrex, and Alderman Newman, started up a new team, Walsall Amateurs in 1889. This was to promote the wholesome Christian principles of pure amateur play and spirit; however, this team still shared the Chuckery ground with its professional rivals. Playing at first in white shirts, navy shorts, they altered the shirts to blue and white quarters, and they continued to receive consistent match reporting into modern times. H. G. Greatrex became a vice-president of the Birmingham Football Association in the 1920s.

To find the site of the Fullbrook ground today, take the West Bromwich Road (Walsall bound, not West Brom) from the Broadway, Walsall's ring road off the A34, and find the Whitehouse Junior School. The houses facing the school, and the streets behind them, were the Fullbrook ground.

For further reading about Walsall FC, suggested reading includes Walsall FC history books by both Geoff Allman and Tony Mathews. However, beware of wrongly identified photographs! In every book I found that every single photo described as ' Walsall Town-Swifts ', 'Walsall Swifts' or Walsall Town, was, in fact not! Clearly the Town-Swifts 1881 pictures in the Allman book are of West Bromwich Albion, and several well-known faces, such as 'Baldy' Reynold, Bob Roberts, the goalie, wearing his England shirt (!), and JEM Bayliss, are clearly identifiable. The English F.A. Cup at the ' Walsall Town-Swifts ' feet should have been a giveaway! The Tony Mathews 'History of Walsall FC' also shows many photographic and factual errors. Any photo showing a Walsall team in a white shirt is certainly not the Swifts, who did not wear a badge on their shirt until 1881.

Walsall Town Swifts 1893

Walsall Town's Green Dragon headquarters

Walsall's Chuckery Ground 1885

Warwick County FC

f.1886-1899

Colours
all blue with yellow stripes; later blue with yellow V yolk

Ground
the Edgbaston County Cricket ground

This was the football team formed by the Warwickshire Cricket Club after they had developed the Edgbaston cricket ground into a proper sports ground with several small grandstands and terracing. The committee decided that it was a financially viable proposition to fund a professional football team during the 1890s even though the cricket teams' balance books were clipping into the red. Only international cricket games were bringing in the crowds of over 5,000. It proved to be a perennial loss-making venture, and the team was dissolved after less than a decade.

Early grounds included:

1. the YMCA ground on Bristol Road Selly Oak
2. the old Pickwick C. C. ground at Camp Hill (This was on St. Paul's Rd, Highgate, also used by the Havelock FC, which became the famous Moseley Rugby Club.)
3. the Wycliffe ground on Pershore Road, Selly Park (the Lloyds Bank grounds?)
4. Edgbaston cricket ground

The team was in the high social class: William Ansell of Ansells Brewery led the committee, and Baron Calthorpe, Earl of Warwick himself was the president.

In 1882, William Ansell (of Ansells Brewery and an Aston Villa director) set up the Warwickshire county cricket club at Leamington-Spa.

In 1885, the Lord Calthorpe gave 5 acres of land, which was rough meadow off the Pershore Rd to be used for sports purposes.

This was developed into a level playing surface and the Warwickshire County cricket club eventually moving its HQ to there after a few years at the Aston Lower grounds cricket and bicycle grounds – (now the site of Nelson Rd etc).

They played their last few seasons in the Midland League.

Most famous players: H. W. Bainbridge. He was on the founding committee for the Warwickshire C. C. C and an international cricketer. Bob Dudley was signed from the Wolves in 1887.

In 1889, Jasper Cowan was all set to sign terms with the Warwick County team, when none other than George Ramsey met him at the train station and persuaded him to sign for his Aston Villa team instead! Ramsay was always said to get his man once he had set his mind on it! Pangbourne was a fast forward who came from Mitchell St. George's but moved on to Walsall Swifts after only one year.

From the outset, the football club were in trouble with the footballing world, as it was perceived, wrongly, that they were attempting to suggest that they represented the whole county, and this flew in the face of nearby Staffordshire and Derbyshire county associations. However, a public letter in the *Birmingham Daily Post* set the matter clear; after all, was there not also a Derby County and a Notts County football team too?

But by the end of 1888, the football team were £100 in the red, according to the cricket club's treasurers' annual report, but it was decided that the football teams' losses could be covered by the Warwickshire CCC for another season or two yet. The cricket club themselves however were in a mess by the turn of the century, with only international matches played at the County ground making the money. They could get 5,000 crowds for that but only a hundred or two for the football team. Aston Villa came to the rescue, when, in 1902, they played a charity match against the (equally) famous Corinthians FC, which raised £112 for the County ground funds, equivalent to around £30,000 today.

Leading player Billy Ollis was sold to Small Heath in 1891, and so too, star forward Pangbourne, who went to Walsall Town-Swifts only weeks after, making a big impression against them in an epic Birmingham Cup tie which went to three games that year. Walsall won the first game by a remarkable 6-5 with Warwick coming back from 0-3 down to 4-4 and nearly snatch a draw, but a replay was ordered on appeal of Warwick. The second game was a good 2-2 draw, and the third game saw Walsall fielding all its reserve side and went down by 3-0.

Pangbourne was the star player in all three games, and he was soon signed up by Walsall Swifts. He was a very speedy winger and had left the Swifts' defenders in his wake. His previous club was Mitchell St. George's of Smethwick. Unfortunately prone to injury, he only played about twenty games for Walsall.

Edgbaston cricket ground of course underwent a multi-million pound redevelopment in 2011 and today bears almost no resemblance to the grand old ground of the twentieth century which most people remember; however, back in the Victorian and Edwardian eras, spectator facilities were much sparser, with only one or two small stands and a main pavilion and clock tower. The large pitch area of course was the same: too big for a football match alone. I expected to find that the footballers had to make do with the other pitches outside the enclosed ground; one on the corner with Cannon Hill Rd (facing Cannon Hill park), and the other at the rear, long since a car park. But no! not only was football played on the hallowed and manicured lawn, but a report from the *Birmingham Daily Post* from 20th October 1890 startles the reader with the fact that there were no less than three different matches all taking place simultaneously: Warwick County v Burton Wanderers by the pavilion, Aston Victoria were playing Brierley Hill, and bizarrely, Aston Old Edwardians were playing Coventry in a rugby match! Spectators were at liberty to wander around the ground and watch portions of whichever match they liked; wonderful value for money indeed! It was reported that of the thousand-plus crowd, only a handful were watching Aston Victoria's game.

Their team which went to Derby County in January 1888, losing 1-4, was:

Shilton (goal); Cant and Mackarness (backs); Talbot, Moore, Page (halfbacks); forwards: Adcock, Stanley (right wing), Webster (centre), Bird and Smart (left wing).

In 1889, W. C. Rose, the Warwick goalkeeper, joined the Wolverhampton Wanderers in 1889. He became a Wolves favourite and was often selected for Representative games which were still going on into the end of the 1890s.

The team of the 1891/2 season was: Hollis (goal); Proffit and Lamsdale (backs); Lillie, Phillips, Ollis (halfbacks); Carter, Hare, Stanley, Cope, Pangbourne, and Forsyth (forwards).

Lillie was the famous Warwickshire and England cricketer, and when the start of the 1891 cricket season began, he reported to the cricketing authorities that he was unavailable for selection due to a bad hand injury sustained in the last match of the football season of the previous Easter!

Biggest defeats:

0-13 away to Derby Midland in November 1887: William Ansell himself acted as umpire when the following team was fielded:

Mason (goal); Webster, Sutton (backs); Munter, Boyce, Page (halfbacks); Talbot, Spears, Moore (centre), Stanley, Asbury (forwards).

It must have been a very sorry experience in officiating in an away game at your own team's humiliation.

0-11 to A. Villa in 8/10/87. At this time, Warwick had only been going three seasons, and the Villa were building their all-conquering team of the 1890s.

FA Cup History – None, Warwick County FC never reached the 1st round proper.

REFERENCES

Birmingham Daily Post

ACKNOWLEDGEMENTS

Phillip Britt, Edgbaston County ground museum

Warwick County's Famous Edgbaston Ground

Warwick County's H.W.Bainbridge

Wednesbury Old Athletic FC

f.1874-1893 revived (1893-1894) and again (1894-1924)

They were founded in the winter of 1874 by scholars of the St. John's night school Athletic Club, Wood Lane, Wednesbury.

They played in four of the first seven Birmingham Cup finals, winning two. They are one of the most successful of all the teams in this book but peaked around 1881, and failure to turn professional early enough in their history – as the Villa did – ultimately cost them their eminent status.

Charles Hatfield was said to be the club founder. He was headmaster at the institute, and it was he who promoted the new game of football to his students. When the institute closed, the football club became an independent outfit. The population of the town in the year 1880 was 20,000, but there were several clubs for the populous to follow.

Their early nickname, the Leather Hands, came about because players worked at the Patent Shaft works and used leather hand protectors in their work. Later this became 'the Old Uns'.

The first original team lasted twenty years, and this is the 'real' WOA which became famous not just throughout the Black Country, but across the footballing Midlands.

It folded in 1924 because it was in a sorry state of being bankrupt after a period in the cash-sapping Midlands League, and crowds which once went past 10,000 were now numbered in the hundreds.

Quickly, a team rose phoenix-like from the ashes when three local minor sides amalgamated and refloated the Old Athletics name, but this was short-lived (about a year), although it did have several men from the original team on its committee.

The third version of Old Athletic came about when the Wednesbury Excelsior team, thought to have started in 1890/1, adopted the Old Athletic name which was vacant. They hoped the Wednesbury people would get behind and support them like the old days. This version was quite successful, spending its life hovering between the Walsall & District League and the Birmingham & District League or Combination. It folded in 1924, by which time, it had been financially forced to revert back to being amateur after crowds dropped to the mid-hundreds, and wages and visitor's gate-share money could not be met.

Colours

1. maroon and white hoops (1877)
2. blue and white hoops (1880)
3. scarlet, blue knicks (1881)
4. scarlet and blue hoops (1884)
5. white, blue knicks (1887)
6. amber and black (1891)
7. black and yellow stripes (1892)
8. amber and black stripes/navy (1893)
9. scarlet and black hoops (at Lloyd St. ground) (1896)
10. white, blue shorts (1910s)
11. red and white stripes, blue (1920s)

Going back to the beginning, they rapidly established themselves as the leading force in the Black Country in the 1870s. They were founder members of the B'ham FA along with Aston Unity in 1875, having formed the Wednesbury FA with local sides Strollers and Elwells.

They won the Birmingham FA Cup final 3-2 v Stafford Road FC in 1877 and again in 1879. In between, they lost the semi-final of 1878. At this time, they were getting the biggest crowd in the Midlands and forging a name for the town as a pace-setting football team. Wednesbury very quickly went football-mad in the 1870s, a century before the same phrase was used about Liverpool.

Early Wednesbury football included elements of the rugby game, i.e. rouges or touchdowns. They played a 2-2-6 formation, not the 1-2-7 formation of other teams at the time.

In the 1870s and early 1880s, they were a free-scoring side, having gained a bit of a reputation for strong play, with shoulder-charging and kick-and-rush tactics still in use long after the combination game had shown itself to be the way to success. Their supporters must have been hoarse with cheering when games such as 16-0 v Cannock, 11-2 v B'ham Excelsior, and 11-4 v Coseley were on display.

Although the 'Old Uns' were, by 1880, the top side in the Midlands with the Aston Villa club, they still couldn't hang on to their best players, for Villa, Albion, and Wolves could afford to play more match money (players were paid by the game in those days). W.O.A had a big squad of players – they ran three teams – and were renting the Oval, all money-drainers.

Star player J. E. M. Bayliss eventually moving to West Bromwich Albion (and FA cup winners' fame), and George Holden too, left for Derbyshire. That broke the 'Wedgbury' fans hearts, but he was back within a year. His 'head for goal and dribble past all of 'em' style was not welcome at Derby Midland, who were more attuned to the new combination (inter-passing play) style, which proved to be the way to success.

During the 1870s and 1880s, the Old Athletic quickly became a powerful force on the scene, and were rampant goalscorers, frequently scoring double-figure wins in friendly matches. An Old Athletic fan would have seen more goals following his side than any other in the Midlands, then or since. So the 1870s and 1880s were happy days, filled with cup successes year on year. Obscure side Boothen were annihilated 20-0 in the Staffordshire Cup; Tipton 11-0, Stoke 12-2, Milton (Stoke) 14-0, and Small Heath (B'ham City) by 7-2. Large crowds gathered at the Oval and in the park; up to 10,000 for games against Walsall, Villa, Blackburn Rovers and their town rivals, the Strollers. In 1880, striker Morley got all 6 goals in the clubs' 6-0 away win at Aston Unity; Morley also hit 4, plus a Holmes hat-trick in their remarkable 10-3 away win at Saltley College two years previously. Even by 1879, WOAC had a reserve side and a Colts team. Even their Colts side were able to beat the youngsters of Perry Athletic 6-0 in December 1879.

They beat Villa 2-1 in 1880 to win the Staffordshire FA cup and probably the title of best team in the Midlands with it. W.O.A. played in the B'ham and District League, then the Midland League in the 1890s but the town couldn't support a professional club, and they sadly disbanded (first time) in 1893. Some players restarted the club but to no avail.

During 1882, their impressive fixture list included such leading teams from today like – West Bromwich Albion, Aston Villa, Bolton Wanderers, Stoke, Blackburn Rovers, Walsall (Swifts), the Wolves, and both Nottingham sides. Only Blackburn Rovers were their superiors that season.

From the 1890s till its final demise, in 1893, the fading club variously played in the Midland League, Birmingham Combination, B'ham & District League, or the lowly Walsall & District League.

By 1883, the club was paying out £45 rent p.a for the use of Elwells' Oval ground, as sizeable chunk of their £340 annual income. However, they had over 150 members each paying 3/6p (17.5p) annual subscriptions, and members enjoyed an annual gala night at the Anchor Hotel on Holyhead Road at the end of each season. Committee members lavishly presented their best players with silver watches and medals from various successful cup runs in the Wednesbury, Staffordshire and Birmingham Cups. This of course was half a decade away from the birth of League football.

Wednesbury folk had got used to successful top flight football matches at the Oval, from both Old Athletic, and to a lesser extent, the Strollers. But it was the WOA who had attained legendary status within the Black Country, with many friendly and cup ties being won by margins of 10-0 and more; WOA persisted with the old formation of 7 forwards long after more scientific 2-3-5 combination play was being introduced. Goals were going in at both ends, which was all right at local level, but when the club made the financially disastrous choice of joining the Midland League in the 1890s, and with star players JEM Bayliss and George Holden gone or retired, they were left exposed as a team behind the progressive times, and by then it was too late to realise the folly of not amalgamating with the Strollers into one professional team which the whole town could get behind with crowds of maybe 3-5,000. Nearly all the other teams in the Midland League were from the east or north Midlands, and WOA could not afford this sort of travelling expenditure on crowds of around 1,500. Sometimes, due to poor fixture arrangements, W.O.A. would play at home for five weeks running, but then seven weeks of away games in which the club received no income. Visiting teams did not get a percentage of the 'gate', only travel and accommodation expenses.

Reformed again in 1893, they won the Staffordshire Junior cup three times in the Edwardian era (1900, 1903, 1905), a sad reminder of when they had won the Senior cup twenty years before. Other minor cups were won in Edwardian times, such as the Walsall, Bilston and Wednesbury cups, and there was a semi-final of the Birmingham Senior Cup in 1908, but the reality was, they were now 2nd class in an ever-expanding football arena where they were once top dogs.

Their biggest win in a senior competitive game was 9-0 v St. George's in 1881, and their biggest ever was an amazing 23-0 destruction of a young Hednesford Rovers side in an 1894 friendly. They entered the FA Cup with limited success in the early 1880s, but didn't get past the qualifying rounds after regionalisation was introduced in 1888.

In 1885, they were the last team to play at the West Bromwich Albion's Four Acres ground, losing 2-3 on 6th April.

GROUNDS

1. 1874-1877: the Well Field (now built over by Rooth Street, opposite Horse & Jockey public house)
2. variously: Brunswick Park and the Trapezium Ground (between Brunswick Park Rd and railway embankment)
3. 1878-1880: the Athletic Grounds – now the large meadow in Wednesbury park nearest to the cemetery
4. 1880-1893: Wednesbury Oval Grounds (still there today although Wood Green College have built on part of it)
5. 1894-1896: the Press Ground Wood Green – location uncertain
6. 1898-1910: the Central grounds, Lloyd Street – now built over by Marks Close off Trouse Lane
7. 1910-1924: the Leabrook grounds (rear Boat Inn P.H) close to Wednesbury Parkway metro station today (Pacific Avenue) – previously known as Harding's ground. Leabrook had a running track (although a part of it ran across the pitch!) and the club spent £100 on a grandstand and general ground improvements.

THE OVAL was also known as 'Wood Green' or 'Elwells ground' because a Mr Elwell had a large forge mill by the stream there before he moved his large works into the town (The Oval is at the edge of the town, near Bescot Station). When Elwells Mill was there, the land was covered with two large lakes which had to be drained away. The Oval was notoriously boggy.

Brunswick Park had been opened in 1875. The adjacent cemetery, opened in 1868, had expanded into the park up to the field known as the Athletic grounds. The 28 acres of park had been purchased the Patent Shaft & Axletree Company for £3,000 by the council and only sixty years previous had been open farmland. The entrance to the ground was near where the park gates are today. Here, the Old Athletics (and the Strollers) would draw crowds of up to 3,000.

Headquarters

1. The Crown & Cushion, High Bullen
2. The Horse & Jockey Pub Wednesbury Road
3. The Boat Inn, Leabrook Road

Star Players: J. E. M. Bayliss (b. 1863 Tipton-1933) sold to WBA 1884-1892. He netted 50 for WBA in 1887/8 season!

J. A. Horton (b. 1866) Also sold to Albion in 1882

George Holden (b. 1859-1925) was a fast right-wing dribbler who got 4 England caps, also chosen for Staffs FA and the B'ham FA representative sides.

Holden started with Wednesbury Old Park FC in 1876, then Wednesbury St James 1877, then left WOA to WBA (1878-86) then came back for 1 season, before ending his career with Derby Midland FC. Holden was a legend in Wednesbury for well over a decade and even above JEM Bayliss, was the best player ever to come out of the town.

Many of the club's best players were snapped up by Albion or Walsall. Wilf Humpage, Frank Wright, George Williams, all moved to the Albion. J. E. M. Bayliss, who came from Tipton, only played for the WOA for two seasons, 1882/3 and 1883/4 before joining the Albion.

1877 saw the Old Un's first piece of silverware on the trophy shelf, when they won the prestigious Birmingham Cup, beating Stafford Road 3-2 in a thrilling see-saw final at the Bournbrook Grounds near Selly Oak. Two years later, the scenario was repeated exactly at Villa's old Wellington Road ground in front of 7,000 spectators. The Old Athletic had a rightful claim to be the Midlands' No. 1 side. However, as the 1880s came, so too did the boys from Aston Villa.

The team at the end of the 1870s was: J. Page (goal); W. Moon (captain and back); Cliffe, Stokes and Hatfield (halfbacks); Reeves, Skidmore, Page, Morley, Holmes, Holden (forwards). Morley was to serve the Wednesbury Association committee for many years to come. By 1883, only Holden and Morley remained, with Groucutt, Woodcock, and Tonks now in attack and Kent between the sticks. Llowarch, who played during the 1890s, was said to be their best ever goalkeeper. He had previously started out with Wolverhampton Rangers in 1882.

During October of 1880, WOA scored a remarkable 51 goals in just 5 games, including 12 past Stoke FC, and they once won fifteen consecutive matches. Other huge wins of note at that time include: 13-0 v Harborne in 1876, 10-3 away at Saltley College in 1878, 11-0 over Tipton in 1879, 20-0 over unknown Boothen in 1880, 12-1 over Rushall Rovers and 15-0 over Walsall Albion during 1880. Even West Bromwich Albion and Aston Villa, Bolton and the Wolves were beaten during 1882. Heady days indeed, and for Wednesbury fans, it should have meant a future history which would have seen them in the Premiership today, but, as we see, wrong decisions by the club, and all too late anyway, left them trailing in the dust of all of those 1882 beaten sides.

The year 1881 proved to be their finest hour, when they entered the English FA Cup and got to the 5th round, or last 8. Well, the last 7 actually, as the FA still hadn't worked out how to give byes in the 1st round in order to get a perfect last 16 in round 4. The FA Cup wasn't officially regionalised until 1888, but in reality, the Staffordshire and Birmingham sides were grouped together until 1 side remained, the same for the east and north Midlands sides. And so it was that the WOA got past local opposition, including the Villa and Small Heath to face mighty Blackburn Rovers in round 5. They had finally met their match, and a 3-1 win for the visiting team, which was to be a giant of the game in the 1880s and 1890s, was no disgrace. A crowd of 8,000 spectators crushed into the Oval without any proper facilities and held back only by ropes swelled the Wednesbury coffers, for the time being anyway.

Their 1883 Birmingham Challenge Cup final v A. Villa drew 10,000 to the Aston Lower grounds on 7th April. Villa won a close game 3-2 to reclaim the Midlands crown. This was probably a turning point for WOA as from this year on, until the Midland League days of 1890, there were more losses than wins, and crowds were falling back to around a thousand, and less for visitors such as Stoke (200), Stafford Rangers (450) and Burton Swifts (250). Only games against Villa, Albion, Walsall Swifts were attracting more than 3,000, and these were the teams that were pulling away from WOA and reducing them to a second-tier club. Alderman Wilson Lloyd gave the club a lift in 1892 when he became a patron and gave them a guinea (£1/1/0), but the reality was that the good days were over, and the team were living on the reputation of the side from the previous generation.

By 1900, the club had an annual income of almost £800; however, expenditure was at least that. Rapidly losing ground to teams who had the foresight to turn professional during the 1880s, WOA were sinking. A bad judgement call to play in the Midland League in the 1890s had lost them a lot of money, for all their opponents were from the East Midlands, and with strange names such as Rotherham and Gainsborough Trinity on the fixture list, crowds dwindled to below a thousand. Eventually, consideration was made to revert to amateur status, and WOA fell from a leading position to a floundering one.

The third incarnation of the Old Athletics spent the 1910s and 1920s variously in the Walsall & District League or the Birmingham Combination or District Leagues, generally struggling, the 1920s being especially embarrassing as they often finished bottom and were sometimes thrashed by 10 goals or more. Fifty years previously, it was they who were doing the thrashing.

Their last ever game ironically was a 5-0 home win over Ironbridge in front of 2,000. Their last ever Birmingham League game in 1924 was on 6 December when Bournville beat them 3-1 at home. They resigned from the league in bottom place and their remaining fixtures were taken on by Nuneaton Town's reserve side.

F A cup history	**1st Round**	**2nd Round**	**3rd Round**	**4th Round**	**5th Round**
1881/2	9-0 B'ham St George	6-0 Small Heath Alliance	Bye	Aston Villa 4-2	Blackburn Rovers 1-3
1882/3	7-1 Spital	1-4 Aston Villa			
1883/4	5-0 B'ham St. George's	4-2 Wolves	4-7 Aston Villa		
1884/5	2-1 Derby Midland	2-4 West Brom Albion			
1885/6	5-1 Burton Swifts	4-3 West Brom Albion (aet)			
1886/7	0-13 Aston Villa (H)				
1887/8	1-7 West Brom Albion (A)				

Honours

Birmingham Senior Cup 1877, 1879
Staffordshire Senior Cup 1880
Staffordshire Junior Cup 1900, 1903, 1905
Walsall Cup 1892
Wednesbury Charity Cup 1881, 1882, 1889, 1890, 1891, 1892, 1893

References

Wednesbury Old Athletic – A Complete History, W. G. Willetts
Wednesbury Free Press
Sandwell Archives, Smethwick Library
The works of Steve Carr, Birmingham football historian writer
Walsall Observer 1870-1900

Wednesbury Old Athletic 1877

Wednesbury Old Park FC

f. 1875-1885, reformed at least once in 1890s-1920?

Colours
red shirt, white sleeves, navy shorts

Ground
Kings Hill, Wednesbury

Origin:The works team from the giant Patent Shaft Steel works, the largest employer in Wednesbury. Away from the main sprawling Patent Shaft steel works across town, the Old Park Ironworks was founded in the 1830s and became known as Lloyds & Fosters. This in turn was bought out by Patent Shaft in 1949, and again by Metro-Cammell in modern times. They made steel castings of all sizes to order, and also made steam engines in the early decades.

Almost nothing is known about this team, as they were a works side, and their matches were hardly ever reported in the Wednesbury press. I believe their old ground is that which is now used by the Wednesbury Rugby Club on Kings Hill. There may well be people still alive who remember playing for this works side in the 1950s and 1960s.

Old Park were the 4th team to emerge in football-mad Wednesbury before 1876, following on from Elwells, Strollers. And Old Athletic. They folded by the end of the 1880s, certainly by 1885, but because they were a works team from the largest steel fabricators in the town, with a workforce of thousands, the team reformed more than once, up until around 1920.

In the early 1870s, they just played against the other Wednesbury teams, and were generally considered to be ranked behind Old Athletic, Strollers, and Elwells, although it is very likely that Old Park shared players with most of those teams.

Team of 1875 – Benton (capt.), Holland, Jay, Dean, Minific, Stokes, Morley, Hill, Cooper, Lowe, Wilkins, Speed, Daniels, Reeves, Horton.

Note the fifteen-man line-up, which was somewhat behind the general times, as the FA cup some four years earlier had stipulated teams of 11-a-side. Of course, at local level, it was into the 'eighties before 11-a-side was universal. Wednesbury teams were 12-a-side until around 1880.

Old Park entered the Birmingham Cup in 1876 for the one and only time. They overcame a team strangely called Harold, from the Perry Barr area in round 1, but went out by 2-0 to town rivals the Old Athletic, probably on Wells' Field on 2nd December.

George Holden, Wednesbury's most famous footballer, started out at Old Park as he was employed at the Patent Shaft Axeltree Works. Axeltree was an early word for the chassis and wheel bearings of a carriage or early motor vehicle. He played for them in 1876.

At Christmas 1915, Old Park stepped in where Willenhall Swifts had failed, and took over their fixture at the second half of the season in the Walsall Combination league, playing opposition such as Bloxwich Strollers, Walsall FC, Cannock Town, Hednesford Town and Darlaston. Old Park participated in a sad affair when they travelled to Willenhall's Portobello ground on 25th April when they were the last ever team to play the Pickwicks team which disbanded the following week. Old Park even defeated former giants and local rivals Wednesbury Old Athletic 3-2 in the last match of the season on their ground in front of a disappointing 500 crowd. But this was on the eve of the Great War, and many teams disbanded during 1916, by which time the playing of football was not socially acceptable when hundreds of thousands of young men who had enlisted were being killed or maimed in action.

One Old Park man who found later fame was William (Billy) Walker who ended up at Aston Villa in 1912 via Hednesford Town. An inside forward, he gained 13 England caps.

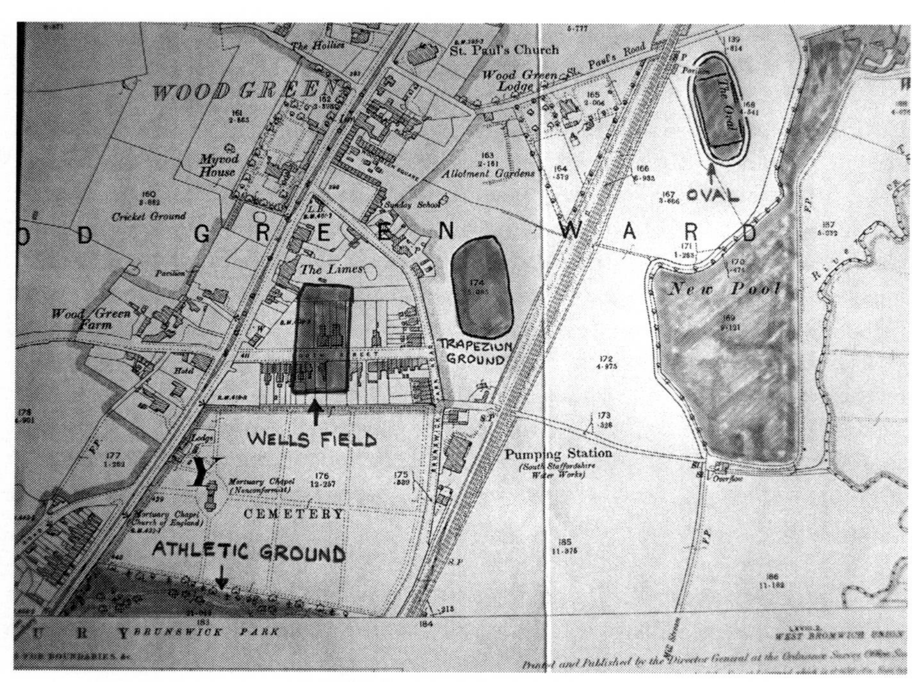

Wednesbury's Football Grounds

Wednesbury Strollers FC

f.1872-1885?

Nickname: 'The Kid Gloves' from the steelmaking trade in the town

Honours
Wednesbury Charity Cup 1884 beating Nottingham Forest 3-0 (replay)

Colours

1. orange** and black hoops (1872-1875)
2. maroon and white hoops (1877)
3. maroon shirts (1877)
4. maroon and white (1880)

Their first ever game was against town rival Wednesbury Old Athletic at Crankhill Farm on the outskirts of the town. Fifteen-a-side was the order of the day! After the inauguration of the Birmingham FA Cup in 1876, they played 12-a-side. Early Wednesbury football was rather on the rough side, with elements of the rugby game included, including mauls, and the ball being charged en masse into the goals. Touchdowns were acknowledged too, as earliest reports talk about winning by 2 goals and 4 touchdowns to nil, etc. The similarity for scoring options between rugby and association are obvious; both have a goal-frame structure into which it is the most desirable element to propel the ball, but both codes recognised that taking the ball to the opponents goal line ('fortress') needed to be receive some merit. We call these corner kicks today of course, but it was a while before the modern structure of play was worked out. Imagine today, if we still counted the number of corner kicks obtained into the scoring process in the Premiership! The match report does however, remind us that some handling and mauling elements from the Rugby games were still in use in Wednesbury football in the early mid-1870s.

Starting out as Wednesbury Town in October 1872, they were founded by town dignitary and author Fred Hackwood. However due to the rise and success of Wednesbury Old Athletic, the team dropped the Town tag and changed its name to Strollers in 1878 as they acknowledge that they were no longer the towns' top team. Original ground was a piece of ground at the highest part of the town on Church Hill, then moving to the expanses offered by Mr Crankhall at his sprawling farm at Mesty Croft, on the Stonecross side of town. At the Crankhall ground, the Strollers wore an orange and black hooped shirt.

Often, they would play on what were called the Athletic grounds; these today form part of Wednesbury park which adjoins the town cemetery. Next came a move to the Trapezium ground, a large field just off Brunswick Park road, with the railway making a boundary on the other side. Today, it's the large back gardens of the houses built in the 1890s between Woden Road East and Brunswick Park Rd, which was known as Cemetery Road in those days. Apart from the Athletic (park) grounds and the Oval, none of their other grounds were up to much; their 1st pitch at the top of Church Hill has a considerable slope both top to bottom and side to side; the Trapezium was probably undersize for a normal 150 × 80 yard pitch, and Crankhall Lane was almost halfway to West Bromwich, near to the old Manor House at Stone Cross.

For the start of the 1878 season, they had added the Strollers tag to their name.

Their first game against 'foreign' opposition was Tipton Town FC, who were actually the Black Country's oldest club, and was where the illustrious J. E. M. Bayliss started his football life. This, like most of their games in 1879 and 1880 were played at the Trapezium ground.

The early team of the mid-1870s was:

S. Tranter (goal); Edward Scott (back) and the rest of the men were forwards: Benjamin Knowles, A. Harvey, Eli Davis, D. Tonks, J. Sutton, Job Edwards, G. Knowles, A. Tonks, J. Duce, and Tom Bryan.

They would play either 15 or 12-a-side according to what their opponents brought along. As was typical of village and small town team, sets of brothers were common. Despite extensive research over two years, no record of their colours could be found. I would suggest that, as the first team in Wednesbury, they didn't need distinguishing shirts, and probably wore white at first. Tantalisingly, a decade after being formed, their club president reports at their AGM that they had changed their colours but once. Job Edwards, who had his own steel-tube factory in the town, was described as the best back in all of Birmingham district in the Midland Athlete newspaper of 1879. He also started manufacturing bicycles from 1869 at which early time, the wheels were made of hickory-wood. Several Strollers men were chosen for the Birmingham and Staffordshire representative sides – an honour which put their club at a disadvantage if it played on the same date! By 1883, three of the Strollers' best men were to leave town and sign for the Aston Villa: Davis, Bryan, and Harvey.

Frederick Hackwood (1851-1926) was head and shoulders, the most eminent person in the thriving town of Wednesbury. A Justice of the Peace, the deputy to the town's Member of Parliament, a M. Stanhope Esq and leading political figure throughout his life. He founded the Wednesbury Institute, the Horticultural Society (FRHS), was secretary at the Freemasons Lodge and was a prolific writer of over forty books, cataloguing and recording every facet of social and political life of Wednesbury town folk.

Reasonable local success ensued for the Strollers, and the club was well-run by local businessmen, some of who were the towns leading political figures. Their main Headquarters were at the Anchor Hotel on Holyhead Road. In a review of their 1881-2 season at the club's AGM and supper party, team captain Knowles reported in the press that between 1872 and 1882, Strollers had played some 303 games, entering the Wednesbury, Walsall and Birmingham cups, but rarely the FA cup. They had won nearly 200 of those games, and the team was justifiably proud of events in its first decade of existence.

Like so many of the amateur teams, Strollers were not No. 1 club in their respective town, the inevitable downhill slide occurred, and by 1880, the Strollers were an insecure fixture on the Wednesbury football map. More than once, they disbanded only to reform, sometimes as the Strollers, and sometimes with the 'Town' tag. It is thus hard to be certain whether a result is by the original Strollers team, by the Town team which used to be the Strollers, or the team which was formed by the reserve side of the Old Athletics breaking away in 1884 and calling themselves the 'Town' too!

Wednesbury Strollers were really a team for the 1870s. Earlier than most, they had a couple of years' start on other nearby teams, and in 1876/7 they reached the semi-final of the Birmingham Cup, being put out by 0-2 to Stafford Road, but going one better in 1877/8 when they reached the final to face unknown Shrewsbury (not Town). In a hard and close game, the Salopians egded home 2-1, but Strollers-in maroon shirts – had got their own back on the railwaymen of SRW by eliminating them 2-1 in a repeat semi-final game. Strollers reached the 4th round twice more, in 1879/80 and 1882/3. Big rivals Walsall Swifts were their nemesis on each occasion. In December 1879, one Garnet Clarke joined them from the famous Wanderers FC, although his name hardly appeared in any 1880 match reports, so perhaps he was consigned to the reserve team.

The Strollers became the first team from Staffordshire to enter the English FA Cup, when in 1878 they travelled to Peterborough to play the famous

Oxford University who despatched them by 7-0; it was said that the wealthy Oxford men helped Strollers with their travel expenses. The Old Athletic team took the national plunge three years later.

In 1884/5 a curious thing happened in the 1st round of the Birmingham Cup; they were drawn against Wednesbury Town! This was a name the Strollers had previously called themselves at the start of the 1870s, but changed it since their rivals the Old Athletic had demonstrated who was king of Wednesbury. And where did this 'new' Town team come from? why – from the breakaway of mostly Old Athletic reserve men who formed their own team, after being disenchanted with their lot at their own club. The new Town easily beat the old Strollers by 5-0, and now, the Strollers were only the 3rd best team in Wednesbury town. And a small town at that.

The team of 1880 was:

Beddoe (goal); Harvey and Scott (backs); Bryan and Jones (halfbacks); B. C. Knowles, Taylor, Burns, Riley, Powis, and Parker (forwards). Strollers were playing in maroon and white hoops.

The club reintroduced the 'Town' tag in 1882/3 as by now, WOA were much more famous and no confusion likely to arise.

In 1883, some Strollers players and most of the Old Athletic reserves team broke away and stated another Wednesbury Town team. This must have been premeditated since they had announced in the Walsall papers that Strollers would not be entering for any cups for the new season. This was judged to be a self-injurious policy.

For a short while, there was a Strollers team, a Town team, and the Old Athletic team in a town of only 20,000 inhabitants.

The continuous history of the Strollers and the Town are hard to unentangle because the original Strollers started out as the Town, the breakaway side called themselves the Town, and much later, another Town team started up after the Strollers had vanished, and the Old Athletics were a shadow of their former selves.

Nonetheless, Strollers were a prolific ambassador for the game in the area. At their annual dinner and awards evening, hosted by leading church figures and town politicians, it was announced that the Strollers had played some

303 matches in their first ten years, had moved grounds three times (park meadow, Oval, Trapezium), and had changed colour once only.

The 1883/4 side was: Hawkins (goal); Morris and Waldron (backs); Bradndrick, Taylor and Yates (halfbacks); Davis, Farmer, Parkes, Higgins, Lunn (forwards). Lunn later joined Walsall Town. Long-serving E. M. Scott was by now the teams' umpire.

In Alf Harvey and Eli Davis, the Strollers had, according to the Villa captain Archie Hunter, writing in his memoirs, 'the finest two left wingers in the district'. This illustrates the forward line-up of the time, with two men on each wing, one backing up the other lest he be tackled and the loose ball could be carried to the corner flag and centred. Another source described Harvey as being 'clever, hard working and dodges well'. Presumably 'dodging' meant body swerves.

Strollers' club president Edward Smith was rightly proud of the team in 1884, for they had secured the impressive trophy which was the Wednesbury Charity Cup for the first (and only) time.

This had been started in 1880 by Isaac Griffiths and was an invitation knockout cup limited to just eight teams, upon application, although strong teams as far away as Nottingham Forest and Shrewsbury subsequently entered the competition. Stollers had re-formed the year before, as Town, and had surprised even themselves when beating arch-rivals Old Athletic 4-0 in round 1.

An even more surprising 3-0 success over a Walsall Swifts side that was making a name for itself was followed by a repeat scoreline against Birmingham St. George's. In the final, they drew 2-2 with a team that was to open up the name of Midlands football to the Old-Boy dominance of the FA cup-Nottingham Forest. In the replay, the Strollers were 3-0 victors. Forest were a bit miffed about the replay not being on their home ground, not understanding that the final was always held at the Wednesbury Oval.

The Wednesbury Charity Cup made the FA cup look like a miniature toy; hand-crafted in the finest Birmingham workshops of White & Hawkins, it was 30" of solid silver and engraved with the finest craftsmanship at a cost of nearly eighty guineas, four times the intrinsic value of the FA cup itself. It was said to be the most impressive trophy competed for in the day, and equivalent to ten years' income for a small club like the Strollers.

The successful team that year was: Tetsall (goal); backs: R. Whitehouse and W. Whitehouse; halfbacks: Shenton and Waldron; the forward line: Mason, Danks, Price, Woodcock, H. Woods, G. Woods. This team is entirely different from the names of only four years before, illustrating just how fluid players' movements were at this time. No doubt, as amateurs, players were free to play for whichever team they liked, and if your best friend was asked to join another team in the town, he probably took his footballing pals with him too.

No team, even wholly amateur, can expect success unless there's a backbone of four or five men who stay with the side year in, year out. Trouble was, as sides like Aston Villa and Walsall Swifts were making rapid progress and offering to pay men 5/ – a game (25p) in the days when a pound was a fortune, small fry stood little hope of hanging on to their best players. Of course, many teams were centred around one or two 'star' players-like Birmingham Excelsior and Aston Unity, and once these men had gone, the heart of the team was gone too.

Prominent players of the late 1870s and early 1880s included – Brian Knowles, Tom Bryan (captain), E. M. Scott, Parker, Byrne, and Oliver Howard Vaughton.

Alf Harvey was their solitary England capped player and he subsequently joined the Villa with Eli Davis in 1882. Vaughton was briefly with Strollers but gained his fame as an Aston Villa player, when he too, went to the 'Perry Park Pets 'with his friend Eli Davis. Vaughton, incidentally owned a successful silversmiths factory in Birmingham's Jewellery Quarter, and it is still in business today, having made thousands of football medals over the past century. You will see this factory if you travel in to Birmingham on the Metro, and look to your right just as the metro is pulling into Snow Hill station.

Benjamin Clive Knowles, who lived at Wolseley House, was also a colleague of Frederick Hackwood, the Strollers' founder, as they were both key member of the committee of the Wednesbury Institute, which the philanthropic Hackwood had set up to educate in all scientific and social matters the ill-educated townsfolk of Wednesbury. Hackwood, like so many others who spread the gospel of football across the Midlands, was a product of Saltley Teachers College. He was there during 1875-77.

Edwin Martin Scott and Benjamin Knowles almost lived next door to each other on Church Hill, which was where their first ground was, at the end of Resevoir passage. Having walked the Church Hill area on foot, it's clear that even without the houses that are now crammed into every nook and cranny of this pathway, there wasn't room for a football pitch. However, the 1902 O.S. map shows that a hundred years ago, Reservoir Passage was twice as long as it is today, and went to the other side of Windmill Street, and thus the ground was between Windmill and Vicar Streets, and no doubt they used the nearby Rose Hill Tavern pub for refreshments or as a headquarters. This ground is now the site of Hardy Road today. Edward Scott was, incidentally, the town's fire brigade captain, and served with Hackwood on the committee of the Wednesbury Institute. With the club's headquarters at the Anchor Hotel, Holyhead Road, it was rather handy for the fire station to be located within the courtyard at the back of that pub! Scott was also the Darlaston town surveyor and a freemason, having come to Wednesbury in 1860 from his native Sheffield. Isaac Griffiths who helped found the club, was also another prominent figure in the town. A Justice of the Peace, and chair of the public gas and water committee, was also on the Schools; additionally, he was co-owner of the Imperial Tube Works which employed almost 300 men. Benjamin Knowles was known in the town as a top breeder of sporting dogs, such as beagles and bloodhounds, and his brother John Knowles was to be mayor of Wednesbury in the mid-1890s.

From some of the above descriptions of prominent players and officials, it can be seen that the Strollers were the town's 'posh' team, of middle-class businessmen, churchmen and local civic officials.

The Strollers' grounds

1. Resevoir Passage, Church Hill
2. Crankhall Farm, Mesty Croft (1875)
3. Blazes Lane (1877)
4. Trapezium grounds, Brunswick Park Rd (known then as Cemetery Road)
5. Wells Field, Rooth St.
6. also Wednesbury Park and Elwells Field (the Oval) depending on pitch availability by other teams.

I spent several days in Wednesbury in June 2011 searching out and visiting all the above grounds, including the Trapezium, much to the surprise/annoyance of the inhabitants of the houses now occupying the old field! I have to say that I was more than pleasantly surprised at the site of the Athletic ground, now within Wednesbury Park. It was one of the nicest and well-kept parks I have ever been to in the Midlands, although the full sun of a hot summer day in the June of 2011 may have had something to do with it.

Their second ground for a short while was described as being a rented field at the bottom of Crankhall Lane. In the 1880s this was a lane which led from Wednesbury cemetery to the small village of Stone Cross, now a surburb of West Bromwich, and so it was really 'out of town'.

On the basis that one would need a 3-acre field for a football match, the 'best fit' on the 1900 O.S. map would be a 2.84-acre oblong field next to farmer Crankhall's allotment field near the canal bridge, just past the Canal Tavern (still there today known as the Friar Park P. H.) This field today is occupied by Eldalade Way. The other possibility is a 3.2-acre field by the farm, itself, now built over as the large Friar Park estate, and Kier Road occupies the spot today. The Crankhall ground became developed over the years, and had a cinder running track which was used by the newly-formed Wednesbury Harriers from 1875. The Harriers, in their green and black hooped vests, became founder members of the Birmingham Athletic Association, along with Birchfield Harriers and Lozells. The ground was also used in later years for athletics, cricket, and wakes until the First World War. Eventually, by the end of the 1930s the whole area was built over as the Friar Park estate.

Strollers had been close to their first trophy when they narrowly lost to the unknown quantity of Shrewsbury in the 1878 Birmingham Cup Final.

They had a severe shock however, at the quality of the Old Boys football sides when they were crushed by 7 goals when they were drawn away to Oxford University in the 1st round of the FA Cup the following season, and by the mid-1880s, the gulf was getting wider between the teams that were going places and those who were standing still when an 11-1 humiliation at the hands of Notts County in late 1882 meant that the Strollers had be satisfied with modest local success.

By the end of 1885, the Strollers' days were over. The Old Athletics had been far more successful, winning all over the Midlands, and at one point (1880) had no equal other then the Villa. There was also this new Wednesbury Town team. No wonder the Wednesbury public didn't know whether to follow WOA or one of two teams variously calling themselves the Town! The young entrepreneurs of the town who founded the team in the early 1870s had now grown too old to play up, or be of any use, and the club had failed to keep a steady stream of players of the same quality coming through the ranks.

Notable games in the early years included tussles with team who went on to become household names:

1882 Wednesbury Charity Cup 1st round: 3-3 (H) WBA (2,000); 1-7 Replay (2,100)

1884 Wednesbury Charity Cup Final: 3-0 Nottingham Forest (The Oval)

Best Players

Eli Davis/Howard Vaughton/John Devey/Tom Bryan/Alf Harvey (Who all went to Aston Villa in 1882)

FA cup history	**1st Round**	**2nd Round**
1878/9	0-7 Oxford University	
1879/80	1-2 Stafford Road W'ton	
1880/1	3-5 Aston Villa	
1881/2	3-1 Stafford Road	1-11 Notts County (after they lodged a protest at losing 2-5 away – they would have been better leaving well alone)

References

The Wednesbury Free Press
The works of F. W. Hackwood
The Wednesbury Papers, Hackwood, 1885
Wednesbury Library
Wednesbury Local History Library
The Wednesbury Herald 1879-1885
Sandwell Archives, Smethwick Library

* Thanks to Steve Carr, historian.

Charlie Perry
Wednesbury Strollers Player

Wednesbury Strollers' Trapezium Ground Remains

Wednesbury Town

f.1883-1884

Ground
Trapezium and the Oval.

Club President:
Edwin Smith

Team Captain:
George Wood

Secretary:
Arthur Wesson

Trainer:
Mr Woodcock

Colours
red and white hooped shirts, blue knickers

Not directly connected to the present team of the same name, who were only formed a few decades ago, and only existed for a calendar year.

Formed when there was a split in the ranks at Wednesbury Old Athletic club in 1883. Alf Woodcock led the break away, taking almost the whole of the reserve team with him in the summer. The Old Athletics only just managed to hold it together, thanks due to their captain and star player of all time, George Holden.

The 'new' Wednesbury Town team had to play sometimes at the dilapidated Trapezium ground or the Oval if no one else was booked to use it.

Scholars of Wednesbury football history can be forgiven if they get confused over the goings-on of the 1880s; the Strollers called themselves the Town for their first couple of seasons, but dropped the Town tag when they saw the Old Athletic were the best team in town; they also re-adopted the Town tag some years later when Old Athletic were the best side with Villa in the West Midlands around 1880-1881, and no confusion was possible. They again dropped the tag just before the above Old Athletic split, and thus the 'Town' tag was available once more, so this Old Athletic break-away FC used it!

However, there was a football microcosm happening in Wednesbury alone, with Strollers, Old Athletic, Town, Old Park, Elwells, and other junior teams, all jostling to prove which one was top dog.

Town didn't have to wait long to make their claim. In 1883, they trounced the Strollers 6-1, but Strollers were on the decline; then came the big clash with Old Athletic on 24th November in the Wednesbury Cup; a 1-1 draw in front of 2,000 at the Oval. The replay wasn't until the following 21st January, when the Town won convincingly 4-0 in front of a huge 5,000 crowd. A year later, Old Athletic squeezed home 3-2 against them in the semi-final of the Walsall Cup.

The new Wednesbury Town worked hard to establish their name during 1884, and played many games, sometimes twice a week. Whether they had someone on board who was connected with the press or just sent in extensive match reports, but the *Wednesbury Herald* of that year hardly ever mention the Old Athletic or Strollers; Wednesbury Town were taking all the highlights for this year at least. So 1884 was the year that football-mad 'Wedgbury' could go watch Town, Strollers, Old Athletics, Elwells or Old Park. It was said that you could find a game of football going on every night or day of the week in Wednesbury, and well into the hours of darkness.

Town were soon hailed as the top team in the district when they won the Wednesbury Charity Cup at the first attempt. It took them two games to overcome the powerful Nottingham Forest, who were said to be one of the top 3 sides in the country, but in doing so, the Town had established a reputation for themselves very quickly. The first final, at the Oval at Wood Green was a 2-2 draw, with Forest scoring two second-half goals. The replay, a week later at the same venue, saw Town exceed themselves and win by 3-0 in front of 2,000 boisterous fans.

However, the short-lived existence of this version of Wednesbury Town ended in August 1884, when it seems that the rift had been healed and the two teams re-joined forces once more into the Old Athletic ranks. This was a very sensible move, since a small town like Wednesbury with its 22,000 inhabitants could barely support one professional club, let alone three or four. Elwells, Old Park and Strollers had all disbanded by the end of the 1880s, although the first named two were re-formed in the 1890s.

The team of 1883 was: Tetsall (goal); Cliff and Whitehouse (backs); Mason, Caddick, and Reed (halfbacks); H. Woods, G. Woods, Woodcock, Reeves, Colley (forwards). Their umpire was Styche, previously with Strollers.

Their 1884 side saw many changes, and ran thus :

Tetsall (goal); R and W. Whitehouse (backs); Mason, Waldron, Sheastone (halfbacks); forwards: Danks and Southwaite (right side), Garbett (centre), H. and G. Woods (right wing). Tetsall had been the Bilston goalkeeper, and Waldron was ex-Strollers.

On 23rd February 1884, Wednesbury Town made another mark when they ousted the Walsall Swifts out of the Wednesbury Cup by 3-1, goals coming from Price and Wood (2) during the second half.

The 'new' Wednesbury Town didn't waste any time in showing they meant business and entered the FA Cup as soon as they were formed, and had a remarkable run in the national cup. Beating a young West Bromwich Albion side 2-0 in round 1, they had another local derby against Walsall Town in round 2. After a 2-2 draw at the Chuckery, they impressively won the replay by 6-0. Derby Midland were their 3rd round opponents, and this time the railwaymen were favourites. However a single goal was enough to send the Tubemen through to round 4. Here, the fairytale came to an abrupt end; the Old Westminsters, one of London's most experienced Old Boys sides beat them 5-0. Their red and white halves included some of London's best amateurs, including Norman Coles Bailey, R. W. S. Vidal, the Rawson brothers, Otter and Sandilands. The new Wednesbury had entered along with all the other established Staffordshire sides and had gone the furthest.

The following year, they stayed together long enough for Aston Villa to put them out by 4-1 in the 1st round. Soon after, the players of this club settled their differences with the Old Athletic club from whom they had sprung, and agreed to re-join their ranks once more.

The team of 1883/4 was: Tetsall (goal): Cliff and Whitehouse (Backs); Mason, Caddick and Reed (halfbacks); H. Wood, G. Wood, Woodcock, Reeves, and Colley (forwards). Styche by this time was either their umpire or reserve player.

FA cup history	1st Round	2nd Round	3rd Round	4th Round
1883/84	2-0 West Bromwich Albion	2-2, 6-0 Walsall Town	1-0 Derby Midland	0-5 Old Westminsters (London)

References

Wednesbury Free Press 1884/5
Sandwell Archives Library

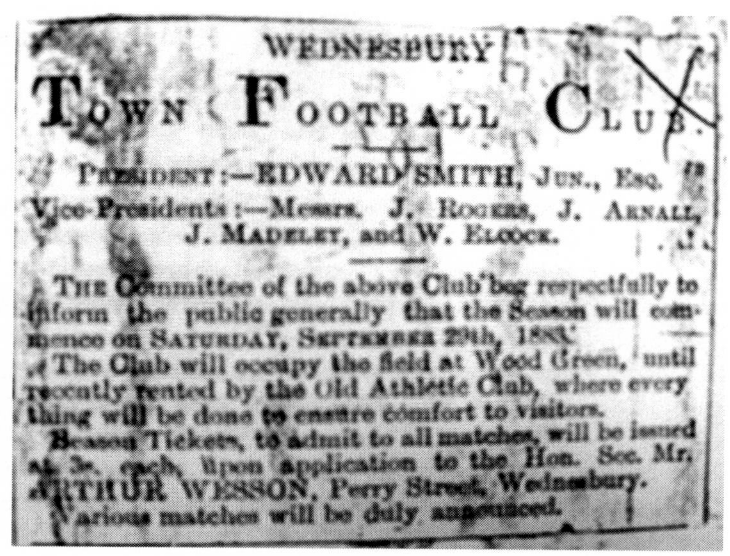

WEDNESBURY

TOWN FOOTBALL CLUB.

PRESIDENT:—EDWARD SMITH, JUN., ESQ.
Vice-Presidents:—Messrs. J. ROGERS, J. ARNALL, J. MADELEY, and W. ELCOCK.

THE Committee of the above Club beg respectfully to inform the public generally that the Season will commence on SATURDAY, SEPTEMBER 29th, 1883.

The Club will occupy the field at Wood Green, until recently rented by the Old Athletic Club, where every thing will be done to ensure comfort to visitors.

Season Tickets, to admit to all matches, will be issued at 3s. each, upon application to the Hon. Sec. Mr. ARTHUR WESSON, Perry Street, Wednesbury.

Various matches will be duly announced.

Wednesbury Town's 1883 Formation

Wellington St. George's (Salop)

f. 1884-1935
Nickname: the Dragons, or the Saints

Home ground:
the Vicarage Field Ground

Colours

light blue shirts 1885
claret shirts circa 1890 claret and blue shirts during 1900;
reverted to claret 1920-32

Honours

Shropshire League champions 1894, 1895
Shropshire County and Charity cups
Welsh Cup semi-finalists 1908
FA Wales Trophy winners 1890 (Welsh Cup)

The football team had been started as a winter offshoot of the St. George's cricket club, by young men who went to the village Institute next to the church.

Wellington St. George's were one of Shropshire's most durable Victorian sides, lasting from about 1884 to the 1930s. They took their name from the St. George's parish church near Oakengates. Visiting teams would have taken the train to Shrewsbury then to Oakengates and done the last part of the journey by horse-drawn taxi carriages. For a while, they vied with Shrewsbury and Oswestry as the county's top side. Amateur village side Wrockwardine Wood were their near neighbours.

In the 1880s, they entered the Birmingham Cup, which by then was really the Midlands Cup, as it was attracting all the top teams from every county from Nottingham to Kidderminster and Shrewsbury to Coventry. Their first assault on the trophy in 1884 saw them have a narrow 4-3 home win over Sandwell in front of nearly 800 spectators, a big crowd for a village team. They went out in round 2 to a strong Wednesbury Town side who had just been formed as a breakaway team from Wednesbury Old Athletic players. 1885 saw Wellington Town join them in the Birmingham Cup, but the powerful Walsall Swifts halted their tracks in round 2 with a 7-0 win after a 2-2 in front of 300 at their Haygate ground. Meanwhile, St. George got past a tricky Calthorpe of Edgbaston by 2-1 but were soundly beaten 6-1 when drawn away to Potteries top side Burslem Port Vale at Moorland Road. In the1886/7 season, both Wellington sides again entered. The competition now regionalised, St. George coming away from Stoke's Victoria Ground with a goal-less draw, but were surprised to be beaten 0-4 at home in front of a whopping 3,000 crowd. The Town side were drawn at home to Shrewsbury Town and lost by 3-1 in front of a 1,000 crowd. The eight teams who came from north Staffordshire and Shropshire were drawn together in what was called the Western Division of the Birmingham Cup after 1887. St. George overcame Ironbridge by the only goal of the game, in front of a big 2,000 crowd, whilst the Town side were put out at home 3-2 by Stafford Rangers. After 1888, entries had risen to over fifty clubs, and it was becoming unmanageable. The B'ham FA at first regionalised the competition, which did cut out all the byes and walkovers, but they then introduced a qualifying tournament to bring the 1st round proper numbers down to about 16. After this point, lesser teams rarely made it through to the competition proper, and it became dominated by Football League and Alliance sides who didn't even bother to field their first teams. St. George's name ceases to appear in the Birmingham cup records after 1887/8.

This side played against Small Heath on 15th November 1886 in the Birmingham Junior Cup-

G. William (goalie); Pickering, Rider (backs); Taylor, Roden, W. Phillips (halfbacks); Williams, J. Phillips, Eames, J. W. Pickering, Murphy (forwards).

In 1889, St. George's travelled to Shrewsbury and defeated the home Town side 2-1 to lift the Shropshire Charity Cup. 2,000 people are said to have assembled 'in a field next to the (old) racecourse' on Saturday 27 April.

They played in the Shropshire League, the Birmingham League, the Welsh Cup, and other minor competitions. They were founder members of both the Birmingham League and the Shropshire League (1893). They played in the Birmingham League from 1889 to 1892 but then went into the new Shropshire League in 1893/4 and were its first champions. They retained the title in 1894/5, and from 1892 to 1896, they were never out of the top 5. In 1908, they got to the semi-finals of the Welsh Cup, losing to Chester by only

2-1. In 1922, they almost got to the 1st round proper of the English FA Cup but were beaten 5-0 by Walsall at the Fifth Qualifying Round.

Being in the Shropshire countryside, a visit to their ground would have felt as good to a trip to the seaside to any of the teams coming over from the Black Country or any of the industrial towns. However, back in the 1890s, rural transport links in Salop would have been nowhere near as advanced as they were in the big Midland towns, and the last leg of the journey from the nearest railway station would have been an unwelcome part of the journey.

Now as a junior side, St. George's joined the Walsall and District League in 1904 and spent the Edwardian era playing teams such as Bloxwich Strollers, Cannock Town, Hednesford, Stafford Rangers (reserves), Darlaston, Bilston, and Wednesbury. Even the nearest of these teams were twenty miles away, so expenses must have been high. It was at this time that they added the word *Victoria* at the end of their name and came to be known as St. George's Victoria for a while. They were very consistent in their anonymity, finishing mid-table in their Walsall League period.

They returned to the Birmingham league in 1924 until their demise in 1931, but they were always a struggling side, their final league positions ranging from 11th at best to finishing in last place for three consecutive seasons, 1927-8/9/30, after which point they resigned from the League and went into liquidation. Wellington Town went on to become a famous amateur side, and eventually they became Telford United.

Their most notable players were:

Frank Peters (b. 1910) came from Coventry City in 1929 and later went on to Charlton Athletic, Swindon and Bristol City, where he scored 75 career League goals.

George Davies (b. 1900-1942), went on to play for Ironbridge (Shropshire), Birmingham City, and Southend throughout the 1920s.

Ben Davies (goalie) played for them in the late 1920s then went on to have a career with Crewe and Port Vale.

Joe Jones (1887-1941) had played for various Welsh teams, before having a long League career with Stoke (200+ games) in the 1910s, and he ended his career in 1925 at Wellington St George's. He was known as a strong defender with a powerful clearance heading ability. His father and uncle had played in the team of the 1890s.

George H. Swift (1870-1956) played for Dragons as a youth. He had a League career with Wolves and Leicester Fosse in the 1890s. He ended up as a manager to Chesterfield and Southampton in the 1910s.

Will Osbourne (1875-1942) was a famous welsh rugby player with 6 international caps. He also played rugby League with Huddersfield and Hull. George retired in 1912 and moved to Oakengates and became Wellington St George's trainer.

Entering the Welsh FA Cup for the first time in 1890/91 season, they went out 1-0 to Oswestry in round 2. By this time, several Salop teams were playing in the Welsh Cup. The following year, neighbours Shrewsbury Town put them out 3-2 at home in round 2. Shrewsbury would have gone on to the final, having beaten Westminster Rovers 4-0 in the semi, but following a protest, the game was replayed and Westminster won 3-1 to reach the final.

Several Salop and Herefordshire teams would enter the Welsh Cup, as they indeed still do. In 1892/3, great excitement was created in the town, when St. George and Wellington Town – the forerunners of Telford United – were drawn against each other. St. George won 3-2 and went on to the 4th round courtesy of some byes and walkovers. Sadly, they met their match when they travelled to Chirk, and they were soundly beaten 9-0. Wellington St. George went out to Shrewsbury again in 1893/4, by which time it was clear that the cup was being regionalised and that the four or five Salop teams would always be drawn against each other. This is a good idea for keeping a team's travelling expenses down, but fans soon get fed up of seeing the same teams year after year. And so would the clubs, no doubt, after all, if you enter the Welsh Cup, you might reasonably expect to meet some teams from Wales occasionally! Unfortunately, the following year, 1894/5, they did, when they met Aberystwith, who won an amazing match on the Vicarage Field ground by 8-3!

In 1896, St. George got to the last 8, losing 0-4 to the eventual winners Bangor City, who incidentally played in a rather nice blue and gold halves with blue shorts. En route, St George had impressively eliminated the strong Druids team, which went on to no less than eight Welsh Cup finals. Neither Wellington St. George's nor Shrewsbury entered the Welsh Cup in

1897, and the Salop flag was carried to the semi-finals by Wellington Town. Only Wellington Town and Ironbridge represented Salop in the Welsh Cup in 1897, and Wellington Town finally won it in 1901/02, then again in 1905/6.

The 1899/90 season saw St. George's finally successful, and they beat Llanwrst in the final to win the FAW Trophy, which was restricted to teams of below level 3, which excluded teams in the Football League, such as Cardiff, Wrexham. The first trophy winners had been a Staffordshire village team, Coppenhall.

During the 1890s, St. George's were founder members of the Shropshire League, and this provided their bread-and-butter match card.

Regular opponents included Hereford, Newtown, Wrockwardine Wood, Ironbridge, Market Drayton, Whitchurch, Shrewsbury, and Oswestry. Oswestry have a good claim to be one of England's oldest clubs, with evidence that they were founded in 1860.

They played in an all-blue strip and lasted right up until 2003 when they were absorbed into the Welsh club, T.N.S who were eight miles away just over the border. After the 1890s, Oswestry preferred to play in the Welsh competitions and often got to the Welsh Cup semi-finals. They played in navy blue and white stripes as early as 1877 at the Victoria Road cricket ground.

St. George's were successful on several occasions in winning both the Shropshire Senior Cup and the Shropshire Charity Cup during the 1890s.

Their 1892 side was: J. Martin, J. Stanworth, J. Norton, A. Evans, J. Roden, A. Dicken, G. Mathews, J. Pinkstone, E. Morris, T. Jones, and F. Jones. At this time, their secretary was Trevor Molyneux, and the club treasurer was R. F. Durie. They were wearing a claret red shirt during the 1890s. Most of the young men would have been employed in the blast furnaces so prevalent within the Shropshire coalfields.

In 1907/8, St. George's re-entered the Welsh Cup but predictably were drawn against Wellington Town and were beaten 2-1 at home. In 1909/10, they got to the 4th round but seem to have been given exemption to the third round. In 1910, St. George's were thrashed 8-0 by Salop neighbours Whitchurch, so it seems that around this date, the Dragons were on the decline, and their best days were behind them The team had grown old together, and there was no new talent coming through.

Their 1906 team was as follows: J. Onions, A. E. Bowles, E. Pickering, S. G. Davies, S. Wakeley, G. Swifts, A. Bailey, R. Picken, W. Plant, H. Hoof, P. Dunkley and A. Morris. Their trainer at this time was George Bryant, and the secretary was M. S. Lee. They had added light blue sleeves to their shirts in the Edwardian era, and thus their colours resembled those of Aston Villa, a club to which they no doubt aspired. They reappeared in 1920 and made the 3rd round, but this proved to be last of their excursions into the Welsh Cup.

Their town rivals, Wellington Town had been formed earlier than the Dragons, in 1879, and by 1920, were making better progress; they had their own ground by 1920 and by 1930 had won or been runner-up of the strong Birmingham League several times. This would have led to the demise of the St. George team as their bigger crowds enabled the Town side to employ professionals.

The odd thing about Wellington St. Georges is they didn't actually come from Wellington itself; the Parish church of St. George is a few miles due east near present-day Priorslee district of Telford and I have found a Frith & Co. sepia postcard which shows the 'football ground and the St. George parish church'. It's a wonderful rural scene with an oval ground with a little wooden ornate stand with a capacity of perhaps a hundred people, with some grassy terrace banking, and the backdrop of farmland all around. A site visit in October 2012 revealed that the old football ground is still there, but now used only by the St. George Cricket Club. Indeed, the whole site has been expanded with hockey, tennis, and playground facilities, and is now the St. George Sports Club run by a board of trustees. I spent the day in the company of Geoff Fletcher, who had taken the trouble to fetch out from the attic, boxes of old photographs, and newspaper cuttings, and we spent the afternoon sifting and sorting them out, and coming across three gems of old Victorian photographs of the football team which are reproduced in the book and on the web site –

(www.morelostteamsofthemidlands.com)

Geoff, a lifelong trustee at the old ground, listened in amazement as I told him that his little village club had received teams such as Stoke, Derby County, Wrexham and attracted crowds of up to 5,000 over a hundred years ago! As I bade goodbye, I could sense a new sense of pride in Geoff's eyes, and he was sure to retell the story at the clubhouse bar for many weekends to come.

St. George is, indeed, its own village within the Telford group of villages; next to the church is the institute, perhaps from which the club sprang, and across the road is the Bell & Bails P. H. which no doubt provided after match refreshments. The pitch was wonderfully flat across the width and length, but the ground seemed lush, and I would imagine that it suffered from being churned up easily in the autumn. Today, even on a heavy autumn day, the pitch is firm, but that is due to a recent ground drainage programme which took place with lottery funding money. The ground originally had two stands: a long stand down the touchline near the church, and a small one facing on the other side by the halfway line. There was also a running and bicycle track around the perimeter, which was banked up behind the goals in the 1910s.

Incidentally, on leaving St. George's, you immediately find yourself in Wrockwardine Wood, an even smaller village; their old ground is now part of the new Telford Sports Centre.

To visit this beautiful old football ground, take the A5 towards Telford, but turn off right when you see signs for St. George's and Oakengates. Head for the Bell & Bails pub, and the ground is opposite next to the church.

FA cup history		**1st Round**
1886	Derby Junction	0-1
1887	Over Wanderers	1-3

References

The FAW Welsh Cup history web site
St. George's Sports Club
Geoff Fletcher at St. George's
History of the Birmingham and District League

Wellington St Georges

Wellington St.Georges 1892

West Bromwich (Dartmouth) FC

f. 1874-1882

Grounds

1. the Four Acres Ground, Seagar Street (see photo)
   Current Birmingham Road ground –across the road from the Hawthorns ground, used from 1920 (cricket team only)

Colours

magenta and blue (hoops?) and matching caps*

The Four Acres ground was next to Christ Church School opposite Dartmouth Park's entrance, which is now Park Crescent, off Seagar Street. There is an old wall, thought to be a remnant of the Four Acres cricket and football ground, at the rear of houses in Summer Street. This old ground had been used by the Dartmouth cricket club for forty years until some of them decided to form a football team at the end of the 1874 cricket season. The football side was very much a side show, with around forty players turning out at football in the team's short nine-year lifespan, suggesting that they never created a settled team, although players such as Tom Smith and George Salter (both goalkeepers), and Mills and Benbow played frequently. The team were made up of a generally higher social class than many others, being comprised of clerks, law clerks, and members of the clergy. Benbow was their star attacker.

The Four Acres ground was at the side of the Christ Church school, to which the Dartmouth had a strong association, with at least one schoolmaster playing an active part in the football team. There was a pavilion at the Seagar Street end. West Bromwich FC had at least two vicars in the side, and several players went on to play for the emerging Albion team, who took over their ground when they folded in the autumn of 1882. Regular opponents during their short eight years of existence included Rushall Rovers, Birmingham FC, Aston Unity, Aston Villa, Calthorpe and the Wednesbury clubs. It has to be said that apart from their final two seasons, where they emerged victorious against better known opposition, they were not one of the leading clubs in the region. One of their best moments came when they won 4-2 away at Wednesbury Old Athletic on 15th March 1880 and a 2-0 home win over Spital (Chesterfield) on 26th February 1881.

Following a site visit in May 2012, and judging by the general topography of the area, there must have been a noticeable slope from one end to the other! Crowds were around the 400 mark, although they went past 1,000 for important cup ties.

WBA at this time were using the Stoney Lane ground, less than 500 yards away, across the road by the Horse & Jockey pub. Both sites are very close to the Dartmouth Park's main entrance today.

Albion were known as the Strollers at this time (1878-80), and the Dartmouth team simply as West Bromwich, but since they ceased winter football to concentrate solely on cricket, and the Strollers became the Albion, there was no confusion after 1881. However, you will find that any team called West Bromwich in newspaper results up to 1881 will be this team and not the Albion.

One man provided a link with West Bromwich Dartmouth, Salters FC and West Bromwich Albion: George Salter. Salter became one of West Bromwich's most prominent citizens and was heavily involved in public life. As well as his famous spring and weighing machine-making company employing thousands, he had a successful political career, becoming a Justice of the Peace in 1888 and Mayor in the 1890s. Salter was a leading figure in the rapid rise of West Bromwich Albion and became chairman of the board of directors and then its honorary president for many years. He, as much as anyone, put the town of West Bromwich on the map, from football, his pioneering spring company and his involvement with cricket.

West Bromwich FC entered the Birmingham AFA cup in 1878, but Walsall's Victoria Swifts (later to become Walsall Town-Swifts) put them out in the 1st round 4-1, after a 2-2 draw in front of 700 at Four Acres. Elwells of Wednesbury put them out the following year after a thrilling 4-4 draw on 6th December ended in a 4-0 replay defeat at the Oval.

Their finest hour came in 1880-81 when they eliminated St. Luke's (4-0), Notts Wanderers (2-0), Saltley College (1-0), and Spital from Chesterfield (2-0), to meet mighty Aston Villa in the semi-final. Sadly, the venue of the Aston Lower Grounds virtually gave Villa home advantage, and the Villains ran out 2-0 winners. They bade farewell to the competition when Notts Rangers put them out 0-4 at home in the 3rd round at the end of January 1882.

After a few years of weak results, 1880 and 1881 became Dartmouth's best spell, with a Birmingham Cup semi-final appearance, followed by making the 3rd round in the Staffordshire Cup in 1881/82. It seems that, very quickly at the end of 1882, they decided not to continue with a football team and concentrate solely on cricket, and once the newly created Birmingham and District Cricket League had started in 1889 – the world's first cricket league – the town was left for the Albion to dominate the scene. This 1882 team, which played Walsall at the Chuckery ground, must have been one of the last their fielded :-

Wyers (goal); Phillips (back); Bushell, Horton, Painter (halfbacks);

forwards: Jessop, Reynolds, Powis, Mills, Wilkes, Williamson

Leading West Bromwich FC players during their brief history were –

Details compiled by Steve Carr

Charles Benbow	51 appearances
S. Mills	48
George Salter	41
J. Bates	37
Eli Horton	32
T. Smith	32
Record victory	9-1 v Calthorpe (Edgbaston) January 1880
Record defeat	1-12 v Elwells (Wednesbury) March 1879

The usual team was: Tom Smith or George Salter (goal)/Harold and Wearing (backs)

Forwards: Billy Carter, Charles Benbow, E. Horton, S. Mills, Baines, Bates, T. Smith, Izon, Bache, Jackson.

Dartmouth would play 15-, 12-, or 11-a-side in the early days, according to the opposition. They kept up a close relationship with West Bromwich Albion, and after the Dartmouth gave up on football to be exclusively a (very famous) cricket club at their Birmingham road ground, they allowed the Albion to use their facilities throughout the 1882/3 season, until they too, moved out to their well-known Hawthorns ground. They no doubt played half-and-half to association and rugby rules with some early clubs, or Birmingham rules in one half and Wednesbury rules in the other half.

There is a long tradition of Dartmouth v WBA cricket and football matches throughout the twentieth century, and these matches drew crowds of several thousands. The club groundsman informs me that the football team played in the colours of the Dartmouth cricket team, which suggests wine red shirts. Well, he was nearly right.

To find the site of the Four Acres ground today, you have to double back on yourself from the A41 Expressway if coming from West Bromwich centre, as Seagar Street is trapped between the Expressway and Dartmouth Park's Lloyd Street entrance. If coming from Walsall, take the A4031 to West Brom and turn left where it says Sandwell Hospital, this is Lyndon Road which, via St. Clement's Lane, becomes Seagar Street.

References

Sandwell Archives Library, Smethwick heavily drawn from *Play Up Brammidge!* Steve Carr, 2004

* Thanks to Steve Carr, a Dartmouth CC member.

Wellington St.Georges' Ground from the Church Roof

Wellington St.Georges' Vicarage Field Ground

West Bromwich Strollers FC

f. 20/11/1878-1880

As is well known, the Albion began life calling themselves the Strollers after finding that no shop in West Bromwich could sell them a football, and they had to walk to nearby Wednesbury. Mind you, in towns where you could, it was common to hire the ball for the day, as many teams could not afford what was then, an expensive item. A lost or burst ball must have been a tragedy. A new leather hand-stiched ball in 1880 cost about 6 or 7 shillings (30p). To give perspective, that was more than two days' pay for a semi-skilled worker.

Albion and the Salter Spring Company of West Bromwich share the same founding story. Almost all of the young men who made the 'stroll' to Wednesbury to buy that ball were all employed at Salters. Indeed a few years later, in 1886, when Albion had won the English FA Cup, seven of the team were still at Salter's Springs.

Their actual founder figure is said to be Charles Perry, no doubt supported all the way by George Salter.

Their 1st committee to run the affairs of the club, albeit only half a dozen games a year in and around Dartmouth Park, comprised:

George Salter/Tom Wilbury (Mayers Green church)/Mr Phillips (Christ Church schoolmaster)/Mr J. Bisseker (secretary).

The first known Strollers team was:

Bob Roberts (goal)/George Bell, J. Stanton (backs)/J. Forrester, Harry Evans (halfbacks); T. Waterfield, J. Siddons, J. Stokes, S. Evans, E. Evans, W. Jones, S. Jones (forwards).

Note there were twelve men, anything from eleven to fifteen still being commonplace at the time. Bob Roberts, at 6'4", at first played in most outfield positions, but it soon became clear that in the days of charging goalkeepers into the net-ball, and all his huge size was a considerable asset against this tactic. He became a stalwart when the West Bromwich Albion became a dominant force on the national scene during the late 1880s.

Harry Aston and Harry Evans were noted early members.

Coopers Hill 'ground'

They began on a patch of ground next to the church in Herbert Street/ Coopers Lane. A remnant of it still exists today, but thanks to the new by-pass, it's hard to see or access. Also, they played in Dartmouth Park, given to the town by Lord Dartmouth, on a pitch to the right of the main entrance facing Herbert Road. Due to the topography of the park, which slopes dramatically from all directions down to the boating lakes, only this top pitch and the cricket meadow were suitable for football or cricket and athletics. The first ever game against opposition was thought to be their 1-0 win over Black Lake Victoria on 13th December 1879. Harry Aston scored that first goal, in Dartmouth Park, home of their employers' cricket club, Salter's Spring Co.

However, recent research discovered a solitary game played in the winter of 1878 – a goal-less draw with Hudson's (soap factory) on 23 November, which would have been only three days after the team's formation, although still quite feasible. I wonder if one James Painter was involved in setting up that game. Before turning out for the West Bromwich FC team in 1881, one of his previous clubs was Hudsons, and after leaving West Bromwich FC, he later played for West Bromwich Albion circa 1883 until 1888, having previously guested for Albion, possibly when they were still the Strollers.

By 1882/3, the Strollers, now Albion, were getting crowds of over 500 and needed a bigger and more permanent pitch. They found their answer when their close rivals Dartmouth decided to relinquish the footballing side and exclusively play cricket.

This was a sound choice, for the Dartmouth CC went on to have a distinguished national career as one of the country's top sides throughout the twentieth century. They allowed Albion to take a long lease on their Four Acres ground.

So the Albionites had walked the three miles to Wednesbury, to the footballing-mad town that already had experienced four years of football, which had four or five teams already. They adopted the nickname of the Strollers, but within three years, chose the tag Albion, as several of their men lived in a small district of the town known as Albion estate.

Their first season colours' were said to be cricket whites, worn with a blue sash and blue cap, and purple socks. In 1880, they tried a maroon shirt, also cardinal red and blue quartered shirts. The year they became Albion, they were wearing yellow and white quartered shirts with a large black Staffordshire knot on the chest. Albion then changed their colours almost every year for the next decade, which must have been very irritating for their fans!

References

Play Up Brammadge! Steve Carr, 2004 various history sites of West Bromwich Albion

West Bromwich Dartmouth's Four Acres Ground Today

West Bromwich Strollers' Dartmouth Park Pitch

Horse & Jockey pub by Four Acres ground

West Bromwich's 3 grounds-4 Acres, Dartmouth Park and Stoney Lane

Willenhall Pickwick FC

Founded: 1884-1919
Nickname: The Picks

Grounds

1. Union Lock ground, Portobello (1884-1915)
2. Springbank stadium (1919-1965)

Colours

1. red and white stripes
2. green shirts/white shorts (as Willenhall in 1916), later red.

Record attendance – 5,000+ v Stockport County, FA Cup 1st round proper 1912

The Picks were the leading team in the town and turned professional within a few years of being formed out of a meeting of interested workmen at the Shakespeare Inn where the pub landlord, Job Broadbent, offered them free use of a large field he owned at Potobello. This became known as the Union Locks ground, as it was behind the factory of that name, famous throughout the country for its locks and keys, etc. It used to be said that half the locks in the world were made in Willenhall. The ground is still there today, sadly overgrown and neglected, but being used by other local teams into the 1970s (see web site photo). The Pickwicks were one of the few teams to choose their colours and never change them throughout the lifetime of the club. Even the stand and fencing at their ground was painted in red and white stripes. At the turn of the century (1900), they were one of the best junior sides in the Midlands. Willenhall folk, like those at Wednesbury, were football-mad and craved success for their team. Stories of their eventually victorious 1894 cup-winning team being carried shoulder high by a joyous crowd all through the town to their HQ at the Shakespeare pub are no exaggeration. For ten years either side of 1900, the Picks were one of the top two or three junior teams in the Midlands.

The Picks, or the Lockmen, as they were sometimes called in the 1890s, had reasonable success at local level. Playing only friendlies and local cup ties for their first decade, crowds would be around 2,000 or 3,000 for Walsall Cup or Staffordshire Junior cup ties and more for their local rivals Willenhall Swifts and Darlaston or Bilston United. Early success came in 1888 when they beat Heath Town (an off-shoot of Stafford Road FC) by 4-1 in the Wolverhampton Junior final. At the end of the 1880s, like many other aspiring teams, they needed a better fixture list and so joined the Walsall & District league until 1907, when they stepped up to the Birmingham Combination. The modestly named Walsall League had a lot of all the leading clubs from the Black Country towns, including at one time Walsall FC themselves, and with many league games being attractive derbies, crowds, income, and the Picks, grew stronger.

They generally fared well in that league, finishing in the top 5 eight of the fourteen years, and were champions three times. In 1907/08, they stepped up to the Birmingham Combination and in what was probably their finest season, won it in 1909, along with the Staffordshire Junior Cup. Again, they generally finished in the top six in the higher league, often enjoying epic tussles with Willenhall Swifts, Cannock, and Wednesbury Old Athletics.

Pickwick had won several of the local town cups, but the one they wanted most was the Staffordshire Junior Cup. After being beaten finalists no less than five times, mostly against Stoke area teams, they finally triumphed in 1909 when they defeated Hanley Swifts 2-1 after being a goal behind at Stoke's ground in front of a record 20,000 crowd. They were finalists again two years later, and the team was on the brink of big things. However, even bigger things were around the corner, in the shape of the First World War. Like many other teams, as several Willenhall men served in France, leagues were suspended, ad hoc games with borrowed players carried the teams through into 1919, but the world had changed. It was time to almost start all over again as if from scratch with the team, although their Portobello ground had steadily seen improvements during the Edwardian era: extra banking, new wooden stands painted in red and white stripes, and improvements to the dressing rooms; the ground had been totally fenced in. Sadly today, there are no remnants of the structures, and the terracing is all overgrown with bushes and trees, despite the fact that works league football was played there from 1920 when Pickwick moved into the Swifts' new Springbank Stadium, until the 1990s.

Rivals, the Swifts, at first their juniors, had entered the Birmingham League before them and had made great strides in the 1890s and were now on an equal footing, having their new stadium. An amalgamation of the town's leading two clubs had already been discussed on the eve of the First World War, and so, at the end of 1919, they re-emerged simply as Willenhall (the Town tag came later, and a change to an all-red strip).

Their side which beat Hartshill Unity to lift the Wolverhampton Junior Cup in 1891 was:

Banks (goal); Wright, Partridge (backs); Moseley, Lowe, Osborne (halfbacks); Loat, Pearson, Southall, Jones, St. Ledger (forwards).

Their side which beat Windsor Street Gas to lift the 1894 Walsall Junior Cup was:

Clarkson (goal); Wright, Partridge (backs); Edwards, Chilton, Southall (halfbacks); Fates, Longmore, Taper. Langford, H. Edwards (forwards).

Their side which beat Hanley Swifts 2-1 to lift to Staffordshire Junior Cup in 1909 was:

Thorpe (goal); Archer, Edge (backs); Downing, Robinson (captain), Wootton (halfbacks); Woollast, Potts, Holt, Heath, Spencer (forwards). This was the Picks' finest ever forward line-up.

Their side which played against Stockport County in 1912 in the Fifth Qualifying Round of the FA cup was: Henworth (goal); Archer, Edge (backs); Wootton, Robinson, Crabtree (halfbacks); Paddock, Mason, Langford, Watton, Round (forwards).

Main Honours

Won the Birmingham Combination in 1908/09, bagging 129 goals in 30 matches and crowds of 3,000-4,000.

Won the Birmingham Junior Cup in 1893/4 with a 4-1 win over Lozells FC

Won the Staffordshire Junior Cup in 1893/4 with a 2-1 win over Hanley Swifts

Semi-finalists Birmingham Junior cup 1888-89-90

Several Pickwick players represented England in Junior Internationals.

Also, either won, or were finalists in the following local cups:

Wednesbury Charity Cup (3 times); Walsall Charity Cup (3); Walsall Senior Cup (2); West Bromwich Cup (1); Bilston Cup (5); Wolverhampton Charity Cup (11); Walsall Junior Cup (6); Staffordshire Junior Cup (7)

Leading players, inevitably were sold for a small sum, or left to join the nearby League clubs.

Tom Knight went to the Wolves in 1886; Albert Fletcher, who joined Pickwick from Fullbrook Saints, a junior team from Walsall went to the Wolves in 1887 for a gold sovereign (!);

Jack Aston (b. 1877-d. 1934) turned pro for Walsall in 1896 till 1899, and went on to score 68 goals in 184 games in the Football League Div II.

The curiously named Gersham Cox came from Villa in 1893 and is sadly credited with netting the Football League's first ever own goal on 8 September 1888. His previous teams included Coventry, B'ham Excelsior and Walsall Town.

Bert Bliss went to Tottenham for the large sum of £50 in 1912. The supporters were far from happy about losing their top prospect, but the club were strapped and needed the money to keep afloat.

The old Pickwicks' swansong was in the 1911/12 Birmingham Senior Cup when they defeated mighty Aston Villa by 2-1, although by this time, most Midland sides fielded a mixture of 1st and reserve team men in their Birmingham Cup sides, and this may have been the case here. Nevertheless, the record books still show 'Villa beaten by the Pickwicks'.

It was at the suggestion of Willenhall's famous FA referee T. G. Bryan that Pickwick and Willenhall Swifts finally amalgamated in 1919 and decided to play in green shirts and white shorts. Pickwick moved into Swifts' Springbank ground at the end of the war in 1919, and the green shirts were chosen because they thought it would bring them luck! This ground subsequently was well-known for dog racing and speedway post the Second World War, and it was situated on the corner of Temple Street and St. Anne's Road. The site was owned by the nearby Lashfords Brewery and, in recent times, the Ladbrookes Corporation.

All that remains of the stadium is the old wall and a cul-de-sac of new houses called Stadium Way after it was demolished to make way for a small estate of houses in 1980.

The new era Willenhall Town team went on to play in the old Amateur Cup final at the old Wembley Stadium in 1981.

A view of the old Union ground is difficult to obtain unless, like me, you get special permission to get on to the roof of the Lock works! (now Assa-Abloy Co). A glimpse can be obtained by walking down the alley at the side of the Balti Nights Indian restaurant on the A454 Walsall Road at Potobello roundabout and looking across the railway tracks and through the trees to the overgrown ground.

ACKNOWLEDGEMENTS

Walsall Observer 1884-1900
The Story of Willenhall Pickwick Football Club, Horace and Peter Davis, 1994, ISBN 0 9523137 07
A–Z of Wolves Players web site

Willenhall Pickwick's HQ-the Shakespeare Inn

Willenhall Pickwick's Portobello Ground

WILLENHALL SWIFTS FC

f. 1900-16 amalgamated with Willenhall Pickwick to form Willenhall (Town). formed as a rival to Willenhall Pickwicks

COLOURS

1. blue and white halves (1900-1905)
2. blue and white stripes after 1905 (see photo).

PLAYED AT THE WAKES GROUND (see web site photo) next to St. Giles' parish church, and later at the SandBank stadium. After 1905, they shared the ground with the Pickwicks, as the Union Lock ground was deemed unsuitable for crowds about more than 2,000 or 3,000.

In post-war years, the Sand Bank stadium was better know as a greyhound and speedway stadium, but being demolished in 1980 to make way for new housing, but suitably called Stadium Way by Willenhall UDC.

Formed in 1900 as a rival to the established Pickwick team by regulars of the Bird In The Hand public house, the Swifts were at first a junior team and entered the Wolverhampton District League, which they won for three years consecutively. They soon moved up a level and were only a notch below their town rivals the Pickwicks within a decade. Most of their team were under twenty years old.

From 1904, they played in the strong Walsall and District League, which included teams such as Darlaston Town, Hednesford Town, Bloxwich Strollers, Cannock Town, and Rushall Olympic. After three seasons of struggling near the foot of the table, the Swifts finally won the title in 1906/7, although crowds were generally less than 1,000, compared to rivals the Pickwick who drew 3,000 or 4,000 for top games and double that for local derbies.

Notable local success came in 1906/7 when they won the Birmingham Junior Cup. By this time, many of the entrants were well-known former big names who were on their way down the ladder, such as Birmingham Victoria, Unity Gas and Wednesbury. They also reached the final of the Wednesbury Cup three years running (1906-7-8) but only won once, against Bilston 1-0 in 1907. Like many other Black Country junior teams of the day, they also entered local cups, such as the Wolverhampton Charity Cup, the Dudley Guest cup, and Walsall and Staffs junior cups.

From 1908, they played in the Birmingham League and were a mid-table side.

From 1911 they joined Pickwick in the stronger Birmingham and District League. This had teams such as Walsall FC, Worcester City, Shrewsbury Town, Wrexham (!) and Kidderminster Harriers, plus the reserve sides of Aston Villa, West Bromwich Albion, and Stoke City. Their five years in the Birmingham League however, were inauspicious, excepting 1912/13 when they finished fourth.

By this time, 1910-14 Swifts were judged to be superior to rivals Pickwicks and crowds were up to the 3,000 mark. However, with the outbreak of the First World War, many signed up as soldiers, and both Swifts and Pickwick spent 1915/16 back in the Walsall Combination. Both Willenhall teams lost many players in the Great War.

Willenhall Swifts resigned from the Birmingham League at Christmas 1915 and after the war was over, and both Willenhall teams amalgamated simply as 'Willenhall' for the 1919/20 season. This had been at the suggestion of Willenhall's well-known FA cup final referee, Mr T. G. Bryan at a club meeting on the eve of the great war.

Swifts for most part of their seventeen years had been junior to their big rivals the Pickwicks, but for their last five or six years, were sometimes the better team, and so had joined forces on an equal footing.

On 27 April 1907, the Wolverhampton Charity Cup final was between the Swifts and their rivals, the Picks. Played at Swifts' new Springbank stadium, the game was a 2-2 draw, suggesting the replay could go either way. It certainly did, for the Swifts were trounced 8-0 at Portobello the following week, with Holt getting four himself!

The biggest attendance at Spring Bank was 5,551 for the visit of the Wolverhampton Wanderers 2nd team at the start of 1920. The homesters were listed as Swifts in the match day programme, although the amalgamation had already been announced, and the team were simply listed as 'Willenhall' in the 1920 Birmingham League final table.

The new Willenhall team had a new lease of life, with Joe Turner, the old Swifts secretary and Harry Fairbank (owner of the Talbot Pub) as new president at the helm, soon won the Birmingham & District League in 1922. However, the good days of the 1920s were contrasted by a disastrous 1930s and the team went rapidly downhill, with finances to match. The club went into liquidation in 1930, after ending its days in the local Wolverhampton works league.

After the Second World War, a new Willenhall Town team was started up in 1950 based at Noose Lane, and they went on to reach the final of the old Amateur Cup (equivalent) at the old Wembley in 1981. They continue today as one of the West Midland's leading non-league sides.

Swifts' most famous players were:

Harry Aston (1881-1938) – centre forward – had a career with W.B.A. (who bought him out of the army to turn professional) and then moved on to Walsall in 1905 before ending his career at Willenhall Swifts in 1907/8.

George Hadley (1893-1963) – a tough rugged halfback who came from local side West Browmwich Victoria around 1910. He gained a Junior International cap for Scotland whilst at the Swifts. He went on to play for Southampton, Villa, and Coventry during 1913-22.

Fred Pentland (1883-1962) who went to Small Heath in 1900 but found greater fame when he moved to Spain and became a successful manager of Athletic Madrid, Bilbao, and the Spanish national side during the 1920s and 1930s.

Arthur Arrowsmith (1869-1954) was an inside right who had a short League career at Stoke City, but when they were relegated in 1908, he was sold to the Wolves. Sadly, he didn't make the grade and was sold down the pyramid to Willenhall Swifts around 1910.

Bert Bliss – who went to Tottenham for £10 in 1912 as an inside forward; other notable players include:

Edward Brueton, a goalkeeper from Small Heath in 1894, and Billy Ellis, Arthur Potts, and John Hallows. Potts (1888-1981) was sold to Manchester United in May 1913 where he spent eight years, but because of the intervention of the First World War, he only scored five times in 28 appearances.

Hallows (1907-63) was a centre forward who came from minor team Liverpool Bluecoats. After a short spell with Swifts, just before the 1919 amalgamation with Picks, he went to West Bromwich Albion, but again, only for a few months. His main career was spent with Bradford City (74 goals) and Barnsley during the 1930s.

'Tippy' Holt and Spencer came from rivals Pickwicks in 1910 to antagonise their former club, and Harry Henworth followed the same route in 1914 along with James Dillard. Sadly, Dillard signed up for front-line duty in France and was killed within weeks, aged only 21.

To view the old Swifts ground today, make for the St. Giles' parish church on the A454 Wolverhampton Road at Willenhall. Turn into the municipal car park. The pitch – and the old Wakes ground – ran from left to right and included the car park and the small football pitch alongside the church today. Nothing remains of the Sandbank Stadium except a part of an old wall on Stadium Way which is off St. Anne's Road near the B4484 Bloxwich Rd North.

No Birmingham Cup history
No FA Cup history

ACKNOWLEDGEMENTS

Willenhall Library
Walsall Observer

Willenhall Swifts' Wakes Ground

Worcester Rovers FC

f. 1877-1900/1

Grounds

1. Flagge Meadow (1877-1886)
2. Thorneloe (from 1887) at the north end of the Pitchcroft district, next to the racecourse.

Headquarters:
The Turks Head P. H Lowesmoor The Union Hotel, Lowesmoor The George and Dragon, Tything

Officers
W. T. Miller (secretary); H. Yoxall (chairman); E.Brown (finance secretary) E. T. Castle (treasurer)

Colours

1880s scarlet and black hoops, black shorts
1890s scarlet and black stripes, white

Following a well-attended meeting of about thirty interested persons at the grammar school, Tything on the last day of August 1877, it was agreed by those present that 'it is desirable that a football club be formed and that it shall be called Worcester Football Club'. Both rugby and Association codes were to be played. Walter Holland was elected president, and a large committee was set up comprising the following men: A. J. Beauchamp, C. F. Binns, E. P. Bowen, L. M. Curtler, A. Hill, J. J. Price, F. W. Grainger, Southall, S. G. Spofforth, J. Stallard, H. Stokes, and W. M. Walmsley. C. W. Griffiths was elected first secretary of the new club, H. S. Seaman its first treasurer. Several men promised or gave money, and several pounds were raised on the day to get things started. Flagge Meadow was the home ground for the first decade, before finding a new home at Thorneloe in 1887/8. Thorneloe being the district primarily around the racecourse which is next to the river, the cathedral being lower down.

I thought I would have a look into the respective beginnings of the rugby and cricket clubs and compare them with the football team, hoping to find some common thread. The football team date of 1877 is later than the claimed history of Worcester Rugby Club, who claim a start date of 8/11/1871 under the leadership of Rev. Francis Eld, with Somerset Place being given as their first ground until 1891, when they moved to New Road for two years. The reason for mentioning this is because Flagge Meadow, Rovers' first ground, belonged to the Royal Grammar School, and Rev. Francis Eld was its headmaster, this suggesting a link between the two organisations. The rugby club also used the Pitchcroft ground, during 1893-94. Somerset Place – a third rugby ground – is now Flagge Meadow Walk. The Worcester Warriors history says that the Pitchcroft ground was the field next to the cricket ground on New Road. If so, then this places 'Pitchcroft' some distance from where I believed it to be, at the top of the Racecourse. To add further confusion, the official history of Worcester (shire) cricket club states that they didn't use New Road until 1899! having played in various parks for their previous forty years. Wherever the Pitchcroft/Thorneloe ground was, it would have been frequently flooded just as the cricket ground (in) famously does today.

So despite the Worcester FC which formed in 1877 stating that they would play both codes, it seems that the Worcester Rubgy Club were founded independently – and six years earlier than the football club. The rugby club disbanded in 1896 for twenty-two years, five years before the football team chrysalised into Worcester City. I used an 1877 and an 1889 map of Worcester, and I was surprised to find that not one of half a dozen known playing grounds for the above three clubs was so described. Even Flagge Meadow was not called such on the 1877 map, and even the 1889 map did not name any of the fields used along the riverbanks.

Worcester Rovers would, like their neighbours the Berwick Rangers, have found opponents few and far between in the county of Worcestershire, as the populous were more interested in cricket and rugby, and rowing, and still are. Newspaper reports from the *Worcester Chronicle* gave more column inches to farming matters and cricket or rugby. Even in the 1890s, match reports would be brief, and Rover's games were reported next to rival Berwick Rangers' games. Apart from the Kidderminster teams, Rovers and Berwick Rangers were the only first-class teams in the county. Other minor sides such as Worcester Olympic and Worcester Excelsior proliferated under their feet.

The Worcestershire County Association had been founded in 1879 under the auspices of the Birmingham FA, probably with the help of Charles Crump, but it didn't gain its 'independence' until 1912.

Flag (or Flagge) Meadow is still there today as a large recreation area, mostly used for cricket, next to the river. It still belongs to the Royal Grammar School. This would have been (and still is) one of the prettiest grounds in the Midlands, in stark contrast to many of the grounds in south Staffordshire and the Black Country which had an array of smoking chimneys, slag heaps, marl pits, and acrid air for their surroundings.

'Thornloe was built over and was next to the racecourse.'

I have not been able to identify with any certainty exactly where this ground was, but the best fit to the description of the previous sentence would be at the end of Pitchcroft Lane, by the allotments and industrial estate. The natural treeline around the allotments is 120 x 85 yards and is thus the right size, but do the allotments constitute the phrase 'built over'? Tempting as it looks, the football ground as used by the Northside Youth FC at the end of Selborne Rd West, although 'next to the racecourse' is clearly not built over. As all their grounds were next to the river and the racecourse; they were probably liable to flooding, leading to cancellations, or ruination of any passing-game style of play. 'Thorneloe ground', as described in the Worcester Warriors history site, places the location directly facing the cathedral on the opposite site of the riverbank.

The first ever Worcester FC match took place on Thursday 20th October 1887 at Flagge Meadow, when their opponents were the 1st Worcestershire Artillery Volunteers. The first ever team then for Worcester football club was:

Bowen (captain), Binns, Cooper, Eaton, Fraser, Glover, Hill, F. Price, Seaman, Southall, J. Southall, Stokes, Tiernay. Notice how most of them just happened to be on the committee! The *Berrow's Worcester Journal*, having no previous experience of publishing a 'team sheet', simply listed the men in alphabetical order. The Worcester team umpire was Mr Whitney Griffiths, and the club colours were scarlet and black hoops.

An early match in 1880 was reported on in the South Staffs Chronicle, in which Rovers travelled to Wednesbury on Saturday 28th November but were beaten 3-0 by the Strollers at the Oval ground. No names were given of the Worcester players.

The following team played against Walsall Town in 1887, being easily beaten by 7-2:

G. Morris (goal); J. Smith & Mills (backs); F. Owen, Andrews, Wilcox (halfbacks); H. Smith, Bradley, Wilkins, Hill and W. Smith (forwards). Note the three Smith brothers.

This 1888 team played host to Oldbury Town on 7th April, the players being: Hardwick (goal); J. Wilkins, Miles (backs); J. Smith, C. Andrews, T. Gough; W. Sherwood, G. Ratcliffe, A. T. Wilcox, W. Smith, H. Smith (forwards). Only 300 spectators witnessed the game, a 1-1 draw, mainly due to the blustery weather, but at least they had a settled side, unlike many of the Aston and Birmingham clubs of the day.

This team went down 1-2 at home to Aston Villa reserve side in the 1893 season of the Birmingham League, the players being: H. Sunderland (goal); S. Sparshott and J. Belcher (backs); W. Wallace, J. Houston, J. Andrews (halfbacks); J. Pickerill, A. Turner, T. Green, A. Gorman, P. Flynn (forwards). Tom Green received a rapturous welcome from the home crowd, having just come back to the team from another. At this time, one Charles Crump (see Stafford Road FC and the Birmingham FA) was turning out for the Worcester Rovers reserve team at halfback despite being in his fifties! He was a Worcestershire man at heart and was known to frequently come over from Wolverhampton to watch the Worcestershire cricket side, turning out if available for Rovers' second strings.

The Rovers 1st team for 1897/8 was:

E. Sheldon, W. Williams, Tom Baugh (captain), C. E. Harley, C. Simmons, Mark Rideout, C. A. Pratt, A. Richards, T. West, W. Greenwood, F. Whitehouse.

At this time, their trainers were C. Jones and E. Lewis (medical); the club treasurer was E. Lewis; the Hon Sec was W. T. Miller; and his assistant was S. T. Castle. The numerous committee comprised: H. Harris, H. Hope, F. Stockhall, H. Booth, W. Hunter, H, Jakeways, T. Radford, C. Warren, F. Price, T. Dinley. Interestingly, the team photo for this year shows few of the players wearing a moustache, but the older committee men mostly do.

Amid rumours that the club wouldn't emerge for the 1899 season, they put an article in the *Worcester Chronicle* on 19th August, proclaiming that the club would compete in the next season, at Thorneloe, and that they had signed E. Baugh from Wellington St. George's – brother of captain Tom Baugh – and F. J. Hadley from Bournbrook FC to add to their small squad of twenty players retained from the previous year. Such small crumbs of comfort were meant to entice the fans back through the turnstyles, but it was result as always that mattered.

Rovers played in the Birmingham & District League from 1893 to 1902 without any real success, their best effort being a 4th place in 1897. Crowds were never enough to maintain a semi-professional club, and the town barely got behind one club, never mind two. When they amalgamated with Berwick Rovers, such was the rivalry between the two sets of supporters that the crowds barely reached 4,000. The *Worcester Chronicle* said that no Berwick Rangers fan would go and watch a Worcester Rovers match, and they were probably right. Regular opposition on the fixture card included Bristol Rovers, Kidderminster, Dudley, Wolves reserves, Small Heath, Wellington Town, Small Heath, and Coventry. They tried to find attractive opposition in order to increase local support and entered cups far and wide, such as the Cannock Chase Foresters cup and the Walsall cup. They were instrumental in setting up the Worcester charity cup in 1893, the trophy having been put up by the Earl of Dudley.

The new combined Worcester City went on to have a famous amateur history, starting with winning the Worcestershire Senior cup for seven consecutive years, 1907-14.

Notable players:

James Deeley – went to Small Heath in 1895

Charlie Simmons – went to West Bromwich Albion in 1898

Tom Green (b. 1863)

A curious set of statistics arose from their 1896 season: played 30; won 10; drew 10; lost 10.

By 1899, rumours that the club were about to disband arose, and at a meeting on 19th August, the perilous finances of the club were revealed, and the inevitable closure occurred just into the new century. It was revealed that poor support had led to many matches drawing revenue of less than £15, which was in itself the total wage bill for the first team. In an effort to keep finances under control, said Miller at the club's 1899 AGM, they would cap any new players to £1 per week. Also mentioned was the bad feeling which existed between themselves and Berwick Rangers. In 1902, Worcester Rovers and Berwick Rangers amalgamated to form a new club, Worcester City. The new team found later success in winning the Birmingham League three times: in 1925, 1929, 1930.

The new club, Worcester City, played its first season at Rangers' old Severne Terrace ground, then moved to the Rovers' old Thorneloe ground for one season (1903), before moving yet again to Flagge Meadow, where they stayed until 1905, when they made their last move to present-day St. George's ground. However, at the time of writing, the lease expires in June 2013 and there are plans to sell out to the developers and move to a new 6,000-seater stadium at Nunnery Way.

Communications with Worcester City FC about the colours of their predecessors regretfully drew a blank.

References

Worcester Chronicle
Berrow's Worcester Journal 1877
Birmingham Daily Post
Lee Gauntlett, Aston Villa historian

Worcester Rovers 1897

Victorian Football Quiz

YOU WILL FIND THE ANSWERS to all these questions within this book. If you can answer half of them without back-checking, you are already a very knowledgable historian yourself! Answers on the next page.

Q1. Which was the first non-League club to knock a League side out of the FA Cup?

Q2. Who sold a player to the Wolves for a gold sovereign?

Q3. Which Shropshire team played its home games in London?

Q4. Which team once played in green and pink quartered shirts?

Q5. Which two Staffordshire teams played on pitches right next to each other?

Q6. Which Black Country team once scored 29 goals in three consecutive games, including 12-1 over Stoke?

Q7. Whose pitch was so bad that visiting cup team often paid a £5 bribe to switch venues?

Q8. Which team's player went to Italy and founded A. C. Milan?

Q9. Which team played home games at Edgbaston Cricket ground?

Q10. Which Derbyshire school played in the FA Cup for several seasons in the 1880s?

Q11. Which Worcestershire team shares its name with a Scottish League club?

Q12. Where was the Trapezium ground?

Q13. Which team were nicknamed the Dragons?

Q14. Which east Staffordshire town has had four different Football League teams?

Q15. Which spring+balance making company gave birth to West Bromwich Albion?

Q16. Who were the Tin-men?

Q17. Which Staffordshire team gave its reserve team a separate name?

Q18. Who played home games at the Molyneux Ground before Wolverhampton Wanderers?

Q19. Which side had Prime Minister Joseph Chamberlain as its Patron?

Q20. Whose home ground was Meadow Lane before Notts County moved in?

Q21. Which famous Birmingham running and athletics club had a football team competing in the Birmingham Cup?

Q22. Where did the original Birmingham Cricket and Football club play its home games?

Q23. Which three teams founded the Derbyshire County Football Association?

Q24. Who were the two pioneering father figures of the Birmingham Football Association?

Q25. Who chanced upon Aston Villa youths in Villa Park and led the club to greatness?

Q26. Which two cycle works teams were Coventry arch-rivals?

Q27. Which Cannock Chase ground was bedevilled by fog?

Q28. Which London Solicitor founded several Shropshire teams and the Welsh Football Association?

Q29. Who beat Hereford 25-0 in the Birmingham Cup?

Q30. Which club claimed that Aston Villa 'stole' their colours?

Q31. Which team played its home games at the Bournbrook Hotel ground?

Q32. Which two teams combined to make Walsall in 1888?

Q33. Whose home ground was at the Cape Hill brewery?

Q34. Which team had a large Staffordshire Knot across its shirts?

Q35. Which ground once had three matches going on all at the same time?

Q36. Which mythical beast links Mitchell St. George's with Walsall Town FC?

Q37. Which Derby Junction player founded Derby County FC?

Q38. Which Birmingham team changed its name twice in three years?

Q39. Which team played in six consecutive Derbyshire Challenge cup finals in the 1880s?

Q40. Which Villa centre forward scored 10 goals past his former club a month after leaving them?

Quiz Answers

1. Warwick County FC. They beat Stoke 2-1 away in the Birmingham cup.
2. Willenhall Pickwick
3. Old Salopians. They had been founded by London old Shrewsbury Grammar school men.
4. Burton United
5. Walsall Swifts and Walsall Town
6. Wednesbury Old Athletic
7. Small Heath
8. Notts Olympic: Herbert Kilpin
9. Warwick County and Aston Victoria
10. Derby Junction St. School
11. Berwick Rangers (Worcester)
12. Wednesbury
13. Birmingham/Mitchell St. George's
14. Burton
15. Salter's Springs Company
16. Hednesford Town/Anglesey
17. Stoke
18. Stafford Road FC
19. Birmingham St. George's
20. Nottingham Rangers
21. Birchfield Harriers
22. Aston Lower Grounds
23. Derby St. Luke's, Long Eaton, Derby Town
24. J. Campbell Orr and Charles Crump
25. William McGreggor
26. Rudge and Singers
27. Hednesford's Cross Keys ground
28. Llewellyn Kendrick
29. Kidderminster Olympic
30. Aston Unity
31. Calthorpe
32. Walsall Swifts and Walsall Town
33. Birmingham/Mitchell St. George's
34. Rushall Rovers
35. Edgbaston County Ground
36. Dragon. It was the nickname of B'ham St. George's and the headquarters of Walsall Town was the Dragon Hotel.

37. William Morley. He left Derby Town to found Derby Midland then left that team to found Derby County.
38. Aston Victoria
39. Staveley FC
40. Arthur Brown: scored 10 against previous team Aston Unity in Villa's 16-0 Birmingham cup win

References

Wikipedia
Football Club History Database
British Newspapers History Online
Historical Football Kits
Charles Alcock's Early Football Annuals 1878-1905
The Story of Football, William Lowndes, London, 1952
The History of Football in Sheffield, Percy M. Young, 1964
Victorian England, J. G. Reader, 1974
The Association of Football Historians
Showell's Directory of Birmingham
Sandwell Local History Archives Library, Smethwick
Walsall Library
Cannock Library
Walsall Local History Centre, Essex Street, Bloxwich
Birmingham City Reference Library
Wednesbury Library & Museum
The History of the Birmingham Senior Cup, Steve Carr
The Old Un's Revisited, Steve Carr
The History of Wednesbury Old Athletics, Cyril Willetts
Walsall Observer & South Staffs Chronicle 1866-1939
Cannock Advertiser 1880-1900
Derby Mercury 1873-1888
Staffordshire Sentinel 1879
Lichfield Mercury 1899
Midland Daily Telegraph 1892
Worcester Chronicle
Wolverhampton Express & Star
Birmingham Daily Post 1869-1899
Wednesbury Herald 1869-1880
The Walsall Free Press 1871-1875
Midland Advertiser
Sheffield Independent 1880
Sheffield Daily Telegraph 1877
History of Birmingham County FA,1975
Burton Evening Gazette
Hereford Times

Belfast News 1895
Dissertation on the Growth of Football in Birmingham 1875-1900, Jack Allen M.A
Aston Unity Cricket Club
Edgbaston County cricket ground museum staff
St. George's Sports Club, Salop
The Official History of the FA Cup, Geoffrey Green, Naldrett Press, 1949
The Code War: English Football Under the Historical Spotlight, Graham Williams, Yore Publications, Uxbridge, 1994
Aston Villa Football Club
Hednesford Town Football Club
Worcester City Football Club
Aston Local History Society
The Minutes & Records of the Wednesbury Football Association 1879-1890
The handbooks of the Birmingham Football Association
Warwickshire County Cricket Club
The Works of Fredrick Hackwood (Wednesbury Press)
Great Bridge Memories, Terry Price, ISBN 0-7509-34468
Old-Maps.co.uk
Kidderminster Victoria Cricket Club
Ordnance Survey Maps of the Midlands 1870-1910
The Deerstalker Magazine (Mitchells & Butlers Brewery)
The photographic collection of Terrance Fletcher (Derbyshire)
The photographic collection of Kevin Powell (Shropshire)
www.midlandspubs.co.uk
www.blackcountryresearch.com
www.olvbirmingham.com

Acknowledgements

With thanks for their help and guidance to:

Mr Roy Burford, Cape Hill, Smethwick, Mitchell St. George's historian
Mr Steve Carr, Birmingham author and historian
Mr Geoff Fletcher, St. George's Club
Mr David Shaw, Hednesford Town FC historian
Mr Terrance Fletcher, Derby football historian
Mr Lee Gauntlett, Aston Villa historian
Mr John Green, Birmingham City Council
The staff at Walsall Local History Centre (Libby, Stuart, Paul)
The staff at Sandwell Local Archives Centre
The staff at Cannock Local History Centre
The staff at Wednesbury Local History Centre

Index

A

B

C

G

H

J

K

L

M

N

O

P

Q

R

S

T

U

V

W

Lightning Source UK Ltd.
Milton Keynes UK
UKOW04n0653291013

219968UK00002B/6/P